FASCISTS AND CONSERVATIVES

TITLES OF RELATED INTEREST

FASCISTS AND CONSERVATIVES

The radical right and the establishment in twentieth-century Europe

edited by

MARTIN BLINKHORN

London and New York

First published in 1990 by Unwin Hyman Ltd.

Reprinted in 2001
by Routledge
2 Park Square, Milton Park, Abingdon, Oxon, OX14 4RN

Routledge is an imprint of the Taylor & Francis Group

Transferred to Digital Printing 2005

ISBN 0-41523-966-4 hbk

Typeset in 10 on 12 point Garamond

Contents

vii

1

Introduction
Allies, rivals, or antagonists?
Fascists and conservatives
in modern Europe

Martin Blinkhorn

During the last twenty years, prodigious scholarly effort has gone into the study of fascism and the right in twentieth-century Europe. Quite apart from the study of particular fascist and national socialist movements and of individual right-wing regimes (Fascist Italy, the Third Reich, Franco's Spain, etc.), scholars have striven to locate the essential nature of fascism; to determine what is distinctive about its ideas, programmes, policies and support; to identify what, if anything, differentiates it from other forms of rightism; and to decide whether a satisfactory definition of 'fascism' can be arrived at – or whether, indeed, the term has any descriptive or analytical value at all.[1]

This volume is intended to assist the further consideration of these and related problems. Whilst paying due attention to 'theories of fascism', the approach of its thirteen contributors is in the main empirical. Its starting-point is the recognition that there existed, in interwar Europe, at the very least a *subjective* distinction between the radical right, as represented in the main by fascism and national socialism, and the conservative right, as represented by constitutional conservatism and various strands of conservative authoritarianism closely or loosely linked to it. Our task has been to examine the relationship between these various strands of the right in a range of European settings, our purpose to analyse the correspondence, or lack of it, between this subjective distinction and objective reality. The settings in question include not only those where fascism or national socialism achieved, or at least shared, power (Italy, Germany, Spain, Austria, Romania) but also others (Portugal, France, Greece, the Nordic countries and Britain) in which the experience of radical fascism, and the fascist–conservative relationship, were in a variety of ways different.

First, it is necessary to go a little further in defining, or at least clarifying, our terms. This is neither an easy nor a satisfying task, since in cases such as

1

those examined here, the definitions, typologies and taxonomies beloved of social scientists tend to fit uncomfortably the intractable realities which are the raw material of the historian. The more closely the data relating to the European right are scrutinized, the more lines stubbornly refuse to be drawn or, when drawn, to remain straight and motionless; exceptions disprove more rules than they prove; and all too rarely do the subjective and the objective coincide.

At the very least, however, we need a point of departure. Let us take fascism first, and begin with what is (almost) incontrovertible: namely, that Italian fascism provides us with models of both a fascist movement and a fascist regime. More or less simultaneously with the emergence of fascism in Italy, there also emerged in other European countries, especially those, like Italy, affected by war, demobilization and revolution or left-wing militancy – Germany, Austria, Finland, parts of the Balkans – significant popular movements with sufficient in common with Italian fascism quickly to be bracketed with it. Then, as time passed and as fascism in Italy ceased to be a mere movement and became a securely established regime, the term 'fascism', and the values, goals etc. associated with it, began to be *deliberately* adopted by new, imitative movements, from London to Athens and from Lisbon to Helsinki.

So far, so good. The picture soon becomes blurred, however, by a number of additional and related factors. It is necessary to recognize, first, that on the interwar European right there existed a plethora of organizations with authoritarian goals, some actually founded before 1914, others newly emerging, some working through parliamentary machinery, others extra-parliamentary and paramilitary in character; and that within the political world of the right, the increasingly modish labels 'fascism' and 'fascist' were employed with little consistency. Secondly, during the course of the interwar period the whole of central, southern and eastern Europe succumbed to rightist, authoritarian regimes of one sort or another, of which few actually called themselves 'fascist' or 'national socialist' but most praised aspects of Italian fascism and Nazism and borrowed selectively from the examples they provided. Third, liberals and leftists, fearful of a general authoritarian trend of which Italian fascism was reckoned to be the standard-bearer, themselves began to apply the term 'fascism' loosely (but understandably) to a variety of right-wing movements, parties and regimes, by no means all of which saw *themselves* as 'fascist'.

To produce a rigorous and consistent definition of 'fascism' against such a background is difficult, perhaps impossible – if only because no single definition will satisfactorily embrace both movements and regimes. Since no definition of 'fascism' can ever be universally accepted or objectively 'correct', what is needed is rather a valid and useful *working approach* which will assist our understanding of the right in general, and of the complex relationships within it. For our purpose

2

it would probably be wisest to suggest (1) that movements and (much more rarely) regimes adopting the labels 'fascist', 'national socialist' and 'national syndicalist', or associating themselves with these causes, present no taxonomic problem; (2) that other movements of the authoritarian right – those, for example, with Catholic origins which claimed not to be 'fascist' – must be considered empirically, in terms of both their subjective and their objective relationship to the radical right; and (3) that ostensibly 'non-fascist' regimes of the right present the most difficulty, since many rightist regimes, not excepting those of Mussolini and Hitler, represented a compromise between self-confessed fascism/national socialism and other forces.

'Fascism' has at least been the object of analytical scrutiny; conservatism much less so.[2] The contributors to this volume have, for the most part, approached this part of their task empirically. The 'conservatives' discussed here are, in the main, those who in the period concerned organized politically or otherwise in order to achieve two principal goals. The first of these was the defence of established social and economic interests, elites, hierarchies, etc., whether within a political system dominated by themselves (Britain, the Nordic countries); within one in which their political grip was shaky and their socioeconomic position threatened (Italy after 1919, Austria under the First Republic, perhaps France in the 1930s); or within one in which sudden political change had handed power – or at least office – to the left (Germany under Weimar, the Spain of the Second Republic). The second goal was the pursuit of modernizing, developmental policies within a 'system of order' in which their own control could be guaranteed and perpetuated. In some cases, 'conservatism' was a largely pragmatic affair; in others, notably that of Germany, it was associated with considerable ideological paraphernalia.

To state what is admittedly obvious, the early twentieth century was an unprecedentedly volatile and turbulent period in the history of Europe. Between the later nineteenth century and the Second World War, although the details and the pace of the process differed considerably from country to country, the dominant classes throughout much of the continent – and those who represented them politically – found themselves facing the arrival of mass politics, political democracy, popular pressure for social reform, and the possibility, at the very least, of left-wing revolution. Two major historical events, the First World War and the Russian Revolution, massively influenced both the sociopolitical realities of Europe and the individual and collective political consciousness of its inhabitants. In the response of Europe's established elites to these and related challenges, fascism – that is, fascist movements and fascist ideas – sometimes played an important and complex part. Complex, since fascism, where it appeared, was at one and the same time a symptom and a product of contemporary

3

change; a possible weapon whereby conservatives might deal with some of the other, unappealing aspects of change, notably the challenge of the left; and a possible threat in itself.

Already before 1914, the confident control of Europe's incumbent elites, variously aristocratic and *haut bourgeois*, 'conservative' and 'liberal', was wavering. Industrialization and urbanization, the capitalist transformation of agriculture, population migration, cultural modernization and secularization: these and related contemporary phenomena were breaking down existing forms of hierarchical and clientelist politics, confronting the politically dominant with the uncertainties of popular politics, the often unwelcome prospect of more genuine democracy, and the fast-advancing threat of socialism. Under these pressures, confidence in existing, mainly liberal-parliamentary, principles and practices was liable to falter.

Throughout much of Europe, 'constitutional' conservatism was already, before fascism became a reality, subject to varying degrees of subversion by ideas and organizations of an authoritarian or corporatist character. The contributions in this volume illustrate, for example, how in the decade before the birth of fascism much of the German right was ideologically 'Pan-Germanized'; how strong was the influence of the Italian Nationalist Association, elitist social theory and the 'Return to the Statute' school in Italy; how Maurassian ideas extended beyond France – where, indeed, their practical importance may if anything have been overstated by historians – to influence conservatives in, for example, Greece and more particularly Portugal. In Austria, the conservative Christian Socials took with them into the 1920s a populist, corporatist, chauvinist tradition, effectively mobilized by Karl Lueger, whilst in Spain the 'alternative conservatism' of Catholic traditionalism continuously beckoned any conservatives whose loyalty to the liberal system was at all shaky.

Of course, it is important not to exaggerate the seriousness of the authoritarian infection *before* 1918. The process was uneven, going furthest in Germany but in several other countries, notably Britain, affecting only the fringes of the established right. Even so, the question as to how much the attachment of conservatives to constitutional, parliamentary systems was a matter of conviction as distinct from self-interest is a very real one. The point is not so much that European conservatism was riddled with authoritarianism before fascism itself came along, as that by then there existed within the broad church of conservatism an authoritarian *ingredient* which, in various ways, was to inform the conservative–fascist relationship from the early 1920s onward. In almost every case these illiberal, usually authoritarian ideas, and those who held them, envisaged little in the way of any surrender of effective power by established elites; rather they represented a variety of notions as to how change might be restrained, negotiated or even directed in such a way as to obviate any loss of real power.

4

Any authoritarian tendencies, whether ideological or merely pragmatic, already present among European conservatives were both intensified and, in some cases, popularized by the complex crisis which hit Europe from 1917 onwards. The scale of that crisis is impossible to exaggerate, involving as it did the Russian Revolution and its impact; the convulsive effects of war, peace and demobilization; the agony of defeat or disappointment with the fruits of victory; radically shifting frontiers and populations; and the advent of new regimes and transformed political circumstances.

In much of postwar Europe, conservatives found themselves operating within a suddenly altered political world in which the control of established elites was overturned or at least seriously threatened. The advent of the Weimar Republic may not have brought down Germany's social and institutional elites, but it deprived them of political dominance and seemed thereby to threaten their total destruction. Austrian conservatives found themselves left with a rump state of questionable national identity, in which socialism was ominously powerful. In Italy, the advent of virtually universal male suffrage and proportional representation thrust the country's 'liberal' and Catholic elites into a mass-political arena for which they were ill-prepared. Greece and Romania, as David Close and Irina Livezeanu respectively tell us, found their polities transformed, the former by the arrival of several hundred thousand refugees from Asia Minor, the latter through the country's doubling in size and population, and its loss of ethnic homogeneity. In both Romania and the newly independent state of Finland conservative anti-socialism was rendered all the more intense by the proximity of the Soviet Union. In situations such as these, in which liberal parliamentarism no longer offered a guarantee of lasting social hegemony, established elites and elements within conservative and sometimes even 'liberal' political parties were liable to find their devotion to parliamentarism wavering.

Nourished by the new climate, authoritarian ideas, groups, even movements and parties, operating on the margins of the 'established' right, proliferated during the 1920s and into the 1930s. The German 'conservative revolutionaries' discussed, from different angles, by Geoff Eley and Jeremy Noakes; the Austrian adherents of Othmar Spann and the assorted Spanish neo-traditionalists; the Portuguese Integralists and, later, the Acción Española intellectuals in Spain: these and other such groups built on existing intellectual and political traditions and stepped up their activities.

The appearance, out of the same postwar crisis – of which they were indeed the creatures – of fascism, Nazism and kindred radical-rightist movements complicated this situation immeasurably. It would be absurd to suggest that Italian fascism, the National Socialist German Workers' Party (Nationalsozialistische Deutsche Arbeiterpartei: NSDAP), the Austrian

Heimwehr, the Romanian student nationalists and other 'new' movements of the 1920s owed *nothing* to previous right-wing, authoritarian ideas and organizations; on the contrary, in almost every instance a common ideological base is visible. Nevertheless in important respects – both ideological and social – they were *different*. For one thing, they were, in Geoff Eley's words, 'more extreme in every way': shriller in their nationalism, more plebeian in composition and style, less respectful of tradition and of established hierarchies, more violent in their behaviour and, specifically and crucially, their anti-leftism. In some, though admittedly not all, cases, they possessed something of a leftist ancestry themselves, and employed as one weapon in their mixed armoury a quasi- or pseudo-leftist rhetoric. This was certainly true of the two movements which must inevitably shape our perceptions of 'fascism', namely, Italian fascism and the NSDAP. At the very least what we may now classify as 'fascist' movements tended to differentiate themselves from what Mosley, in the next decade, was to label the 'old gang' of conservative and liberal politicians and notables. Whatever may have happened later, these were genuine differences, both subjectively and objectively speaking.

The more or less spontaneous emergence of radical-rightist movements in the 1920s – spontaneous in the sense of being autochthonous and non-imitative – was later, mainly after the onset of economic depression in 1929, followed by the much more deliberate, even calculated, foundation of fascist, national socialist, or clearly *fascisant* movements inspired by the example and supposed success, first of Italian fascism and later of Nazism. The British Union of Fascists, the Juntas de Ofensiva Nacional Sindicalista (JONS) and Falange Española in Spain, Norway's Nasjonal Samling, Portuguese National Syndicalism, the Parti Populaire Français: these are just a few examples of the imitative fascism of the 1930s. It is important to stress the obvious, but all too often ignored, distinction between organizations such as these, and their predecessors which grew, so to speak, organically out of the postwar environment.

Discussion of the radical and the conservative right from the start of the 1920s must take account of divisions within the latter among convinced authoritarians, convinced constitutionalists and those who oscillated somewhere between. As John Stevenson makes clear, the vast majority of British Conservatives never seriously faltered in their attachment to a parliamentary system which was long-established, had evolved gradually and was dominated for much of the interwar period by a powerful Conservative Party. Save on the most uninfluential fringes, Britain lacked an 'authoritarian' tradition, and its interwar social order was considerably less convulsed than was the case in much of continental Europe; politically and constitutionally speaking, interwar Britain appears to have been almost in its entirety 'conservative'. Although authoritarianism

6

clearly exercised a greater influence among Conservatives in the four Nordic countries examined by Stein Larsen, ultimately constitutionalism appears to have held firm there also, even in Finland where it was seriously threatened in the early 1930s. In France, too, as Roger Austin shows, the weight of influential conservative opinion seems to have remained somewhat unenthusiastically loyal to the Third Republic. And it would be unjust to deny that significant numbers of political conservatives, and 'establishment' figures generally, in other European states retained a genuine, and not merely contingent, attachment to liberal freedoms, whatever the alternative temptations or punishments.

The fact remains that in many of the countries examined in this volume, conservative parties and the interests they represented shifted perceptibly rightwards after 1919. Quite apart from the radicalization of the German conservative right, we may observe the shift of Austrian Christian Socials towards 'Austrofascism' from the late 1920s on; the welcoming of dictatorship in Spain (1923) and Portugal (1926); the Clerico-Moderates' embrace of authoritarianism in Italy; the Greek Populists' drift towards authoritarianism in the early and mid-1930s; and the failure of conservative republicanism in the face of Catholic corporatism in the Spanish Second Republic.

The relationship of this process to fascism is far from straightforward. Fascism's achievement of power in Italy probably could not have occurred without the complaisance of a variety of elite groups, conservative-liberal politicians, etc. While regarding Mussolini's movement with considerable suspicion, these elements were nevertheless impressed by its patriotism, youthful energy, mass base and strike-breaking capacity, and convinced that, even if given a taste of power, it could be manipulated in the establishment's interests. In this, as John Pollard writes of the Italian Catholic right, they suffered from an 'erroneous perception' of fascism. Something of a pattern was established in Italy in 1921/2 that was to be repeated elsewhere, though not always with the same outcome. A decade later in Germany, Conservative politicians and elite groups were just as confident that they could 'tame' Nazism, and even more mistaken. Other instances, however, were more favourable to the conservative right. The Austrian Christian Socials and sections of the fascist Heimwehr existed from the outset in a state of symbiosis. In the case of France, Austin shows how conservative manipulation of Doriot's Parti Populaire Français (PPF) seems to have fulfilled most of the aims which lay behind it, while more serious problems for the Fédération Républicaine and the Radicals arose when La Rocque's Parti Social Français (PSF) moved away from its earlier 'street' fascism towards a more orthodox position. The attractiveness of fascism as the hard edge of conservatism was even briefly apparent in Britain, though it is doubtful if Lord Rothermere's ephemeral enthusiasm for the British Union of Fascists (BUF) really reflected a much broader

Conservative position; this is not, of course, to suggest that in conditions of political instability and a deteriorating economy – the reverse of those which obtained in the Britain of the mid-1930s – the situation might not have been different.

It is not, however, simply a matter of what attitude conservative parties, their supporters and the interests they represented took towards autonomous fascist parties. The installation of the Fascist regime in Italy, especially after the erection of a dictatorship in January 1925, created a model which served not merely for would-be imitators such as Mosley or Quisling but also, albeit usually in a more selective way, for elements within the conservative right itself. This operated in a variety of contexts, affecting conservative parties within parliamentary systems as well as authoritarian regimes with non-fascist, essentially conservative, origins. Larsen shows the extent to which fascism and national socialism ate into Nordic conservatism, inspiring a rash of *fascisant* splinter-groups and interest associations, and in particular infecting conservative youth movements. He also shows, however, that constitutional conservatives successfully beat off the radical-rightist challenge. In Spain, the Confederación Española de Derechas Autonomas (CEDA), on behalf of policies which its leaders insisted were not fascist, employed a 'style' which certainly was; here too the party's youth movement, the Juventud de Acción Popular (JAP), suffered at the very least what Stanley Payne has called 'the vertigo of fascism' – and arguably more. Explicitly authoritarian movements of the conservative right were naturally even more prey to fascist influence, in terms of both style and acceptance of extreme solutions; just as Italian Nationalism and conservative Catholicism quickly found a home in the Fascist regime, so in Spain the monarchist right under the Second Republic developed its own brand of 'monarcho-fascism' and leaders such as Calvo Sotelo happily donned the 'fascist' label. The Austrian Heimwehr, while implicitly fascist in style and operation throughout its existence, adopted an explicitly fascist programme in 1930.

'Non-fascist' regimes, too, were affected, though by no means all in the same way. Primo de Rivera's dictatorship, in the Spain of the 1920s, may have originated in a straightforward military coup and been essentially conservative-paternalist in character, yet its luminaries borrowed selectively from the Italian model and in some cases explicitly sought to create 'fascism from above'; the pattern, unsuccessful in Primo's case, was to be followed, with varying degrees of superficiality and success, by others from Metaxas in Greece to King Carol of Romania. This last example highlights a further complication. Just as some dictatorships attempted to 'fascistize' themselves, so they or others sometimes found themselves at odds with more radical-rightist elements of what might be regarded as more authentically 'fascist' character. King Carol's suppression in 1938 of the Romanian Legion, whose origins are examined here by Irina Livezeanu, is merely one of the more brutal examples of such a conflict and its resolution; in the dictatorship of Salazar, depicted by Tom Gallagher as predominantly Catholic in inspiration and conservative in character, Rolão Preto's blue-shirted National Syndicalists emerged as a radical fascist opposition – and were also unceremoniously, if in this case peacefully, suppressed.

Such developments created, during the course of the 1920s and 1930s, a situation at once simple and confused. For many on the left it was simple: since the 'objective' role of interwar right-wing authoritarianism was the defence of capitalism through the violent destruction of the left, all its manifestations could be regarded as 'fascist' whether they accepted the label or not; or, to put it another way, 'fascism' referred to the role of certain kinds of regime rather than to a particular kind of political movement or set of ideas, and 'fascists' were all those who, by whatever route and with whatever ideological inspiration, sought to create or perpetuate such regimes. Given the fate suffered by leftists at the hands of various kinds of rightist regime, not all of which devotees of analytical rigour would regard as fascist, such an attitude is at least understandable. For those seeking a more rigorous understanding of 'fascism', confusion reigned, since the differences among a whole host of rightist movements and parties, and an increasing number of rightist regimes, tended to be subtly nuanced and constantly shifting.

On the basis of what has been examined so far, it is clearly reasonable to confirm the existence of a distinction, at the level of ideas and movements, between the radical or 'fascist' right and the conservative right, even when the latter gave birth to authoritarian movements of its own. However, for the reasons just discussed, not merely was a boundary between fascists and authoritarian conservatives never drawn with total clarity, but it became more blurred with every year that passed. Matters become more difficult still, however, when we come to examine the fascist–conservative relationship in the context of those regimes to which fascist or national socialist movements made a major contribution or, indeed, which they actually created.

Few analysts of fascism would wish to quarrel with the proposition that the Italian Fascist regime provides us with a template for use in assessing the nature of other rightist dictatorships. Yet, as Roland Sarti points out, if the measure of 'fascism' in power is the power of the fascist movement within the regime, then Fascist Italy was an only partially fascist state. Both the contributions on Italy in this volume make it clear that Mussolini's regime represented a compromise between various forms of fascist radicalism, notably those associated with syndicalism, corporatism and *squadrismo*, but also embracing republicanism and anti-clericalism, and

9

essentially conservative forces. The latter included powerful economic interests (bankers, industrialists and *agrari*); the monarchy; the Vatican, the Church and their Clerico-Fascist supporters; and the 'new right' of Italian Nationalism. The results of this compromise included the resolution of the 'Roman Question'; the abandonment of syndicalist and, in any serious sense, corporatist radicalism in deference to the economic establishment; the retention of the monarchy; the creation of a state that conformed to Nationalist rather than strictly fascist prescriptions; and the allocation to the Fascist Party and its associated organizations of a role that, whilst undeniably important, stopped well short of the actual exercise of power, formulation of policy, or pursuit of a 'fascist revolution'.

Leaving aside for the moment the unique case of the Third Reich, other regimes of the interwar and wartime right arrived at their own compromises, though by a variety of routes and, naturally, with different results. The Franco regime – the only European regime with a *major* radical fascist ingredient to survive long beyond 1945, and studied here by Paul Preston – is a useful example. Notwithstanding the aforementioned *fascisant* tendencies within the Spanish Catholic and monarchist right, radical fascism, in the form of the Falange (fused from 1934 with the JONS), was weak until 1936 when it began to expand rapidly, not least through the recruitment of disillusioned JAP-ists. From the start of the Civil War the Falange's growth became explosive. In April 1937 Franco, as effective head of state of Nationalist Spain, fused the Falange with the Carlists, monarchists and the rest of the right to form the single party of his regime: a process, though differently conducted, somewhat similar to Italian fascism's fusion with Nationalism and Clerico-Fascism after 1922. The product, like the Italian Fascist regime, was a compromise between radical fascism and conservative authoritarianism, in this case with unambiguous military and Church support. As Preston indicates, Falangism played a superficially prominent and important role for as long as it suited Franco, that is, until the mid-1940s, thereafter to be shunted into the sidings of Spanish political life.

In both the Italian and Spanish cases, fascist radicals writhed with impatience at the non-appearance of the 'revolution' or total takeover of the state of which they dreamed. In Italy during the late 1930s, fascist radicalism was channelled into Germanophilia and racism, without the essential nature of the Fascist state altering significantly; as Sarti points out, there is as much reason to suppose that Mussolini was planning to strengthen the state *vis-à-vis* the Fascist Party as the opposite. The bizarre experience of the Italian Social Republic confirms both the existence of a distinctive 'fascism' and its marginalization during the previous twenty years. In Spain, the frustration of devoted Falangists from the late 1940s onward was unable to assume potent political form. In both cases, of course, vast numbers of fascist/Falangist activists settled contentedly for whatever rewards the regime could offer them.

10

Other regimes offer different perspectives. The Austrian *Ständestaat* studied by Jill Lewis was, as its origins made likely, a comfortable blend of Christian Social and Heimwehr elements: one form of fascism, she argues, confronted and ultimately confounded by another, Nazism. Vichy, as depicted by Roger Austin, whilst its ideological atmosphere may have betrayed its conservative origins, in its 'strongly executive character', attempts at mass mobilization, and surveillance policies appears to have advanced closer to 'fascism' than is sometimes supposed.

The vital feature of all these and other regimes, whatever their provenance and outward characteristics, is that in all of them conservative interests and value-systems proved either dominant or capable of coexisting with an official 'fascism'. This is not to suggest that in Italy during the 1930s or Spain during the early 1940s, conservatives, whether driven by monarchism, Catholicism, or material interest, were not often irked by fascist display, vulgarity and office-holding or, indeed, anxious lest full-scale 'fascist revolution' might yet be unleashed. The fact remains that no serious conservative attempt to overthrow Mussolini occurred until wartime defeat transformed political realities, while monarchist machinations against the Franco regime were both unsuccessful and dictated more by self-interest than ideology or principle.

The fall of Mussolini and the protracted final agony of Francoism may at first sight seem to have little in common. One feature, however, they do share: the willingness of conservatives to abandon dictatorship when its advantages cease to be apparent, just as they or their predecessors embraced it and lived with it when it seemed in their interests to do so.

Despite the fact that German national socialism appears to belong to the same category of political *movement* as Italian fascism, Falangism and the rest of the radical right, the Third Reich, whether or not we choose to classify it as 'fascist', stands on its own as a *regime*. Whilst the process remained incomplete (in twelve years, how could it be anything else?), the German state, and elite corps such as the army and the bureaucracy, were subjected to 'Nazification' in a way not approached, or even seriously attempted, by fascists elsewhere. Despite emulative gestures in the Italian Social Republic, under Vichy, and even during the Second World War in Salazar's Portugal, the advancing role of the SS *within* the Third Reich was also unparalleled elsewhere. If fascism was 'more extreme in every way', then Nazism and the Nazi regime were more extreme still. This is not the place to pursue very far the question of *why* Nazism produced a qualitatively different kind of regime, as it surely did, from Mussolini's or Franco's. Suffice it to say that Nazism possessed an ideological content and thrust which most if not all other fascisms lacked; that Nazi ideology, as

11

both Eley and Noakes make clear, represented the most extreme version, organized more successfully and externalized in more extreme ways, of an already radicalized nationalist ideology; and that many, probably most, German Conservatives had by 1933 also placed themselves at various points on the same broad radical-nationalist spectrum.

Jeremy Noakes illustrates graphically the complex relationship of German Conservatives with Nazism and the Third Reich. While mistrustful of Nazism's turbulent plebeianism and 'socialist' overtones, most of the individuals and groups he examines recognized in it a common yearning for national self-respect and *Volksgemeinschaft*. Confident of 'taming' Nazism, the Conservative elites allowed it access to power. The sheer extremism of Nazism, however, provoked more in the way of Conservative opposition, and ultimately resistance, than occurred, until the last minute, in Italy. The denial of human rights, determination upon war, and of course encroachment upon Conservative prerogatives: these were among the causes of Conservative divergence from Nazism. Even so, to suggest a sharp and consistent Nazi–Conservative cleavage in the Third Reich would be going much too far. Noakes is careful to point out that the individuals whose disillusionment, criticism, opposition, resistance and, in some cases, executions he itemizes were often anything but typical of the sectors – Junkers, army officers, bureaucrats – from which they came. Considering the extremes to which Hitler had driven Germany by 1944/5, what is striking is not the extent of Conservative resistance but its limitations and utter failure.

The authors represented in this volume make abundantly clear how complex, fluid and subtle was the relationship between the radical and the conservative right in twentieth-century Europe. In the light of what their chapters tell us, two extreme views of that relationship must surely be rejected. The first, taking fascist anti-conservatism as seriously as its anti-leftism, holds that fascism does not belong on the right at all, that it somehow stands outside the established left–right spectrum. The second holds that distinctions within the non-democratic right are so superficial as to be scarcely worth considering; fascism is either an appropriate term for all manner of authoritarian rightist movements and regimes, or else is meaningless as a term of definition or description. To accept the first view involves deliberately or unthinkingly denying the nature of a relationship resting upon a significant measure of common ground and shared antagonisms, and without which no fascist or Nazi regime, and significantly fewer conservative-authoritarian regimes, could ever have been created. To embrace the second involves artificially smoothing the contours of the right, and ignoring very real differences, tensions and downright enmities within the admittedly very broad church of European rightism.

It cannot seriously be denied that as movements, parties and political ideologies, conservatism and fascism occupied very different positions within the early and mid-twentieth century European right, converging at some points and conflicting at others. In certain circumstances, especially characteristic of the 1919–45 period, convergence outweighed conflict, and the uneasy coupling of fascism and conservatism spawned a new kind of political regime. With fascists often showing a tendency to succumb to a cosy conservatism, and conservatives sometimes embracing the rhetoric (or more) of fascism, such regimes exhibited a kaleidoscopic variety of tendencies of which the rarest was what might be termed 'pure' fascism. In many cases, genuine – that is to say self-consciously radical – fascists were a negligible force and any 'fascist' elements at most merely cosmetic. Elsewhere, notably in Spain, assorted conservatives proved capable of displacing radical fascism. In Fascist Italy, surely the paradigmatic fascist regime, conservatives co-existed with fascists, survived largely unscathed, and when given the opportunity overthrew the Fascist regime. Only in Germany did the conservative right come close to being devoured by the tiger it had chosen to ride.

NOTES

1 The general bibliography on fascism is now vast. The following is intended merely as a selective guide: F. L. Carstens *The Rise of Fascism* (London, 1967); S. G. Payne, *Fascism. Comparison and Definition* (Madison. Wis., 1980); N. O'Sullivan, *Fascism* (London and Melbourne, 1983); M. Kitchen, *Fascism* (London, 1976); J. Weiss, *The Fascist Tradition. Radical Right-Wing Extremism in Modern Europe* (New York, 1967); E. Weber, *Varieties of Fascism* (Princeton, NJ, 1964); S. J. Woolf (ed.), *Fascism in Europe* (London, 1981) [an earlier edition appeared in 1968 as *European Fascism*]; S. J. Woolf (ed.), *The Nature of Fascism* (London, 1968); A. J. Gregor, *Interpretations of Fascism* (Berkeley Calif., 1974); W. Laqueur (ed.), *Fascism. A Reader's Guide. Analyses, Interpretations, Bibliography* (London, 1976); H. R. Kedward, *Fascism in Western Europe 1900–45* (New York, 1971); N. Poulantzas, *Fascism and Dictatorship* (London, 1979); M. Vajda, *Fascism as a Mass Movement* (London, 1976).
   On the fascist–conservative relationship, see H. Rogger and E. Weber (eds), *The European Right. A Historical Profile* (London, 1965); E. Nolte, *Three Faces of Fascism* (London, 1963); Barrington Moore Jr, *Social Origins of Dictatorship and Democracy. Lord and Peasant in the Making of the Modern World* (London, 1967).
   Two recent volumes examine in detail the social base of fascism: S. U. Larsen, B. Hagtvet and J. Myklebust (eds), *Who Were the Fascists? Social Roots of European Fascism* (Bergen, Oslo and Tromsø, 1980) and D. Mühlberger (ed.), *The Social Basis of European Fascist Movements* (London, New York and Sydney, 1987).
2 On conservatism see H. Rogger and E. Weber (eds) *The European Right. A Historical Profile*; N. O'Sullivan, *Conservatism* (London, 1976); J. Weiss, *Conservatism in Europe, 1770–1945* (London, 1977); R. Kirk, *The Conservative Mind* (London, 1954); S. P. Huntington, 'Conservatism as an ideology', *American Political Science Review*, vol. LI (1957), pp. 454–73; C. Rossiter, 'Conservatism', in D. L. Sills (ed.), *International Encyclopedia of the Social Sciences* (New York, 1968), Vol. iii, pp. 290–4; P. Viereck, *Conservatism Revisited* (New York, 1965). See also two issues of the *Journal of Contemporary History* devoted to 'A century of conservatism': vol. 13, no. 4 (October 1978) and vol. 14, no. 4 (October 1979).

2

Italian fascism: radical politics and conservative goals

Roland Sarti

Explicit professions of conservatism have been fairly rare in Italian politics. Ever since national unification was achieved under conditions of near-revolution, political movements have sought to gain credibility and support by proposing strategies of change that were more or less radical in nature. Indeed, even in those few instances when the conservative label has been borne with pride the object has been to bring about change in the established political order. On the whole, Italian conservatives have shown little Burkean respect for institutions and processes received from the distant past. Conservatism in Italy may express itself as an abiding loyalty to family, local community, land, or religion, and to the values and social relationships based on respect for these institutions, but much less often as an attachment to specific political institutions and processes. The general reluctance to endorse specific political forms except in the very short run means that in Italian politics conservatism tends to reside largely in the eyes of beholders. Participants prefer to be known as advocates of change, modernization and progress.

The perceptions of beholders and participants were strikingly different in the case of fascism. In the early days of the movement left-wing critics of fascism found enough evidence of collusion between Fascists and landowners, particularly after 1921, to describe fascism as conservative or reactionary in spite of its origins in the revolutionary tradition.[1] The accusation was hotly denied by Fascists who insisted on the revolutionary character and mission of their movement. According to Giuseppe Bottai, fascism was the only revolutionary movement of the twentieth century because of its roots in the cultural reaction against nineteenth-century rationalism. More commonly, Fascist intellectuals preferred to emphasize the alleged uniqueness of their movement, which they claimed enabled it to transcend conventional distinctions between left and right. That view was perhaps stated most effectively by Sergio Panunzio who, while acknowledging the movement's conservatism on such matters as the importance of strong family ties, propagation of Catholicism among the masses, respect for the authority of the state, the role of women within the family, and restriction of popular initiatives, argued nevertheless that 'in other respects fascism is innovative to such a degree that conservatives fear it, particularly when it affirms its commitment to establish the syndical state and demolish the parliamentary state'.[2]

Such subjective perceptions, whether favourable or unfavourable, help us to understand the nature of the political debate but not necessarily the nature of fascism or, least of all, any possible connections with conservatism. Discussion of their relationship is complicated by the fact that neither is easy to define. The common tendency to use the term 'fascist' as a political epithet and 'conservative' as a synonym for retrograde or reactionary does not help. But scholars who usually avoid such loose language also find it difficult to come up with generally acceptable definitions, probably because fascism lacks a clearly recognizable fountainhead in the world of ideas and conservatism encompasses attitudes and phenomena that go beyond ideology and politics. Clinton Rossiter's definition of conservatism, for instance, distinguished between three basic varieties. The first, temperamental conservatism, manifests itself according to Rossiter as a disposition to resist dislocating changes in the routines and structures of daily life. The second, situational conservatism, is said to reflect a more deliberate and systematic opposition to disruptive change in the realm of social mores, hierarchic relationships and religion. Political conservatism, the third form, differs from these other varieties in at least one important respect. Often referred to as 'the right', political conservatism can exist only in modern society, as an organized force surrounded by other organized political forces competing to direct the course of change.[3]

Let us dwell on this last definition. If it is true that political conservatism is indeed a modern phenomenon, then we would not expect conservative movements to renounce the principles and techniques of modern politics, including pursuit of popular support, development of mechanisms for mass mobilization, courting of specific interest groups for political purposes, and use of mass media to convey political messages. It may be suggested that in their acceptance of modern technology, such as the use of computers in our own time, and of mass-mobilization techniques, movements of the right are not basically different from any other movements. In modern politics massive assaults on the autonomy and conscience of individuals are not the prerogative of any particular current. While the forms may range from mass rallies to paid commercials, manipulative techniques are employed systematically from left to right. For that reason they are not particularly useful for purposes of distinction and classification. We can therefore express legitimate reservations about interpretations that place fascist regimes outside the conservative tradition because of their undeniably original use of mobilization and propaganda techniques.[4] Techniques are, after all, only means to an end. Our discussion of fascism concerns itself more with ends than means.

Using history as a guide, we can say that starting with the French Revolution conservatives have pictured themselves as defenders of established
institutions, social relationships, or values against the forces of change.
Describing conservative goals in this deliberately general manner is
preferable to positing a necessarily antagonistic relationship between
right and left, not only because right and left may often practise the
same kind of politics but, more to the point in the case of Italy, because
both conservatives and Fascists have perceived enemies on many different
points of the political spectrum. In the context of Italian politics, the
forces of change could be plausibly perceived as being represented
by Communists, Socialists, liberals, or even politically active Catholics.
Against the push for change orchestrated by one or more of these
groups, conservatives have generally upheld the need for a principle
of order, the value of social distinctions and the legitimacy of private
property, and have expressed suspicion of purely rational remedies,
majority rule and egalitarian notions. Probably the best way to approach
a discussion of conservatism and fascism is to try to relate the choice of
means to the attainment of such generic, but economically and socially
meaningful, goals.

Efforts to present fascism as a specific form of conservatism have always
run into difficulties, for fairly obvious reasons. To revert to Rossiter's
distinctions, if we perceive conservatism as an attitudinal phenomenon
we risk not being able to relate it to any specific form of political
activity. The tendency to resist dislocations in the routines and structures
of daily life manifests itself in most political movements, including the
most radical. Fascists and communists can be equally adverse to changes
in eating habits, pastimes and work schedules. Furthermore, we can
safely assume that a movement like the fascist whose ideology professed
enthusiasm for adventure, risk and aggrandizement must have attracted
more than its share of temperamental iconoclasts. 'Me ne frego' ('I don't
give a damn') is not a sentiment likely to appeal to temperamental
conservatives.

In the case of Rossiter's second category, that of situational conservatism, it is perhaps easier to see similarities with fascism. Here we are
dealing with attitudes towards aspects of the public order like religion,
law, contract, and social hierarchy. Fascist legislation on church–state
relations, relations within the family, the role of private property, and
labour relations on the whole bolstered these principles, but anti-clerical,
anti-monarchist and anti-bourgeois tendencies were never extinguished
and actually served the regime by prolonging the hope, dear to some,
that fascism would some day turn radical.[5] Attempts to see fascism as a
projection of authoritarian personality traits raise troublesome questions.
A good case in point is Theodore Adorno's *The Authoritarian Personality*

(1950), which ultimately blurs distinctions between conservatism, authoritarianism, fascism and totalitarianism.[6]

Distinctions being an essential part of historical reasoning, we should explore the relationship between conservatism and fascism with due regard for the specifics of place and time. That was the message of Karl Mannheim's well-known essay of 1927 on 'Conservative thought', wherein he cautioned that

> Conservative action ... is always dependent on *a concrete sense of circumstances*. There is no means of knowing in advance what forms a conservative action in the political sense will take ... how a conservative will react can only be determined approximately *if we know a good deal about the conservative movement* in the period and in the country under discussion.[7]

The country under discussion being Italy, we immediately face the problem of having to identify a conservative tradition in a context where, as previously noted, open professions of conservatism have been rare and a broadly based conservative movement has never materialized. Since self-confessed conservative Fascists were rarer than Venetian gondoliers in the Gulf of Naples, we must investigate the question by looking beyond the realm of stated intentions.[8]

We begin with Mannheim's observation that conservative action is always dependent upon a set of concrete circumstances. The circumstances of Italian political life after national unification made it almost impossible for leaders and governments to present themselves as conservative. In international relations Italy's position as the least of the great European powers put pressure on the political class and its representatives to come up with strategies of expansion and to test their effectiveness on a fairly regular basis. Italy's African campaigns in the nineteenth century, the Italo-Turkish War of 1911–12, the First World War, the reconquest of Libya in the 1920s, the Italo-Ethiopian War (1935–6), the intervention in Spain (1936–9), the annexation of Albania (1939) and finally the Second World War, make Italy the European power most ready to engage in combat during that period. The invocation of the *Hymn of Garibaldi* that Italy cease to be a land of music and song and resume its ancient role as a warrior nation was realized in the first half of the twentieth century with unexpected suddenness and intensity.

Such activism in foreign policy did not accord with conservatism at home. Long before the Fascists came to power the Italian state used its considerable resources to instil a sense of national pride in the people and to develop the economic muscle needed to play an active role far from home.[9] Protective tariffs, government subsidies and contracts on

17

behalf of steel, armaments and shipbuilding made the Liberal state the most revolutionary agent in Italian society.

Following Italy's humiliation at Adowa in 1896 the connection between activism abroad and radical change at home became explicit. Enrico Corradini's political review *Il Regno* (1903–6) called for reforms that would foster political unity at home to strengthen Italy's posture abroad. In the thinking of frustrated nationalists like Corradini, the stronger the desire to gain international stature the greater the propensity to demand radical transformations of the system of government. Members of the Italian Nationalist Association (hereafter referred to as Nationalists), which Corradini helped to found in 1910, thought along these lines, but so did many other figures and groups, including Futurists, D'Annunzians of various stripes, and even Liberal critics of Parliament like Gaetano Mosca and Vilfredo Pareto, all of them considered precursors of fascism.[10] Although we often refer to them as belonging to the right, it was a right that showed little reverence for the institutions of government inherited from the previous generation of Risorgimento leaders. They were not conservative in that sense, but we should not rule out the possibility that, as Mannheim suggests, their politics may have been conservative in ways that must be understood in reference to a specific historical context.

The context is provided by the circumstances of national unification. Achieved against the wishes of the Church, the Bourbons and the Habsburgs, and without much popular support outside of urban society, national unification drove genuine conservatives out of national politics. The outcasts included legitimists who remained loyal to the deposed dynasties, clericals, segments of the nobility, the clergy and all but the wealthiest peasants. Most Italians were deliberately excluded from politics by a narrow franchise that gave the vote to less than 2 per cent of the population in 1861 and reflected the fear of the governing Liberal minority toward the rest of society. Conservatives who under different circumstances could have played a constructive role as a party of opposition were in fact absent from national politics for some forty years after national unification. They were present in local politics where they often found considerable support, but their presence at the grassroots level only reinforced the Liberals' fears towards the *paese reale*, the 'real society' that was seen as being hostile or indifferent to the laws and institutions that made up the *paese legale*.

The call to bridge the gap between the two societies came first from the conservative wing of the Liberal establishment. The use of the term 'conservative' is justified in this case by the fact that it was borne proudly by the movement's founder, Catholic senator Stefano Jacini. His conservatism was actually an idiosyncratic version of the dominant liberalism, for while criticizing the Liberals for misgoverning the country, Jacini accepted national unification as irreversible and parliamentary government as desirable. Jacini feared that the gap between *paese reale* and *paese legale* would isolate the state from the people. His proposals for strengthening the state included extending voting rights, encouraging local self-government, and invigorating the economy by modernizing agriculture.[11] The National Conservative Party that was to promote this programme was virtually stillborn in the early 1880s, but Jacini's politically premature attempt at national reconciliation is nevertheless interesting as an anticipation of future expressions of conservatism. In this first manifestation, Italian conservatism displayed a recurring concern for strengthening the state, a suspicion of Liberal politicians elected by narrow constituencies and of political cliques entrenched in the elective Chamber of Deputies, and the expectation that disenfranchised citizens could be relied upon to help correct the abuses of government and the weakness of the state.

Conservative hopes of finding popular support would be undercut by political developments that followed the demise of the National Conservatives. By the early 1890s it was clear that the Socialists also enjoyed broad popular support. Parliamentary conservatives, fearful of popular support for both Socialists and Catholics, had to rethink their political tactics. Their goal was still, as it had been in Jacini's time, to strengthen the state, but now they sought to strengthen it by institutional reform at the centre of government rather than by electoral reform in the country at large. Several measures adopted during Francesco Crispi's second administration of 1893–6, most notably the purging of 847,000 voters from the electoral lists, were indicative of growing conservative fears of popular participation in public life. But the clearest expression of the new conservative fear of the *paese reale* appeared in Sidney Sonnino's call of 1897 for a 'Return to the *Statuto*', the original Piedmontese constitution of 1848 which gave the Crown far more independence than was the case in Italian politics in 1897. Like Jacini before him, Sonnino singled out the Chamber as primarily responsible for misgoverning the country, but his attack on the only elected branch of Parliament reflected a more general fear of popular participation in government and grassroots organizations. He confided these fears to his diary, writing that it was his ultimate intention to stop the gains of Socialists and Catholics, 'especially the former who are organizing powerfully', and to restrict those laws that gave 'dominance to the numerically larger classes'.[12]

The 'Return to the *Statuto*' approach signalled a quantitative rather than a qualitative shift in conservative politics, for conservatives like Sonnino and Antonio Salandra, the landowner from Apulia who served as Prime Minister in 1914–16, never abandoned attempts to secure broad popular support for a conservative programme. Sonnino's course during the protracted parliamentary crisis of 1899–1900 also envisaged, besides curbing Parliament and strengthening the Crown, launching a new Conservative Party that would rally support for administrative and social reforms. The repeated failure of such efforts in years to come forced Sonnino, Salandra and their parliamentary supporters to remain within the Liberal camp, which was dominated by the more pragmatic and resourceful Giovanni Giolitti. In the Liberal camp they were neither fish nor fowl, for while profoundly at odds with Giolitti's tactics of dealing with Socialists and Catholics as parliamentary needs dictated, they were at the same time unable to play the role of consistent and principled opposition to which they aspired. Unable to emerge as a fully autonomous party of opposition, they may indeed have brought Italy into the First World War in May 1915 in the hope that a rapid victory would give them the political leverage denied to them by the normal course of parliamentary politics.[13] But whatever their intentions may have been in the spring of 1915, it seems clear that the absence of a Conservative Party firmly committed to parliamentary government opened the way to the emergence of new groups on the right who were both hostile to Parliament in principle and determined to bring about change by political action outside Parliament. This was the political vacuum that was filled 'first by Nationalists, and later by other forces among which fascism would eventually emerge the winner'.[14]

There were no organizational ties between this new right and the older right of Sonnino and Salandra. The old right was made up of seasoned parliamentarians who accepted the ground-rules of parliamentary government, the new right of brash young intellectuals who rejected Parliament and liberalism, and asserted the need for a bold, expansionist foreign policy.[15] They sought support not in the halls of Parliament or among the disenfranchised but, rather, among the intelligentsia, businessmen, and iconoclasts of all ages. But in some respects the old and new right were closer than is sometimes argued.[16] Both were suspicious of the political force that resides in numbers (and the number of eligible voters was growing: from 2 million in 1882 to 2.9 million in 1909 and 8.4 million in 1913); both saw the affirmation of socialism as a direct result of mass mobilization; both held liberalism primarily responsible for the country's alleged drift to the left; both believed that freedom of speech and association, and Giolitti's recognition of the workers' right to strike, led to the emergence of a state within the state by promoting the growth of trade unions, chambers of labour, co-operatives and rural leagues. In spite of their undeniable differences, old and new right were one in their commitment to a strong state capable of resisting popular pressures. It is that commitment that justifies placing both within the same tradition of conservative politics.

Probably the most significant difference between the old and new right was the latter's awareness that the dawning age of mass politics required new forms of political mobilization. That awareness was particularly evident in the writings of Alfredo Rocco, the Nationalist jurist who elaborated the most systematic alternative to the Liberal state based on an integral view of society.[17] The strong state envisaged by Rocco had to reach deep into the *paese reale* without making concessions to the principle of independent initiative capable of resisting the power of the state. Achieving that goal required new forms of mass mobilization that did not exist in the Liberal state. Among Nationalists, designing those new forms became the task of theoreticians like Rocco, while devising the political tactics to achieve those goals became the concern of effective power brokers. In the latter role, Luigi Federzoni would distinguish himself when he became Minister of the Interior under Mussolini in 1924–6.

Although in the long run the Nationalists influenced fascism in decisive ways, their role was by no means predetermined. In its early years fascism was a movement of vigorously competing currents and factions. Thus, when the Nationalist and Fascist parties merged formally in February 1923, the former Nationalists encountered within the Fascist Party entrenched rivals who were by no means prepared to defer to the newcomers.[18] Among these competitors, the Nationalists stood out in many ways: they were committed to gradual reform of the state, were determined that any changes be carefully controlled by representatives of the state and believed that the state must assume important responsibilities to secure social justice for the people. They abhorred initiatives, popular or otherwise, that the state could not control, insisting that everything occur within, and nothing against, the state. They were conservative not in the sense of being opposed to change, but of wanting to retain control of those changes that were an inevitable part of the process of modernization. It is only in this sense that one can speak of Fascist conservatism: change carefully controlled from above, making no concessions to pluralism and independent initiative. For Rocco, who served as Fascist Minister of Justice from 1925 to 1932, this meant nothing less than carrying out a 'conservative revolution'.[19]

Most Fascist leaders preferred to avoid the conservative label altogether, concentrating instead on pushing alternative versions of revolution. The names of Giuseppe Bottai, Roberto Farinacci and Massimo Rocca come perhaps most readily to mind in this regard. Each played an important role in the 1920s in a race to see who would eventually dominate the course of the Fascist revolution. Their activities are well documented in the first two volumes of Renzo De Felice's ongoing biography of Mussolini. But none of them had convincing credentials as would-be revolutionists, and only Farinacci had an independent basis of power that gave him a measure of security. The former Nationalists' most serious and worrisome rivals were the syndicalists, some of them former Marxists who had found a place in fascism. They had experience, organization and support among workers and peasants. The rivalry between these labour leaders and former Nationalists recreated within fascism some of the ideological and class tensions that had bedevilled the old Liberal regime.

In discussing the syndicalists' role within fascism the most difficult task is to ascertain their degree of influence. The revolutionary thrust of their ideas has been well demonstrated.[20] There can be little doubt that on ideological grounds they were the nemesis of all the conservative interests that flocked to fascism after the March on Rome. The rediscovery of this revolutionary component of fascism corrects crude Marxist interpretations of fascism as a pliable tool in the hands of capitalists. At the same time, concentrating attention on one strand of fascism raises the danger of an opposite distortion, for while it is sufficiently clear at the current stage of research that the syndicalists were indeed strong enough to leave their mark on the regime, it is no less apparent that their major proposals for restructuring Italian society were decisively defeated in the 1920s. The works that provide the best understanding of what the syndicalists did and failed to do are those that pay close attention to the rivalries, confrontations and compromises that marked the internal history of fascism.[21] Also useful but perhaps less definitive because of the difficult issues they address are works that try to assess the impact of the Fascist labour movement on wages, standard of living, popular perceptions of the regime, and economic development.[22] The Fascist labour movement played a significant role in these areas where the syndicalists had to devise strategies that reconciled the interests of labour with the political needs of the regime.

Regimes born of revolution face the dilemma of how to prolong their credibility as carriers of revolution while at the same time erecting a new system of order. All the currents present in fascism, whether potentially revolutionary or conservative, were dominated by the logic of a system that had to appear revolutionary while simultaneously implementing measures for law and order. The resulting dynamics made it expedient for conservative Nationalists to pose as a party of revolution and for revolutionary syndicalists to claim that their chief concerns were social stability and economic productivity. In both instances it was the apparent ability to reconcile contrasting claims that made them particularly useful to fascism and Mussolini. The original encounter between Mussolini and the revolutionary syndicalists occurred in 1914–15 when they all argued for Italian intervention in the war against the Central Powers. The founding of the Unione Italiana del Lavoro (UIL) in November 1914 gave the syndicalists a narrow basis among workers that they would expand after the war largely through the efforts of Edmondo Rossoni. Rossoni's recruitment among land-workers succeeded largely because of his working relationship with Fascist leaders, particularly Italo Balbo in Ferrara during 1921–2.[23] In January 1922 Rossoni became secretary-general of the Confederation of National Syndicates, which worked closely with the Fascists. In December 1922 the merger was sealed and the organization renamed the General Confederation of Fascist Syndical Corporations.

Rossoni had vast ambitions for his confederation. His immediate objective of making it the largest labour organization in the country was achieved fairly readily in the climate of intimidation that prevailed before and after the March on Rome. Between 1920 and 1924 the membership of the Socialist General Confederation of Labour declined from 2.3 million to 200,000, and that of the Catholic Italian Confederation of Workers from 1.2 million to 400,000, while the membership of the Fascist Confederation rose from 250,000 to 1.8 million. At that level, its membership exceeded that of the Fascist Party which claimed only 650,000 members in 1924, and the disparity alarmed party leaders for obvious reasons. Rossoni's confederation had become the largest organization in the country outside of the Catholic Church and seemed poised to take over fascism itself. That prospect pleased few people outside the ranks of syndicalism. Rossoni and labour threatened too many vested interests to be allowed to grow unchecked.[24]

With this large organization to give him leverage, Rossoni seemed bent on controlling the course of the continuing Fascist revolution. On 12 November 1922 *Il Popolo D'Italia* quoted him as saying that only the Fascist syndicates could complete the revolution. Through them would emerge the political leaders of the future, they would provide the basis for a new system of political representation based on occupation and production, and they would inculcate a strong productivist ethic in both workers and employers that would replace counterproductive class loyalties. They would accomplish all this by enrolling workers and employers in the same organizations of 'mixed syndicates' or 'corporations'. Through them all citizens would eventually find social fulfilment in their respective roles as producers. Productive man would replace political man as the social ideal: the crowning achievement and lasting contribution of fascism to the problems of industrial society.[25]

Rossoni's vision clearly exceeded his grasp. The membership of the syndicates was large but their organization in the first years of the regime left much to be desired. As a leader, Rossoni was more adept at creating passing furores with his firebrand rhetoric than at planning for the long term. His opponents were not taken in by what they feared was mere lip-service to the principle of class co-operation. Opposition came from many quarters, some within and some outside fascism. Formally outside but working their way toward a close working relationship with the regime were businessmen who used the General Confederation of Italian Industry (Confindustria) as their mouthpiece and bargaining agent. Through the Pact of Palazzo Chigi in December 1923 they were able to wrest from

Rossoni the recognition that employers and workers would retain separate organizations. They also promised mutual co-operation, but the agreement in effect pushed the realization of Rossoni's corporate state into the dim and distant future.[26]

Because it was politically useful the corporatist ideal was not renounced, but the battle was on among competing Fascist groups to give it concrete content. Party leaders, speaking through a resolution of the Fascist Grand Council on 1 May 1923, had already indicated that they expected the corporatists to represent qualified minorities rather than large numbers ('sindacalismo di minoranza qualitativa e non di numero') and not to aim at a monopoly of labour representation.[27] The party obviously did not want to face a large, popular and independent labour movement, all the more dangerous because it bore the Fascist label. Equally opposed, although for different reasons, were the Nationalists who wanted to protect the integrity not of the party, which they disliked and feared, but of the state, which they worshipped. They too wanted to launch a new labour movement and a corporatist society based on the principle of class collaboration and on the rewarding of individual merit rather than the advancement of class interests. To the extent that both revolutionary syndicalists and Nationalists endorsed these ideas they had something in common.[28] These similarities nevertheless disguised deep-seated differences of temperament and approach that made syndicalists and Nationalists arch-rivals within fascism. More than any other single development, the outcome of their rivalry would control the direction of change in Fascist Italy.

The positions of both syndicalists and Nationalists were seemingly strengthened by the outcome of the political crisis that gripped the country after the assassination of Giacomo Matteotti by the Fascists on 10 June 1924. The crisis, which lasted almost six months and threatened to topple Mussolini, convinced him to abandon attempts at reconciliation with the regime's enemies and rely instead on declared supporters who had not wavered during the crisis. Both syndicalists and Nationalists sat on the committees that studied institutional reforms, but the dominant role of the Nationalists is evident from the recommendations that emerged. They reaffirmed and strengthened the role of the Crown, limited that of Parliament, and within Parliament suggested a strengthening of the appointive Senate at the expense of the elective Chamber. This version of a 'return to the *Statuto*' disappointed too many expectations to prevail, but is nevertheless indicative of the influence wielded by conservatives. The reforms that were legislated in 1925–6 probably went further than conservative ministers like Federzoni and Rocco would have liked. Rossoni obtained his monopoly of representation over labour and forced employers to accept the principle of compulsory arbitration of labour disputes by special courts. Federzoni and Rocco, on the other hand, managed to protect the state bureaucracy from party control, expand the power of the prefects, curb what remained of the Fascist squads, and reaffirm the principle of orderly change directed from above.[29]

In retrospect it seems clear that the institutional reforms of 1925–6 owed more to the authoritarian reformism of the former Nationalists that to the revolutionary spirit of the syndicalists. But no one took the defeat of the syndicalists for granted at the time. With the new power of exclusive representation of labour, Rossoni headed a single national labour confederation of considerable power. Much to Mussolini's displeasure, in September 1927 Rossoni publicly criticized the government for failing to lower the cost of living after having imposed extensive wage cuts. At a time when wage cuts were the order of the day owing to the government's deflationary policy, employers did not like having to deal with a unified labour movement. Party secretary Augusto Turati insisted that the party must have supremacy over the syndicates. For Giuseppe Bottai, soon to be Minister of Corporations, the syndicates were remnants of the old class mentality that kept labour and management apart. He did not wish to abolish the syndicates, but neither did he want them to have too much power. Clearly, there was enough hostility towards Rossoni and his organization to sustain a concerted campaign to discredit him and break up his confederation. The dismemberment (*sbloccamento*) took place in December 1928 and was immediately followed by Rossoni's forced resignation as head of the labour movement. From that point on, to quote De Felice, 'Fascist syndicalism practically left the scene and became a mere instrument deprived of autonomy, power, and prestige'.[30]

The judgement that Fascist syndicalism practically disappeared from the scene after 1928 is perhaps too extreme. The *sbloccamento* put an end once and for all to the syndicalists' hope of acting as the driving force of the revolution but did not deprive them of the power to act and react in the area of labour relations. There are several first-hand accounts that stress the vigour with which a younger generation of labour leaders spoke out on bread-and-butter issues of interest to workers.[31] By 1937 the national economy had entered an expansionist and slightly inflationary phase that facilitated the work of labour negotiators. Wage increases negotiated in 1936, 1937 and 1939 brought real wages in industry back up to the levels of the early 1920s. But the most significant and lasting gains occurred in social insurance and public health, with improvements in illness and disability benefits, introduction of family subsidies, increases in piece-work rates, and end-of-the-year bonuses and compulsory payment for national holidays. Many of these innovations became permanent features of a national social insurance scheme which to this day relies heavily on state and employer contributions. Such gains indicate that industrial workers in particular were not left unprotected, but also how effectively the syndical movement was deflected from its revolutionary course. By the late 1930s syndicalism was an effective mainstay that showed a remarkable capacity to avoid fundamental issues of social organization. The labour movement had become an instrument of social conservation.

A similar fate awaited other currents of fascism that also aspired to lead the revolution. The corporatists, who had Bottai as their most articulate and intellectually sophisticated spokesman, were given a series of reforms between 1930 and 1934 that fell far short of what they expected. The corporations that finally emerged looked impressive enough on paper but were denied the powers of control and planning that were essential to the fulfilment of their economic role. While the defeat of the corporatists is easy to understand, for they were after all isolated intellectuals with no following outside their own circles, the ease with which the Fascist Party was rendered politically innocuous is more puzzling. The explanation may be found in Mussolini's growing prestige, sense of personal infallibility, and irritation towards collaborators who showed independence of mind. By the early 1930s he may have felt that he needed an organization capable of carrying out his own policies, not one that could produce its own leadership and generate ideas. Whatever the reason, following the appointment of Achille Starace as its secretary in December 1931 the party increasingly took on a choreographic role that made it extremely visible and ultimately irrelevant. Article 1 of the party charter of 1932 described the party as 'a civilian militia at the orders of the Duce and in the service of the Fascist state'.[32]

The state that the party was expected to serve was considerably less Fascist than these words suggest. Its Fascist character was evident in the vast organizational network that enrolled youngsters, students, teachers, public employees, peasants, city workers and housewives. Whether joined voluntarily or under pressure, these organizations were not irrelevant to their millions of members, for at the very least they drew ordinary men, women and children out of their daily routines and exposed them, however briefly, to collective experiences that did not revolve around the traditional institutions of family, church and local community. But the atmosphere that ordinary people found in these new organizations was not intended to encourage spontaneity and initiative from below. This was particularly true of the largest popular organization of the 1920s, the Opera Nazionale Dopolavoro, which in 1939 listed more than 3.8 million members. In Victoria De Grazia's words, the Dopolavoro ultimately fostered 'a static acceptance of the regime' and proved to be incompatible with the 'dynamic expansionist and imperialist mentality' that was supposed to be the distinguishing trait of fascism.[33] Popular acceptance of authority had been an early aim of the Nationalists who, to secure it, had been willing to practise the radical politics of mass organization. In that sense, the Fascist regime delivered what modern-minded conservatives usually seek: popular support without popular initiative.

At the level of government the conservative approach that aimed at strengthening the state was also still very much in evidence by the late 1930s. Of the two grand figures of Nationalism, Rocco left office in 1932 and died three years later. He had nevertheless worked well as Minister of Justice, for the institutional reforms that he inspired and directed were able to contain any moves to fascistize the state. Federzoni stayed on, serving as President of the Senate until 1939 and voting for Dino Grandi's motion of 25 July 1943 that called upon the king to take over from Mussolini. In his memoirs, published in 1967, the year of his death, Federzoni expressed serious reservations over the alliance with Germany, the racial laws, conduct of the war, and Mussolini's diminishing sufferance towards the Crown.[34] He feared a radicalization of the regime, a fear that was also based on what appeared to be a recrudescence of Mussolini's old anti-bourgeois sentiments. Businessmen shared those fears after 1935, but it is important to remember that they were fears for the future. Mussolini's course and the regime's actual record of reform were something else. It is quite possible that genuine radicalization was very far from Mussolini's mind; there are indications that he was planning to expand further the role of the state bureaucracy in Italian life at the expense of party and militia. The war did precisely that up to July 1943, strengthening the regular army, prefects, police, and state planning agencies that took charge of price controls, food requisitioning, rationing, surveillance, and allocation of industrial raw materials. The key figures were usually administrators whose actions conformed to state law rather than to political directives.[35]

Perhaps the experience of the German-controlled Italian Social Republic of 1944–5 shows that the radical-revolutionary current within fascism had not disappeared. Nevertheless, Mussolini's puppet regime can tell us little about what might have been the 'normal' evolution of fascism in the absence of military defeat. In the short-lived history of the Social Republic, businesses were nationalized, workers received a voice in the management of enterprises, the so-called 'traitors' who had voted for Grandi's motion were condemned to death, and fascism returned to its original republicanism. Most importantly, the police were given unprecedented powers to deal with internal subversion and the armed Resistance. Thus, in its final phase fascism may have created the police state that brought to the fore its totalitarian tendencies. But it is highly unlikely that the Fascist regime could have turned in that direction spontaneously. A more likely outcome in the absence of war and German prodding is that *fascismo* would gradually have been taken over and vanquished by *mussolinismo*. The record shows that *mussolinismo* meant, above all, a strong bureaucratic state based on law rather than a police state driven by a revolutionary vision of a future society. No doubt not only Rocco, but even Jacini, Crispi and Sonnino would have intuitively understood the spirit if not all the manifestations of the Fascist regime.

NOTES

1 On the early interpretations of fascism, see R. De Felice, *Le interpretazioni del fascismo* (Bari, 1974), pp. 167–91.
2 S. Panunzio, 'Il doppio aspetto del fascismo', in R. De Felice (ed.), *Autobiografia del fascismo* (Bergamo, 1978), p. 185. This important collection of texts emphasizes Fascists' perception of themselves as revolutionists.
3 See Clinton Rossiter's entry on 'Conservatism' in the *International Encyclopedia of the Social Sciences* (1968).
4 Interpretations that stress the manipulative aspects of fascist regimes often also see them as being closely related to movements of the left, and therefore revolutionary in character. Such interpretations usually employ the concept of totalitarianism as a unifying device. Trend-setting in this respect was C. T. Friedrich and Z. K. Brzezinski, *Totalitarian Dictatorship and Democracy* (Cambridge, Mass., 1956). More subtle interpretations that also point to the novel and revolutionary aspects of fascism are E. Weber, *Varieties of fascism* (New York, 1964) and S. G. Payne, *Fascism: Comparison and Definition* (Madison, Wis., 1980). J. Weiss, *The Fascist Tradition* (New York, 1967) sees fascism as an updated version of nineteenth-century conservatism. Somewhat different in emphasis is P. V. Cannistraro, *La fabbrica del consense. Fascismo e mass media* (Bari, 1975) which sees Italian fascism as aspiring but ultimately failing to secure radical change through the use of mass media and mobilizing techniques.
5 The literature on fascism's dealings with the Church, labour, business, army and monarchy is too vast to be discussed here. Useful overviews appear in G. Quazza (ed.), *Fascismo e società italiana* (Turin, 1973). The persistence of radical currents within fascism well into the 1930s is evident from M. A. Ledeen, *Universal Fascism* (New York, 1972) and R. Zangrandi, *Il lungo viaggio attraverso il fascismo* (Milan, 1964).
6 Historians of Italian fascism have shown little desire to explore possible links between individual or collective psychology on the one hand and authoritarianism or fascism on the other. Some provocative psychohistorical suggestions emerge from the long and brilliant essay by novelist Carlo Emilio Gadda, *Eros e Priapo. Da furore a cenere* (Milan, 1967).
7 All references are to Mannheim's English-language volume *Essays on Social Psychology* (London, 1953), p. 95 (original emphasis).
8 One Fascist who comes close to being a self-confessed conservative is Dino Grandi. In his diary of 1944 he proclaims unswerving loyalty to the monarchy, religion and orderly process. He claims never to have believed in fascism, totalitarianism and other 'inconsistent fetishes' invented by Mussolini. See his *25 luglio quarant'anni dopo* (Bologna, 1983), p. 141. Still, as a young Fascist he had argued for what many would consider to have been revolution, including the overthrow of liberalism and Parliament, and their replacement by a government based on labour. See his *Le origini e la missione del fascismo* (Bologna, 1922), p. 70.
9 The links between economic and political expansion are stressed in R. A. Webster, *L'imperialismo industriale italiano. Studio sul prefascismo* (Turin, 1974); also S. Romano, *Giuseppe Volpi, industria e finanza tra Giolitti e Mussolini* (Milan, 1979).
10 Texts from the writings of fascism's many precursors appear in A. Lyttelton, *Italian Fascisms from Pareto to Gentile* (London, 1973). According to Lyttelton, the diversity of sources and inspiration was a political asset because 'different phases of fascism required different ideological justifications' (p. 11).

11 See Francesco Traniello's introduction to the reprint of Jacini's writing of 1870, *Sulle condizioni della cosa pubblica in Italia dopo il 1866* (Brescia, 1968). For a general discussion of Italian conservatism, see Rosario Villari, *Conservatori e democratici nell'Italia liberale* (Bari, 1964).
12 S. Sonnino, *Diario, 1866–1912*, Vol. I (Bari, 1972), pp. 323, 332, 356.
13 This argument has been presented most recently by S. Jones, 'Antonio Salandra and the politics of Italian intervention in the First World War', *European History Quarterly*, vol. XV, no. 2 (April 1985), pp. 157–73.
14 H. Ullrich, 'L'organizzazione politica dei liberali italiani nel Parlamento e nel paese, 1870–1914', in R. Lill and N. Matteucci (eds), *Il liberalismo in Italia e in Germania dalla rivoluzione del '48 alla prima guerra mondiale* (Bologna, 1980), p. 444.
15 On the new right, see A. J. De Grand, *The Italian Nationalist Association and the Rise of Fascism in Italy* (Lincoln, Nebr., 1978).
16 The differences between the old and new right are stressed in S. Saladino, 'Italy', in H. Rogger and E. Weber (eds), *The European Right. A Historical Profile* (London, 1965), pp. 208 ff.
17 See Paolo Ungari, *Alfredo Rocco e l'ideologia giuridica del fascismo* (Brescia, 1963).
18 For a thorough account of these internal conflicts, see R. De Felice, *Mussolini il fascista*, I: *La conquista del potere, 1921–1925* (Turin, 1966).
19 A. Rocco, 'La trasformazione dello Stato', in *Scritti e discorsi politici*, Vol. III (Milan, 1938), pp. 771–88.
20 See D. D. Roberts, *The Syndicalist Tradition and Italian Fascism* (Chapel Hill, NC, 1979) and J. J. Roth, *The Culture of Violence. Sorel and the Sorelians* (Berkeley, Calif., 1980), esp. pp. 197–211 and 223–35.
21 Most useful are F. Cordova, *Le origini dei sindacati fascisti, 1918–1926* (Bari, 1974) and B. Uva, *La nascita dello stato corporativo e sindacale fascista* (Assisi, 1974).
22 Noteworthy studies that try to assess the impact of the Fascist labour movement are G. Merlin, *Com'erano pagati i lavoratori durante il fascismo* (Rome, 1970); G. Sapelli, *Fascismo, grande industria e sindacato. Il caso di Torino* (Milan, 1974); C. Vannutelli, 'Le condizioni di vita dei lavoratori italiani nel decennio 1929–39', *Rassegna di Statistiche del Lavoro*, vol. X (May–June 1958), appearing in English in R. Sarti (ed.), *The Ax Within. Italian Fascism in Action* (New York, 1974), pp. 141–60.
23 On Rossoni and Balbo, see P. Corner, *Fascism in Ferrara, 1915–1925* (London, 1975), pp. 188–92, and G. B. Guerri, *Italo Balbo* (Milan, 1984), pp. 81–2, 98–9. On Rossoni, see the comprehensive profile by Cordova in F. Cordova (ed.), *Uomini e volti del fascismo* (Rome, 1980), pp. 337–403.
24 On the development of the syndicates, see E. Malusardi, *Elementi di storia del sindacalismo fascista* (Lanciano, 1938), which contains important first-hand information, and the informative study by C. Schwarzenberg, *Il sindacalismo fascista* (Milan, 1972).
25 A compact source for Rossoni's early ideas on Fascist syndicalism is his *Le idée della ricostruzione. Discorsi sul sindacalismo fascista* (Florence, 1923).
26 See R. Sarti, *Fascism and the Industrial Leadership in Italy, 1919–1940* (Berkeley, Calif., 1971), pp. 58–66.
27 Partito Nazionale Fascista, *Il Gran Consiglio nei primi cinque anni dell'Era Fascista* (Rome, 1928), p. 41.
28 The account of Fascist syndicates by one-time Nationalist Mario Viana, *Sindacalismo* (Bari, 1923), pp. 79–90, shows considerable sympathy for the syndicalists' aims.
29 Discussions of these reforms appear in A. Aquarone, *L'organizzazione dello Stato totalitario* (Turin, 1965), pp. 52–63, and Adrian Lyttelton, *The Seizure of Power. Fascism in Italy, 1919–1929* (New York, 1973), pp. 277–99.
30 R. De Felice, *Mussolini il fascista. L'organizzazione dello stato fascista, 1925–1929* (Turin, 1968), p. 336.
31 On the subject of syndicalist tactics, many interesting revelations and observations are to be found in P. Capoferri, *Venti anni col fascismo e con i sindacati* (Milan, 1957); G. Cavatorta, *Ieri, oggi, domani. Dal taccuino di un sindacalista* (Rome, 1950); and T. Cianetti, *Memorie dal carcere di Verona* (Milan, 1983).

32 Text in Aquarone, *L'organizzazione dello Stato*, pp. 518–29. On the role of the Fascist Party in the 1930s, see R. De Felice, *Mussolini il duce*, I: *Gli anni del consenso, 1929–1936* (Turin, 1974), pp. 216–28.

33 Victoria De Grazia, *The Culture of Consent. Mass Organization of Leisure in Fascist Italy* (Cambridge, 1981), pp. 226–7.

34 Luigi Federzoni's *L'Italia di ieri per la storia di domani* (Milan, 1967) provides a detailed account of the Fascist Grand Council Meeting of 24–5 July 1943, but also discusses fascism in general terms.

35 See the comments in R. De Felice, *Mussolini il Duce*, II: *Lo stato totalitario, 1936–1940* (Turin, 1981), pp. 47–63.

3

Conservative Catholics and Italian fascism: the Clerico-Fascists

John Pollard

During its rise to power in the early 1920s Italian fascism attracted the support of several small but politically important groups of conservative Catholics. These Catholics, who were given the name 'Clerico-Fascists' by Don Luigi Sturzo, leader of the Catholic Partito Popolare Italiano (PPI),[1] played a role in the consolidation of Mussolini's regime between 1922 and 1925 which was out of all proportion to their numerical strength. In addition, they made an important contribution to the advent of the *Conciliazione*, the reconciliation between church and state which was finally achieved in 1929.

Despite their political importance, however, the Clerico-Fascists have received scant attention from historians. Although there exists a considerable monograph literature concerning the Catholic response to the rise of fascism in Italy, very little of it has dealt with the Clerico-Fascists. Rather, the emphasis has been on the 'acceptable face' of Italian Catholicism in the 1920s and 1930s, embracing, for example, the rise and fall of the PPI; anti-fascism in the Catholic University Students' Federations (FUCI); the anti-fascist Movimento Guelfo D'Azione; and the relations between Catholics, Catholic organizations and fascism at a local level. As one historian of the Catholic movement has remarked:

> It is in fact no accident that everything or nearly everything is known about the exile of F. L. Ferrari, or about the writings of G. Donati, but nothing or very little about E. Martire and the *Rassegna Romana*, in other words about the Clerico-Fascists.[2]

Since Camillo Brezzi wrote these words in 1978, the gap has been filled as far as Martire is concerned by a fine political biography.[3] Indeed, the very limited literature on the Clerico-Fascists has been almost entirely biographical: there are studies of Stefano Cavazzoni, who led the major Clerico-Fascist breakaway from the PPI;[4] of Giovanni Grosoli, whose control of a large part of the Catholic press gave him such influence in Catholic circles;[5] and of Carlo Santucci, who became a powerful Clerico-Fascist intermediary between the Vatican and fascism.[6] However, whilst a biographical approach is useful in studying Clerico-Fascism, which was very much a movement of influential individuals and cliques, it does have its limitations. What is also needed is the kind of closely detailed study of Catholic politics which has been carried out for Turin in the 1920s.[7]

These are not the only serious gaps in our knowledge of the Clerico-Fascists. We still know next to nothing about Carlo Cornaggia Medici and the first Clerico-Fascist organization to appear on the political scene, the Unione Nazionale. Nor, as yet, does there exist a fully researched account of the most important of all the Clerico-Fascist organizations, the Centro Nazionale Italiano. As for the political influence wielded by the Clerico-Fascist journalist and parliamentary deputy, Paolo Mattei-Gentili, we are only in a position to guess at it. Nevertheless general interpretations of the Clerico-Fascist phenomenon are not lacking.[8] The most useful is provided by Richard Webster:

> The new Clerico-Fascists of 1923–4 were but the old Clerico-Moderates writ large.[9]

Whilst it would not be true to say that *all* the Clerico-Fascists had been Clerico-Moderates before the First World War, any more than that all Clerico-Moderates became Clerico-Fascists, Webster's thesis is substantially correct and provides a key to understanding why so many Catholic conservatives eventually went over to fascism.

Although, despite the need for further research, it is possible to reconstruct in some detail the crucial contribution of the Clerico-Fascists to the triumph of fascism, this can only be properly understood in the broader context of the part played by Catholics in Italian politics during the 1920s. Whilst the emergence of Catholicism as an organized force in Italian politics dates essentially from Sturzo's foundation of the PPI in 1918, Catholics had begun to enter Parliament on an individual basis from 1904 onwards. This was as a result of the relaxation of the papal decree *Non Expedit* of 1874, which forbade Catholics from taking part in Italian politics as a protest against the way in which the Church had been treated by the Liberal ruling class and in particular the destruction of the temporal power, the pope's sovereignty over the Papal States.

By the beginning of the twentieth century, the Vatican had come to regard the emerging working-class movement as more of a threat than the anti-clericalism of the Liberals. Thus in 1904 Catholics in some dioceses of northern Italy were allowed to stand for Parliament and Catholic voters were permitted, even instructed, to support Liberal candidates in order to keep out candidates of the left. After the 1913 election there were about thirty Catholic deputies in the Italian Parliament, of whom the majority were Clerico-Moderates, that is to say Catholic conservatives committed to the defence of the existing economic, social and political order, and therefore willing to co-operate with Liberal governments. Where the Clerico-Moderates differed from their Liberal allies was obviously in the field of church–state relations, for one of the major goals of the Clerico-Moderate strategy was to achieve a solution of the 'Roman Question', as the church–state conflict was called in Italy.

The Catholic parliamentary contingent also contained a small minority of Christian Democrats, like the Catholic peasant leader Guido Miglioli, whose political objectives encompassed a radical and wide-ranging pro-gramme of economic, social and political reforms – a far cry indeed from the programme of the Clerico-Moderates. If Christian Democracy was poorly represented in the ranks of the Catholic deputies, it was very much stronger in the Catholic movement as a whole. Christian Democrat leaders like Sturzo were suspicious of the Clerico-Moderate enthusiasm for alliances with the Liberals, regarding these as a cynical misuse of the voting power of the Catholic masses. Sturzo eventually led the Catholic masses on to the political stage at the 1919 general election, and in so doing revolutionized Italian politics.

Backed by the Catholic press and trade unions, and uniting both Clerico-Moderates and Christian Democrats, the new PPI proved capable of fully mobilizing the Catholic electorate. Thanks to this, and to the introduction of proportional representation, the party won a fifth of the votes and came second after the Socialists. It also prevented the Socialists from achieving a greater electoral triumph and helped destroy the parliamentary majority which the Liberals had enjoyed since Unification. Because the Socialists would not co-operate with 'bourgeois' parties, the PPI now became vital to the functioning of the parliamentary system; without it no government could be formed or kept in power.

But the newly found unity between the Clerico-Moderates and the Christian Democrats did not last long. The Catholic conservatives, like other Italian conservatives during the 'Red Two Years' of 1918–20, saw the greatest threat to Italy as that of Bolshevik revolution and the country's greatest need as being for a strong, stable government capable of solving the many serious problems facing it. Sturzo's intransigent refusal, at the elections of 1920 and 1921, to allow his party to enter into prewar-style alliances with the Liberals, the right-wing Nationalists and the Fascists against the Socialists consequently produced the first intra-party tensions between the Clerico-Moderates and the Christian Democrats. It also strained relations between the party and the Vatican.[10]

The PPI's equally intransigent parliamentary tactics during the minis-terial crises of 1922, which led to the downfall of one government, that of Facta, and the stillbirth of another, that of Giolitti, alienated

Catholic conservative opinion still further. In June Cornaggia Medici made his first attempt to establish a conservative alternative to the Catholic party by founding the short-lived Unione Costituzionale. In July Prince Francesco Boncompagni-Ludovisi resigned the *popolare* whip and joined the Nationalists. And in September, the eight *popolare* senators protested to Sturzo about the party's flirtations with the Reformist Socialists.[11] The direction in which the conservatives, both inside and outside the party, were moving was that of *popolare* participation in an emergency government of 'national concentration', headed by a leading Liberal such as Giolitti, Salandra, or Orlando, and including all right-wing forces, the Fascists not excepted.

The conservatives achieved their aim in November 1922 when three *popolare* ministers entered Mussolini's first government and the party voted for it in Parliament. Predictably, Sturzo opposed this move, and the left wing of the party continued to oppose it, insisting that a national congress be called to review the decision. Cavazzoni and the right wing sought in vain to defer the congress which, when it did meet, in Turin, voted for only 'conditional' collaboration with fascism. In reply, Mussolini dismissed the *popolare* ministers and declared war on their party.

In the aftermath of the congress, two leading pro-fascists, Tovini and Pestalozza, resigned from the PPI and formed a rival organization, the Partito Nazionale Popolare (PNP). The PNP seemed to have a rosy future ahead of it, for by spring of 1923 the Vatican had become convinced of the need for Catholic political pluralism. Whilst it did not desire the elimination of Sturzo's party, according to a secret envoy of the Italian Foreign Office 'it wishes to see alongside it a Catholic party of modern conservatism'.[12] Mussolini also favoured the breakaway movement, instructing prefects to give it all assistance.[13] But the PNP failed to attract a significant following and folded within three weeks. Its founders had chosen the wrong moment. The majority of the pro-fascists inside the PPI preferred to soldier on in the hope that the party could be persuaded to return to a policy of co-operation with fascism.

The other Clerico-Fascist organization to emerge in 1923 was the Unione Nazionale, essentially a re-run of Cornaggia Medici's effort of the previous year. It too had Mussolini's backing, and was looked upon with considerable favour in the Vatican.[14] Like the PNP, however, it failed to establish itself as a credible alternative to the PPI. In part this can be attributed to the fact that the Unione was too elitist in character, being essentially a federation of aristocratic and fervently monarchist cliques in Turin, Milan and Naples together with the 'black' or papal aristocracy of Rome. Indeed, over half the signatories of the April 1923 manifesto of the Unione Nazionale were aristocrats, prompting the comment from Gaetano Salvemini that 'with all the animals on their crests it would have been possible to put together a complete heraldic bestiary'.[15] The programme and philosophy of the Unione were also far removed from those of a modern conservative party. Even the pro-fascist newspaper *Il Momento* of Turin was forced to admit that Cornaggia Medici and his friends were notorious for their 'hostility towards the workers and towards trade union organizations'.[16]

The final showdown between the pro-fascist elements inside the PPI and their anti-fascist opponents took place during the debates on the Acerbo Law – the electoral reform designed to give Mussolini a solid, safe parliamentary majority. The smooth passage of the bill through Parliament was dependent upon the attitude of the PPI, but Sturzo and the majority of *popolare* deputies were determined to oppose it. This opposition was effectively neutralized by the forced resignation of Sturzo as party leader. As a result of pressure exerted by Mussolini and the pro-fascist *Corriere D'Italia*, the Vatican ordered Sturzo to withdraw from politics. This he duly did out of canonical obedience to his ecclesiastical superiors.

Sturzo's departure had the desired effect of demoralizing the PPI, which now fell easy prey to the machinations of its pro-fascist 'fifth column'. Having persuaded the parliamentary caucus to abstain in order to preserve party unity, Cavazzoni and the right-wingers then betrayed their colleagues by voting for the bill.[17] Mussolini's 'swindle' passed safely into law. This was perhaps the Clerico-Fascists' most important contribution to the Fascist consolidation of power. As Santarelli points out:

> If the *popolare* group had not split ... proportional representation would not have been abandoned, and in that case Mussolini might not have been able to make use of those lists of 'national concentration' which in the elections of 1924 permitted him to consolidate his power.[18]

The Clerico-Fascists made a further contribution to the consolidation of the Fascist regime in the 1924 general election. After the débâcle over the Acerbo Law, the PPI began to disintegrate at both national and local level. In July 1923 all those who had voted for the law were expelled from the party, and when Parliament was dissolved in March 1924 nearly a quarter of the 108 *popolare* deputies had either been expelled or had seceded.[19] The entire *popolare* senatorial contingent also defected, taking with it the newspapers of Grosoli's trust.

The disintegration at national level quickly spread to the provinces. Prefectoral reports reveal bitter struggles for power between Clerico-Fascists and *popolare* loyalists.[20] In the majority of cases the struggles resulted in the Clerico-Fascists' expulsion. As the list of signatories to the Clerico-Fascist manifesto of 24 March demonstrates, many *popolare* communal or provincial councillors followed local Clerico-Fascist deputies out of the party.[21] Mussolini made strategic use of the geographical spread of Clerico-Fascist support in the 1924 election, assigning fourteen places in the Fascist list to Catholic candidates: one to the Union Nazionale and the remainder to former *popolare* deputies who still possessed a strong local following.[22]

Wider Clerico-Fascist support for the Fascist list was mobilized in other ways. On 24 March 1924 a Clerico-Fascist appeal to the Catholic electorate, signed by 150 Catholics (mostly former *popolari*) from all regions of Italy, appeared on the walls of Rome and other major cities. The appeal not only drew attention to the benefits of the government's ecclesiastical measures, but also stressed the good which Mussolini was doing for the nation as a whole. The signatories declared themselves duty-bound to support a 'national' government which was making progress in the 'moral and material reconstruction' of the country and had also re-established Italian prestige abroad. While admitting that 'the normalization of national life' was proceeding slowly, they argued that it would be achieved by supporting fascism, not by opposing it.[23] The appeal was given massive publicity by the Fascist Party and press, and was also carried by the Clerico-Fascist newspapers in the great cities.[24] In fact, by the spring of 1924 the Clerico-Fascists had control of virtually the whole of the Catholic daily press, which they used to give vigorous support to Mussolini's election campaign.

It is very difficult to assess the effects of Clerico-Fascist support for Mussolini in the 1924 general election. What is known, however, is that the Catholic candidates in the Fascist list obtained a total of 107,000 personal preference votes, suggesting that overall Catholic support of fascism was considerably greater. Their contribution to Mussolini's victory was, therefore, far from negligible.

The Clerico-Fascists were to render Mussolini another very important service during the summer of 1924 when, as a result of the crisis provoked by the Matteotti murder, Mussolini's government was tottering on the brink of collapse. In an operation designed to show the continuing support of conservative forces for Mussolini, the Clerico-Fascists entered the government along with two Liberals, Casati and Sarocchi. The Lombard banking magnate Cesare Nava became Minister of Finance and Paolo Mattei-Gentili, editor of *Il Corriere D'Italia*, became Under-Secretary at the Ministry of Justice. In Parliament, and in their press, the Clerico-Fascists remained steadfastly loyal to Mussolini, and it is a measure of their confidence in him and his government that they should have chosen to found their new political organization, the Centro Nazionale Italiano, in August 1924 at the height of the Matteotti crisis.

After the end of the crisis, the Clerico-Fascists accepted Mussolini's destruction of the institutions of parliamentary democracy in Italy, and faithfully supported the legislation setting up the Fascist dictatorship.

Cavazzoni justified this by recourse to the 'emergency situation' argument:

> If in a period of strong government we succeed in resolving all the vital problems of Italy (and more or less all great states have been created or reinforced in periods of authoritarian government) then we must look to the future to restore liberty.[25]

The arguments of another Clerico-Fascist, the journalist and senator Filippo Crispolti, were based less on expediency than on his criticisms of the workings of parliamentary democracy in Italy. He condemned its 'extreme parliamentarism and excessive individual personal and civil liberties which are not in theory acceptable to Catholics'.[26] In addition there were those Clerico-Fascists, like Piero Misciateli, who positively rejoiced in the downfall of democracy and the establishment of dictatorship, because they considered democracy to be a system essentially northern, Anglo-Saxon and Protestant in origin and conception, and accordingly unsuitable for a Latin, Catholic country like Italy.[27]

These attitudes confirm Webster's judgement of conservative Catholics in the prewar period:

> The Clerico-Moderates accepted the 'strong state' of the Sonnino–Salandra conservative, constitutional tradition, with its high evaluation of the national, Catholic 'moral sentiment'. The Clerico-Moderates repairing to Salandra's standard foreshadowed their rallying in 1923 to another 'strong state' and submitting to its demolition of Parliament.[28]

The authoritarianism of so many Catholic conservatives was reinforced by their contacts with prewar Nationalism. It is hardly surprising that the Clerico-Fascists so readily accepted the nationalistic programme and rhetoric of fascism, because many of them had begun to gravitate into the orbit of the Nationalist Association. The Libyan War of 1911–12 was for many Clerico-Moderates the departure point in their voyage towards fascism via Nationalism. The leading Catholic bank, the Banco di Roma, had a massive commercial investment in Libya; it also had effective financial control of Grosoli's Trust and was thus able to ensure that a large part of the Catholic press would support Giolitti's colonial venture in North Africa. Ernesto Vassallo, Libyan correspondent of *Il Corriere D'Italia* and later Clerico-Fascist deputy for Sicily, was particularly active in the propaganda campaign on behalf of Italy's 'fourth shore'.[29] A similar, though more restrained, position was adopted by Fernando Nunziante in the *Rassegna Nazionale*.

The aftermath of the Libyan War saw the development of political contact and even co-operation between Catholics and Nationalists. In

1913 Egilberto Martire was one of a number of young Catholic intellectuals involved in public debates with the Nationalists,[30] and in the general election of that year two Nationalists were elected in the Rome constituency, thanks to the support of the local Clerico-Moderates.[31] A year later, Alfredo Rocco publicly enunciated the Nationalist movement's new attitude towards the Church. Rejecting the entrenched anti-clericalism of the Liberal ruling class, he accepted the need to recognize and protect the interests of the Church in Italy which, he argued, 'would serve the Italian nation for its expansion in the world'.[32] Rocco was paving the way for the future alliance between the Church and fascism, and also laying the intellectual foundations for the Clerico-Fascist acceptance of the Mussolinian 'Myth of Rome' which, during the 1930s, Martire was so vigorously to uphold in the *Rassegna Romana*. When the majority of Clerico-Moderates voted for intervention in 1915 all the ideological preconditions for the conservative Catholic alliance with fascism had been fulfilled.

The defence of economic interests was one of the most powerful motives impelling Italian conservatives to throw in their lot with fascism in the 1920s. In this regard the Clerico-Fascists were no exception. The rise of the Clerico-Moderates to positions of influence in the Catholic movement in the 'Giolittian Era' had been accompanied by a parallel development, namely their emergence as a powerful economic interest group in their own right.[33] As a result, the Clerico-Fascists of the 1920s and 1930s were, by and large, a very wealthy, privileged elite, a kind of Catholic plutocracy with a very substantial stake in the Italian economy.

Banking was the sector of the economy in which the Clerico-Fascists were most strongly represented. In 1924 five Clerico-Fascist deputies (Tovini, Imberti, Martire, Boncompagni-Ludovisi and Nunziante) and five Clerico-Fascist senators (Passerini, Nava, Santucci, Grosoli and Soderini) controlled eight of the twenty large and medium-sized Catholic banks, including the 'big four' – the Banco di Roma, the Banco Ambrosiano of Milan, the Credito Nazionale and the Istituto Italiano di Credito.[34] Moreover, through their dominant influence in the Unione Delle Banche Cattoliche, and their network of personal connections with the smaller Catholic banks, the Clerico-Fascists had for many years very successfully channelled the deposits of the Catholic small saver in the local *casse di risparmio* into capitalist investments on a larger and often national scale.[35]

Banking matters, in this case the affairs of the Banco di Roma, provided the motive for the first measure of serious co-operation between the Catholic conservatives and the Fascist government. In late January 1923 Mussolini and the Vatican's Cardinal Secretary of State, Gasparri, met secretly in Rome. The significance of this encounter goes beyond the fact that it was the first direct contact between the Vatican and fascism, for it took place in the Roman palace of Carlo Santucci. As the last president of the former Unione Elettorale, as president of the Banco di Roma, as a member of Grosoli's Trust and of the papal court, and as a Senator of the Kingdom, Santucci was probably the most influential Catholic layman in Italy. Thus it was in his house that the Clerico-Fascists commenced their historic role as intermediaries between the Vatican and fascism.

More importantly, it was at this meeting that Mussolini confirmed his agreement to one of the measures with which he had bought *popolare* support for his first government back in 1922: the salvage of the collapsing Banco di Roma. The bank was not only the largest Catholic bank, it was also the linchpin of the whole Catholic banking system. If it had been allowed to collapse then a large part of that system would have gone with it. In addition, it would have had a catastrophic effect on the finances of the Vatican for which the bank held large deposits.

In return for a Treasury-backed rescue operation Mussolini demanded that the Banco di Roma 'conform to the policies of the Fascist Regime'.[36] To ensure this, he further insisted that Santucci be replaced by Francesco Boncompagni-Ludovisi as the bank's president. In this way Mussolini hoped to cut off the financial support which he believed the Banco di Roma was giving to the PPI. There is no evidence that the party was receiving such support, but Mussolini's salvage of the bank did have important political consequences. Through it fascism was able to exercise a strong influence on the Catholic banking world, and in as much as the Catholic banks worked together to sustain Grosoli's Trust, Mussolini was able to ensure that many Catholic newspapers would switch their allegiance in time for the 1924 general election.

In the long term the Clerico-Fascist 'investment' in fascism yielded a handsome dividend. During the mid- and late 1920s Italy's economic difficulties had serious repercussions for the Catholic financial world. By the end of the decade a total of 74 Catholic banks and *casse di risparmio* closed their doors, with a loss to their customers of over 1,000 million lire.[37] The Clerico-Fascists, however, succeeded in persuading the Treasury to help the banks under their control.[38] Eventually, they won the endorsement of the Banca D'Italia for a project aimed at securing the future of all surviving Catholic banks through the establishment of a new controlling institution, the Istituto Centrale di Credito, headed by two leading Clerico-Fascists, Stefano Cavazzoni and Francesco Mauro.[39] The *popolare* journalist, Ignini Giordani, was not very wide of the mark when he wrote in 1925 that the Clerico-Fascists were merely 'dei cattolici, apostolici (banco) romani'.[40]

Although the Clerico-Fascists also had interests in insurance, manu-facturing and foreign trade,[41] their other main economic concern was agriculture. Edoardo Soderini and Giovanni Grosoli, for example, both very active in national politics in the 1920s, had large agricultural holdings in Emilia-Romagna and Le Marche respectively, as did Mattei Farinà in the Campania, Fernando Nunziante in Calabria and Romano Gianotti in Piedmont. Numerous examples can also be cited of locally important Clerico-Fascists whose family fortunes were tied to the land.

The response of men such as these to the growing strength of rural socialism in 1920 and 1921 was not dissimilar from that of other Italian *agrari*. They were just as hostile to the activities of the Socialist and Catholic peasant leagues and just as active in combating them during the many agrarian disputes of this period. In pointing out that Grosoli was one of the leading lights in the local landowners' association in Ferrara, Paul Corner quotes his early appreciation of the activities of the Fascist squads:

> When I stop to consider the work of these young men, who for the defence of the freedom of others, go to their deaths with a generosity without limits ... I am profoundly impressed by the rectitude of their intentions and the nobility of their aims, which go far beyond simple material and factional interests.[42]

But Corner also doubts whether Grosoli's hostility to socialism was purely a matter of defending freedom: 'As a landowner in his own right he undoubtedly appreciated the reasons which pushed the *Federazione Agraria* towards fascism.'[43]

The same can be said of other Clerico-Fascist landowners, for example Carlo Malvezzi of Bologna[44] or Filippo Sassoli de Bianchi, 'Owner of ·the Buton and of vast holdings in the Mugello, who left the Partito Popolare of Grosseto before the 1920 local elections'.[45] In the south, Farina, Nunziante and Zaccharia-Pesce (a Catholic who was elected in the Fascist list for Apulia in 1924) had all belonged to Liberal groups in the prewar period. They were also landowners who jumped on the 'bandwagon' of the PPI in 1919 because this moderate mass party seemed to offer the best defence of agrarian interests in a regime of proportional representation.[46] They abandoned the party in 1923 when it became clear that it was in decline and that fascism was in the ascendant.

These examples indicate the weakness of the PPI as an inter-class party representing both *agrari* and large numbers of small peasant farmers, sharecroppers and even the day-labourers of Miglioli's Catholic peasant leagues. While much further research into the relations between Catholic landowners and Catholic peasants is still needed, it is already clear that their unnatural and uncomfortable political alliance was breaking down all over Italy, and that the sole beneficiary of this process was agrarian fascism.

While the Clerico-Fascists clearly had a great deal in common with other Italian conservatives who rallied to fascism, as *Catholics* they also possessed some interests of their own. Above all, they had *religious* motives for supporting Mussolini. For the Clerico-Fascists, the resolution of the 'Roman Question' was a uniquely important political goal. They therefore reacted very positively to the radical change which took place in Mussolini's religious policy in 1921. Mussolini's transformation from a rabid, violent anti-clerical into a professed admirer of the Church and its values was as sudden as it was unexpected. In his maiden speech to Parliament in May 1921, Mussolini brazenly declared that 'Fascism neither practises nor preaches anti-clericalism'. He went on to praise the conservative and patriotic values of Catholicism, offering the Church improvements in its material position if it would abandon its 'temporalistic dreams'.[47]

Like other Clerico-Fascists, Piero Misciateli was convinced of Mussolini's good faith:

> From the historical and religious point of view it is important to understand that Mussolini is a convert, or, as William James defined it, a man born again.[48]

But Mussolini's change of heart was entirely political. There is absolutely no evidence that he had renounced his lifelong atheism or anti-clericalism. With the same cynical opportunism that had motivated his other shifts to the right during his rise to power, namely, his abandonment of socialism and republicanism, Mussolini set out to win the Vatican's approval for his movement and thus outflank one of his major political competitors, the PPI.

From the Vatican's point of view, one of the chief defects of the new Catholic party was precisely, and ironically, that its policy on the 'Roman Question' was unsatisfactory. As an avowedly 'aconfessional' party the PPI played down the significance of the 'Roman Question'.[49] This policy led to a right-wing revolt at the party's first congress in Bologna in 1919, and several of those who spoke out on the issue joined the Clerico-Fascists in 1923–4.[50]

Given this dissatisfaction with the party's religious policy, the package of ecclesiastical measures which Mussolini announced in November 1922 was bound to be received favourably in the Vatican and in Catholic, conservative circles. The reintroduction of religious instruction into primary schools, the increases in the salaries of those clergy paid by the state, and the placing of the crucifix in public buildings, to mention only the most important of these measures, far exceeded anything that Liberal governments had done for the Church since Unification and amounted to nothing less than a revolution in the Italian state's religious policy.[51]

41

Mussolini was doing something which his Liberal predecessors, tied as they were to the anti-clerical traditions of the Liberal state, had not dared to do; he had, in the words of Pius XI, 'abandoned the anti-clerical fetishism of the Liberal ruling class'.

The various Clerico-Fascist *manifesti* of 1923–4 demonstrate the powerful impact of Mussolini's ecclesiastical measures on conservative Catholic opinion. The manifesto of the Unione Nazionale, for example, argued that fascism aimed at nothing less than the establishment in Italy of 'a lasting social Christian and Italian order'.[52] The pre-election Catholic manifesto of March 1924 was even more explicit in recognizing the benefits of Mussolini's new ecclesiastical policy:

> How can we fail to take account of the fact that this government ... by reintroducing religious instruction into the schools, by restoring the crucifix to public buildings, and by declaring war on the freemasons, and by other demonstrations of its respect for our Catholic institutions, has shown that it is ready to fulfil our most fervently held aspirations and that it wishes to establish in our country a new atmosphere of spirituality and religious liberty.[53]

The ecclesiastical measures of November 1922 fulfilled a large part of Mussolini's pledges of May 1921. They also confirmed the instinctive feeling of those Clerico-Fascists who nostalgically hankered after the secure, ordered and hierarchical world of the *ancien régime* that a Catholic, confessional state could now be reconstituted under the aegis of an authoritarian, Fascist regime. They had every reason to feel confident that Mussolini could be persuaded to go further and settle the 'Roman Question' itself. In the face of the demand of Farinacci, the Fascist Party Secretary, in 1925 that the Clerico-Fascists formally merge with the Fascist movement,[54] they insisted on retaining their separate political identity in the Centro Nazionale. Their belief that they had a role to play in the developing rapprochement between church and state convinced them that they still required autonomy outside the Fascist Party.

Between 1925 and 1929 the Clerico-Fascists did indeed make an important contribution to the processes which ultimately led to the *Conciliazione*. Despite the failure of the Centro Nazionale to attract a large following,[55] its very existence and activities gave an appearance of Catholic support for fascism at a time when the Catholic masses were either indifferent or hostile. This illusion was reinforced by the Clerico-Fascist press which became increasingly influential in the Catholic world owing to the fact that anti-fascist Catholic newspapers were being closed down by the authorities.[56]

The Clerico-Fascists also rendered the Church a great service at this time. During the mid- and late 1920s, when the Vatican was fighting for the survival of Catholic Action against the regime's attempts to eliminate or at least 'fascistize' all voluntary organizations in Italy, Mussolini was becoming impatient with the continued presence of *popolari* in the Catholic associations. As a guarantee of the political reliablity of Catholic Action, Clerico-Fascists were introduced into key positions in the organization at local and national level.[57]

A more direct Clerico-Fascist attempt to resolve the 'Roman Question' was made in 1925 by Carlo Santucci, who offered his proposals to both the former Nationalist Rocco, now Minister of Justice, and the pope. This initiative, which essentially consisted of a bilateral revision of the 1871 Law of Guarantees, failed thanks to the pope's pessimism, but it did keep the 'Roman Question' on the table.[58]

Of greater long-term value was the work of Mattei-Gentili. His appointment to the Ministry of Justice, along with Rocco, was designed to reinforce Mussolini's religious policy. It was Mattei-Gentili who presided over the next stage of that policy in his capacity as chairman of a commission established to carry out a wholesale revision of Italy's ecclesiastical laws. When the pope publicly announced that he could not accept a unilateral revision of those laws, it seemed as if the work of the commission had been aborted. However, when the text of the Lateran Pacts was published in 1929, it became clear that Mattei-Gentili's efforts had not been in vain, for the Concordat incorporated many of the reforms, notably those relating to Church property, which had originally been drafted by his commission.[59]

The announcement of the signing of the Pacts in February 1929 was an occasion for particular jubilation on the part of the Clerico-Fascists. One contemporary observer reported that 'The Clerico-Fascists are exultant, the *popolari* are demoralized and disorientated.'[60] The Clerico-Fascists might well have been exultant, for the *Conciliazione* represented the realizations of their greatest hopes and the vindication of their whole political strategy since 1923. Their feelings of triumph were short-lived, however, for while the *Conciliazione* marked the success of their political strategy, it also meant they had now served their purpose for both the Vatican and the regime. In consequence, during the 1930s the Clerico-Fascists were unable to play a very active or important political role.

The Centro Nazionale had already fallen out of favour with the Vatican in 1928, owing to the political ineptitude of its leadership. At its national congress in March of that year Egilberto Martire rather incautiously suggested that church and state had been equally to blame for the origins of the 'Roman Question', a remark that was especially unwelcome in the Vatican because negotiations for the Lateran Pacts had reached a delicate stage at precisely this point. Pius XI was swift and crushing in his response, which was interpreted in Catholic circles as a public disavowal of the Clerico-Fascists.[61] The regime, too, abandoned the

Clerico-Fascists shortly after the *Conciliazione*, but not before the Centro Nazionale and the Unione Nazionale had performed one last service by supporting the Fascist list in the election, or 'plebiscite', of March 1929. The Clerico-Fascists received scant reward for their loyalty, being assigned only four out of the 400 places on the list. The elevation of half a dozen Clerico-Fascists to the Senate was poor recompense. The truth was that whereas Clerico-Fascist support had been very necessary to the success of fascism in the 1924 election, in 1929 it was of only marginal significance given the fact that both Catholic Action and the Catholic press urged Catholics to vote for fascism.

The last major link between clerico-fascism and the regime was broken in September 1929 when Mattei-Gentili was dropped as Under-Secretary for Justice in a general Cabinet reshuffle. Mattei-Gentili's departure from the government had fatal consequences for *Il Corriere D'Italia*, the last surviving Clerico-Fascist daily newspaper, for government subsidies were cut off shortly afterwards. On 22 September the *Corriere* announced that this was to be its last edition, and with undisguised bitterness it reminded its readers that 'From the March on Rome ... the *Corriere* has supported the regime with exemplary loyalty.'[62]

In the summer of 1930 the leaders of the Centro Nazionale, forced to accept the logic of their position, dissolved their organization on the grounds that 'the original aims and objectives of the Centro Nazionale Italiano have been fully realized in the achievements of Mussolini and Fascism'.[63] The only Clerico-Fascist organization now left was the Unione Nazionale, which survived as a loose grouping of Cornaggia Medici's friends in the Senate. Indeed, from 1929 onwards the focus of Clerico-Fascist political activity shifted to the Upper House, the surest sign of the political impotence of the Clerico-Fascists in the 1930s.

The effective demise of clerico-fascism as a political force in 1929 was paralleled by the virtual elimination of its influence in Catholic circles, and especially in Catholic Action. Many of the Clerico-Fascists who in the mid-1920s had been placed in key positions at diocesan level within Catholic Action had been replaced by the beginning of 1929, and in September of that year Luigi Colombo, a Clerico-Fascist sympathizer and close friend of Stefano Cavazzoni, resigned as national president.[64] Thus the 'bridge' between the Church and fascism, which had served both sides so well in the years leading up to the *Conciliazione*, was removed, and the Clerico-Fascists were unable to resume their role as intermediaries during the very serious crisis in relations between the Vatican and the regime which arose in 1931.

It is emblematic of the fate of the Clerico-Fascists in the 1930s that in 1939 their sole remaining deputy, Egilberto Martire, was carried off to prison and later sent into 'internal exile'. Martire's alleged offence was to have claimed that Galeazzo Ciano, Mussolini's son-in-law and

Foreign Minister, had the evil eye.[65] In fact, Martire had fallen foul of Ciano for rather more serious reasons, namely his public criticism of the regime's foreign policy. Having earlier supported Fascist imperialism in the pages of the *Rassegna Romana*,[66] by 1938 Martire had become profoundly disturbed by Mussolini's increasingly close relationship with Hitler. When the Nazis occupied Catholic Austria, Martire's bright vision of Fascist Italy as the leader of a bloc of Catholic powers between the atheistic communism of the Soviet Union and the neo-paganism of Nazi Germany began to fade. Mussolini's entry into the war on the side of Germany in June 1940 completed Martire's disillusionment.

The relationship between the Clerico-Fascists and fascism was a very complex one. It was also, obviously, one of mutual self-interest. For their part, the Clerico-Fascists achieved most, if not all, of the objectives which had motivated their support for fascism. Mussolini seemed to have exorcized the Bolshevik threat; he had restored law and order; and the Clerico-Fascists believed that through their alliance with fascism they had succeeded in protecting the economic interests that they held so dear. In particular, they had managed to salvage a large part of the network of Catholic financial institutions. However, it can be argued that the crisis which overtook the Catholic banks in the 1920s was at least partly of Mussolini's making, the result of his obstinate insistence on revaluing the lira.[67] Furthermore, the Clerico-Fascists' success in this field had its limits; they were unable (or unwilling?) to prevent the destruction or 'fascistization' of many of the Catholic movement's other economic and social organizations, such as the peasant leagues, the co-operatives and the trade unions.

For the Clerico-Fascists the most important and enduring result of their alliance with fascism was, of course, the *Conciliazione*. As one of Cavazzoni's Milanese colleagues remarked after the dissolution of the Centro Nazionale:

> Even the *Centro Nazionale* has gone: the last dyke has been broken; but what does this matter? The 11th of February remains.[68]

Yet even in this area the Clerico-Fascists were to be disappointed. The Catholic, confessional state which so many of them desired did not materialize, as is demonstrated by their carping criticisms of the public morality policy of the regime and its attitude towards the Protestant minorities.[69]

It was obviously the Fascist regime that derived the greater profit from its relationship with the Clerico-Fascists. It is difficult to see how Mussolini could have consolidated his power so smoothly in the crucial period between the March on Rome and the end of the Matteotti crisis without the help of the Clerico-Fascists, whose treacherous intrigues divided and effectively neutralized the PPI. And when, after the *Conciliazione*, Mussolini no longer needed Clerico-Fascist support, he was able to cast them aside with little difficulty. It may be argued, on the other hand, that the Clerico-Fascists managed to preserve their political autonomy longer than any other group which supported fascism. The Centro Nazionale, after all, was the only non-fascist organization of a strictly political character to be allowed to nominate candidates for the 1929 election. Nevertheless, it is indicative of the cynical ease with which Mussolini 'squashed' clerico-fascism in 1929 that few former members of the Centro Nazionale succeeded in obtaining a Fascist Party card after its demise.[70]

The Catholic conservative *ralliement* to fascism was founded upon an erroneous perception of the nature of Fascist ideology. In the early 1920s the Clerico-Fascists had no problems in coming to terms with the 'darker' side of fascism, with its theory and practice of violence, or with its totalitarian pretensions. In common with other Italian conservatives, they were able to dismiss the violence of fascism as an adolescent disorder, and they regarded totalitarianism as being largely rhetorical. The development of the regime after 1925 seemed to confirm the wisdom of these judgements. Fascism became 'normalized', and the achievement of the *Conciliazione* and the establishment of the corporate state seemed to suggest that fascism was implementing an essentially conservative programme. Only the development of the Rome–Berlin Axis revealed to the conservatives that fascism was not the 'safe', permeable and conservative ideology which they, and Pius XI for that matter, had thought it to be.

In any case, by the late 1930s it was too late; the Clerico-Fascists had played out their role in Italian history. That role may be summarized as follows. The gradual rapprochement between church and state in Italy had gone hand-in-hand with a progressive reunification of the Liberal and Catholic wings of its ruling class. In the Giolittian Era, the emerging working-class movement had posed a threat to the institutions of both church and state. It had also threatened the economic interests of both the Liberal and the Catholic bourgeoisie. The Clerico-Moderates thus entered Italian politics as the defenders of the Church and of their own economic interests: hence their growing economic and political collaboration with the Liberal ruling class. The Clerico-Moderates' political role was only temporarily eclipsed by the establishment of the PPI under Christian Democratic leadership in 1919. The threat of revolution, and the concomitant rise of fascism, gave them the opportunity to recover their role. When it became clear that they could not carry on that role inside a party dominated by progressive, reformist, and even pro-socialist elements, 'the old clerico-moderate faction', in Candeloro's words, 'seceded from the *Partito Popolare* and transformed itself into a Clerico-Fascist group'.[71]

Through their dedication to fascism the Clerico-Fascists were able to bring to a successful conclusion the process of reuniting the two wings of the Italian ruling class.

NOTES

1 Sturzo first used the term in an interview with *La Stampa*, 10 February 1924. It should be stressed that this chapter is concerned with the Catholic, lay politicians who went over to fascism in 1923–4, rather than with pro-fascist members of the clergy, or with Catholic intellectuals who strongly supported fascist policies in the 1930s: for an account of the activities of the latter, see P. Ranfagni, *I Clerico-Fascisti: Le riviste dell'Università Cattolica negli anni del Regime* (Florence, 1975).

2 C. Brezzi, 'Sul Clerico-Fascismo', in A. Monticone (ed.), *Cattolici e Fascisti in Umbria* (Bologna, 1978), p. 415.

3 D. Sorrentino, *La Conciliazione e il 'fascismo cattolico'* (Brescia, 1980).

4 S. Cavazza, *Stefano Cavazzoni* (Tortona, 1981).

5 R. Sgarbanti, *Ritratto politico di Giovanni Grosoli* (Rome, 1959).

6 G. De Rosa, *I Conservatori Nazionali: Biografia di Carlo Santucci* (Brescia, 1962).

7 B. Gariglio, *Cattolici democratici e Clerico-Fascisti a Torino, 1922–27* (Bologna, 1978).

8 For a survey of interpretations, see *Dizionario storico del movimento cattolico in Italia (DSMCI)*, Vol. I, Tome I (Turin, 1981), pp. 79–84.

9 R. A. Webster, *The Cross and the Fasces: Christian Democracy and Fascism in Italy* (Stanford, Calif., 1961), p. 89.

10 For an example of this unease in conservative Catholic circles, see the editorial by Paolo Mattei-Gentili in *Il Corriere D'Italia*, 10 December 1920.

11 See J. N. Molony, *The Emergence of Political Catholicism in Italy* (London, 1977), pp. 130–1.

12 Quoted in R. De Felice, 'Nuovi documenti su alcuni primi contatti fra il mondo cattolico e il fascismo dopo la marcia su Roma', *Il Cannochiale*, nuova serie, Vols IV–VI, p. 163.

13 See the police reports in Archivio Centrale Dello Stato, Ministero Dell'Interno, DGPS, AA.GG.RR. (1923), Busta 70, *Partito Popolare Filo-Fascista*, 17 April 1923.

14 The list of signatories to the June manifesto reads like a roll-call of the papal household. It is inconceivable that all these men would have signed without papal approval.

15 G. Salvemini, *Chiesa e stato in Italia* (Milan, 1968), p. 284.

16 *Il Momento*, 5 July 1923, 'Perplessità e confusioni'.

17 G. De Rosa, *Il Partito Popolare Italiano* (Bari, 1974), p. 251, and Molony, *Political Catholicism*, p. 169, both claim that nine *popolare* deputies voted for the Acerbo Law; the true figure was sixteen: see *Atti Parlamentari*, Leg. XXVI, Sessione 1921–3, Discussioni della Camera, p. 10, 683.

18 E. Santarelli, *Storia del movimento e del Regime fascista*, Vol. I (Rome, 1967), p. 359.

19 In addition to those who voted for the Acerbo Law, another nine deputies left the party.

20 See the reports from the prefects of Como (8 August 1923), Cuneo (10 October 1923) and Rome (1 January 1924), Archivio Centrale Dello Stato, Ministero Dell'Interno, DGPS, AA.GG.RR. (1923), Busta 70, *Partito Popolare Filo-Fascista*.

21 Of the 150 signatories, 57 described themselves as provincial or communal councillors, *assessori*, or *sindaci* (mayors).

22 Gianotti and Imberti (Piedmont); Cavazzoni and Preda (Lombardy); Olivi and Tovini (Veneto); Mattei-Gentili (Le Marche); Boncampagni-Ludovisi and Martire (Lazio and Umbria); Nunziante (Calabria and Basilicata); Zaccharia-Pesce (Apulia); and Vassallo (Sicily).

23 *Il Popolo D'Italia*, 23 March 1924, 'Vibrante Appello' etc.

24 *L'Avvenire D'Italia* (Bologna), *Il Momento* (Turin), *Il Cittadino* (Genoa), *Il Corriere D'Italia* (Rome) and *La Libertà* (Naples).
25 Quoted in L. Cavazzoni (ed.), *Stefano Cavazzoni* (Milan, 1955), p. 87.
26 Quoted in Sorrentino, *La Conciliazione*, p. 97, n. 118.
27 P. Misciateli, *Cattolici e fascisti* (Rome, 1924), p. 90.
28 Webster, *The Cross and the Fasces*, p. 49.
29 M. G. Rossi, *Le origini del Partito Cattolico* (Rome, 1977), pp. 212–13.
30 Webster, *The Cross and the Fasces*, pp. 36–7.
31 Rossi, *Le origini del Partito Cattolico*, p. 362.
32 As quoted in A. Lyttelton, *Italian Fascisms from Pareto to Gentile* (London, 1973), p. 37.
33 Rossi, *Le origini del Partito Cattolico*, ch. 6.
34 *Annuario delle banche cattoliche* (Milan, 1924), pp. 91–185. These clerico-fascist politicians were assisted in their control over the banks by a number of other clerico-fascist financiers the most notable of whom were the Caccia–Dominioni brothers of Milan and the Zilieri brothers of Vicenza.
35 Rossi, *Le origini del Partito Cattolico*, p. 286.
36 As quoted in F. Margiotta-Broglio, *L'Italia e la Santa Sede da Porta Pia alla Grande Guerra* (Bari, 1966), p. 442.
37 A. De Stefani, *Baraonda Bancaria* (Milan, 1960), p. 426.
38 Letter from Bonaldo. Stringher, director-general of the Banca D'Italia, to Padre Tacchi-Venturi, the Vatican's special envoy to Mussolini, in which Mussolini agreed to save the Banco di Piccolo Credito of Ferrara, of which Grosoli was president: Margiotta-Broglio, *L'Italia e la Santa Sede*, doc. 141, pp. 442–3. A Caroleo, *Le banche cattoliche* (Milan, 1976), p. 145, cites the cases of two other Catholic banks saved by the regime: the Credito Meridionale, controlled by the two leading Clerico-Fascists in Naples, the Duke of Santaseverina and the Count of Caracciolo, and the Banca Cattolica della Calabria, whose auditor was Fernando Nunziante.
39 Caroleo, *Le banche cattoliche*, pp. 143–6.
40 I. Giordani, *La rivolta cattolica* (Turin, 1925), p. 72.
41 Rossi, *Le origini del Partito Cattolico*, chs VI and VII. Rossi's picture of the breadth of clerico-moderate economic interests is confirmed by the biographical information contained in *DSMCI*, Vol. II.
42 Quoted in P. Corner, *Fascism in Ferrara, 1915–1925* (Oxford, 1975), pp. 127–8.
43 ibid.
44 Anthony A. Cardoza, *Agrarian Elites and Italian Fascism: the Province of Bologna, 1901–1926* (Princeton, NJ, 1983), p. 295.
45 P. L. Ballini, *Il movimento cattolico a Firenze* (Rome, 1969), p. 380.
46 M. Bernabei, *Fascismo e nazionalismo in Campania* (Rome, 1975), p. 132, lists the interests of Farina, 'above all a great landed proprietor'. In 1919 Farina and the *agrari* of Salerno province entered the PPI *en masse* instead of founding their own party.
47 Quoted in Margiotta-Broglio, *L'Italia e la Santa Sede*, p. 52.
48 Misciateli, *Cattolici e fascisti*, p. 14.
49 The 'Roman Question' was referred to in just one sentence of the seventh article of the party programme: 'Liberty and independence for the Church in the fulfilment of its spiritual mission'; quoted in G. Sabatucci (ed.), *La crisi italiana del primo dopoguerra* (Rome and Bari, 1976), p. 230.
50 De Rosa, *Partito Popolare*, pp. 22–3.
51 For the full list of measures, see A. C. Jemolo, *Chiesa e stato in Italia negli ultimi cento anni*, 3rd edn (Turin, 1963), p. 256.
52 The text is in G. B. Naitza and G. Pisu, *I cattolici nella vita pubblica in Italia, 1919–1943* (Florence, 1977), pp. 63–4.
53 *Il Popolo D'Italia*, 27 March 1929.
54 R. De Felice, *Mussolini il fascista*, II: *L'organizzazione dello stato fascista, 1925–1929* (Turin, 1968), p. 47.
55 Membership figures for the Centro Nazionale in 1927 are quoted in P. Borzomati, *I Giovani Cattolici nel Mezzogiorno d'Italia dall'Unità al 1948* (Rome, 1970), pp. 143–5.

56 J. F. Pollard, *The Vatican and Italian fascism, 1929–32: A Study in Conflict* (Cambridge, 1985), pp. 117–19.

57 For examples, see Gariglio, *Cattolici democratici e Clerico-Fascisti*, p. 232 and S. Tramontin, 'Popolari, cattolici e fascisti a Treviso (1919–23)', *Civitas* (September–October 1978).

58 P. Scoppola, *La Chiesa e il fascismo: documenti e interpretazione* (Bari, 1971), p. 111.

59 For the text of the Concordat, see Pollard, *The Vatican and Italian Fascism*, Appendix III.

60 Letter from an anonymous friend to G. Donati, reproduced in G. Rossini (ed.), *G. Donati: scritti politici*, Vol. II (Rome, 1965), p. 356.

61 Pollard, *The Vatican and Italian Fascism*, p. 59, n. 60.

62 *Il Corriere D'Italia*, 22 September 1929.

63 Quoted in Cavazzoni (ed.), *Stefano Cavazzoni*, p. 232.

64 ibid.

65 M. Muggeridge (ed.), *Ciano's Diary, 1939–1943* (London, 1947), pp. 29–30.

66 Sorrentino, *Il Conciliazione*, pp. 163–7.

67 Caroleo, *Le banche cattoliche*, p. 141.

68 Quoted in Cavazzoni, *Stefano Cavazzoni*, p. 82.

69 Pollard, *The Vatican and Italian Fascism*, pp. 109, 114.

70 Sorrentino, *La Conciliazione*, p.107, n. 199.

71 G. Candeloro, *Il movimento cattolico in Italia* (Rome, 1953), p. 361.

4

Conservatives and radical nationalists in Germany: the production of fascist potentials, 1912–28

Geoff Eley

I

The recourse to political violence – to repressive and coercive forms of rule, to guns rather than words, to beating up one's opponents rather than denouncing them from the speaker's platform – was ultimately what distinguished fascism, in Germany and elsewhere, from existing forms of right-wing politics. Of course, the coercive apparatuses of the state had always been used against certain kinds of opposition, whether via routine applications of the law for the protection of persons and property or the maintenance of public order, or by curtailment of civil freedoms under conditions of national emergency, such as wartime or a general strike, or by more restrictive or authoritarian systems of public policing. Coercion in this sense is a normal dimension of legally constituted public authority, whether more liberal or more authoritarian. It provides necessary sanction against activity transgressing the established boundaries of social and political dissent. Privately organized coercion had also been common, in the form of strike-breaking, vigilantism, economic paternalism, servile labour in agriculture, and so on. But fascist violence was new. In Germany the Anti-Socialist Law (1878–90); harassment, deportation and imprisonment of left-wing agitators; curtailment of the right to strike; the setting of police or troops on to strikers and demonstrators: these were one thing. But *terror*, first through a militarized and confrontationist style of politics, then as a principle of state organization, was another.

In this sense, the years 1914–23 marked a crucial watershed in the politics of the German right. The disaster that befell the latter in 1918 – the double trauma of military defeat and revolution – viciously radicalized its ideological temper. During the civil war that prevailed for much of the period 1918–23 there was ample scope for the resentful activism of the returning right-wing 'front-soldiers' and their civilian compatriots, simultaneously elevated and brutalized by the experience of the war, morally outraged by the dissolution of traditional values that seemed to accompany the revolutionary turbulence of the Republic's foundation. The burgeoning paramilitary formations that appeared from the end of 1918 were the practical medium of this counter-revolutionary anger, together with the *völkisch* and anti-Semitic associations that mushroomed during the same period. Much of this momentum carried over into the years of so-called 'relative stability' between 1924 and 1928–9, and in its institutionalized forms made a major contribution to the take-off of the Nazi Party between 1928 and 1930. The complexities of this transition from the counter-revolutionary confusion of Weimar's early years to the growing concentration of popular right-wing energies around the National-sozialistische Deutsche Arbeiterpartei (NSDAP) in the years of the Republic's demise, require detailed explication beyond the range of this chapter. But certain basic truths need stating lest they become obscured in the exposition that follows. Primary among them is the anti-communist and anti-socialist impetus behind Nazi political violence, which in its motivations and direction was also to a great extent anti-working class.[1]

To put it bluntly: *killing* socialists rather than just arguing with them, or at most legally and practically restricting their rights, was a new departure. The radicalism of this break can hardly be exaggerated. Before 1914 anti-socialism was certainly one of the German right's defining preoccupations. The earlier repertoire of anti-socialist politics extended from 'exceptional legislation' on the model of the Anti-Socialist Law and other flexible forms of legal harassment, through routine discrimination via the state apparatuses, manipulated welfare legislation, private systems of company paternalism, and systematic propaganda offensives among the working class, to the renewed speculation concerning a 'corporative' revision of the democratic franchise that surfaced on the eve of the First World War. But Wilhelmine anti-socialism stopped short of the terroristic interventions that became all too familiar in the years 1918–23 and 1928–34. It presumed a practical pluralist consensus that came together between the late 1890s and 1911–12 during a process of cumulative but partial parliamentarization, which allowed public life to arrange itself within the existing framework of the Bismarckian Constitution.

It was the collapse of this emergent consensual framework between 1912 and 1920, within a polarized public climate and a postwar context of working-class insurgency, that called the fascist option to the stage. In both sets of circumstances – before 1914 in the imperfect but democratically elected parliamentary arena of the Empire, and after 1918 in the full-scale parliamentary democracy of the Weimar Republic – the left-right polarization worked heavily to the left's advantage, so long as the political process remained organized along electoral and constitutional lines. Thus even when the Weimar centre-right managed an unstable parliamentary majority between 1924 and 1928, the liberal Weimar Constitution's pluralist logic tended to impose a practical scenario of compromise and negotiation, to the anger of the intransigent anti-republicans on the right of the German-National People's Party (DNVP), and at the cost of serious splits in the latter when it joined the government in 1924–5 and 1927–8.

In a crisis, this circumstance – right-wing alienation from a polity structurally tilted towards the left – could be extremely dangerous. In fact, it gave the major push towards right-wing political violence: initially in 1918–23, when working-class militancy threatened to radicalize the parliamentary-democratic content of the revolution; and then later in 1930–3, when the welfare state, the defensive positions of the trade unions, and the mobilized popular resources of the Social Democrats and Communists obstructed Germany's economic and political recovery as the right had come to conceive it. Fascism emerged as a radicalized form of authoritarian politics in a situation where liberal-constitutional forms of government seemed to have exhausted their capacity for stabilizing an extreme and protracted domestic crisis.

If we formulate these observations into an abstract generalization, the definition of fascism falls into two parts: (1) a formal descriptive one, stressing the kind of politics fascism involved; and (2) a situational or conjunctural one, specifying the kind of crisis in which fascist politics became a realistic option.

In the first of these respects, fascism was simply more extreme in every way. It involved a qualitative departure from existing conservative practice, replacing traditional notions of hierarchy with corporatist notions of social organization, combined with fresh ideas of a centrally directed authoritarian state and a 'new kind of regulated, multi-class, integrated national-economic structure'. Above all, fascism stood for an ideal of national concentration, in which nationalist loyalties were celebrated as the supreme public good. Allegiance to the nation liquidated all forms of sectional identification, while older ideas of clerical, aristocratic and bureaucratic authority subsided before the new ideal of the race-community, whose integrity could be guaranteed only through a biologically determined struggle for existence against corrupt foreign influences.

Moreover, this process had a domestic and a foreign dimension. In the foreign sphere fascism entailed an extreme programme of aggressive imperialist expansion, legitimated in racist and national-Darwinist terms; domestically it appeared as the necessary solvent of socioeconomic discontent. In addition, fascism was self-consciously and blusteringly plebeian, rhetorically clothing itself in a crude and violent egalitarianism appropriate to its broadly based popular appeal. Fascism stood for activism and popular mobilization, in a distinctive political style. This included 'an aesthetic structure of meetings, symbols and political choreography'; militarized forms of mass display; the celebration of violence, masculinity and youth; and 'a tendency towards an authoritarian, charismatic, personal style of command'. Negatively speaking, fascism defined itself against liberalism, social democracy and communism, or any creed which seemed to tolerate difference, division and conflict against the essential unity of the race-people as the organizing principle of social and political life.[2]

Secondly, this kind of politics only materialized under a definite set of conditions. Here we need to stress a concatenation of immediate circumstances which defined the 'conjunctural specificity' of the fascist phenomenon – why it happened when it did. Briefly, these included: the impact and outcome of the First World War; the European revolutionary conjuncture of 1917–23; the unprecedented gains of the left, in both revolutionary and reformist terms; and the breakdown of parliamentary institutions. The German military disappointment of 1918, coming as it did after the extraordinary success of the drive to the east following the Bolshevik withdrawal from the war and the Treaty of Brest-Litovsk (March 1918), but in a developing context of general popular war-weariness, provoked in the autumn of that year a fundamental crisis of the unity and popular credibility of the dominant classes. This opened up a gaping space for radical political solutions. During the German Revolution the radical right then defined itself against the double experience of thwarted imperialist ambitions and ignominious domestic retreat, in which each resentment relentlessly stoked the other.

In right-wing perceptions, the postwar situation was dominated by the public accommodation of organized labour, whose political and trade union aspirations appeared to be in command: trade unions acquired an unprecedented corporative legitimacy; the national leadership of the Social Democratic Party (Sozialdemokratische Partei Deutschlands: SPD) controlled the levers of government and generally occupied the centre of the political stage; and considerable movements to the left, increasingly dominated by the newly founded Communist Party, maintained a frightening level of popular insurgency. Under these circumstances, liberal and parliamentary methods of political containment were shown to have exhausted their effectiveness, guaranteeing neither the political representation of the dominant classes nor the mobilization of adequate popular consent. In such circumstances fascism materialized as an extreme, extra-systemic solution to the crisis.

More abstractly, it can be stated that fascism prospered under conditions of general crisis which paralysed the state's ability to dispatch its vital organizing functions, in relation both to the economy and to the larger business of maintaining cohesion in society. In the extremes of the crisis (in the German case, between 1930 and 1933) the paralysis extended to the entire institutional framework of politics, including the parliamentary and party-political forms of representation. This was true in two ways. On the one hand, the political co-operation of the dominant classes and their major economic fractions could no longer be successfully organized within the given forms of parliamentary representation and party government. The usual forms of parliamentary coalition-building consequently became unbearably complicated, so that politics became increasingly factionalized into a series of manoeuvres for influence and control over the high governmental executive. In the process a gap opened between an increasingly unrepresentative governmental politics, disastrously divorced from any stable basis of popular legitimacy, and a febrile popular electorate, increasingly mobilized for action but to diminishing political effect. On the other hand, therefore, the popular legitimacy of the same institutional political framework simultaneously passed into crisis. Broadly speaking, this was what characterized Germany between the suspension of normal parliamentary government in March 1930 and the appointment of Hitler to the chancellorship in January 1933. In the context of the Weimar crisis, adjustments within the existing institutional arrangements looked increasingly futile. More radical solutions beyond the bounds of the system consequently became more appealing.[3]

Two points arise from this way of defining fascism. The first concerns the sociology of fascist support. The above remarks have deliberately abstained from what is probably the commonest approach to the problem of a general definition, namely, the reference to social functions and the social bases of fascism's mass appeal. Here, of course, the overwhelming emphasis has been on the petty bourgeoisie and its discontents.[4] Now, my own scepticism about this reflects no hostility to sociology as such, whether in the form of social theory or social scientific methodology. Nor is it meant to diminish the importance of carefully analysing the fascist movements' social composition at its different levels, a process which has largely confirmed the salience of the petty-bourgeois appeal.[5]

The argument is not about the greater susceptibility to fascist political appeals of the petty bourgeoisie as such, whether small-scale owners and producers or the new categories of salaried employees (lower-grade civil servants, junior managerial and technical personnel, teachers, clerical workers, parts of the professions, etc.), but about the part this should play in fascism's basic definition. The danger of making the 'lower-middle-class' thesis central is that it closes our minds to the presence of other social groups, both in the fascist movements themselves and in their strategies of mobilization. Where we find evidence of such groups – for example, the working class – it inclines us to seek special explanations, or even to explain them away, and at any event to minimize their causal significance. It also encourages reductionist explanations of fascist ideology and its appeal, attributing fascist success to the 'reactionary protest potential' of 'traditional strata' damaged by the process of 'modernization'.[6] While persuasive within limits, this attributes too powerful a fascist disposition to the petty bourgeoisie – implying that they were always headed for a

54

radical right destination in the German situation, forming the natural or essential constituency for a fascist movement – and leaves us ill-equipped to understand why other social groups might also find fascist ideas attractive. Its view of ideology is too structural and too behaviourist, occluding the autonomy of ideological process and simplifying the shaping of an individual's political subjectivity. For these reasons, it is better not to prejudge the social direction of the fascist movement's ideological appeal. Only when the latter has been sorted out can we then go on to determine its varying sociology, in highly specific analysis of concrete situations.

The second point arising from my approach concerns the importance of the Weimar period as a whole, rather than the immediate circumstances of the Nazis' rise to power in 1930–3. Fascist potentials were *already* being generated in the earlier circumstances of revolutionary turbulence during 1918–23. The descent into counter-revolutionary violence *already* occurred with the Free Corps during the suppression of the Spartacist and related insurgency of January–March 1919, while the public climate was simultaneously radicalized by the proliferation of *völkisch* and anti-Semitic activity signified by the Pan-German League's launching of the Deutschvölkischer Schutz- und Trutzbund in February 1919. In both respects an anti-system politics was being constituted. It displayed all the specific ideological characteristics noted above. It aimed to concentrate popular right-wing aspirations on a showdown with the new republic behind a double programme of nationalist resurgence and anti-Marxist repression. It was directed as much against the liberal and Social Democratic architects of the nascent republican order as against the insurrectionary utopianism of the German Communist Party (Kommunistische Partei Deutschlands: KPD) and the neo-syndicalist ultra-left. As it happened, this renascent right drastically overplayed its hand by trying to seize power prematurely in the ill-fated Kapp Putsch of March 1920. After an initial success the putsch was defeated by a general strike in defence of the Republic, thus gaining the unwanted distinction of having provoked virtually the only concerted example of a united left front in the history of Weimar.[7]

The comparison with Italy is instructive in this respect. There, by contrast, it was the revolutionary left that brought events to a climax in the occupation of the factories in September 1920. But this initiative remained isolated in the northern industrial triangle of Turin–Genoa–Milan. The left failed to carry either the trade union federation or the Italian Socialist Party as a whole behind a full-blooded revolutionary strategy. Consequently, the factory council movement failed to generate some continuing national-political momentum, and having sown the storm its leadership reaped the whirlwind in the guise of a brutal fascist counter-mobilization. The Italian Socialists achieved the worst of both worlds – an imposing regional dominance in the north, whose revolutionary and maximalist rhetoric evoked the extremes of anti-socialist anxiety in the propertied classes, and an actual reformism on the part of the majority, which never covered itself by serious coalition-building, involving either the equally mobilized peasantry of the centre and south, or the acutely threatened northern 'middle strata'. As the insurrectionary wave broke during the autumn of 1920, it was the Fascists who capitalized on the resulting left-wing demoralization, breaking the power of the trade unions, co-operatives and Socialist local government bastions in the northern countryside, and eroding the broader resonance of Socialist political ideals. The culmination of this process, of course, was Mussolini's March on Rome in October 1922 and the consolidation of a Fascist regime during the following three years.

In Germany this was not the outcome of the revolutionary conjuncture of 1918–23. The greatest single difference from Italy was the SPD's ability to function as a factor of order, permitting a much broader basis of co-operation around the emergent republican order at a time when the right's ideological direction and organizational cohesion, particularly at its *völkisch* and paramilitary extremes, remained far from clear. By comparison the PSI as a party stood much further to the left, which allowed a process of right-wing concentration around the redemptive potential of a radical nationalist and anti-socialist terror to become far more advanced. In Italy, the patent inability of Giolittian liberalism to meet the challenge of working-class insurgency allowed the Fascist cadre to become a more important pole of attraction for larger circles of the dominant classes and others feeling threatened by the reigning social turbulence.

In this respect the closer analogue to Italy in 1918–22 is the Germany of 1930–3, when the situation of the SPD was highly reminiscent of the Italian Socialist Party's ten years before. It provoked the right to anger and anxiety with the same immobilizing combination of characteristics: entrenched reformism, obstinately bunkered in the defensive apparatus of social legislation, labour law, and local government influence, which blocked the necessary measures of ruthless capitalist stabilization; and continuing rhetorical militancy, articulated through the visionary Marxist-reformist strategies of the party intelligentsia and the anti-fascist activism of the Reichsbanner militia. The liberal state collapsed into a similar paralysis. The social fear engendered by the post-1928 gains of the KPD replicated the Italian anti-socialist panic of 1918–22. So if in 1920 the Italian September had reversed the signs of the German March, in 1933 Germany provided the delayed equivalent of 1922.

At this stage of our knowledge, the more interesting issue is thus not the immediate rise to power of the Nazis, which has been exhaustively researched and discussed in the last two decades, but the larger process of transition from a more conventional to a more radicalized form of right-wing politics – that is, from a conservative authoritarianism pragmatically observing the parameters of liberal legality to a radical authoritarianism seeking completely to overturn that framework.[8] We ought, in short, to

concern ourselves with the generation of fascist *potentials*. In line with
the most stimulating scholarship produced on the Imperial period since
the 1960s, we should perhaps focus on the overall unities of the Imperial
and Weimar periods taken as a whole (*c*. 1890–1933), and the questions
(so to speak) to which Nazism eventually became the answer.

This direction of analysis would be consistent with one extremely influential body of interpretation since the mid-1960s, which has stressed the
importance of authoritarian continuities in German history between Bismarck and Hitler. Such an approach has focused on the survival of so-called
'pre-industrial traditions', located in the old 'ruling elites' (landowners,
military, bureaucracy) and their continuing dominance in the Imperial
political system. However this homogenizes the period 1871–1933 into an
overall unity, across which certain fixed patterns of authoritarianism work
themselves out, and within which specific conjunctures and processes of
innovation become less important. For my part, I wish to retain the stress
on a larger and deeper historical context for studying the origins and
dynamics of fascist radicalization, while opting for a much tighter focus on
a more limited founding period, roughly 1912–20, which stands in a fairly
radical discontinuity with the bulk of the Imperial period that preceded it.

II

To understand the character of the fascist departure, we thus need to
begin with an earlier period of right-wing radicalization. The context
of fascism in Germany was not just the immediate circumstances of the
world economic crisis and the suspension of parliamentary government
between 1929/30 and 1933/4, but the entire period of the Weimar Republic
and particularly the founding years of revolutionary turbulence between
1918 and 1923. All the forms of fascist politics that appeared with the
rise of the Nazis were basically prefigured in the earlier conjuncture,
particularly if we compare the latter with other examples of radical
authoritarian and counter-revolutionary mobilization in the same period,
of which the Italian case is obviously the most important. To a great extent,
moreover, this new configuration of the right was also anticipated in the
final years of the Empire, overdetermined by a combination of foreign
and domestic difficulties. From this point of view, the years 1919–20 may
be defined as a critical period of radicalization, in which one concept
of the right was replaced by another. To illustrate what I mean by
this, I wish to consider a number of closely interrelated questions.

1

In the Weimar Republic 'conservatism', in the traditional sense of the
Wilhelmine Conservative Party – as the political representation of an

East Elbian landowning interest structurally privileged in its access to state power – had become a negligible quantity. The German Revolution removed its basis and reduced large-scale landed property to one fraction of the dominant classes among others (and far from the most important, economically and politically). With the foundation of the German National People's Party (Deutschnational Volkspartei: DNVP), which was avowedly a larger coalition party of the right, the East Elbian landed interest was placed at a new disadvantage. The dyed-in-the-wool traditionalists were left marooned on an isolated rock of ideological 'Prussianism', while the agricultural lobbyists of the Agrarian League astutely sank their futures in the new process of right-wing coalition-building. Soon, even the most inveterate defenders of pre-1918 traditions either tacitly or explicitly adjusted to the new political landscape. Graf Kuno von Westarp, one of the leaders of the pre-1918 Conservative Party, who entered the new era obstinately defending the integrity of his party's past, is a good example. He became the second chairman of the DNVP in 1924, consistently argued the need for tactical participation in the Weimar political process, and left the party in 1928 as a bitter opponent of Alfred Hugenberg's new confrontationist course. Westarp's positions nevertheless exhibited a personal consistency, since he remained hostile to the populist and demagogic posture of 'nationalist opposition', whether in the form of the radical nationalist drive for right-wing unification between 1912 and 1918 or Hugenberg's version after 1928.

Ironically, however, the Conservative national committee, which Westarp had carefully preserved in 1918 as a defence against rampant populism in the DNVP's new politics, proved one of the strongest sources of radical nationalist support for Hugenberg's leadership bid in 1928. Nothing could have illustrated more dramatically the ideological capitulation of traditional Conservatism to the new exigencies of right-wing politics under Weimar, despite the isolated stand of an individual like Westarp. The desire for a Hohenzollern restoration often remained, but this was a distinctly secondary consideration against the immediate priority of dismantling the hated Weimar/Versailles system. East Elbian traditionalists managed a minor regroupment around Hindenburg's presidency after 1925, but even here the dominant ideological perspectives had more in common with the radicalized authoritarianism produced by the 1912–20 watershed than with the more narrowly conceived 'Prussianism' it supplanted.[9]

Two separate processes were important to this marginalization of the old Conservative tradition. The first began with the founding of the Agrarian League in 1893 and amounted to the pursuit of agrarian interests within the larger political arena of the Reich. Its effect was to impose a quite different set of political priorities on the Agrarian League's leaders, involving them in a much broader and more complicated set of political and ideological relationships than the East Elbian leadership of the Conservative Party itself had ever needed to confront. In turn, this permitted greater openness to both anti-Semitic and radical nationalist influences and eased the Agrarian League's involvement in the unification initiatives of the right after 1912. The long-term outcome was the second process, involving the decisive separation of agrarian politics from Conservative party politics of the traditional monarchist kind, and amounting to a 'Pan-Germanizing' of the Conservative political vision that remained. As Jens Flemming has shown, this was readily apparent in the manoeuvres of 1927–8 which brought Hugenberg to the DNVP chair.[10] Thus, after the dust of the revolutionary years 1918–23 had settled, even the residual Conservatism of the East Elbian network preserved by the Conservative national committee had been thoroughly transformed. Between the wheels of agrarian interest-politics and radical nationalist ideology the Conservative political tradition of the Empire had been ground to nought.

2

The ideological transformation of East Elbian Conservatism is worth exploring in more detail. How did party-political Conservatives come to abandon their hostility to the ideas and realities of mass politics, a resistance which remained very marked during the Wilhelmine era, and which constitutes one of the most important factors separating conservatives from fascists? We can appreciate the significance of this question if we remember that for most of the Wilhelmine period there were serious tensions between agrarian Conservatives and radical nationalists, quite apart from the disdain of the Conservative upper crust for the rabble-rousing type of popular anti-Semitism. Basically, radical nationalist aspirations legitimized – indeed celebrated – exactly those processes of socioeconomic development that were threatening the East Elbian landowning interest in its traditional form.

Thus the big navy symbolized industrialism in the discourse both of its supporters and its opponents, and was ideologically linked in all manner of ways to the promotion of industrial and commercial interests. Moreover, high arms spending raised the spectre of a comprehensive finance reform, and Conservative efforts to evade and partially assimilate the consequences of this connection dominated much of the political process between 1908 and 1913. Another plank of the radical nationalist platform, the struggle against 'Slavdom' in the east, also infringed Conservative interests, because consistent anti-Polish measures required severing the cheap migrant labour market for the eastern estates. The integrity of big landed property in the east was also threatened by internal colonization (the settling of healthy German peasants on inefficiently run large estates), which had been in the Pan-German programme since the late 1890s, and which entered more general currency on the eve of the war. But in general the whole ideological posture of 'national opposition', which combined criticism of the government and Kaiser with a strident belief in popular mobilization, rising in a crescendo of divisive polemics on the right between 1904 and 1908, was profoundly unsettling for the deference-oriented outlook of traditional Conservatives.

Such tensions remained a major obstacle to the unification of the right between the 1890s and the First World War, and contributed to the instability of the various right-wing coalitions that actually materialized during that period: for example, the *Sammlungspolitik* of 1897–1902 or the Bülow Block of 1907–9. They were partially overcome in the aftermath of the second Moroccan Crisis of 1911 and the Reichstag election of 1912. The most obvious explanation for this new development was the anti-socialist panic ignited by the SPD's electoral success (bringing it 110 seats out of the Reichstag's 397) and the simultaneous reduction of the parliamentary right (Conservatives, Free Conservatives and the right wing of the National Liberals) to an unprecedented low of 62 seats, supplemented by another 24 or so anti-Semites, independent agrarians and miscellaneous particularists. For the first time this created serious fears of a centre-left realignment of the German polity, constructed from the Catholic Centre Party (91 deputies), the National Liberals (only five of whose 45 deputies stood unequivocally on the right), the left liberals (41 deputies, freshly unified into the Progressive People's Party in 1910), and whatever portion of the Social Democrats could be won for such a 'realistic' course. The serious prospects of such a realignment may have been low, but the right's fears were no less real for that. Under these circumstances, when the left had made great strides and the government seemed incapable of a dynamic response, urgent pressure developed for a common organizational and ideological front of the right.

Secondly, international developments also assisted the cause of right-wing unification. After the disappointments of the second Moroccan Crisis there occurred a definite shift from *Weltpolitik* back to *Kontinentalpolitik*, and from naval to military armaments, as the main focus of German foreign policy. Aside from the army's historic place in Conservative affections, this return to a programme of landward expansionism created a framework of thinking in which specifically Conservative interests, that is, agrarian ones, could be more easily accommodated. The prospects of eastward expansion brought a new discourse of imperialist speculation – involving territorial conquests, new living space, settlement policies, the creation of a 'frontier peasantry', meeting the Russian threat – that was far less inimical to Conservative ears. At the very least, radical nationalist ideas on internal colonization could now be displaced outwards, to be realized at the expense of Tsarist Russia (and Russian, Polish and Ukrainian landowners), without disturbing the social relations of the East Elbian countryside.

Thirdly, there emerged a new activist grouping in the Conservative Party around Wolfgang Kapp, the origins of which remain unclear but which seemed willing, for winning the support of the peasantry and *Mittelstand*, to develop a more imaginative and constructive policy based on material incentives as opposed to rhetoric alone. These efforts focused on co-operative insurance schemes and various forms of paternalistically structured self-help, and converged with the movement for internal colonization in which Kapp was also heavily involved. Given the contacts concurrently opened up between the Pan-Germans and the Agrarian League, these initiatives created a new common basis, quite outside the given basis of Conservative party politics, for political co-operation with the radical nationalist right. After 1912 the Pan-Germans also began seriously recruiting individual East Elbian Conservatives for the first time in their history. This process accelerated during the war, particularly once the more grandiose prospects of eastward expansion opened up, and as the radical nationalist front found itself pushed further into opposition to the civil government. The disorientation produced by the Kaiser's abdication and the military defeat in the west then combined with the radicalizing effects of the revolution to leave Conservatives still more vulnerable to Pan-German and radical nationalist ideology.

In other words, beneath the exigencies of the new anti-socialist policies after 1912, and within the framework of an expanded German imperialism in eastern Europe, the former tensions between the Conservatives and radical nationalists ceased to be as serious an obstacle to right-wing concentration. Some of the old hostilities obviously remained. 'What does German-national [*deutschnational*] really mean? I am three times more of a Prussian than I am a German', declared one old East Elbian DNVP Reichstag deputy in exasperation at the new tenor of right-wing politics.[11] But, on the whole, Conservative thinking during Weimar now proceeded within well-established radical nationalist parameters.

3

The radicalization and unification of the right during 1912–20 occurred through the complex interactions of an 'old' and a 'new' right, which at different times during the previous two decades had exploded into serious political conflicts. The interactions occurred on several different levels: (i) between 'notables' (*Honoratioren*) and a new type of activist politician (a mixture of professional politicians, pressure-group and interest-group functionaries, career-making freebooters, and ideological enthusiasts); (ii) between the dominant classes (the capitalist class in the strict sense, landowners and the upper strata of the military, bureaucracy, judiciary, and professions) and the petty bourgeoisie (the organized old and new *Mittelstand*); and (iii) between an establishmentarian conservatism and a new ideology of 'national opposition'. Generalizing, we can say that the first two of these levels (the more institutional and sociological) were overdetermined in the third (the ideological), because the radical-right critique of the existing establishment was fuelled above all by the belief that the dominant classes (represented in the political arena by stultified party notabilities) had become incapable of the imaginative and determined politics now necessary for realizing Germany's interests in the world and meeting the challenge of the left. In *Reshaping the Germany Right* I argued that a fully fledged national opposition then emerged in two distinct phases: (i) the growth of a dissident and largely anti-parliamentary radical nationalist public, defining itself against the conventional governmental and party-political right via a dynamic, populist conception of political mobilization (roughly 1890–1908); followed by (ii) the rather unexpected readmission of that radical nationalist public to the right-wing mainstream under conditions of unprecedented disaffection of the dominant classes from the government and unprecedented electoral weakness of the right-wing parties, on ideological terms set increasingly by the radical nationalists themselves (beginning in 1907–8, with a quickening after the second Moroccan Crisis and the 1912 election).

Now, the political sociology of this process involved a concerted effort to ground the putative right-wing front in a mobilized petty-bourgeois base. Indeed, right-wing political strategy had become powerfully focused on the necessity of integrating both the old and the new petty bourgeoisie within the structures of the emerging anti-socialist concentration (*Sammlung*); and one of the most distinctive features of the 1913 Cartel was the conjunction of the older forms of industrial-agrarian co-operation with the freshly organized Imperial-German *Mittelstand* League (Reichsdeutscher Mittelstandsverband: RMDV) and the mass support of the nationalist pressure groups. Unfortunately, discussion of this question has become bogged down in an increasingly unhelpful polemic regarding the 'manipulated' versus the 'autonomous' character of this petty-bourgeois support, with one group stressing 'manipulation from above' by the 'traditional elites', and the other stressing processes of 'self-mobilization from below'.[12] The terms of this debate have become oversimplified and unnecessarily dichotomous. For example: by seizing on the term 'self-mobilization' and isolating it from the larger context of careful argumentation, some critics of *Reshaping the German Right* implied that I see the self-consciously mobilized petty bourgeoisie as somehow being the dominant factor in the right, which effectively called the shots. But this is really to reify just a single term within a more complex argument, which has always insisted on the dialectical nature of the interactions between the old and new right. It was from the tensions between dominant and subordinate classes, which were constitutive for right- as well as for left-wing politics, that radicalization came.

We can perhaps make this clearer by focusing more concretely on the agencies that sought to mediate the interaction. In this sense three categories of political actors may be distinguished. The *first* were the more far-sighted representatives of the classic industrial–agrarian coalition and their allies, in the two Conservative parties and the National Liberal right, who now appreciated, owing to parliamentary weakness and the growing mobilization of the *Mittelstand* in its own right, that the formal framework of *Sammlungspolitik* had to be adjusted in a more popular direction. At the same time, their intentions and the model of politics these reflected were clearly manipulative. This was a case, in straightforwardly instrumental terms, of 'officers' trying to find 'troops'. In other words, these were the intelligent representatives of the 'old right', the spokesmen of *Sammlungspolitik* in the old Bismarckian mould.[13]

The *second* group might be called the political brokers of the right, who played the key part in ideologically re-equipping the right for these new needs and opportunities. Here ought to be included (i) the radical nationalists around the Pan-Germans; (ii) a cognate category of functionaries and ideologists in and around the Imperial League Against Social Democracy and the so-called patriotic labour movement; and (iii) the Kapp group in the Conservative Party. All had a highly developed conception of popular mobilization and became technically extremely skilled and experienced at their work. But this conception was also an *authoritarian* as opposed to a *participant* one, and therefore beyond a certain point was also 'manipulative' in relation to the 'masses' properly defined. This was especially true of the Pan-Germans under Heinrich Class and Alfred Hugenberg, his *éminence grise*, who both held a cynical view of the masses themselves. Rather than agitating the latter directly, they preferred a combined strategy of working for influence in high places and mobilizing the masses at one remove (through agencies they influenced and if possible secretly controlled). As Lohalm has shown, the Deutschvölkischer Schutz- und Trutzbund after 1919 was a classic embodiment of this strategy.

Lastly, there emerged an autonomous category of petty-bourgeois politicians, whom in *Reshaping the German Right* I tentatively (and no doubt slightly cryptically) called 'organic intellectuals of the petty bourgeoisie in Gramsci's sense'.[14] This concept cannot be elaborated here, but does emphasize the independent political cast and social affiliations of those concerned. They emerged from two interlocking milieux between the 1880s and the First World War: first, political anti-Semitism, with its social base in the central German peasantry and urban shopkeepers, tradesmen and artisans; and, second, the dense network of artisanal, retailing, co-operative and petty entrepreneurial organizations that became so important under the national and regional umbrella of the RMDV and its predecessor, the German *Mittelstand* Association (Deutscher

Mittelstandsverband: DMV) of 1904. Moreover, the new *Mittelstand* also contributed organizations to this second milieu, themselves generating (as in the case of the German-National Commercial Assistants Association [Deutschnationaler Handlungsgehilfenverband: DHV]) their own cultural functionaries and intellectual cadre. The special-interest parties, of which the Wirtschaftspartei was the most important, and the *völkisch* movement were the linear descendants in the Weimar Republic of these interconnected Wilhelmine milieux.

The interaction of these three political elements – each commanding key political resources and popular constituencies – produced an extremely volatile situation. Intelligent politicians of the old guard (category one) saw that in a crisis of ruling-class disunity and diminishing popular support a lasting stabilization required new concessions to the principle of popular mobilization. However, this very process required delegating a high degree of autonomous political initiative to activists and ideologists (the 'brokers' in category two) whose antics became very difficult to control. This scenario was basic both to the history of the Agrarian League and to the experience of the Pan-Germans, the Navy League and other nationalist pressure groups in the 1890s and 1900s. In 1913 the process was taken a stage further, because now the brokers themselves were dealing with a more popular formation (category three) engaged in asserting its own independence and passing out of direct control.[15] During the Weimar Republic the same unstable and contradictory relationship proved to be a critical weakness of the DNVP, which failed to establish its undisputed moral-political leadership over the Protestant *Mittelstand* and never became the organic representation of its myriad local and regional organizations.

But the real legacy of Wilhelmine radical nationalism, where a very broad degree of integration *was* achieved, was ideological. If the radical nationalist 'brokers' were ultimately unable to go the whole hog by integrating 'organic' politicians from the *Mittelstand* and the patriotic labour movement as equal partners in the process of concentration – for example, by including them in the real leadership bodies of the Fatherland Party, as opposed to its cosmetic larger executive – their ideological innovations were none the less radical for that. An appeal to the 'will of the people' was something quite *new* for the right. Appeals to the national interest were obviously the common stuff of German politics. But in the official language of Wilhelmine conservatism they normally connoted ideas of harmony of interests or 'estates'. The rhetorical syntax of traditional Bismarckian *Sammlungspolitik* left no room for any notion of popular legitimacy as such. Radical nationalism's political novelty was not only that it introduced such a notion into the practice of the right, but that it did so in confrontation with the right's existing institutions, in a highly innovative organizational and agitational way. During the radicalization of 1912–20 the Pan-German panacea – the ideal of a united race-people mobilized for battle with internal and external foes, obliterating the divisiveness of class-sectional, particularist and confessional loyalties via the fanatical pursuit of German aggrandizement – entered the discourse of the right as a whole. The revolutionary years 1918–23 witnessed the escalation of the tone and content of these ideas, and also extended and solidified this diffusion.

By the early 1920s, therefore, a brutalized form of the radical nationalist legacy was the common property of the German right, reaching from the Conservative wing of the DNVP to the paramilitary formations and the extreme *völkisch* sects. But this remained an *ideological* achievement, because the radical nationalists never proved capable of organizing the 'race-people' into a new and internally cohesive *social* bloc. This limitation ultimately vitiated the potential effectiveness of the Fatherland Party in 1917–18, and that of the Deutschvölkischer Schutz- und Trutzbund, which while numerically impressive never managed the transition from ideological to fully political mobilization. Most of all, it vitiated the effectiveness of the DNVP.

4

This brings us, finally, to the organizational question. For the fusion of the old and new right was achieved far more successfully at a level of ideology than at that of institutions or organized social forces. Arguably, this discrepancy between the *extent of ideological radicalization* (which permeated the dominant classes as a whole after 1912–20 as well as the petty bourgeoisie) and *the persistence of organizational and sociopolitical fragmentation* (with continuing tensions between radical nationalist notables and the right's broader popular constituency) goes a long way towards explaining both the contempt of the Nazis for the old political gang and the ease with which they eventually superseded them. Hitler in particular was contemptuous of the Wilhelmine radical nationalists' well-meaning but ultimately elitist attempts to win the masses. In his mind this extended from the Pan-German coterie of Hugenberg in the DNVP to the *völkisch* splinters of the Deutsch-völkisch Freiheitspartei (DFVP) and its fellows. He compared the latter explicitly with the radical nationalist activity of Wilhelmine days, for

> Just as in those days, control [over the *völkisch* movement] was acquired by entirely honourable but fantastically naive scholars, professors, *Land-, Studien-* and *Justizräte*, in short middle-class idealists. It lacked the warm breath of youthful energy. The impetuous drive of enthusiastic hotheads was rejected as demagogy. As a result the new movement was a *völkisch* but not a popular movement.[16]

This was a perceptive commentary. Whatever the original aspirations of radical nationalists between the 1880s and 1900s, by the 1920s they had settled for an exterior and authoritarian relationship to the masses. Indeed, Hugenberg's strategy for controlling the DNVP was predicated on explicit disregard for the popular constituencies the party had already managed to assemble.

In this respect, the Nazi Party was quite different. Of course, the Nazis were in their own way every bit as contemptuous of the masses in the democratic sense. But they were at the same time aggressively plebeian in outlook, and managed a degree of broadly based popular mobilization which, with the possible exception of the SPD in 1918–20, was unmatched during the Weimar Republic on any part of the political spectrum. The really striking feature of the Nazis' success after 1928 was not so much its disproportionate dependence on a single social group, the petty bourgeoisie, as its integration of diverse social support. This was a major constructive achievement. The various elements of the German right precisely lacked a strong tradition of consummated solidarity in the political sphere, and the unification process after 1912 failed to resolve the various histories of hostility and mutual suspicion. Consequently, its ability to overcome such contradictions in a rising wave of electoral success between 1928 and the summer of 1932 made the NSDAP a popular political phenomenon on the right with no precedent in German history. It not only subsumed the organizational disunity of the right, but also gave the latter an exceptionally broad popular base, centred on the peasantry and petty bourgeoisie but extending far into the wage-earning population.

The NSDAP's success in rallying the variegated constituencies of the right into a unitary organizational framework made it unique in modern German politics. In this sense, it 'succeeded where the traditional parties of the bourgeois centre and right had repeatedly failed, becoming the long-sought party of middle-class concentration'.[17] As is well known, the Nazis prospered at the expense of the liberal parties and the DNVP, obliterating the former at the polls altogether and slashing the latter's support from 14.2 per cent in 1928 to a mere 5.9 per cent in July 1932. But, as we have seen, this did not represent the dissolution of a stable and solidly founded entity. From the beginning the DNVP had been a thoroughly unstable formation, and in any case had never managed to gather in anything like the full coalition of support attained by the Nazis. It experienced an early drainage of strength to the Wirtschaftspartei and the DVFP, and had never adequately integrated the local forms of special-interest and *völkisch* activity. As Tom Childers has shown, this fragmentation 'actually intensified and·broadened during the so-called Golden Twenties', as the DNVP's support succumbed to 'the rising appeal of parties that renounced the integrative aspirations of the larger, socially complex and ideologically oriented parties and championed the interests of specific occupational, economic, or regional groups'. The crisis of the DNVP was accordingly already visible in the 1928 elections, *before* Hugenberg's drive for control, which exacerbated the situation by poisoning relations with the party's remaining popular groups. The NSDAP then emerged from the pack between 1928 and 1930 as the dynamic agency capable of unifying this volatile and disparate range of constituencies into a single movement.[18]

For future discussion, the key question thus becomes not the process by which the NSDAP succeeded in overcoming much (though not all) of the instability by recombining the elements of the right into the long-needed sociopolitical bloc, because by now we know much about what happened between 1928 and 1934. If the argument of this chapter, concerning the fascist tendencies of the Weimar period as a whole and the long-term difficulties of the establishment's relations with the petty bourgeoisie, is accepted, the significance of the later period becomes somewhat relativized. The immediate conjuncture of the depression and the associated political crisis of the Weimar Constitution will always remain crucial to our understanding. But for now the more interesting questions perhaps concern the years 1918–28, when a synthesis *seemed* possible under the aegis of the DNVP, but came to nothing.

From this point of view, it was significant that Hugenberg's victory in the DNVP's leadership struggle in 1928 was also a victory for the Pan-German strategy – 'anti-parliamentary' in its aims, 'extra-parliamentary' in its political base. The resources mobilized by Hugenberg were recruited to a striking degree from a 'non-partisan' radical nationalist public, primarily the Stahlhelm, the United Patriotic Leagues, and of course the Pan-Germans. In effect, this amounted to a resurgence of the radical nationalist cadre first assembled during 1912–20. As such, it drew on the basic components of the Wilhelmine 'new right', with the key exception of the most recent additions to the latter, the *völkisch* groups and the Christian Socials. Socially, it reassembled the same coalition that sustained the 1913 Cartel: landowners, businessmen, retired officers, civil servants, the commercial and agricultural *Mittelstand*, and the free professions. In this way, the tenacity of the Wilhelmine radical nationalist strategy emerges very strongly.[19] But this was not the continuity of a traditional 'pre-industrial elite' and its manipulations reaching back to Bismarck. It was a dramatic synthesis of more recent provenance, which began to acquire its final form only in the post-1912 conditions of anti-socialist weakness.

However, this radical nationalist victory occurred only on a badly reduced *popular* base. In raising the standard of uncompromising 'national opposition', Hugenberg consciously set himself against the organized interests who had set the tone under Westarp between 1924 and 1928. Not only were the DNVP's popular lobbies (DHV, Christian labour, etc.) now in opposition to his leadership, but their own popular constituencies were beginning to desert the party. Between the two elections of 1928 and 1930 the DNVP's popular credibility plummeted. Organizationally, the putative coalition of 1918 completely fragmented. Thus although Pan-Germans and other radical nationalist activists were now finally in full command, and the programme of the early 1900s was to that extent fully realized, the populist groundswell they had always hoped to ride was now flowing elsewhere. In 1930 the DNVP lost another 2 million votes on top of the 2 million already lost in 1928. The Nazis were already waiting in the wings.

NOTES

This chapter represents a development of arguments in the final chapters of my book, *Reshaping the German Right. Radical Nationalism and Political Change after Bismarck* (New Haven, Conn., and London, 1980), and complements another essay, 'What produces fascism: pre-industrial traditions or a crisis of the capitalist state?', in *Politics and Society*, vol. 12 (1983), pp. 53–82, reprinted in Geoff Eley, *From Unification to Nazism. Reinterpreting the German Past* (London, 1986), pp. 254–82.

1 Stressing the anti-working-class character of Nazi political violence in no way precludes acknowledging the Nazis' substantial recruitment of working-class support, particularly through the *Sturmabteilung* (SA). More specifically, that violence was directed against the traditional class consciousness of the classical labour movement in all its party-political, trade union, and subcultural manifestations. This can easily be obscured by too simple an emphasis on the anti-capitalist and anti-bourgeois aspects of Nazi rhetoric and the plebeian origins of Nazi rank-and-file support after 1930. These issues have given rise to heated historiographical debate, especially arising out of the work of Conan Fischer. See, for example, C. Fischer, 'Class enemies or class brothers? Communist–Nazi relations in Germany, 1929–33', *European History Quarterly*, vol. 15, no. 3 (July 1985), pp. 259–79, and the ensuing exchange between Fischer and Dick Geary in ibid., vol. 15, no. 4 (October 1985), pp. 453–71.
2 For a more detailed discussion of the characteristics of fascist ideology and politics, from which the present formulations are adapted, see Eley, 'What produces fascism', esp. p. 271. For a useful discussion of fascist ideology, see S. G. Payne, *Fascism. Comparison and Definition* (Madison, Wis., 1980), pp. 195 ff., 6 ff., whence the phrases in quotation marks are drawn.
3 This way of formulating the problem – as the conjunction of a dual crisis, a crisis of representation and a crisis of hegemony or popular consent – derives from the work of Nicos Poulantzas, *Fascism and Dictatorship* (London, 1979). The most stimulating exploration of that approach in relation to the crisis of Weimar is David Abraham's *The Collapse of the Weimar Republic. Political Economy and Crisis*, rev. edn (New York, 1986).
4 Broadly speaking, the same has been true of non-Marxist and Marxist accounts, allowing for the tendency of older Marxist versions to see the fascist mass movement in overly functional terms as an instrument of big capitalist interests. David Beetham (ed.), *Marxists in the Face of Fascism. Writings by Marxists on Fascism from the Interwar Period* (Manchester, 1983), is an excellent introduction. The classic sociological version of the 'lower-middle-class thesis' is S. M. Lipset, *Political Man. The Social Basis of Politics* (New York, 1960; rev.edn, Baltimore, Md, 1981), esp. ch. 5, pp. 127–79 and the new afterthoughts, pp. 488–503, which reaffirm the original argument. Research broadly

confirms the petty bourgeoisie's disproportionate role. See especially Michael Kater, *The Nazi Party. A Social Profile of Members and Leaders, 1919–1945* (Cambridge, Mass., 1983) and Thomas Childers, *The Nazi Voter. The Social Foundations of Fascism in Germany, 1919–1933* (Chapel Hill, NC, 1983). The main empirical account dissenting from this view, Richard Hamilton's *Who Voted for Hitler?* (Princeton, NJ, 1982), which argues the disproportionate importance to the Nazis of upper-class support, provides no evidence for discounting the lower-middle-class thesis, and is actually quite compatible with it.

5 Childers, *Nazi Voter*, and J. W. Falter, 'Wer verhalf der NSDAP zum Sieg', in *Aus Politik und Zeitgeschichte*, B28–79 (14 July 1979), pp. 3–21, and 'Wählerbewegungen zur NSDAP 1924–1933', in O. Büsch (ed.), *Wählerbewegungen in der europäischen Geschichte* (Berlin, 1980), pp. 159–202. The most comprehensive assembly of evidence for European fascisms as a whole, which largely reinforces the 'lower-middle-class' view, is S. U. Larsen, B. Hagtvet and J. P. Myklebust (eds), *Who Were the Fascists? Social Roots of European Fascism* (Bergen, Oslo and Tromsø, 1980). An earlier essay of my own, which attempted to define the sociopolitical dynamics of right-wing radicalization in Germany between the 1870s and 1930s, took much the same line; see Geoff Eley, 'The German right, 1860–1945: how it changed', in Eley, *From Unification to Nazism*, pp. 159–202 (originally published in R. J. Evans (ed.), *Society and Politics in Wilhelmine Germany* (London, 1978), pp. 112–35.

6 For typical examples: J. Kocka, 'Ursachen des nationalsozialismus', in *Aus Politik und Zeitgeschichte*, B25–80 (21 June 1980), pp. 3–15; H. A. Winkler, 'German society, Hitler, and the illusion of restoration', in G. L. Mosse (ed.), *International Fascism: New Thoughts and New Approaches* (London and Beverley Hills, Calif., 1979), pp. 143–60; H.-J. Pühle, *Von der Agrarkrise zum Prafäschismus* (Wiesbaden, 1972); H.-U. Wehler, *The German Empire 1871–1918* (Leamington Spa/ Dover, NH, 1985), esp. pp. 230–46. For an extended discussion of the deeper historical perspectives of 'political backwardness' and 'failed modernization' implied by this approach, see Eley, 'What produces fascism', and D. Blackbourn and G. Eley, *The Peculiarities of German History. Bourgeois Society and Politics in Nineteenth-Century Germany* (Oxford, 1984).

7 There are no detailed accounts of the Kapp Putsch in English. See J. Erger, *Der Kapp-Lüttwitz Putsch* (Düsseldorf, 1967); E. Konnemann and H.-J. Kirsch, *Aktionseinheit contra Kapp-Putsch* (Berlin, 1972); E. Lucas, *Märzrevolution 1920*, 3 vols. (Frankfurt, 1970, 1973 and 1978); H. A. Winkler, *Von der Revolution zur Stabilisierung. Arbeiter und Arbeiterbewegung in der Weimarer Republik 1918 bis 1924* (Bonn, 1984), pp. 295–342.

8 Hitler's parliamentary and 'legal' strategy following the fiasco of the Munich Putsch in November 1923 was very far from the practical parliamentarism of the Conservative parties before 1914. Whereas the Wilhelmine right observed the rules of liberal political discourse until shortly before 1914, the Nazis treated them with complete and bare-faced cynicism. Hitler made no bones about exploiting parliamentary procedures simply to destroy them. Moreover, the Nazis' strategy of 'legality' was always accompanied by systematic violence against opponents and against the very principle of political pluralism. The repudiation of the parliamentary legitimacy that had previously constrained the right from this kind of extremism is the essence of the transition described here, and for large sections of the German (as of the Italian) right it had clearly been accomplished in 1918–23.

9 The Conservative agrarian politician Elard von Oldenburg-Januschau, whose career spanned the Wilhelmine and Weimar periods, is an excellent example. Superficially the crustiest of traditional Junkers who after 1925 became a confidant of Hindenburg, in the late 1920s he actually became a strong advocate of Hugenberg's politics.

10 J. Flemming, 'Konservatismus als "nationalrevolutionare Bewegung". Konservative Kritik an der Deutschnationalen Volkspartei 1918–1933', in D. Stegmann, B.-J. Wendt and P.-C. Witt (eds), *Deutscher Konservatismus im 19. und 20. Jahrhundert. Festschrift für Fritz Fischer zum 75. Geburtstag und zum 50. Doktorjubiläum* (Bonn, 1983), pp. 295–331.

11 General von Kleist of Wendisch-Tychow, quoted by Werner Liebe, *Die Deutschnationale Volkspartei 1918–1924* (Düsseldorf, 1956), p. 128.

12   The first position is associated with, for example, Hans-Ulrich Wehler, Jürgen Kocka, Hans-Jürgen Puhle and Heinrich August Winkler. The second has become attached to a small grouping of British German historians including David Blackbourn, Richard J. Evans and myself, though it is questionable how far a common position in this regard is actually present in our works. For good introductions to the question, see R. G. Moeller, 'The *Kaiserreich* recast? Continuity and change in modern German historiography', *Journal of Social History*, vol. 17 (1983–4), pp. 655–83, and W. Mock, '"Manipulation von oben" oder Selbstorganisation an der Basis? Einige neuere Ansätze in der englischen Historiographie zur Geschichte des deutschen Kaiserreichs', *Historische Zeitschrift*, vol. 232 (1981), pp. 358–75.

13   The classic account of this politics is D. Stegmann, *Die Erben Bismarcks. Parteien und Verbände in der Spätphase des wilhelminischen Deutschlands. Sammlungspolitik 1897–1918* (Cologne, 1970). See also Stegmann's 'Zwischen Repression und Manipulation. Konservative Machteliten und Arbeiter- und Angestelltenbewegung 1910–1918', *Archiv für Sozialgeschichte*, vol. 12 (1972), pp. 351–432, and his subsequent essays on the late Weimar period: 'Zum verhältnis von Grossindustrie und Nationalsozialismus 1930–1933', in ibid., vol. 13 (1973), pp. 399–482; 'Kapitalismus und Faschismus in Deutschland 1929–1934', in *Gesellschaft. Beiträge zur Marxschen Theorie*, vol. 6 (Frankfurt, 1976), pp. 19–91; and 'Antiquierte Personalisierung oder sozialökonomische Faschismusanalyse?', *Archiv für Sozialgeschichte*, vol. 17 (1977), pp. 275–96. The last two items formed part of a polemic with Henry Ashby Turner: see H. A. Turner, 'Grossunternehmer und Nationalsozialismus', *Historische Zeitschrift*, vol. 221 (1975), pp. 18–68.

14   Eley, *Reshaping*, p. 358.

15   ibid., p. 359.

16   W. Jochmann, *Nationalsozialismus und Revolution. Dokumente* (Frankfurt, 1963), pp. 88 ff.

17   Childers, *Nazi Voter*, p. 262.

18   T. Childers, 'Interest and ideology: anti-system politics in the era of stabilization, 1924–28', in G. D. Feldman (ed.), *Die Nachwirkungen der Inflation auf die deutsche Geschichte 1924–1933* (Munich, 1985), p. 3.

19   From this point of view, the most illuminating account of Hugenberg's campaign for the DNVP leadership is H. Holzbach, Das *'System Hugenberg'. Die Organisation bürgerlicher Sammlungspolitik vor dem Aufstieg der NSDAP* (Stuttgart, 1981).

5

German Conservatives
and the Third Reich:
an ambiguous relationship

Jeremy Noakes

On 21 March 1933, a wreath-laying ceremony was held in the Garrison Church at Potsdam to mark the opening of the new Reichstag elected on 5 March.[1] In front of the tomb of Frederick the Great, the holiest shrine of Conservative Prussia, the new Reich Chancellor, Adolf Hitler, leader of the Nazi Party, joined Field-Marshal Paul von Hindenburg, Reich President and the living symbol of the Prusso–German Conservative tradition, in a ritual of dedication for the new regime. It was attended by four of the six sons of the former Kaiser and a chair was symbolically left vacant for the exiled Wilhelm II. A guard of honour was provided by detachments of the *Reichswehr*, the Nazi *Sturmabteilung* (SA) and *Schutzstaffel* (SS), and by the Stahlhelm, the conservative veterans' organization, of which Hindenburg was honorary president. After an address, in which Hitler referred to 'the marriage between the symbols of past greatness and the vigour of youth', he bowed to and shook hands with Hindenburg in a gesture of homage from the new Germany to the old. Broadcast live to the nation, the occasion moved some members of the middle class to tears.[2]

Eleven years later, on 20 July 1944, an abortive attempt was made to assassinate Hitler. Most of those involved in the attempted coup came from the traditional German elites, the army and the civil service, and many were from noble families.[3] Yet many had begun by sharing the illusions associated with the Potsdam ceremony, participating to a greater or lesser extent in the regime. The Potsdam ceremony of March 1933 and the bomb plot of July 1944 thus represent the two poles in the relationship between the German Conservatives and the Third Reich and raise a number of questions. Why did so many Conservatives welcome the new regime with enthusiasm? At what points did their co-operation with it break down and for what reasons? And, finally, did any Conservatives remain immune to its temptations and, if so, why?[4]

The rise of the Nazi Party reflected the political bankruptcy of German Conservatism, the culmination of its failure to adjust to the age of mass

71

politics and to acquire and sustain a broadly based popular constituency. Before 1918, Germany had failed to develop a strong Conservative party.[5] Indeed, the divisive effects of national unification had led to the creation of two parties: the German Conservative Party, dominated by East Elbian landowners (the Prussian Junkers), and the Free Conservatives, supported by sections of heavy industry, some northern and western Protestant landowners, and a small section of the *Bildungsbürgertum*. Neither of these parties had succeeded in acquiring a wide appeal. The Conservative Party had relied on its close links with the Agrarian League to mobilize mass peasant support; but this narrow agrarianism tended to alienate it from other sections of the community.[6] Attempts to develop a reformist Conservatism along Christian Social lines in the 1880s and early 1890s came to naught and, during the prewar years, both Conservative parties found themselves increasingly obliged to come to terms with a 'new right' embodied in nationalist 'leagues' such as the Pan-German League.[7]

This 'new right' expressed both the aspirations of a rising middle class, which objected both to the exclusiveness of the traditional elite and to its alleged political weakness at home and abroad, and the resentments of traditional groups – peasants, artisans, and small retailers – at the impact of modernization. It differed from traditional Conservatism in locating the basis of political authority not as hitherto in the state or in the monarchy as its embodiment, but rather in the nation (*Volk*). At the core of this ideology was an ethnic or *völkisch* nationalism which regarded the interests of the German *Volk*, an entity defined by language and culture or 'race' rather than by citizenship, as the supreme value.[8] Deploring what they saw as the drift towards liberal democracy, which through the encouragement of a degrading egalitarianism and a selfish and atomistic individualism would undermine the strength and solidarity of the *Volk*, its members advocated a powerful authoritarian state to ensure a tough defence of German interests abroad and a hierarchical political and social order at home.

The Conservative establishment endeavoured to sustain its authority by harnessing the new right. It adopted much of its extreme rhetoric – the attacks on 'outsiders' (Jews, 'Manchester Liberals' and Social Democrats) – and made minor gestures in favour of its clienteles (e.g. the partial reintroduction of guild controls for artisans in 1897), while endeavouring to rule as before.[9] However, by apparently legitimizing the new right, the traditional Conservatives enabled it to impose its own definition of the values of a patriotic German, summed up in the term *national*: anti-liberal, anti-Semitic, anti-Marxist, and above all chauvinist. Moreover, after 1914 this definition was reinforced by its identification with the values for which Germany was fighting: the 'ideas of 1914' in contradistinction to the values of the enemy, the 'ideas of 1789'.[10] During the war, for example, Thomas Mann had claimed that 'Conservative and *national* are one and the same thing'.[11] The leading spokesman of postwar 'revolutionary conservatism', Moeller van den Bruck, agreed: 'The Conservative counter-movement ... places the idea of the nation above all other ideas – even above that of the monarchy.'[12] The sense of 'national community' (*Volksgemeinschaft*) engendered by the outbreak of war had formed the core of the 'ideas of 1914' and, after the virtual civil war of 1918–20 and their experience of an extreme version of pluralist democracy under Weimar, in which Bismarck's 'enemies of the Reich' appeared dominant, all sections of the right were at one in yearning for its revival. It was the assumption that a *Volksgemeinschaft* was about to be achieved which generated the euphoric response to the Potsdam ceremony of 21 March 1933.

The Conservatives were no more successful after 1918 than before in establishing an effective political organization. The founding of the German National People's Party (DNVP), in 1919 represented an attempt to unite the various prewar Conservative groups and extend the social basis of political Conservatism – hence the inclusion of the word *Volk* in the party's new title.[13] The word *Deutschnational* in the party's name marked the influence on the values of the 'new right'. However, the DNVP was deeply flawed by its origins as an umbrella organization, and Weimar's extreme form of proportional representation encouraged its fissiparous tendencies. Relations between the 'old' and the 'new' right had always been strained. Before the war, the former often deplored the political irresponsibility of the extreme nationalists and despised and feared their populist radicalism; the latter criticized the arrogance, political weakness and social exclusiveness of the old elite. After 1918, the focus of disagreement lay on the respective attitudes towards participation in Weimar governments. Government participation by the DNVP and the compromises involved (Locarno and lower tariffs) alienated the ultras and the agrarian supporters of the DNVP. The final blow occurred in 1928 with the takeover of the party by its Pan-German wing under Alfred Hugenberg.[14] Hugenberg's hard-line policy of 'nationalist opposition' to the Republic split the party, leaving him with a rump of ultra-Conservatives and Pan-Germans whose reactionary image alienated the party's white-collar constituency, leaving it – like the peasants – vulnerable to the appeal of Nazism. Moreover, the arrogance and intransigence of the new DNVP leadership represented a major obstacle to the formation of a bourgeois bloc of the middle-class parties as a basis for a non-Nazi regime of the right.[15] Instead, it was to the Nazis that the rump DNVP looked for support in their vicious campaign against the Republic.

The decision of Hugenberg and of non-party Conservatives such as Neurath and Schwerin von Krosigk to ally with the Nazis represented the culmination of the German Conservative establishment's attempt to harness the forces of the populist 'new right' which had been under way since the 1890s. Ironically, Hugenberg, a co-founder of the Pan-German

League, found himself in the position of an establishment Conservative being outflanked by Hitler, who now represented the challenge of the radical right formerly posed by the Pan-German League. However, Hugenberg decided to ally with the Nazis not only because they possessed the mass support which he lacked, but also because he and many other Conservatives assumed that, as members of the 'nationalist opposition' against Weimar, they all shared basic values and goals. In the sense that both Nazism and postwar German Conservatism were products of the right-wing ideological consensus which had developed during the years 1890–1918 under the impact of the 'new right', this assumption was correct. The problem was that Pan-Germans like Hugenberg, for all their rhetoric, were essentially solid *Bürger* of the prewar era, men whose political style and practice on the whole reflected the civilities of that age. Hitler and his Nazis, on the other hand, were the product of war and revolution, an altogether harsher political climate which produced an altogether tougher and more ruthless political animal.

This fact undermined the two further assumptions on which the Conservatives had entered the coalition with the Nazis: first, that their political experience and their administrative and economic expertise would enable them to outmanoeuvre the inexperienced and heavily outnumbered Nazis; and, secondly, that they could count upon the support of the Conservative elites in general and of Reich President Hindenburg in particular. In short, they thought they could tame the Nazis and use them as a kind of public relations machine for an authoritarian regime of the right. In the light of these assumptions, they preferred an alliance with the Nazis to the alternative solution of a right-wing authoritarian regime based on the army, police and civil service, with the Reichstag reduced to impotence, which risked alienating large sections of the population and causing civil war.

This patronizing strategy reflected both a social and an intellectual arrogance *vis-à-vis* the Nazi *arrivistes* and a fundamental misunderstanding of the nature of Nazism. Above all, however, it represented a grave miscalculation of the balance of forces between the two groups for, in the event, the Nazis proved far shrewder and more effective politicians, ruthless and single-minded in their pursuit of political power. The Conservatives in the cabinet not only lacked an independent mass base – the DNVP had only 8 per cent of the vote – but were also a disparate collection of individuals with a predominantly civil service background and mentality, who made no attempt to co-ordinate their actions or develop a coherent Conservative strategy. Hugenberg, for example, buried himself in his departmental responsibilities which, since he combined the four portfolios of the Reich and Prussian ministries of Economics and Agriculture, were certainly onerous. However, his assumption that, by solving the economic crisis, he could win over Hindenburg and establish an impregnable power base proved an illusion, while his clumsy performance in office alienated his fellow Conservatives. This division among his rivals played straight into Hitler's hands, ensuring Hugenberg's isolation when he resigned on 26 June 1933.[16]

Although the sentiments associated with the Potsdam ceremony reflected the predominant mood among the German upper and middle classes in 1933, it was not universal. The DNVP's decision to enter a coalition with the Nazis had been Hugenberg's alone, reflecting the autocratic structure he had introduced on becoming party leader. It was contrary to the advice of some of his closest colleagues who, after their negative experience of trying to co-operate with the Nazis during 1931–2, pressed for an authoritarian regime without Hitler.[17] Among these perhaps the most interesting was Ewald von Kleist-Schmenzin.

Kleist was an archetypal Junker.[18] Born in 1890 of a distinguished Prussian family and raised on a remote estate in Pomerania in an atmosphere saturated with Prussian aristocratic tradition, Kleist's main political objective was to restore the Hohenzollern monarchy and establish a political system in which, in effect, the patriarchal conditions on his own estate would be reproduced at national level. He played a leading role in the ultra-Conservative 'Main Association of German Conservatives' which united the remnants of the pre-1918 German Conservative Party within the DNVP and represented the social elite of rural East Elbia.[19] It had close links with the *völkisch* and Pan-German wings of the party and, in the leadership struggle of 1928, threw its support behind Hugenberg and the Pan-Germans as the most committed opponents of the Republic. In April 1929, Kleist took over the chairmanship of the association and, as a representative of the war generation, tried to modernize its stance by adopting modish 'revolutionary conservative' concepts, shifting its emphasis from preserving tradition towards becoming a 'national revolutionary movement'.

Although some members of the Main Association established informal contacts with the Nazis in the hope of utilizing them in the campaign against the Republic, others, including Kleist, remained sceptical. Indeed, in the summer of 1932, he published a pamphlet, *National Socialism – A Threat*.[20] It was clearly prompted primarily by his experience of the disruptive impact of Nazism on his estate and local community. Thus, he complained that the Nazis had perverted Conservative workers by expressing socialist demands in a nationalist guise. As a result, workers who had hitherto been reliable now neglected their work, while the younger peasants and small tradesmen would soon end up as socialists or even communists. Even the youth of the educated classes which had fallen for Nazism were now alienated from their parents. Moreover, through their intolerance, divisiveness and contempt for traditional procedures the Nazis had undermined the community. Decisions which had been reached constitutionally were often ignored – even those of non-political organizations: 'in short, everywhere there is destruction of the conditions of social and public life'. Kleist regarded this development as 'even more dangerous than Social Democracy'. Finally, in summing up the crucial distinction between Nazism and Conservatism, Kleist drew on the traditional religious foundation of Prussian Conservatism:

> It is the attitude to religion which separates and must always separate Conservative thinking from National Socialism. The basis of Conservative politics is that obedience to God and faith in him must also determine the whole of public life. Hitler and National Socialism adopt a fundamentally different position ... It is a fact that Hitler – even if he occasionally says something to the contrary – acknowledges only race and its demands as the highest law governing state activity. That is a materialism irreconcilable with faith and Christianity.

Kleist fought hard against the Nazi takeover. He tried to persuade Hindenburg not to appoint Hitler and urged Hugenberg not to join a coalition with the Nazis. Hugenberg, however, accused him of being 'too much of an ultra'.[21] On 13 February 1933, he summed up his position in a letter of resignation from the DNVP addressed to Hugenberg:

> I have not fought against the parliamentary system and for an authoritarian state in order to replace a party government of the left with a party government of the right under an authoritarian disguise, but rather as a Conservative honestly working for a truly independent and of course decisively patriotic government.[22]

To a friend he was blunter:

> Do not think that when you board an express train, the driver of which is deranged, you can somehow take over the controls. You may well travel very fast, but when the train reaches the points it will suddenly be derailed. The fundamental mistake is the pretension to total power: that is the devil at work. Only God can claim total power. If a human being does so then the perversion of power must follow.[23]

Although initially Kleist accepted that 'everyone must use all their energies to co-operate with the new order so that as many sensible things as possible can be implemented',[24] he himself retired to his estate, later becoming a leading member of the resistance until his execution in January 1945.

Although Kleist had adopted the 'revolutionary conservative' rhetoric current among his generation, his Conservatism was essentially rooted in the archaic social order and the Prussian traditions of Pomerania. The challenge by the Nazis to that order alerted him to their revolutionary nature and his ultra-Conservative principles immunized him against the temptation, to which both middle-class Conservative intellectuals and more pragmatic Conservative politicians were vulnerable, of believing that the Nazis were part of the same 'nationalist opposition' and that they could be tamed and used. Thus, despite his co-operation with Hugenberg and the Pan-Germans, in his eyes they were tainted with National Liberalism, and his sense that the Nazis were exploiting nationalism for 'socialist' ends led him to repudiate the glorification of the interests of the *Volk* as the highest good, the cardinal feature distinguishing the new right from the old. For Kleist the highest good was 'not calculable in terms of national expediency . . . the nation as such is not the ultimate measure, but rather the will of God which commits us to living for the nation. That is the fundamental distinction.'[25]

In adopting a position of uncompromising hostility to Nazism, Kleist was exceptional among his fellow Junkers. Indeed, a number had already established contacts with the Nazis prior to 1933.[26] Most, while resenting the *Gleichschaltung* of the Stahlhelm and the radical rhetoric and parvenu manners and pretensions of party officials, were to a varied extent reconciled to many of the new regime's policies. Thus, they welcomed its destruction of democracy in general and the left in particular, and its reassertion of German power and pride. For, unlike Kleist, many Junkers had substituted the nation for God as the core of their value system or at least assumed the nation was God's chief instrument on earth: an idea in which they were encouraged to believe by a substantial section of the Protestant clergy, and an indication of the thorough Germanization of Prussia since 1871. Last but not least, they welcomed policies which ensured the profitability and above all the survival of their estates, many of which were on the verge of bankruptcy in 1932. As with the Weimar Eastern Aid Programme, the large estates benefited disproportionately from the Nazi government's agricultural debt clearance measures of 1933–4.[27] Hitler gave priority to agricultural production and substituted the programme of *Lebensraum* in the east for Weimar plans to settle peasants on bankrupt Junker estates, thereby frustrating the Nazi peasant lobby under Darré which was hostile to the Junkers. A few Junkers, for whom the SS in particular provided a favoured sphere of operation, became committed Nazis; some joined the party in a defensive move to preserve their authority within the local community; others went into 'inner emigration' on their estates. As a group, the Junkers suffered a drastic decline in influence in the Third Reich, preparing the way for their destruction after 1945.

The hostility to Nazism of the ultra-conservative Prussian, Kleist-Schmenzin, had its South German counterpart in the response of Bavarian monarchists such as the influential journalist, Erwein von Aretin.[28] Like

Kleist, Aretin came from a distinguished noble family. His conservatism was rooted in Bavarian tradition and in his Catholic faith, from which he deduced that monarchy was the only form of state corresponding to God's will. He disliked Weimar as a democratic republic whose constitution had reduced Bavarian independence. However, he was also opposed to anti-Catholic, north-German, *deutschnational* Conservatives who wished to ride roughshod over Bavarian state rights in the name of the Reich. Finally, ever since the Munich putsch of 1923 he had despised Hitler, regarding the Bavarian Nazis as 'down and out Jacobins' most of whom 'differed little from Communists'.[29] During February 1933, the Bavarian monarchists devised a plan to block the *Gleichschaltung* of Bavaria by appointing Crown Prince Rupprecht General State Commissioner with dictatorial powers, preparatory to a restoration of the Bavarian monarchy.[30] The idea even gained support from some Bavarian Social Democrats. Amateurish planning, and failure to win over the Bavarian premier, Held, let alone Hindenburg and the *Reichswehr*, wrecked the scheme. Aretin paid for his anti-Nazi activities with a spell in Dachau followed by official exile from Bavaria, while later resistance activities by Bavarian monarchists were crushed by the Gestapo.[31]

As with Kleist, a combination of aristocratic pride, loyalty to traditions independent of and, to some extent, at odds with German nationalism, and the conviction that his political beliefs conformed to the divine will, enabled Aretin to resist the temptations associated with National Socialism. In this, however, they were hardly typical of the German nobility, who were guided more by opportunism than by Conservative principles. The lead was given by the German royal family. During 1932, the ex-Kaiser and the crown prince had competed for Nazi support for a restoration of the monarchy and, in 1933–4, a representative of the Hohenzollern family approached Hitler on three separate occasions, only to be fobbed off with vague promises.[32]

The hopes vested in Nazism by the Prussian royal family were shared by a substantial section of the German aristocracy, particularly that of North and East Germany.[33] Many had lost most or all of their land over the previous century; after the 1918 revolution they also lost the protection of the monarchy and the remnants of their noble privileges. Finally, under the new democratic regime and the Versailles treaty, which limited the officer corps to 4,000, entry into their traditional professions – the army and the civil service – had been severely restricted. This section of the aristocracy came increasingly to adopt the views of the new right. Indeed, as early as 1920 the leading association of the nobility, the Deutsche Adelsgenossenschaft (DAG), had adopted a so-called Aryan clause excluding those of Jewish ancestry from membership. By 1930 the DAG had become committed to the 'nationalist opposition' of Hitler and Hugenberg. It saw the Weimar crisis as a fundamental crisis of all those forces of the modern world – liberalism, democracy, materialism – which were undermining the position of the aristocracy. The Nazi regime appeared to offer the chance to put the clock back, to return to the aristocracy its monopoly of the higher ranks of the civil service and of the officer corps, and thereby restore its position as the dominant elite and *the* prime estate of the realm.

After Hitler's appointment, therefore, the DAG made desperate efforts to ingratiate itself with the new regime. To demonstrate its members' eligibility to be the new elite it introduced a much tougher Aryan clause, requiring the membership to prove non-Jewish ancestry back to 1750. The DAG's chairman announced:

> We are being asked to make a big sacrifice, dispensing with some valuable and highly regarded members. But the general interest of the aristocracy demands this step. Once more the hour of decision has struck for the nobility and, as far as we can tell, it will not strike again ... We must exploit the present situation, however uncertain it may be, as a springboard, using it for our own purposes. If we ignore this hour, we shall ignore the historic hour of the nobility ... But if we boldly seize our opportunity then the great goal which has been out of reach for a hundred years will come again within our grasp – the nobility will once more become a political estate.[34]

Initially, Hitler was happy to encourage such delusions. However, although various nobles found jobs within the regime, and Himmler, in particular, was sympathetic to the nobility as a source of 'good blood' for his SS elite,[35] the DAG failed in its attempt to restore the nobility to its position as *the* elite. The Nazis wanted an open elite. In place of the traditional German elite criteria of birth, property and education, they advocated new criteria of race, biological fitness, achievement and ideological commitment.[36] The DAG found itself increasingly forced to adjust to these demands. Thus, attempting to deflect criticism by Nazi militants of the allegedly reactionary nature of the aristocracy, the DAG began to abandon its traditional commitment to the monarchy and even to Christianity. However, these concessions at last began to provoke opposition from some members. By 1938, Prince Bentheim, chairman of the DAG, was urging that 'the membership should strive everywhere and with all means to strengthen the Conservative elements – Conservative in the true and not the reactionary sense'.[37] Too late the DAG had begun to appreciate the revolutionary nature of Nazism.

During the first eighteen months of the regime, most Conservative hopes of taming the Nazis were pinned on Papen, Vice-Chancellor and Reich Commissioner/acting Minister-President of Prussia. However, with

Göring's appointment as Prussian Minister-President on 7 April 1933, Papen had lost his main power base, for there was no provision in the constitution for a Vice-Chancellor and hence no Vice-Chancellery.[38] By the end of May, this had been partially rectified through the efforts of Papen's assistant, Fritz von Tschirschky. Tschirschky used his personal connection with the Reich Minister of Finance to secure the establishment of an office for the 'Reich Chancellor's Deputy', colloquially known as the Vice-Chancellery. This was then staffed by a group of young Conservative aristocrats, who used Papen's authority to develop a wide range of contacts with the administration, *Reichswehr*, police, press and Catholic Church. Their aim was to assert a Conservative influence on the regime, and their intellectual mentor was Papen's speech writer, a well-connected Munich lawyer and influential publicist, Edgar Jung.[39]

Papen, Jung and their aristocratic colleagues had hoped to exploit Papen's close links with Hindenburg to conduct their strategy of taming Hitler. Papen summed up his view of the coalition in a notorious comment to Kleist-Schmenzin: 'What do you want? I have Hindenburg's confidence. In two months we shall have squeezed Hitler into a corner until he squeaks.'[40] Lacking either official recognition in the constitution, or an adequate power base in the government machine, Papen did indeed depend for influence entirely upon Hindenburg's support. However, the aged Hindenburg, anxious to divest himself of governmental responsibilities, was encouraged to do so by his entourage. Moreover, Papen's frequent absences from Berlin persuaded Hindenburg to revoke his previous insistence on the Vice-Chancellor's attendance at his interviews with Hitler, which, in any case, soon became few and far between.[41] Hindenburg restricted his interventions to a few issues which aroused his particular interest, notably the army.[42]

During 1933, Papen's office was deluged with complaints, mainly from the upper ranks of German society, about the behaviour of the Nazis.[43] Although its officials managed to assist in a number of cases, they became increasingly frustrated at their relative impotence. In short, Papen's colleagues were well placed to observe both the reality of Nazi rule and the bankruptcy of the 'taming' concept in view of the inexorable growth of Nazi power. This prompted them to reappraise their political strategy and, in Jung's case, his ideological assumptions.

Before 1933 Jung had been a member of the Young Conservatives, a political group which formed a branch of the 'revolutionary conservative' movement.[44] The term 'revolutionary conservative' had been applied by Hugo von Hoffmansthal in a speech to Munich University students in 1927. He referred to a 'legion of seekers' who sought

> not freedom but communal bonds ... Never was a German fight for freedom more fervent and yet more tenacious than this fight for true

coercion, this refusal to surrender to a coercion that was not coercive enough ... The process of which I am speaking is nothing less than a conservative revolution on such a scale as the history of Europe has never known. Its aim is to achieve a form, a new German reality in which the whole nation can take part.[45]

Their views were derived primarily from Nietzsche and the vitalist philosophy of the late nineteenth century and from the experience of the war and postwar years, which had convinced them of the bankruptcy of the capitalist economic order and of bourgeois society. Although their recipes for the future ranged from the neo-feudalism of the Young Conservatives to the more technocratically oriented 'third way' between capitalism and socialism of the 'Tat' circle and Ernst Niekisch's National Bolshevism, the movement's members shared two broad convictions: hostility to the Weimar Republic and what they saw as the hegemony of liberalism, by which they meant the secular, rational, moral tradition of the West; and a vision of national redemption through a new 'Third' Reich containing a new post-bourgeois order. Whilst also differing in the extent of their sympathy for Nazism, all, including Jung, welcomed the political energies which it had unleashed against the Republic.

The title of Jung's major work, *The Rule of the Inferiors*,[46] was a description of Weimar which expressed the resentment of members of the middle-class German intelligentsia at the deterioration in their economic position and social status under the Republic. In his view this 'mass rule' of liberal democracy must be 'overcome by a new Conservatism, freedom by integration, leadership and subordination, with rights according to achievement, the inequality of men, hierarchy and order'.[47] Although not personally involved in Hitler's appointment, Jung too had advocated an intellectual version of the 'taming' concept. Thus, in June 1932, he acknowledged that the Nazis had 'the historic honour of having liquidated the Republic, such a tremendous feat that the gratitude of the Conservatives is assured'. Nevertheless he insisted that

the intellectual preconditions for the German revolution were created outside National Socialism. National Socialism has undertaken so to speak the 'mass movement portfolio' in this great collaborative effort ... I have respect for the primitiveness of a popular movement, for the fighting energy of victorious Gauleiter and storm leaders. But their success does not give them the right to consider themselves the salt of the earth and to despise the intellectual avant garde [of Conservatism].[48]

Jung naively hoped that the 'revolutionary conservative' intelligentsia would acquire an intellectual hegemony over the new regime, with 'the victory of the German revolution' being achieved through 'the merging of the German mind with the dynamic of the mass movement'.[49] Unlike those 'revolutionary conservatives', such as the 'Tat' circle, who regarded mass mobilization as vital, were attracted by the 'socialist' pretensions of Nazism, and preferred a revolution to a restoration, Jung was concerned to 'depoliticize' the masses and subordinate them to an authoritarian elite.[50] This made him less vulnerable to the appeal of Nazism, placing him closer to more traditional Conservatives such as Kleist-Schmenzin. Although himself a Protestant, Jung had already been influenced by Catholic social and political philosophy, from which he was able to develop a critical perspective on the cult of nationalism as a secular religion characteristic of both the *deutschnational* and the 'revolutionary' Conservatives. Thus, in place of 'fascist nationalism' and autarky, Jung began to advocate a European federation of nations, in which he assumed Germany would play a leading role, but which would respect the various cultures and operate a common market for their mutual benefit.[51] Nazi ideology with its racist and ethnic exclusivity and arrogance was, he argued, unsuitable as a philosophy for such a Europe, which must be based on Christianity and a Conservatism derived from it. Similarly, he rejected the 'total state' of the Nazis and opposed their attempt 'to politicize all spheres of life, to subject them to regulation by the state'.[52] Above all, his experience of Nazi contempt for human rights made him aware for the first time of their importance:

> Those who fight against human values must never forget that alongside the version enshrined in the Rights of Man of 1789, there is also the natural law version of Christianity on which European culture is based.[53]

Jung expressed his growing disillusionment with the regime most bluntly via Papen's address to the University of Marburg on 17 June 1934.[54] By the summer of 1934 he had become convinced of the need to act before it was too late and felt it incumbent on the Conservatives to do so. As he remarked to a friend: 'We are partly responsible for "this chap" coming to power: we must get rid of him.'[55] He intended Papen's Marburg speech to focus the widespread dissatisfaction among the Conservative elites about the regime and galvanize them into action, provoking an SA revolt and a declaration of martial law by Hindenburg. However, the plan of the Vice-Chancellery staff was flawed by its dependence on the actions of others – the SA, the *Reichswehr* and Hindenburg – over whom they had no control. Moreover, while Jung aimed to remove Hitler, his colleagues were anxious to avoid making him a martyr.[56] They preferred a new version of the 'taming' concept, in which, after the Nazi 'radicals' had been arrested, Hitler and Göring would be included in a 'directory', together with Generals von Fritsch and von Rundstedt, former chancellors Papen and Brüning, and the Lord Mayor of Leipzig, Carl Goerdeler.

Papen's critical speech was enthusiastically applauded by his university audience. It was broadcast live on Frankfurt radio, and a summary was published in an early edition of the *Frankfurter Zeitung*.[57] Although further publication was banned by ·Goebbels, a thousand copies had already been printed and received a sympathetic response from many upper- and middle-class Germans. Papen threatened to resign and take the matter up with Hindenburg if the ban were not lifted. Typically, however, he lacked the will to follow through, allowing himself to be mollified by Hitler's ·suggestion of a joint interview with Hindenburg – which naturally never took place.[58]

Hitherto, Hitler had refrained from moving against the 'bastion of reaction' in the Vice-Chancellery out of deference to Hindenburg.[59] However, with Papen's Marburg speech the Conservative opposition appeared to be throwing down the gauntlet, and Papen's subsequent indolence, together with Hindenburg's absence at his estate in East Prussia, encouraged Hitler to pick it up. He ordered Jung's arrest on 25 June; five days later Jung and his colleague, Herbert von Bose, were murdered during the Röhm purge.[60] The Vice-Chancellery was peremptorily abolished. After a feeble protest, Papen adjusted to the situation, accepting the post of ambassador to Austria. He was accompanied to Vienna by the remaining members of his staff, who established a kind of Conservative opposition in exile. They developed existing contacts with Austrian legitimists, contacts which had served the Gestapo as the pretext for Jung's arrest, and cultivated links with the circle round the Conservative Catholic theorist, Othmar Spann. After the Anschluss the Gestapo quickly broke up the group, murdering one of its members, Freiherr von Ketteler.[61]

The Conservative politicians in the cabinet and the Reichstag had assumed they could count on the support of the traditional elites – the civil service and the army – in taming the Nazis. However, in addition to sharing common goals in the destruction of parliamentary democracy and the revival of German power, these elites believed they could use the Nazis to achieve their own particular aims. Thus, they were happy to dispense with Conservative politicians such as Hugenberg and Papen.

The civil service's response was initially determined primarily by its negative perceptions of the Weimar Republic. Before 1918, the civil service had dominated public affairs. Ministers were civil servants not party politicians, restricted to a largely critical role in Parliament. Moreover, since the eighteenth century German civil servants had developed an exalted view of their role as highly trained and objective servants of a state which embodied the general interest of the nation, whereas they regarded politicians as unskilled representatives of selfish parties trying to press their narrow interests at the expense of the community as a whole and making demagogic appeals to the ignorant masses.

Under Weimar this situation changed drastically. Party politicians now formed the government, with civil servants reduced to a subordinate role in a system characterized by extreme pluralism and unstable government. They had to negotiate and bargain between the numerous parties and pressure groups representing the different interests and ideologies of a highly fragmented society which, in their view, were trying to colonize the state for their own ends.[62] An illuminating diagnosis of the situation from the standpoint of the senior ranks of the civil service was given on 26 April 1933 in a lecture to the Mittwochsgesellschaft, an elite discussion group, by the Prussian Finance Minister and a later resistance member, Johannes Popitz.[63] Confronting the fragmented society of Weimar, he declared, was

> a powerless state, alienated from the nation and with only a formal, inconsistent, polycratic constitution, a civil service which lacked a common ethos, with organs which either, like the continually changing governments, were without any common ideology, or, like the Reichstag and its parties, were only a screen concealing forces hostile to the state.

This situation had aroused a 'growing nationalist opposition' against 'these pluralist, interest-oriented forces which lacked any total ideology', an opposition which included those committed to Hitler. The crisis had called for either reform or revolution. The presidential governments of 1930–3, from Brüning to Schleicher, had tried to base themselves on the only part of the state untouched by pluralist forces – the Reich President. They had failed 'because a leading personality was lacking and they had not established contact with the popular movement'. So the only path left was that of revolution being carried out by the new regime, a revolution which had involved 'overcoming the pluralist forces linked to material interests by ruthlessly exploiting the abolition of all freedoms, thereby removing from these forces their basis in the pressure groups, parties and public opinion'.

Like many civil servants, Popitz had welcomed this revolution while reserving judgement about the future. He was concerned

> whether the leader of the revolution will succeed in maintaining the authoritarian leadership for the work of reconstruction and, further, whether the upsurge of patriotism will lead to a new and lasting mental attitude in the nation, or whether a materialist outlook will reassert itself leading to the misuse of the movement for the purpose of securing special interests aimed at guaranteeing lucrative positions.

He was also concerned about what room would remain for 'the values of personality and personal initiative' and whether events would follow the Italian Fascist example, or whether a ruling class would emerge 'based on a sense of responsibility and expertise linked to and serving the nation'.

While civil servants such as Popitz would have preferred Papen's authoritarian 'new state' to a Nazi regime, those of the younger generation tended to have a somewhat different perspective formed by 'revolutionary conservative' theory. Fritz-Dietlof von der Schulenberg, for example, the scion of a distinguished Prussian Junker family, became a Nazi in March 1932.[64] Strongly influenced by Spengler's *Prussianism and Socialism*,[65] Schulenberg rejected the reactionary attitudes of the DNVP and, unlike Popitz, was attracted by the 'socialist' aspects of National Socialism. These he interpreted in terms of a paternalist policy of state welfare for the deserving poor and the creation of an 'organic' and hierarchical society but one with an open elite from which the traditional barriers of birth and wealth had been removed. Above all, he hoped for a restoration of an idealized version of the civil service of eighteenth-century Prussia. Then, Schulenberg claimed, civil servants had been 'leaders of the people', a creative elite with an *esprit de corps*, representatives of a dynamic state committed to the public interest, whereas now they had degenerated into a mere bureaucracy, functionaries of a state whose policy emerged from a compromise between the egoistical interests of the government parties. 'The civil service must combine National Socialist drive with Prussian administrative experience.'[66]

By far the most important of the Conservative elites in terms of its potential impact on the balance of power between the Nazis and the Conservatives was the army.[67] In view of the numerical superiority of the SA and SS over the Conservative paramilitary forces, the Stahlhelm and the Bismarckbund, and the fact that, by the middle of March 1933, the Nazis controlled all the police forces in the Reich, the army alone had the power to enable the Conservatives to regain control over events. Thus, its attitude towards the new regime was vital.

The army's response was determined by a combination of political, social and professional concerns. Before 1918 it had been the most politically powerful and socially prestigious of all the German elites. After 1918, however, it found itself operating in a very different climate. Its political position was weakened since it was now subject to parliamentary control, and its social prestige had declined in the more democratic atmosphere. In short, it had become just another functional elite. Even more serious, in the view of the more technocratically oriented officers who came to dominate the army during the 1920s, was the failure of the Weimar Republic to provide a satisfactory framework within which the armed forces could secure their interests and realize their goals.

The parameters within which the army was obliged to operate were determined, first, by the provisions of the Versailles treaty, limiting it to 100,000 men and imposing restrictions on the numbers and categories of its weapons; and, secondly, by the new kind of industrial warfare demonstrated between 1914 and 1918. In such a war all the nation's resources had to be mobilized; total war not merely involved the professionals but also required the harnessing of the economy and of society as a whole.

After an uneasy relationship during the stormy years 1919–23, the *Reichswehr* leadership had endeavoured to reach a *modus vivendi* with the Republic on the basis of a modest rearmament programme which could be painlessly financed during the relatively prosperous period of 1924–8.[68] However, this policy was wrecked by the economic collapse of 1929–33 and the consequent breakdown of the political compromise between the various political, economic and social forces which had existed since 1924. The years 1929–33 saw the army drawn further and further into the political arena in an attempt to establish a new political basis on which to realize its goals. Its main concern was to secure a regime able not only to provide a framework of political and financial support for rearmament at government level, but also to neutralize the left and, above all, secure the widespread popular acceptance for such a programme, that is the mental rearmament (*Wehrhaftmachung*) which would be vital to its ultimate success. However, not only did the army leadership fail in its attempt to establish such a regime between 1930 and 1933, but its increasingly overt intervention in politics through General von Schleicher's activities jeopardized the army's position as a symbol of national unity and strength. As a result, there was a growing desire among officers to escape from politics and to concentrate on their professional role.

On coming to power, Hitler cleverly responded to those needs by proposing a relationship between the army and the regime, in which the state would rest on two pillars – the army and the Nazi Party; the state itself would be represented by President von Hindenburg.[69] To many officers this seemed an ideal solution: Hitler would handle the political side, creating a framework conducive to the development of the armed forces, while the military concentrated on their professional tasks. It seemed almost like a return to Imperial Germany, with Hindenburg, to whom Hitler and the army leadership would both be responsible, acting as an *ersatz* Kaiser: a model symbolically represented in the Potsdam ceremony of 21 March 1933. Differences were to arise between the army leadership and the War Ministry concerning how far the army should attempt to preserve its own traditions within the regime, but there was no support for Conservative politicians attempting to play an independent, let alone a dominant, role. Thus, the War Minister, General von Blomberg, told the generals on 1 June 1933 that 'the claim of the DNVP to equal rights was mistaken', since the NSDAP deserved the whole credit for the revolution. 'It will be all to the good if this movement soon achieves the total power which it seeks and DNVP and Centre disappear.'[70]

The blindness of the traditional elites to the revolutionary nature of Nazism was encouraged by the apparent security of their position until 1937–8. The Röhm purge of 30 June 1934 had represented a major turning point in the Conservative–Nazi relationship.[71] During the first half of 1934, discontent had grown among the elites about the trend of events in general and the role of the SA in particular. Röhm's undisguised ambition to swamp the professional *Reichswehr* by merging it into a mass army controlled by his SA threatened the basis of the 'two pillar' concept. The activities of 'SA delegates', assigned to supervise government offices, were resented by the civil service as unwarranted interference. And, last but not least, the unruly behaviour of the SA undermined the image of respectability which Hitler had been endeavouring to create: the impression of a moderate and responsible statesman who led a party containing radical elements which he would find impossible to restrain without co-operation from the elites. They had provided that co-operation and now, in effect, he was expected to fulfil his side of the bargain. Through his SA purge Hitler reassured them, thereby enabling him to crush with impunity the Conservative opposition based in the Vice-Chancellery, even to the extent of murdering two generals, von Schleicher and von Bredow.

During the period of economic recovery and diplomatic insecurity, however, Hitler remained anxious to secure the co-operation of the traditional elites and lacked the self-confidence to assert his complete dominance over them. They, in turn, were so preoccupied with the professional opportunities opened up by the new regime, after years of frustration under a poorly functioning pluralist democracy, that initially they were inclined to overlook or play down its negative features.

A good example is the *Oberbürgermeister* of Leipzig, Carl Goerdeler, a member of the Conservative *Grossbürgertum*.[72] Like Popitz, Goerdeler had welcomed the chance to implement far-reaching constitutional and administrative reforms. In a memorandum to Hitler of August 1934 he praised the Nazi Party for 'the elimination of the party system' and 'the removal of the boundaries between the German peoples' through the effective ending of federalism.[73] With his appointment as Reich Price Commissioner in November 1934 and the key role accorded him in the drafting of the new Reich Local Government Law of 30 January 1935, Goerdeler gained the impression that the new regime was responsive to his ideas. Hitler went out of his way to flatter him, and he found that the views of Nazi experts on local government (though not those of the party's cadre organization) broadly coincided with his own. Finally, in Leipzig itself he 'worked with the NSDAP during the early years after

1933 with complete confidence in it', thanks to a competent Nazi district leader.[74]

The turning-point in Goerdeler's relations with the regime came in 1936–7. In 1936 he found his economic proposals for a deflationary policy, minimum government interference and a closer integration in the world market rejected in favour of what he saw as an irresponsible programme involving accelerated rearmament and autarky. In 1937 he resigned as *Oberbürgermeister* because of the local party's insistence on removing a statue of Mendelssohn on the grounds that he was a Jew: in his view both an encroachment on his sphere of authority and a blow to Germany's cultural reputation.

Goerdeler had already become increasingly aware of the negative aspects of the regime – administrative confusion, lawlessness, errors in economic and financial policy, attacks on the Churches, the moral decline in party and state, and its totalitarian ambitions – and his memoranda to Hitler had contained muted criticism. However, hitherto he had believed the 'signs of degeneration were offset by positive features'.[75] Now, in July 1937, disillusioned by the rejection of his advice and by his resignation in somewhat humiliating circumstances, he gave full vent to his disappointment in a letter to an English friend:

> National Socialism had the opportunity of making the high ideal of comradeship in life and work the basis of our national life. It had the opportunity of unifying Germany's states internally as well. By inscribing achievement and comradeship, decency and justice on its banners, it had the opportunity of actually assuming the moral leadership in a world undergoing social change. It could have secured Germany's vital interests abroad. As a party it made the mistake of dictators: it demanded power, it seized power and it abused power. It is our task to prevent this misuse of power from causing damage to the German people … For through its totalitarian claims it affects the natural roots and the moral foundations of human life; it must find itself in an insoluble contradiction to them.[76]

Like Popitz and the younger Nazi civil servant, Schulenburg, Goerdeler became disillusioned with the regime precisely because it represented an affront to his professional ethos. The extent to which that ethos had atrophied within the civil service and been replaced by a purely functional conception of its role and by 'secondary virtues' such as duty and loyalty devoid of ethical content, helps explain the exceptional character of such opposition. For Goerdeler's response cannot be described as typical of the bureaucratic elite in general. It may be that his position as *Oberbürgermeister* of a great city gave him a broader perspective and a more ambitious view of his role in national life than that of the average senior ministerial official who, despite his pretensions, had in practice largely renounced the traditional claims of the German civil service to political leadership.[77]

. After 1937, Goerdeler's disillusionment with the regime acquired an additional intensity in response to the course of German foreign policy. Born in eastern Prussia, Goerdeler shared the Nazis' determination to revise the eastern frontiers at Poland's expense, by force if necessary. However, he was appalled by the prospect of involvement in a major war which in his view Germany could not win. His realization that Hitler was bent on such a war encouraged him to move from loyal opposition to active resistance. For, in jeopardizing Germany's future as a great power, Hitler posed a threat to the heart of modern German Conservatism: its pride in and commitment to the German nation-state.

This combination of professional ethos and concern for Germany's future was also evident in the decision of members of the other major Conservative elite, the army, to break with the regime. Here Goerdeler's counterpart was General Ludwig Beck.[78] Like Goerdeler, Beck had welcomed the 'political transformation' wrought by the Nazis, writing to a friend in March 1933: 'I have longed for it for years and am pleased that my hope was not deceptive: it is the first glimpse of light since 1918.'[79] Appointed Chief of the General Staff in October 1933, he had welcomed Hitler's 'two pillar' concept, which corresponded to his own view that the army and the political leadership must be equal partners in the state. It was a view which derived both from the Prussian military and state traditions and from what Beck saw as the requirements of modern industrialized warfare, in which the boundaries separating the military and the civilian spheres had largely broken down.

The turning-point in Beck's relationship with the regime came in 1938. The Blomberg–Fritsch crisis in March represented the first major challenge by the regime to the prestige and professional integrity of the army.[80] For many of those officers who were to join the resistance it was this, as much as the dubious ethics of the affair, which initiated their disillusionment with the regime. However, the affair could be interpreted as the result of the machinations of the Gestapo and SS, in which Hitler himself had not been personally involved; this is what Beck and many others preferred to assume. Much more serious from Beck's point of view was the divergence over policy towards Czechoslovakia which developed between Hitler and himself over the following months. Beck did not differ from Hitler concerning the goal: the destruction of Czechoslovakia. 'It is correct', he wrote, 'that Germany needs a larger living space both in Europe and in the colonial sphere. The first of these can only be acquired through war.' And he agreed that Czechoslovakia posed a threat to Germany which would have to be removed 'if necessary by war'.[81] However, he strongly disagreed with Hitler's decision to attack Czechoslovakia in

1938, believing this would provoke a war with the Western powers which Germany could not win. Blaming this decision on Hitler's 'radical advisers', he endeavoured to dissuade him through memoranda. To these, however, Hitler remained impervious, thereby prompting him to resign.

Apart from jeopardizing the nation and its future greatness, Hitler's behaviour represented in Beck's view a repudiation of his professional ethos as Chief of the General Staff. For, instead of allowing him, as the representative of the army, to participate in major strategic decisions on equal terms, Hitler was demanding that the armed forces subordinate themselves to the political leadership in the shape of the Führer, since March the Supreme Commander of the *Wehrmacht*. He clearly regarded their professional role as that of mere military technicians. While Keitel, Jodl and other generals were prepared to accept this, Beck found such a role intolerable:

> There are ultimate decisions concerning the fate of the nation at stake here. The military leaders will go down in history with blood on their hands if they do not act in accordance with their professional and political knowledge and conscience. Their duty as soldiers to obey is qualified in cases where their knowledge and conscience and their sense of responsibility forbid the execution of an order.[82]

Even then, however, Beck still maintained a distinction between Hitler and the SS and party bosses: 'There can and must be no doubt that this struggle is being fought for the Führer.' The line must be

> For the Führer, against the war, against the party bosses, peace with the Churches, freedom of speech, an end to Cheka methods, justice once more in the Reich, reduction of all contributions by half, no more building of palaces, housing for all national comrades, integrity and simplicity.[83]

As with Goerdeler, Beck's shift from loyal opposition to subversive resistance occurred only with his realization that Hitler himself was bent on a major war which Germany could not win and that he must be personally identified with all the negative aspects of the regime.

The timing of the disillusionment of members of Conservative elites, such as Goerdeler and Beck, in 1937–8 reflected a shift in the balance of power within the regime which occurred during those years and a radicalization of its policies.[84] With the resignation of Schacht in November 1937 and the fall of Blomberg, Fritsch, Neurath and other generals and diplomats in the spring of 1938, the relationship between the Nazis and the Conservative elites had ceased to be an entente of more or less equal partners and had become the clear subordination of one to the other.

The traditional elites exhibited a broad spectrum of responses to this development. Many of their members accepted the role of functionaries whose responsibility was limited to carrying out the orders, whatever their nature, of the political leadership. To a degree, this represented a recognition of the extent to which their traditional claim to a dominant *political* role had been rendered anachronistic during the previous decades, thereby undermining their self-confidence. For the traditional elites – the 'public servants' (*Staatsdiener*) – had lost the basis of their legitimacy as *the* political elite in the context, first, of parliamentary democracy under Weimar, and then of a charismatic dictatorship operating through a party with totalitarian ambitions. Their acceptance of this was facilitated by the fact that, in part at any rate, their goals continued to coincide with those of the regime: the aggrandizement of Germany and later the war against Bolshevism. Some justified their continued obedience by dissociating Hitler as head of state from those aspects of the regime which they despised.

Some members of the elites, however, retained their traditional professional ethos which involved not only functional efficiency and personal integrity, but also a sense of responsibility for the nation's welfare rooted in the German tradition of state authority. For these, growing disillusionment during the mid-1930s turned into loyal opposition in 1937–8 and then, in a few cases, into determined resistance.

Loyal opposition might be defined as an attempt to defend the rule of law and traditional Conservative values against Nazi militants without challenging the authority of the regime. A case in point was Franz Gürtner, Reich Justice Minister until his death in 1941.[85] A Bavarian Conservative who shared the general outlook of men like Popitz, like them he had welcomed the demise of Weimar and the opportunity it provided to rationalize the legal structure by establishing a uniform system for the Reich. During 1933–4 he had prevented the takeover of the ministry by the leading Nazi candidates – Hans Frank, Hans Kerrl and Roland Freisler – and from then onwards resisted as best he could the inexorable encroachment of Himmler's SS apparatus on the powers of the judiciary, and not simply out of departmental egoism. Nevertheless, Gürtner's respect for established authority was such that he refused to challenge Hitler's authority to make law. For example, he acknowledged his own impotence in relation to the 'euthanasia' programme, remarking: 'It is a catastrophe for a Reich Minister of Justice to be reliably informed that murders are being carried out all the time in the country for which you are responsible and yet you don't know anything about it.'[86] However, when he learned that Hitler had approved the programme, he declined to assist a judge who was trying to prevent it, commenting: 'Well, if you do not acknowledge the Führer's will as a source of law, as a legal basis, then you cannot remain a judge.'[87]

The transition from loyal opposition to determined resistance was encouraged by the regime's refusal to tolerate opposition beyond narrow bounds. But for most it was a difficult path, involving a painful reappraisal of their values. For some Conservatives, such as Popitz and the former German ambassador to Rome, Ulrich von Hassell, it was prompted in part by resentment at their displacement from office or influence, which was further increased by concern at the process of social levelling associated with the regime.[88] However, it also represented a reaction against what they saw as the Nazis' challenge to their professional ethos not only through incompetence and corruption but also through the launching of a catastrophic war which jeopardized the nation.

However, Conservative resistance to the regime was ultimately fuelled by more than professional concerns even in the broadest sense. There was also growing anxiety about the regime's totalitarian ambitions, which threatened the relative autonomy of the traditional elites not only professionally but, through such organizations as the Hitler Youth, even socially. The fact that members of the Conservative resistance were predominantly public servants from an exclusive social milieu meant that professional, social, even family networks provided an invaluable source of solidarity for a profoundly isolated group, not only facilitating conspiratorial activity but also providing mutual reinforcement for their convictions.[89]

Finally, moral concerns played an increasing role in Conservative justification of resistance.[90] Often only properly awakened by professional disillusionment, through which for the first time they had acquired a sense of perspective, moral revulsion was stimulated by the regime's growing inhumanity both at home and, above all, abroad as it fought a war of racial extermination in the East. Underpinning this moral stance was a new or reawakened religious faith.[91] Religion increasingly provided the foundation for a Conservative critique of the regime which now appeared as the extreme culmination of trends associated with modern industrial and urban society – materialism, secularism, social atomization, and alienation – which they had opposed under Weimar and had assumed Hitler would overcome by creating a new organic *Volksgemeinschaft.* Instead, he had betrayed the promise of Potsdam by launching a 'revolution of nihilism'[92] in his demonic drive for total power and his materialist obsession with race. Above all, however, religion proved vital in a situation where Conservatives found themselves not only engaging in high treason but doing so at a time when the vast majority of their fellow countrymen identified the interests of the nation with Hitler as Führer. Thus, their high treason (*Hochverrat*) against him would be regarded as treason against the whole nation (*Landesverrat*), the greatest of crimes for most early twentieth-century German Conservatives. In their extreme isolation, and constantly aware of the possibility of having to pay the supreme penalty for their actions, Conservatives turned increasingly to religion. For, as Helmuth von Moltke put it: 'The degree of danger and of self-sacrifice now required of us presupposes more than good ethical principles.'[93]

NOTES

1 See K. D. Bracher, W. Sauer and G. Schulz, *Die Nationalsozialistische Machtergreifung. Studien zur Errichtung des totalitären Herrschaftssystems in Deutschland 1933/4* (Cologne and Opladen, 1960), pp. 149 ff.

2 See E. Ebermayar, *Denn heute gehört uns Deutschland... Persönliches und politisches. Von der Machtergreifung bis zum 31. Dezember 1935.* (Hamburg and Vienna, 1959), p. 47. On this atmosphere see also H. Mommsen, 'Der Mythos des nationalen Aufbruchs und die Haltung der deutschen intellektuellen und funktionalen Eliten', *Merkur*, vol. 38 (1984), pp. 97–102.

3 The literature on the July plot is enormous; see in particular P. Hoffmann, *Widerstand, Staatsstreich, Attentat, Der Kampf der Opposition gegen Hitler* (Munich, 1969).

4 On the relationship between Nazism and the Conservatives see Mommsen, 'Der Mythos des nationalen Aufbruchs'; E. Nolte, 'Konservatismus und Nationalsozialismus', *Zeitschrift für Politik*, vol. 2 (1964), pp. 5–20; K. Fritzsche, 'Konservatismus im gesellschaftlich-geschichtlichen Prozess' (II), *Neue Politische Literatur*, vol. XXXIV, no. 3 (1979); J. Flemming, 'Identitäts und-Interpretationsprobleme konservativer Politik. Anmerkungen zum Verhältnis von Konservatismus und Nationalsozialismus', *Gesellschaft und Wissenschaft, Teil I: Gesellschaft.* Ringvorlesung (Hamburg, 1983), pp. 113–26; H. Mommsen, 'Der Widerstand gegen Hitler und die deutsche Gesellschaft', in J. Schmädecke and P. Steinbach (eds), *Der Widerstand gegen Nationalsozialismus. Die deutsche Gesellschaft und der Widerstand gegen Hitler* (Munich, 1985), pp. 3–23; K.-J. Müller, 'Nationalkonservative Eliten zwischen Kooperationund Widerstand', in ibid., pp. 24–49; K.-J. Müller, 'Zur Struktur und Eigenart der nationalkonservativen Opposition bis 1938 – Innenpolitischer Machtkampf, Kriegsverhinderungspolitik und Eventual-Staatsstreichplanung', in ibid., pp. 329–44; A. Schildt, 'Die Illusion der konservativen Alternative', in ibid., pp. 151–68; and F. Stern, 'National Socialism as temptation', in F. Stern, *Dreams and Delusions. The Drama of German History.* (London, 1988), pp. 147–91.

5 See in particular J. N. Retallack, *Notables of the Right. The Conservative Party and Political Mobilization in Germany 1876–1918* (London, 1988).

6 H.-J. Puhle, *Agrarische Interessenpolitik und preussischer Konservatismus im wilhelminischen Reich 1893–1914. Ein Beitrag zur Analyse des Nationalismus in Deutschland am Bespiel des Bundes der Landwirte und der Deutsch-Konservativen Partei* (Hanover, 1966).

7 Cf. D. Stegmann, *Die Erben Bismarcks: Parteien und Verbände in der Spätphase des wilhelminischen Deutschlands. Sammlungspolitik 1897–1918.* (Cologne and Berlin, 1970); D. Stegmann, 'Vom Neokonservatismus zum Protofaschismus: Konservative Partei, Vereine und Verbände 1893–1920', in D. Stegmann *et al.* (eds), *Deutscher Konservatismus im 19. und 20. Jahrhundert. Festschrift für Fritz Fischer zum 75. Geburtstag und zum 50. Doktorjubiläum* (Bonn, 1983), pp. 199–227; G. Eley, *Reshaping the German Right. Radical Nationalism and Political Change after Bismarck* (New Haven, Conn. and London, 1980); and R. Chickering, *We Men Who Feel Most German. A Cultural Study of the Pan-German League 1886–1914* (London, 1984).

8 Chickering, *We Men Who Feel Most German*, pp. 75 ff.

9 D. Blackbourn, 'The politics of demagogy in Imperial Germany', *Past and Present*, vol. 113 (November 1986), pp. 152–84.

10 K. von Klemperer, *Germany's New Conservatism. Its History and Dilemma in the Twentieth Century* (Princeton, NJ, 1957), pp. 47 ff.

11 Quoted in ibid., p. 53.

12 Quoted in ibid., p. 164.
13 W. Liebe, *Die Deutschnationale Volkspartei 1918–1924* (Düsseldorf, 1956); L. Hertzmann, *DNVP. Right-Wing Opposition in the Weimar Republic 1918–1924* (Lincoln, Nebr., 1963); A. Thimme, *Flucht in den Mythos. Die Deutschnationale Volkspartei und die Niederlage von 1918* (Göttingen, 1969). ·
14 F. Hiller von Gaertringen, 'Die Deutschnationale Volkspartei', in E. Matthias and R. Morsey (eds), *Das Ende der Parteien 1933* (Düsseldorf 1960), pp. 544 ff.; J. A. Leopold, *Alfred Hugenberg. The Radical Nationalist Campaign against the Weimar Republic* (New Haven, Conn. and London, 1977), pp. 45 ff.; H. Holzbach, *Das 'System Hugenberg'. Die Organisation bürgerlicher Sammlungspolitik vor dem Aufstieg der NSDAP* (Stuttgart, 1981), pp. 192 ff.
15 L. E. Jones, 'Sammlung oder Zersplitterung. Die Bestrebungen zur Bildung einer neuen Mittelpartei in der Endphase der Weimarer Republik', *Vierteljahrshefte für Zeitgeschichte* (March 1977), pp. 265–304.
16 Hiller von Gaertringen, 'Die Deutschnationale Volkspartei', pp. 609 ff.; Leopold, *Alfred Hugenberg*, pp. 145 ff.; A. Ritthaler, 'Eine Etappe auf Hitlers Weg zur Ungeteilten Macht: Hugenbergs Rücktritt als Reichsminister', *Vierteljahrshefte für Zeitgeschichte* (August 1960), pp. 196 ff.; and J. L. Heinemann, 'Constantin von Neurath and German policy at the London Economic Conference of 1933: background to the resignation of Adolf Hitler', *Journal of Modern History*, vol. 41 (1969), pp. 164 ff.
17 Hiller von Gaertringen, 'Die Deutschnationale Volkspartei', pp. 567 ff. Hugenberg had last-minute doubts when confronted with Hitler's demand for new elections, but was persuaded by the other Conservative Cabinet members that the Reich President could not be kept waiting; see K. D. Bracher, *Die Auflösung der Weimarer Republik. Eine Studie zum Problem des Machtverfalls in der Demokratie* (Villingen/Schwarzwald, 1960), pp. 726–7.
18 For what follows see B. Scheurig, *Ewald von Kleist-Schmenzin. Ein Konservativer gegen Hitler* (Oldenburg, 1968).
19 J. Flemming, 'Konservatismus als "nationalrevolutionäre Bewegung". Konservative Kritik an der Deutschnationalen Volkspartei 1918–1933', in Stegmann et al. (eds), *Deutscher Konservatismus*, pp. 295–331.
20 Printed in Scheurig, *Kleist-Schmenzin*, pp. 255–69.
21 See 'Selbsterlebte wichtige Begebenheiten aus den Jahren 1933 und 1934', in ibid., pp. 264–9.
22 Hiller von Gaertringen, 'Die Deutschnationale Volkspartei', p. 636.
23 Scheurig, *Kleist-Schmenzin*, p. 214.
24 See above, n. 18.
25 Scheurig, *Kleist-Schmenzin*, p. 260.
26 For the Junkers' response to Nazism, see Flemming, 'Konservatismus als "nationalrevolutionäre Bewegung"; K. Gossweiler and A. Schlicht, 'Die Junker und die NSDAP 1931/32', *Zeitschrift für die Geschichtswissenschaft*, vol. 15 (1967), pp. 650 ff.; B. Buchta, *Die Junker und die Weimarer Republik. Charakter und Bedeutung der Osthilfe in den Jahren 1928–1933* (Berlin, 1959); D. Gessner, *Agrardepression und Präsidialregierungen in Deutschland 1930–1933. Probleme des Agrarprotektionismus am Ende der Weimarer Republik* (Düsseldorf, 1977); R. Thévoz, H. Branig and C. Lowenthal-Hesel, *Pommern 1934–35 im Spiegel von Gestapo-Lageberichten und Sachakten (Darstellung)* (Berlin, 1974), pp. 70–89; S. Baranowski, 'Continuity and contingency: agrarian elites, conservative institutions and East Elbia in modern German history' *Social History* (October 1987), pp. 306–8; F. L. Carsten, *Geschichte der Preussischen Junker* (Frankfurt am Main, 1988), pp. 174 ff.
27 J. E. Farquarson, *The Plough and the Swastika. The NSDAP and Agriculture in Germany 1928–45* (London, 1976), pp. 146 ff.; J. E. Farquarson, 'The agrarian policy of National Socialist Germany', in H. G. Moeller (ed.), *Peasants and Lords in Modern Germany* (Boston, Mass., 1986), pp. 250 ff.; A. Bramwell, *Blood and Soil. Walther Darré and Hitler's Green Party* (Bourne End, 1985), pp. 106–7.
28 For what follows, see E. von Aretin, *Krone und Ketten. Erinnerungen eines bayerischen Edelmannes* (Munich, 1958).
29 ibid., p. 374.

30 K. Schwend, 'Die Bayerische Volkspartei', in Matthias and Morsey (eds), *Das Ende der Parteien*, pp. 481 ff.

31 J. Donohoe, *Hitler's Conservative Opponents in Bavaria 1930–1945* (Leiden, 1961).

32 W. Gutsche and J. Petzold, 'Der Verhältnis der Hohenzollern zum Faschismus', *Zeitschrift für die Geschichtswissenschaft*, vol. 29 (1981), pp. 917–39.

33 For what follows, see G. H. Kleine, 'Adelsgenossenschaft und Nationalsozialismus', *Vierteljahrshefte für Zeitgeschichte* (January 1978), pp. 100–41.

34 ibid., pp. 119–20. The DAG contained around 17,000 of the 85–95,000 persons of noble birth in Germany.

35 See, for example, Himmler's speech of 18 February 1937 to SS *Gruppenführer* in B. F. Smith and A. E. Peterson (eds), *Heinrich Himmler, Geheimreden 1933 bis 1945* (Frankfurt, 1974), p. 61. In 1938, of the 117 highest-ranking SS leaders 15 (12.9 per cent) were noble, of whom 7 belonged to the DAG; see H. Höhne, *The Order of the Death's Head. The Story of Hitler's SS* (London, 1969), pp. 123–4.

36 On Nazi elite ideas see W. Struve, *Elites Against Democracy* (Princeton, NJ, 1973), pp. 202 ff. and R. Zitelmann, *Hitler. Selbstverständnis eines Revolutionärs* (Stuttgart, 1987), pp. 399 ff.

37 Kleine, 'Adelsgenossenschaft und Nationalsozialismus', p. 135.

38 For what follows, see F. G. von Tschirschky, *Erinnerungen eines Hochverräters* (Stuttgart, 1972); and F. von Papen, *Memoirs* (London, 1952).

39 On Jung see K. M. Grass, 'Edgar Jung, Papenkreis und Röhmkrise 1933/34', dissertation, University of Heidelberg, 1966; B. Jenschke, *Zur Kritik der konservativ-revolutionären Ideologie bei Edgar Julius Jung* (Munich, 1971); and E. Forschbach, *Edgar J. Jung, ein konservativer Revolutionär* (Pfullingen, 1984).

40 Scheurig, *Kleist-Schmenzin*, p. 267.

41 Tschirschky, *Erinnerungen eines Hochverräters*, pp. 234–5.

42 One of Hindenburg's most important interventions was his letter to Hitler of 4 April 1933 requesting the exclusion from dismissal under the proposed Civil Service Law of those Jews who had fought at the front or had lost sons in the war, a request that was met in §3 (2) of the law when published on 7 April 1933. For the letter see W. Hubatsch, *Hindenburg und der Staat* (Göttingen, 1966), pp. 375 ff.

43 Tschirschky, *Erinnerungen eines Hochverräters*, pp. 103–4; Grass, 'Edgar Jung', p. 50.

44 On 'revolutionary conservatism', apart from other works referred to elsewhere, see A. Mohler, *Die Konservative Revolution in Deutschland 1918–1932* (Stuttgart, 1950); K. Sontheimer, *Antidemokratisches Denken in der Weimarer Republik* (Munich, 1962); F. Stern, *The Politics of Cultural Despair. A Study in the Rise of the Germanic Ideology* (New York, 1965); O.-E. Schüddekopf, *Linke Leute von Rechts. Nationalbolschewismus in Deutschland 1918–1933* (Frankfurt, 1972); J. Petzold, *Konservative Theoretiker des deutschen Faschismus. Jungkonservative Ideologen in der Weimarer Republik als geistige Wegbereiter der faschistischen Diktatur* (Berlin, 1982); and J. Herf, *Reactionary Modernism. Technology, Culture and Politics in Weimar and the Third Reich* (Cambridge, 1984).

45 H. von Hofmannsthatl, *Das Schrifttum als geistiger Raum der Nation* (Munich, 1927), p. 31.

46 *Die Herrschaft der Minderwertigen. Ihr Zerfall und ihre Ablösung durch ein neues Reich* (Berlin, 1929/30).

47 Quoted in Jenschke, *Kritik der konservativ-revolutionären Ideologie*, p. 154.

48 E. Jung, 'Neubelebung von Weimar?', *Deutsche Rundschau* (June 1932).

49 ibid., p. 158.

50 E. J. Jung, *Sinndeutung der deutschen Revolution* (Oldenburg, 1933), p. 29. On the 'Tat' circle see K. Fritzsche, *Politische Romantik und Gegenrevolution. Fluchtwege in der Krise der bürgerlichen Gesellschaft. Das Beispiel des 'Tat' Kreises* (Frankfurt, 1976).

51 Grass, 'Edgar Jung', pp. 214 ff. and Forschbach, *Edgar J. Jung*, pp. 106 ff.

52 Quoted in Grass, 'Edgar Jung', p. 209.

53 ibid., p. 222.

54 The text of the speech is printed in Forschbach, *Edgar J. Jung*, pp. 154–72.
55 The comment was made to Rudolph Pechel, editor of the *Deutsche Rundschau*; see Grass, 'Edgar Jung', p. 47.
56 Tschirschky, *Erinnerungen eines Hochverräters*, pp. 188 ff.
57 Papen, *Memoirs*, pp. 307 ff.
58 See Grass, *Edgar Jung* and Tschirschky, *Erinnerungen eines Hochverräters*.
59 H. G. Seraphim (ed.), *Das politische Tagebuch Alfred Rosenbergs aus den Jahren 1934/5 und 1939/40* (Göttingen, Berlin and Frankfurt, 1956), p. 33.
60 Tschirschky, *Erinnerungen eines Hochverräters*, pp. 188 ff.
61 H. Graml, 'Vorhut konservativen Widerstands. Das Ende des Kreises um Edgar Jung'. in H. Graml (ed.), *Widerstand im Dritten Reich. Probleme, Ereignisse, Gestalten* (Frankfurt, 1984), pp. 172–82.
62 J. Caplan, 'The imaginary universality of particular interests: the tradition of the civil service in German history', *Social History*, vol. 4 (1979), pp. 299–317; and P.-C. Witt, 'Konservatismus als "Überparteilichkeit". Die Beamten der Reichskanzlei zwischen Kaiserreich und Weimarer Republik 1900–1933', in Stegmann *et al.* (eds), *Deutscher Konservatismus* pp. 231–70.
63 K. Scholder, *Die Mittwochsgesellschaft. Protokolle aus dem geistigen Deutschland 1932 bis 1944* (Berlin, 1982), pp. 254–8. On Popitz see H. Dieckmann, *Johannes Popitz. Entwicklung und Wirksamkeit in der Zeit der Weimarer Republik* (Berlin, 1960) and L.–A. Bentin, *Johannes Popitz und Carl Schmitt. Zur wirtschaftlichen Theorie des totalen Staates in Deutschland* (Munich, 1972).
64 On Schulenburg see A. Krebs, *Fritz–Dietlof Graf von der Schulenburg. Zwischen Staatsräson und Hochverrat* (Hamburg, 1964); H. Mommsen, 'Fritz–Dietlof Graf von der Schulenburg und die preussiche Tradition', *Vierteljahrshefte für Zeitgeschichte*, 1977, pp. 213–39; and U. Heinemann, 'Fritz-Dietlof Graf von der Schulenburg. Das Problem von Kooperation und Opposition und der Entschluss zum Widerstand gegen das Hitler-Regime', in Schmädecke and Steinbach (eds), *Die Widerstand gegen Nationalsozialismus*, pp. 417–35.
65 *Preussentum und Sozialismus* (Berlin, 1919).
66 Quoted in Mommsen, 'Schulenburg', p. 482.
67 On the army and Nazism see K.-J. Müller, *Das Heer und Hitler, Armee und nationalsozialistisches Regime 1933–1940* (Stuttgart, 1969); K.-J. Müller, *Armee, Politik und Gesellschaft in Deutschland 1933–1945, Studien zum Verhältnis von Armee und NS System* (Paderborn, 1978); and M. Messerschmidt, *Die Wehrmacht im NS-Staat. Zeit der Indoktrination* (Hamburg, 1969).
68 M. Geyer, *Aufrüstung oder Sicherheit. Reichswehr und die Krise der Machtpolitik 1924–1936* (Wiesbaden, 1979), pp. 85 ff.
69 Müller, *Das Heer und Hitler*, pp. 54 ff.
70 ibid., p. 65. Blomberg implied by the word 'total' a concentration of all the 'nationalist' forces rather than 'totalitarian'.
71 On the Röhm purge see Bracher *et al.*, *Die Nationalsozialistische Machtergreifung*, pp. 897–972; C. Bloch, *Die SA und die Krise des NS-Regimes 1934* (Frankfurt, 1970); H. Bennecke, *Die Reichswehr und der Röhm-Putsch* (Munich, 1957); Müller, *Das Heer und Hitler*, pp. 64 ff.; and H. Höhne 'Mordsache Röhm' (Stuttgart, 1985).
72 On Goerdeler see G. Ritter, *Carl Goerdeler und die Deutsche Widerstandsbewegung* (Stuttgart, 1954) and M. Krüger-Charlé, 'Carl Goerdelers Versuche der Durchsetzung einer alternativen Politik 1933 bis 1937', in Schmädecke and Steinbach (eds), *Die Widerstand gegen Nationalsozialismus* pp. 383–404.
73 Ritter, *Goerdeler*, p. 452.
74 Quoted in Krüger-Charlé, 'Carl Goerdelers Versuche', p. 386.
75 Ritter, *Goerdeler*, p. 67.
76 ibid., pp. 63–4.
77 On the position of *Oberbürgermeister* in the Third Reich see H. Matzerath, *Nationalsozialismus und kommunale Selbstverwaltung* (Cologne, 1970), pp. 229 ff., and J. Noakes, 'Oberbürgermeister and Gauleiter: city government between party and state', in G. Hirschfeld and L. Kettenacker (eds), *Der 'Führerstaat': Mythos und Realität* (Stuttgart, 1981), pp. 194–225.

78 On Beck see K.-J. Müller, *General Ludwig Beck. Studien und Dokumente zur politisch-militärischen Vorstellungswelt und Tätigkeit des Generalstabschefs des deutschen Heeres 1933–38.* (Boppard/RH., 1980).

79 ibid., p. 339.

80 H. C. Deutsch, *Hitler and his Generals: The Hidden Crisis, January–June 1938* (Minneapolis, Minn., 1974); J. Schmädecke, 'Die Blomberg-Fritsch-Krise: Vom Widerspruch zum Widerstand', in Schmädecke and Steinbach (eds), *Der Widerstand gegen Nationalsozialismus*, pp. 368–82; and Müller, *Das Heer und Hitler*, pp. 295 ff.

81 Müller, *Beck*, p. 521.

82 Ritter, *Goerdeler*, pp. 171–2.

83 Memo of 19 July 1938 in Müller, *Beck*, pp. 555–6.

84 M. Broszat, *The Hitler State* (London, 1981), pp. 294 ff.

85 For what follows, see L. Gruchmann, *Justiz im Dritten Reich. Anpassung und Unterwerfung in der Ära Gürtner* (Munich, 1987).

86 ibid., p. 507.

87 ibid., p. 512.

88 See, for example, the entries for 17 and 29 September 1938 in *The Von Hassell Diaries 1938–1944* (London, 1948), pp. 9, 13.

89 H. Mommsen, 'Der Widerstand gegen Hitler und die deutsche Gesellschaft', in Schmädecke and Steinbach (eds), *Die Widerstand gegen den Nationalsozialismus*, pp. 8–9.

90 P. Steinbach, 'Wiederherstellung des Rechtsstaats als zentrale Zielsetzung des Widerstands', in ibid., pp. 617–36. This was particularly true of the younger generation of officers who had been initially more enthusiastic about the regime and for whom the later disillusionment was correspondingly sharper. See W. Schieder, 'Zwei Generationen im militärischen Widerstand', in ibid., pp. 447–8.

91 K. von Klemperer, 'Glaube, Religion, Kirche, und der deutsche Widerstand gegen den Nationalsozialismus', in *Vierteljahrshefte für Zeitgeschichte* (March 1980), pp. 293–309.

92 The title of the Conservative critique of Nazism by the former Nazi President of the Danzig Senate, Hermann Rauschning, *Die Revolution des Nihilismus. Kulisse und Wirklichkeit im Dritten Reich* (Zurich and New York, 1938).

93 Klemperer, 'Glaube, Religion...', p. 304.

6

Conservatives and fascists in Austria, 1918–34

Jill Lewis

The Austrian First Republic was founded in 1918 following the collapse of the Habsburg Empire and was officially destroyed by the German invasion in 1938. The term 'First Republic', however, actually encompasses three political phases: the democratic republic (1918–33), the dictatorship (1933–4) and the 'Austrofascist' *Ständestaat* (1934–8).[1] Throughout most of this twenty-year period the national government was dominated by the Christian Social Party. The purpose of this chapter is to examine the relationship between that party and the growth of fascism in Austria. It will be argued that the Christian Social leadership swung towards fascism in the late 1920s as a result of domestic political and economic problems, developing in the process a form of 'Austrofascism' that was distinct from both German and Italian fascisms. Essential to this argument is the debate within Austria on the still politically contentious term 'Austrofascism'.

The first of the chapter's three sections examines the discussion on the nature of the *Ständestaat*, arguing that the rejection of the term 'Austrofascism' in this context is based on too rigid and too German-oriented a definition of fascism. In particular, the emphases on German nationalism and anti-Catholicism have obscured the role which Catholic populism, a strong trend in Christian Social ideology, played in the development of Austrofascism. This is the theme of the second part of the chapter. Finally, by tracing the relationship between the party and the Heimwehr, it is argued that the Christian Social leaders were not reluctant allies of this small, 'native fascist' party, but actively supported its paramilitary activities in a battle to destroy the Social Democratic movement and, much later, to forestall the growth of National Socialism. In Austria during the 1930s, the division between 'conservative' and 'fascist' thus became blurred.

On 1 March 1933 the Austrian railway unions called a two-hour strike in protest at the railway authority's announcement that the payment of wages and pensions would be suspended for the second time in a year. The authority's stated reason was lack of cash owing to the economic crisis; nevertheless the lack of prior consultation meant that the announcement broke the collective contract between employer and unions.[2] What was ostensibly a purely industrial dispute also bore marked political overtones. To many Austrians it epitomized a general political crisis, for the railways were state-owned and the management's decision was supported by the national government, a coalition of Christian Social, Agrarian League and fascist Heimwehr members. The major opposition, the Social Democratic Party, supported the railway workers. The Socialist railway union was not only Austria's largest trade union, it was also crucial to the strength of organized labour and hence to the party itself. In a period of increasing political polarization the Social Democratic leaders argued that their final weapon in defence of parliamentary democracy was the general strike. Without the support of the railway workers a general strike could not succeed.

The dispute, and the government's attempts to outlaw future railway strikes,[3] provoked a parliamentary crisis which was only resolved when the government prorogued Parliament and resorted to dictatorship. Between March 1933 and May 1934 Austria was ruled by decrees based on the 1917 War Economy Emergency Powers Act. Austrians lost the rights to demonstrate, to strike and to the freedoms of speech and the press. In May 1933 the Chancellor, Engelbert Dollfuss, announced the birth of a new political movement, the Fatherland Front, which was intended to envelop all bourgeois parties and paramilitary groups. During 1933 bans were placed, first on the Communist Party and then, after a number of bombing incidents involving Nazi members, on the Nazi Party. Finally in February 1934, on the pretext of a rumoured Socialist putsch, government forces attacked Socialist party buildings throughout the country and this, the largest political party in Austria, to which some 10 per cent of the population belonged, was also banned.[4]

Although Austria ceased to be a parliamentary democracy in March 1933, its democratic constitution was not officially overturned until May 1934. It was then replaced by a corporate constitution designed to create a 'Social, Christian, German state, Austria, founded upon estates under strong authoritarian leadership': the *Ständestaat*.[5] Parliament was replaced by six councils: those of state, culture, the economy and the provinces, plus a federal diet and assembly. The first four possessed only advisory powers, while the membership of five out of the six was nominated by either the Chancellor's office or the president. The exception was the federal diet, whose members were chosen by the provincial governors and financial officers, the mayor of Vienna and, in the absence of a Viennese financial officer, a person 'well informed about the city's finances'. The apparent independence of this body was illusory, for the governors were appointed by the Chancellor and the financial officers by the governors.[6] All council members had to be 'loyal citizens' as proved by their membership of the Fatherland Front. The Front, therefore, controlled political participation. It also represented the mass element in Austrofascism, mediating in labour disputes and organizing demonstrations of loyalty. By 1936 its membership was 2 million, in part because it was impossible to obtain a job or unemployment benefit without quoting a Fatherland Front number.[7]

Theoretically the councils represented only part of the new political system. The constitution also contained references to six occupational corporations, drawing representatives from both employers and workers, which would regulate the economy and advise the government on policy.[8] Only two of these were ever set up; in practice the existing employers' associations continued to act as representatives of industry and finance, thereby maintaining the relationship, essentially one of strife, which had existed between employers and employees under the democratic republic.[9] What differences there were favoured the employers; with workers deprived of the right to form their own unions and engage in free collective bargaining, employers could lower labour costs without fear of the resistance previously encountered.

Finally, the constitution accorded a privileged position to the Catholic Church, allowing it independence over internal affairs and appointments and increasing its role in public schooling. Particular stress, indeed, was placed upon the religious aspects of the *Ständestaat*, whose founders intended it to create a new 'Austrian ideology', German yet Catholic, embodying the finer features of Austrian intellectual and imperial traditions and combining them with the spiritual superiority of religion. This it was hoped would rally the Austrian people, 90.5 per cent of whom were at least nominal Catholics, and distance them from both socialism and the German but racist and irreligious creed of National Socialism.[10] In Dollfuss's view these goals could be achieved simultaneously; in March 1933 he stated that the only way to halt the 'Brown Wave' *and* defeat the Socialists was to carry out what the Nazis had promised in Germany, while moderating it in certain ways. 'Only then will we succeed in teaching the majority of Socialist Party members that they no longer have any power and they will leave the Socialist Party.'[11] The first stage in this strategy was the abolition of Parliament, the second the establishment of the *Ständestaat*.

The nature and origins of the *Ständestaat* are controversial issues in Austrian historiography, despite – or perhaps because of – the fact that until recently academic research into the entire period has been badly neglected. The very term '*Ständestaat*' is contentious for, although it was the official title of the Austrian state between 1934 and 1938, it invokes an image of a pre-industrial society or, more concretely, a society unfettered by modern class divisions, while also emphasizing its Catholic roots. This image, which the state itself sought to foster, still pervades much of the writing on the period, especially that which rejects the whole notion of Austrofascism. For instance, while the corporate nature of the 1934 constitution may be indisputable, many historians draw an emphatic distinction between the 'Catholic' corporatism of Austria and the 'fascist' corporatism of Mussolini's Italy or Hitler's Germany. The Austrian constitution was influenced, they argue, by the 1931 papal encyclical *Quadragesimo Anno*, and was adopted not as a move towards fascism but as a defence against it.[12] The Austrian government resorted to dictatorship in 1933 as an act of national self-protection at a time of crisis. Parliament had become unworkable and Hitler's assumption of power in Germany and National Socialist regional electoral victories at home in 1932 both indicated a growing domestic threat. Had the democratic constitution remained, new national elections would have been called and these, it was feared, would have swept the Nazis to power.[13] Austrian corporatism was therefore inherently anti-Nazi and, by extension, anti-fascist. The outward expression of fascism, the destruction of Parliament, the political opposition and the unions, and the establishment of the Fatherland Front, reflected instead a traditional conservative dictatorship which adopted the trappings of fascism for pragmatic reasons – in order to appease both the Italian fascists and the Heimwehr, on whom the government relied for support. But the structural base and dynamism of 'true' fascism were missing.

This view, and the entire approach on which it is based, have been challenged by Klaus-Jörg Siegfried. Their proponents, he alleges, have concentrated excessively upon external (i.e. German and Italian) forces promoting Austrian fascism, and insufficiently upon internal economic factors.[14] He argues that the economic instability of the 1920s, the inflation of 1922–3, the stabilization crisis, shortage of capital, and the weakness and eventual collapse of the banking system forced Austrian industry, and hence the government, to increase their reliance on Anglo-French capital. This necessitated accepting the investing states' condition of renouncing all possibility of a customs union with Germany. The resultant split of 1932 in the ruling alliance between the Christian Social and Pan-German parties jeopardized bourgeois control of Parliament.[15] The *Ständestaat*, therefore, arose from a crisis of capitalism, with the function of maintaining bourgeois power while destroying the Socialist labour movement and so reducing the social costs of labour. The 'clerical dictatorship' was thus a form of fascism.

Siegfried differs from most historians in adopting a functional rather than a descriptive concept of fascism itself. Questioning the use of typological definitions or models, he points out that, in the Austrian context, these concentrate on *German* characteristics of fascism and the National Socialist system imposed after 1938. From this starting-point it is simple to isolate those aspects of the *Ständestaat* which differed from National Socialism and then conclude that the earlier system was not fascist.

This has been common practice in the study of Austrofascism. For example, the *Ständestaat* was authoritarian but never fully totalitarian, allowing the Catholic Church internal autonomy.[16] Anti-clericalism was completely absent. The mass movement, the Fatherland Front, was not a source of the dictatorship but was created only after it had been declared.[17] There was no attempt to restructure the economy because, although a corporate system existed on paper, it was never fully implemented.[18] Nor was there any policy of autarky or militaristic imperialism, both of which characterized the domestic and foreign policies of Nazi Germany and Fascist Italy.[19] More doubtful is the assertion that the *Ständestaat* was not supported by industry and finance but rested upon the Church and army.[20] Clearly the *Ständestaat* did not conform to the models of fascism which are frequently used as definitions: according to such criteria it was at most an alliance between the fascist principles of the Heimwehr and the clerical conservatism of the Christian Social Party, designed to preserve 'the social and religious traditions of Austria' against the 'revolution of nihilism' from both left and right and to 'restore Austria's traditional social structure':[21] conservatism cloaked in fascist attire.

Yet, as Siegfried has pointed out, the very use of such rigid, descriptive definitions is problematical, since they depend so heavily upon the specific circumstances in which German National Socialism in particular developed that they effectively preclude comparative analysis. This is uniquely true in the case of Austria, where similar cultural characteristics and a shared language tend to mask basic differences between the two countries, such as those involving the political roles during the nineteenth century of religion and nationalism. In any case, some of the criteria used to dismiss 'Austrofascism' are of dubious validity even when applied to the two 'true' fascisms of Italy and Germany. Examples of this are the insistence on a functioning corporate economy, full totalitarianism and anti-clericalism, all of which would be difficult to establish in the Italian case.[22] Even where the models do reflect 'true' fascism, they ignore political, cultural and economic differences which might give rise to *varieties* of fascism. For instance, the Austrian economy was small, structurally weak, relied heavily on foreign capital and trade, and lacked the diversity which would have allowed a policy of economic autarky. Rather than ruling out the possibility of fascism, this simply suggests that an Austrian fascist regime would adopt other economic policies in an attempt to promote domestic capital.[23] The final criticism of the typological approach is that although its users are scrupulous in attempting to define 'fascism', the term which is frequently adopted in its place, namely 'conservatism', has received far less analytical attention and frequently lacks any definitional rigour whatsoever.

This last point is amply illustrated by the case of the Christian Social Party which, with its Catholicism, influential monarchist wing and strong rural support, is commonly held to have represented the 'conservative' as distinct from the 'nationalist' or 'socialist' camps in Austrian politics.[24] Yet the party had other characteristics which undermine the appropriateness of the 'conservative' label, especially when this is used to distinguish it from the 'fascism' of the Heimwehr. These include a radical populist tradition and a corporatist ideological strand which became increasingly influential in the 1920s as the economy floundered and class tensions increased, and had much in common with the Heimwehr. It was this which led to the Austrofascism of the *Ständestaat*. In terms of the narrow descriptive definitions of fascism, Christian Socialism remained essentially conservative with fascist overtones. As we have seen, however, narrow definitions cannot accommodate the idea of different forms of fascism and have become academically sterile. A wider approach is needed.

'Fascism' is not just a political state, it is also an ideology which, like all ideologies, can exist independently of the state. The beliefs of which fascist ideology consists are radical, populist, culturally chauvinist and authoritarian, seeing class conflict and individualism as the principal causes of decay in modern society. To overcome this fascists advocate an economy organized above class interests and based on a corporatist organizational ethos. The economy remains in private hands but under state direction, serving the common and united interests of the people as identified by the state. Fascist ideology fuses the anti-modern and anti-capitalist corporatism of the late nineteenth century with the pro-capitalist centralism of the twentieth, while remaining stridently anti-liberal and anti-socialist. These precise trends had been present from birth in the Christian Social Party. In the late 1920s they came to the fore, reaching their culmination in the *Ständestaat*, no simple military dictatorship but an authoritarian state which bourgeois politicians, supported not only by Church and army but also by most sections of Austrian capital, sought to legitimize in terms of populism and chauvinism. Rather than being borrowed from Italy, via the Heimwehr, or from Germany, the *Ständestaat*'s corporatist populism and chauvinism had their roots in Austrian political ideology and particularly that of Christian Socialism. The Catholic nature of Austrian corporatism, far from establishing its conservative origins, represented a specifically Austrian form of populism with radical traditions. Austrian fascism was not, therefore, the product of an alliance between the Italian-sponsored Heimwehr and the conservative Christian Social Party, but developed within Austrian bourgeois parties with the support of Austrian capital. In short, it was home-grown.

The remainder of this chapter will seek to demonstrate this by establishing (1) that Christian Social populist traditions fostered a distinct form of fascist thought which contributed to the creation of the *Ständestaat*; (2) that the

Heimwehr's role was as support for the Christian Social leadership and not as a competitive or dominant force; and (3) that the object of the *Ständestaat* was to undermine the strength of the working class. Austrian fascism was doubtless less radical and less successful than its German counterpart, but fascism it nevertheless remained.[25]

Central to this argument is the political role of religion within the Christian Social Party. Although in the Republic the links between the party and the Church establishment were unusually strong, this had not always been so. The original Christian Social movement had been distinctly anti-establishment, stemming from the revolt of the Viennese petty bourgeoisie after the 1873 stock market crash and depression. This had presented a former Liberal politician, Karl Lueger, with the opportunity to galvanize the newly enfranchised 'five gulden' men into a movement able to challenge and eventually defeat the Liberal Party in Vienna's council elections.[26] Lueger's own charisma was one reason for his success, but another was the platform on which he built his campaign: a bombastic religious anti-Semitism with which he won the support of anti-Liberal, anti-capitalist elements within the petty bourgeoisie, as well as the lower clergy.[27]

Linked to Lueger's movement was the Catholic neo-romantic corporatism of Karl Vogelsang. Both Lueger and Vogelsang based their politics on hostility towards anti-Catholicism, modern capitalism and – most important for Lueger – the Liberal Party which was associated with both.[28] There were also sharp differences between them, especially regarding religion. Vogelsang developed a highly Utopian, backward-looking panacea in which the evils of modern society and its lack of Catholic morality would be transformed by a system of economically based corporations.[29] Lueger's Catholicism was more pragmatic and was used to unite the previously fragmented Viennese petty bourgeoisie against the anti-clericalism and pro-capitalism of the Liberals. His earliest electoral themes were religious anti-Semitism, a non-plebeian form of populism, and a rabid denunciation of 'corrupt' (i.e. Jewish) capitalism. But the success of Lueger's party lay also in its political *style*, whereby the clubland culture of Viennese politics was replaced with a dynamic, mass-based organization.[30] The movement grew following a series of campaigns aimed at specific groups – teachers, lower government officials and the large and influential block of Viennese landlords – who felt they had a grievance against the city council.[31] Once in office the Christian Socials consolidated their support through a programme of 'communalism' in which the council established its own companies to provide gas, water and electricity and to raise income for the municipal budget. Lueger's corporatist ideas were useful symbols rather than genuine goals; unlike Vogelsang he aimed to reform capitalism, not to replace it. His use of Catholicism was equally pragmatic, since it provided his movement with a 'quasi-religious façade' and an air of moral superiority – as well as votes. Above all, the Christian Social Party displayed a populist and corporatist hue from birth.

Whilst the links between Lueger and Vogelsang and the political Catholicism of the *Ständestaat* should not be exaggerated, nor should they be ignored. 'Lueger, protector of the people', albeit the non-working-class people, was a common theme of Christian Social politics during the Republic. Even more readily played was the role Lueger had assumed for his party as defender of Christian values, since this provided a popular stance from which to attack non-Catholic parties – in the 1890s the Liberals and in the 1920s the Social Democrats. In both periods the political power of religion was more important than its spiritual element. Links also existed between Vogelsang's Catholic corporatism and Christian Social intellectual thought under the Republic, notably the writings of Othmar Spann.[32]

Spann was probably the most important corporatist thinker of the day; when professor of political economy at Vienna University he was said to have 'exercised a lasting influence on "almost the entire non-Marxist, politically interested younger generation", whether it was German nationalist or Catholic conservative'.[33] The latter group included the future chancellor, Engelbert Dollfuss.[34] Spann shared Vogelsang's rejection of capitalism and also proposed to replace it with a system of corporate bodies; however where Vogelsang had envisaged the disappearance of the state through corporatism, Spann argued in favour of a strong authoritarian state. This would oversee a political and economic system based upon five separate and hierarchical corporations, ranging from one for manual workers at the bottom to one for 'intellectual heroes', teachers and educators, at the top. Although the system included safeguards intended to ensure decentralization and so prevent dictatorship, the only group which represented the 'entire nation' and therefore had overall control was the political leadership.[35]

Spann's influence over the Heimwehr has long been acknowledged. When the paramilitary movement finally adopted a political programme in May 1930 in the form of the Korneuburg Oath, Spann was said to be its spiritual father.[36] The oath rejected parliamentary democracy and demanded in its place

> the self-administration of the estates and a strong leadership of the state which will be formed not from the representatives of the parties, but from the leading persons of the big estates and from the ablest and best men of our movement ... Every comrade knows three powers: faith in God, his own hard will and the word of his leaders.[37]

Its publication followed a series of lectures and courses on Spann's theories which the Heimwehr had organized for its members during 1929.

But Spann's influence was by no means limited to the Heimwehr. Ignaz Seipel, the Christian Social leader during the 1920s, came into contact with the Spann circle when he was developing his theory of 'True Democracy'. This rather ambiguous theory dismissed democracy as being unaccountable to the people, but appeared to be synonymous with straightforward dictatorship; its links with Spann are therefore tenuous.[38] It was a different matter with the Catholic students' organizations, whose anti-parliamentarian, anti-liberal and *völkisch* trajectory owed much to Spann's theories. Out of this developed the concept of an 'Austrian ideology', a missionary nationalism based upon Austrian culture and Catholic religion, which underpinned the ideology of the *Ständestaat* and distinguished Austrian national zeal from the biological racism of German nationalism.[39]

The specifically Austrian and Christian Social origins of the *Ständestaat*'s Catholic corporatism were shared by the Heimwehr but were not exclusive to it. Whilst Dollfuss may have said that his state was based on *Quadragesimo Anno*, the latter emphasized the need to eradicate class conflict through 'autonomous' bodies or free associations and said that men should be free to choose the type of government they wanted. This was clearly not the case in the *Ständestaat*. *Quadragesimo Anno* also attacked those employers 'who even abuse religion itself, cloaking their own unjust impositions under its name, that they may protect themselves against the clearly just demands of their employees': a situation which actually developed in the period 1934–8.[40] However the most telling evidence that the 1934 constitution arose from an anti-democratic tendency in the party which predated the encyclical was the party programme of 1926 which indicated a clear move towards an authoritarian, corporatist and *Stände* policy. When *Quadragesimo Anno* was published in 1931, Christian Social leaders proudly declared that there was no need to alter their 1926 programme since it already conformed to the encyclical's teachings.[41] This was only partially correct: the encyclical had already criticized Italian fascism for misusing the corporate concept for political rather than social purposes, something that was equally true of the Christian Social Party.

As well as corporatism, and indeed running counter to it, the Christian Social Party and its ideology also contained social reformist and federalist strands. During the 1920s, however, the corporatist tendency grew increasingly powerful, thanks partly to the party's structure and partly to the political situation. The structural factor derived from the very nature of the national party, which had been founded in 1907 as an alliance between Lueger's Viennese party and the more conservative Catholic party of the provinces. There were therefore two Catholic movements, the first urban and radical, the second rural and traditional, representing German-speaking, property-owning Catholic farmers, the landed aristocracy and sections of the bourgeoisie.[42]

In the first years of the Republic this division was reflected in the conflict between the monarchist and centralist Viennese wing and the predominantly federalist and anti-monarchist provincial factions. With Vienna controlled after 1918 by the Social Democrats, the Christian Social Party's electoral power lay in the provinces. Even so, it was the Viennese wing of Ignaz Seipel which dominated the coalition governments.[43] Conflict between the agrarian federalism of the provinces and the centralism of the party leadership was one feature of Christian Social internal politics in the early 1920s, but differences also surfaced over such crucial issues as *Anschluss* with Germany, relations with the Social Democratic Party, and later those with the Heimwehr. In essence the party functioned as an electoral club of diverse groups which were united in defence of 'Christian values' against the secular Social Democratic Party. Early electoral campaigns were based on this principle – the reintroduction of compulsory religious education in schools, the abolition of Glöckl's education reforms in Vienna, reform of the marriage laws – as well as involving more direct attacks on the fiscal and housing policies of 'Red Vienna' and the Tenants' Protection Act.[44] Slogans were couched in terms of an urban–rural battle between piety and the devil, with Vienna sucking the provinces dry. In the 1927 election campaign political Catholicism was definitely overshadowed by anti-socialism when the party formed an electoral pact with other anti-socialist parties, including the anti-clerical Pan-Germans.[45] Twelve months later, Seipel began his 'True Democracy' campaign, announcing that its main champion was the Heimwehr.[46]

The heterogeneous character of the Christian Social Party, and the shift in political power from the provinces to the national leadership, help explain its abandonment of democracy in favour of authoritarianism. This is not a complete explanation, however. The notion that Parliament had become a sham also grew after 1927 in the provinces, as the political situation deteriorated rapidly amid increased right-wing fears of a Socialist electoral victory or revolution. Hitherto the Social Democratic Party and the anti-socialists had maintained an uneasy relationship in which the former controlled the industrial areas, including Vienna, but remained in opposition in Parliament, while national power was held by a series of coalitions dominated by the Christian Socials in alliance with the Pan-Germans and the Agrarian League. But the size of the Social Democratic Party, its dominance of the capital and its apparent militancy remained constant thorns in the side of the bourgeois parties.[47] One basic problem was economic policy. In 1922 the national government attempted to stop hyper-inflation and stabilize the currency by raising foreign loans and pursuing deflationary policies dictated by the League of Nations. At the same time the Viennese council carried out an experiment in socialist economics based on high taxation and high public sector spending.[48] While the countryside saved, the capital spent.

The Socialists, moreover, were highly visible, staging rallies and demonstrations, organizing their own militia, and maintaining close links with the Free Trade Union movement. Even after high levels of structural unemployment cut the unions' membership by over 25 per cent in the mid-1920s, the Social Democratic Party increased its membership and parliamentary representation. In the 1927 election the Socialists, despite their opponents' unity and a vociferous and violent 'run-up', actually gained three seats while the Unity List lost seven.[49] Soon afterwards, violence flared. In July 1927, eighty-eight people were killed in the middle of Vienna when a Socialist demonstration ended in a battle between police and workers. A 24-hour protest strike was then broken up, apparently by the Heimwehr.[50] These events instilled even greater fear in the Christian Social Party. The Social Democratic presence in Parliament had already been sufficient to prevent the government from abandoning some postwar reforms – rent protection and employment laws in particular. After the election the apparently greater prospect of a shift in political power away from the right, in the streets if not in Parliament, encouraged the Christian Social Party's national leaders to increase support for the right-wing paramilitary Heimwehr.

In relation to this point a number of historians have referred to an *alliance* between the conservatism of the Christian Social Party and the fascism of the Heimwehr. This assumes an independence for the latter which did not exist.[51] The ideological links between the two, already examined, represented only one area of overlap. In political terms their relationship was even closer, for, although regional variations existed within both movements, to all intents and purposes the Heimwehr emerged in the 1920s as the paramilitary wing of the Christian Social Party, sharing rank-and-file members and, in some instances, leaders. In the industrial belt of Upper Styria it also developed a second function as an anti-Socialist trade union force, which brought it the support of sections of Austrian banking and industry.[52] It is in this context that the political influence of the Heimwehr must be seen, for when civil war broke out in February 1934 it was the result of *government* action against the Socialists, in which the Heimwehr acted as an auxiliary force rather than as the main aggressor. Indeed throughout its history the Heimwehr depended upon Christian Social support, particularly the protection of the national government. If a mutual dependence developed after 1927 it was only in part the result of Italian influence, for the Heimwehr provided the manpower to challenge the Social Democratic movement on the streets.[53] This became the main goal of both industry and the Christian Social leadership in the late 1920s and above all after the 1930 election, when it seemed that, despite the depression, the political power of the Socialists could not be defeated within the existing constitution.

It is important to stress that the relationship between the Heimwehr and the Christian Social Party did not stem from the escalation in class conflict after 1927. It can be traced back to the immediate postwar period, when small defence groups sprang up throughout the countryside to protect rural communities from looting by ex-soldiers trekking back from the front and by ex-prisoners of war. These, the original *Heimwehren*, were issued with arms by local government officials and with the approval of the provisional government in Vienna, on the grounds that the units were apolitical and that self-protection was necessary in the chaos of the time; by 1919 it was reported that in Styria 70 per cent of all communes had raised such units and that contact had been made with nationalist ex-soldiers fighting on the borders.[54]

The apolitical character of the Heimwehr proved shortlived, for two reasons. The first was the introduction of requisitioning of cattle and grain, which were sent to the cities where hunger was rampant. This was carried out by the army and workers' councils, both dominated by Social Democratic supporters. To many farmers there was little difference between requisitioning and looting. The second reason was that a schism broke out within the provisional government over Socialist influence in the army. In the spring of 1920 the Christian Socials attempted to reduce this by introducing a bill federalizing the army and so bringing it under the control of non-Socialist provincial governments. When this failed several provincial governors sought and gained financial support for local Heimwehr groups from industry and from anti-socialist groups in Hungary and Bavaria.[55] The motivation for this was fear of a 'Bolshevik' revolution, and support continued even after the Socialists left the coalition. Three years later Heimwehr forces were used to break a strike in Styria, provoking Socialists to form their own militia, the Schutzbund.[56] This Heimwehr, however, was very different from the earlier units, comprising nationalist students, members of the petty bourgeoisie and ex-army officers. It was extreme in its actions and fanatically anti-socialist.[57]

Several points arise from this. First, the early Heimwehr was not a single movement but a collection of small groups, some supported by the Christian Social Party and others by the Pan-German Party. The consequent internal feuding prevented unity until 1927. However the Pan-German sections were mainly confined to northern Styria and Carinthia, whilst in the other provinces the Christian Social sections dominated – to the extent that in the Tyrol the Heimwehr was led by Christian Social Party leaders, the majority of its members were Christian Social supporters, and part of its funding came from Christian Social coffers.[58] Secondly, the Heimwehr's industrial support came via the Christian Social Party and carried the provision that the movement should support the government. In 1922 the Central Association of Industrialists began paying 150 million crowns monthly to various Heimwehr units and channelled this through the Chancellor's office. The Chancellor, Seipel, tried to unite the various factions of the Heimwehr into a single movement which was to be a 'reliable instrument of power', 'to serve as a kind of auxiliary police, if the army proved weak or unreliable'.[59] Although the attempt failed and relations between the Christian Social leaders and the Heimwehr cooled until 1927, they were never broken.

The year 1927 marked a watershed in the Republic's history. Prior to the election of that year political tensions had been high, but both sides had restricted their activities to their own areas of support – the Christian Socials and the Pan-Germans were active in the provinces and the Social Democrats in the cities. After 1927 the national government encouraged Heimwehr attempts to challenge the Social Democrats by holding marches and demonstrations in Socialist strongholds in a bid to reclaim the cities or to provoke the Socialists into a violent response which could be forcibly suppressed. The Heimwehr were the obvious choice, for the 1927 general strike had been broken in Styria when Heimwehr units had marched against the strikers and destroyed what the government considered to be a potential revolution. In the autumn of 1927, despite the dubious legality of the Heimwehr's actions and strong rumours that the goal of its Styrian leader, Walter Pfrimer, had been to march on Vienna, Seipel once more arranged meetings with bankers and manufacturers to raise funds for the Heimwehr.[60] At the same time he was striving to increase Christian Social influence within the movement, and beginning to champion it as the protector of 'True Democracy'. He and other members of the government resisted pressure from Britain and France to introduce a general disarmament bill, despite the high number of clashes between the Heimwehr and the Schutzbund and the threat that, without such a law, foreign loans might not be forthcoming. According to the British ambassador this was because such a bill would have to have covered both movements. Instead raids were carried out by government troops and the Heimwehr on Schutzbund weapon stores; the bulk of what was seized was handed to the Heimwehr.[61]

In this way the Heimwehr came to act as the quasi-legal shock force of the Austrian government. Four months after the movement had publicly rejected 'Western democratic parliamentarism' in favour of a corporate state, the Christian Social chancellor, Vaugoin, invited two of its leaders to join the Cabinet, even though the Heimwehr had, at that time, never stood for election, had no deputies in Parliament and was anti-democratic. Unlike both the Agrarian League and the Pan-German Party, the Christian Social leaders told their members that there was no apparent inconsistency between the Korneuburg Oath and their party's principles.[62] When 14,000 armed Heimwehr men attempted a Putsch in

September 1931, the government failed to act until Social Democratic leaders threatened to call out the Schutzbund. Troops took three hours to travel thirty miles from Graz to Bruck an der Mur, enabling the putschists to disperse. The Christian Social governor of Styria dismissed the whole event as 'tipsy twaddle'.[63] Finally in 1932, when the Christian Social/Pan-German coalition collapsed, Dollfuss formed a new government with the support of nine Agrarian League and eight Heimwehr deputies who had been elected in 1930. Fey, a Heimwehr leader, was given the Ministry of Public Security, from which he authorized more raids on the Socialists.[64]

The government's majority of one depended on the Agrarian League and the Heimwehr. According to C. Earl Edmondson, this led to the 'tragedy of Dollfuss's having to allow them [the Heimwehr] to drive a wedge between him and the Socialists, who before Fey's appointment had tacitly tolerated his government'.[65] But Edmondson does not explain why the Heimwehr's influence was so much greater than that of the Agrarian League, which objected to the extent of the fascists' participation; nor does he provide evidence to support his theory that Dollfuss would have preferred a democratic solution to the political dilemma, one which included the Social Democrats. Indeed, Schuschnigg, Dollfuss's successor, wrote that a coalition with the Socialists had been rejected as impractical by the Christian Social leaders since 1931.[66] More telling is Dollfuss's own explanation of his move towards populist authoritarianism: 'Many things will change . . . [We will] do everything step by step to force the Marxists to their knees.'[67] Nor is there evidence in his other speeches and actions to suggest that he was a reluctant ally of the Heimwehr. He was continuing a Christian Social policy of support for the movement. But the Heimwehr remained, as it had always been, the junior partner in the relationship. It was the Christian Social leaders who chose between an alliance with their traditional enemies, the Social Democrats, and so maintaining the parliamentary republic, or jettisoning democracy in favour of fascism. If their predominant fear had been the growth of the National Socialist Party it is difficult to see why they decided to turn first on the one party which might have been able to stem that growth. But fear of socialism was older and much stronger than fear of National Socialism.

Anti-socialism was also popular with allies outside Austria. A major advocate was the Italian government which began to give arms and money to the Heimwehr in 1927 on condition that the movement conquered its internal differences and concentrated on building a political rather than a purely paramilitary movement.[68] But domestic financiers, Austrian industry and banking were making the same demands, discouraging talk of putsches and encouraging the movement to widen its base.[69] Relations between the Heimwehr and employers had been close since the 1922 stabilization crisis when the government had stemmed hyper-inflation by forcing the unions to accept longer working hours, pay-cuts and so higher unemployment.

Unsure of the loyalty of the army, provincial governments had allowed the Heimwehr to police and break strikes against this policy. Over the next few years union strength declined but the labour movement retained the rights to representation, unemployment pay and other social welfare benefits which employers considered an uneconomic drain and the cause of Austria's economic plight. In order to remove these it was necessary to break the Free Trade Unions and, ultimately, the political power of the Social Democratic Party in Parliament which effectively defended these laws. The Heimwehr developed a dual role in this battle, first as anti-unionists and later as provocateurs of the Socialist rank and file.

The prime example of economic battle occurred in the iron and steel region of Upper Styria, in the works of Austria's largest private employer, the Alpine Montangesellschaft. This company, a subsidiary of the German Vereinigte Stahlwerk, led the campaign in the 1920s against the Eight Hour Day Law, collective contracts and union rights. In 1925, following a strike, the company set up a 'social-political' programme designed to influence the political attitudes of its workers and to instil feelings of company and national loyalty, both of which were heavily tinged with German nationalism.[70] The 'Alpine' training schools became centres of Heimwehr activity, encouraged by the management. Several weeks before local government and factory council elections in May 1928 the Styrian Heimwehr announced that it had reached an agreement with the company restricting new employees in several mines to its members. Two months later it established the euphemistically named 'Independent Union Federation', the first programme of which argued that class conflict led to physical and spiritual exhaustion, demanded Anschluss with Germany and a directly elected president, whilst maintaining that it was politically independent. In 1929 it added two new demands – a strong authoritarian state and the reorganization of the economy on a corporate basis.[71] At the same time that it set up the 'Independent Unions' the Heimwehr also opened employment exchanges to provide firms with 'loyal' workers. The Alpine Montangesellschaft negotiated a new wage contract with the Independent Union in 1929, despite the fact that the union did not command a majority on the factory council. The company's management subsequently became one of the staunchest defenders of the German-oriented section of the Heimwehr.

The activities of the Alpine Montangesellschaft and its sponsorship of the Styrian Heimwehr illustrate one way in which political attitudes had changed. Before the war the company had refused to recognize unions, but had been forced to do so by law under the Republic. In 1925 it tried to ignore this legislation as it had successfully ignored the Eight Hour Day, but this led to a strike in which Christian Trade Union members defied their leaders and joined Free Trade Union colleagues.[72] In response the company turned to the Heimwehr to found a union which would comply with the law but represent management interests. The language of politics had changed so that even repression had to appear just and representative. What was true for the Independent Unions was later true for the *Ständestaat*.

It is necessary here to clarify one point: although the Styrian movement was a part of the national Heimwehr, it was not part of its Christian Social wing and in 1932 broke away to join the National Socialists. The Alpine Montangesellschaft management was also in sympathy with the Nazis, in favour of Anschluss and opposed to the Christian Social Party.[73] But the events in Styria were important to the Christian Socials, for one consequence of the Alpine Montangesellschaft position was that the Heimwehr appeared to build up a working-class following in Upper Styria: without a Heimwehr card it was not worth applying for a job and, as unemployment soared, this became a major incentive to join. This area thus provided the single outright electoral victory in 1930 which, under Austrian electoral law, allowed the Heimwehr to enter Parliament and gave Dollfuss the eight votes which secured his majority.[74]

The Alpine Montangesellschaft was not the Heimwehr's only industrial backer. The Central Association of Bankers also gave financial aid, although this was more pragmatic and aligned with Austrian as opposed to German economic needs. In return for the money, the Heimwehr was to provide a 'physical force against internal anarchy and external threats'.[75] Funds were increased in 1927 at Seipel's request and in the same year industrialists put pressure on Heimwehr leaders to prevent a putsch, fearing that this would trigger a flight of foreign capital. In 1929 the collapse of Boden Kreditanstalt almost stopped further payments, until Seipel intervened again.[76] According to Karl Haas, it was the financiers' interpretation of the attitude of foreign investors which most influenced their political decisions. Having preached caution in 1927, the same men privately offered government officials support for a non-parliamentary political system in 1932, as long as this was based on an economically sound programme and did not involve compromise with the Social Democrats.[77] An interesting comment on this appeared in the private papers of the vice-president of the Central Association of Industrialists, Robert Erhart. Making notes on a meeting between his association and the Chancellor, Buresch, in January 1932, Erhart wrote that three political possibilities had been discussed: a new bourgeois coalition with the Pan-Germans, which he said would accomplish little; a coalition between the Christian Social and Social Democratic parties, which would split the Christian Socials but not solve the economic problems; and a non-parliamentary government.

> It is doubtless true that not only politicians but also broader circles have become familiar with this idea. Events in other countries have shown that if the legitimate government begins to exercise such measures,

the resistance is surprisingly low and people fairly soon accept the situation. This is true only if the legitimate government does this. If it is necessary to seize power first this process takes longer, as can be seen with the National Socialists in Germany, because the demagogues in the opposition use the identification of the economy and industry with fascism to create very effective political slogans. Thus (3) must be followed by propaganda to cultivate the ground, meaning that the population must be shown again and again that the present conditions cannot continue and something will have to change. This will have to take place in addition to the more subtle long-term work of the Central Association of Industrialists. Such propaganda activities must be independent of the Association so that they can retain the freedom of movement which is necessary if they are to extend beyond what has already been done.[78]

This was written fourteen months before the proroguing of Parliament and twelve months before the Nazi victory in Germany. The very fact that such issues were raised in a meeting between politicians and industrialists is evidence of the hardening attitudes against parliamentary democracy in both camps. Ten months later Dollfuss told a peasants' meeting that 'the fact that it is possible for the government to put urgent measures into effect at once, without endless preliminary parliamentary struggles, will contribute materially to restoring our democracy to health'.[79] It was a case of dictatorship being more 'democratic' than parliamentarism.

This last point is part of the dilemma of fascism as a form of bourgeois political dictatorship in which populism is used to justify the destruction of democratic institutions. The state is said to embody the 'spirit of the people' rather than merely representing a variety of social groups or classes. Underlying this is the belief that there is such a 'spirit of the people' which differentiates one nation from another. In Austria, where concepts of nationality were problematical, this spirit was identified by the Christian Social leadership as German but Catholic, thus separating it from non-Catholic German nationalism. The explanation was religious but the factors which led to the *Ständestaat* were political and economic and lay in a fear found amongst politicians and businessmen that political power might slip out of the hands of the bourgeois parties. This process began in 1927, intensified in 1930, and was the reason for the increase in support for the Heimwehr from both financiers and the Christian Social leadership. The Heimwehr was not the instigator of policy and its influence appears to have been exaggerated, thus diminishing the role of the Christian Social Party itself in the progression towards fascism. Parliamentary democracy in Austria was destroyed in order to wipe out the Social Democratic movement, not to protect the country against fascism. The result was a form of fascism itself: Austrofascism.

NOTES

1 Literally translated: 'State of Estates'.
2 *Arbeiter-Zeitung*, 2 March 1933.
3 ibid.
4 *Jahrbuch der österreichischen Arbeiterbewegung 1932* (Vienna, 1933), p. 85.
5 C. A. Gulick, *Austria from Habsburg to Hitler*, Vol. 2 (Berkeley, Calif., 1948), p. 1404.
6 ibid., p. 1443.
7 E. Talos and W. Manoschek, 'Politische Struktur des Austrofaschismus 1934–1938', in E. Talos and W. Neugebauer (eds), *'Austrofaschismus': Beitrage über Politik, Ökonomie und Kultur 1934–1938* (Vienna, 1985), p. 104.
8 G. Jagschitz, 'Die österreichische Ständestaat 1934–1938', in E. Weinzierl and K. Skalnik (eds), *Österreich 1918–1938. Geschichte der Ersten Republik*, Vol. I (Vienna, 1985), p. 501.
9 Talos and Manoschek, 'Politische Struktur', p. 93.
10 E. Hanisch, 'Der Politische Katholizismus als ideologischer Träger des "Austrofaschismus"', in Talos and Neugebauer (eds), *'Austrofaschismus'*, p. 55; A. Staudinger, 'Austrofaschistische "Österreich"-ideologie', in Talos and Neugebauer (eds), *'Austrofaschismus'*, p. 309.
11 Dollfuss, speech of 25 March 1933, quoted in W. Goldinger (ed.), *Protokolle des Klubvorstandes der Christlichsozialen Partei 1932–1934* (Vienna, 1980), p. 212.
12 C. Earl Edmondson, *The Heimwehr and Austrian Politics, 1918–1936* (Athens, Ga, 1978), p. 199; A. Wandruszka, 'Österreichs politische Struktur: Die Christlichsoziale-Konservative Lage', in H. Benedikt (ed.), *Die Geschichte der Republik Österreich* (Vienna, 1954), p. 334–7.
13 R. J. Rath, 'Authoritarian Austria', in P. Sugar (ed.), *Native Fascism in the Successor States 1918–1945* (Santa Barbara, Calif., 1971), pp. 24–43; see also U. Kluge, *Die österreichische Ständestaat 1934–38* (Vienna, 1984) and a review of this work by R. G. Ardelt, *Zeitgeschichte*, vol. 13, no. 3 (December 1985), pp. 109–19.
14 K.-J. Siegfried, *Klerikalfaschismus* (Frankfurt, 1979), pp. 1–7. Similar approaches have been taken by W. Holzer, 'Faschismus in Österreich', *Austriaca* (July 1978), pp. 80 ff. and S. Mattl, 'Die Finanzdiktatur. Wirtschaftspolitik in Österreich 1933–1938', in Talos and Neugebauer (eds), *'Austrofaschismus'*, pp. 133–59.
15 Siegfried, *Klerikalfaschismus*, p. 23.
16 Hanisch, 'Der Politische Katholizismus', p. 53.
17 Talos and Manoschek, 'Politische Struktur', p. 97.
18 Jagschitz, 'Die österreichische *Ständestaat*', p. 501.
19 E. Holtmann, *Zwischen Unterdrückung und Befriedigung* (Vienna, 1978), p. 15.
20 G. Botz, *Gewalt in der Politik*, 2nd edn. (Vienna, 1978), pp. 237–8.
21 Edmondson, *Heimwehr*, p. 182.
22 Jagschitz, 'Die österreichische Ständestaat', p. 498; Martin Kitchen, *The Coming of Austrian Fascism* (London, 1980), p. 278. On Italy see Adrian Lyttelton, 'Italian fascism', in W. Laqueur (ed.), *Fascism: A Reader's Guide* (London, 1976), pp. 91, 95, 97.
23 Mattl, 'Die Finanzdiktatur', pp. 136–49.
24 Wandruszka, 'Die Christlichsoziale-Konservative Lage', pp. 312–32.
25 John Rath and Carolyn Schum have argued that the Dollfuss–Schuschnigg regime was not fascist because, amongst other things, its attack on civil liberties was less extreme than those of the Nazi or Italian Fascist states. They comment that although Dollfuss set up a concentration camp in Wöllersdorf in 1933, 'even G. E. R. Gedye, who was anything but a friend of the Dollfuss regime, admits that life was relatively easy [there]'. J. Rath and C. Schum, 'The Dollfuss Regime: fascist or authoritarian?', in S. U. Larsen, B. Hagtvet and J. P. Myklebust (eds), *Who Were the Fascists? Social Roots of European Fascism* (Oslo, Bergen and Tromsø, 1980), p. 252.
26 J. W. Boyer, *Political Radicalism in Late Imperial Vienna* (Chicago and London, 1981), p. 275. The Viennese franchise was based on a curia system and the right to vote

depended on the level of tax paid. In 1885 the lowest threshold was reduced from 10 to 5 gulden, enfranchising lower artisans and shopkeepers.

27 Boyer, *Political Radicalism*, pp. 160–4. Adolf Hitler wrote about Lueger at length in *Mein Kampf*, comparing his policies and tactics with those of the German nationalist leader Schönerer. In all the important areas in which Schönerer failed, Lueger, he said, succeeded. Adolf Hitler, *Mein Kampf* (Munich, 1939), pp. 105–34.

28 Boyer, *Political Radicalism*, p. 223–5.

29 ibid., p. 177.

30 Gulick, *Austria from Habsburg to Hitler*, Vol. 1, p. 26.

31 Boyer, *Political Radicalism*, p. 419.

32 E. Weinzierl, 'Kirche und Politik', in Weinzierl and Skalnik, *Österreich 1918–1938*, pp. 471–2.

33 F. L. Carsten, *Fascist Movements in Austria* (London, 1977), p. 168.

34 Staudinger, 'Austrofaschistische "Österreich"-ideologie', p. 295.

35 A. Diamant, *Austrian Catholics and the First Republic 1918–1934* (Princeton, NJ, 1960), p. 240.

36 Edmondson, *Heimwehr*, p. 72. Carsten (*Fascist Movements in Austria*, p. 171) argues that Italian fascism was more influential than Spann. See also K.-J. Siegfried, *Universalismus und Faschismus. Das Gesellschaftsbild Othmar Spanns* (Frankfurt, 1974), p. 84.

37 Gulick, *Austria from Habsburg to Hitler*, Vol. 2, p. 895.

38 R. Stöger, 'Die christliche Führer und die "wahre Demokratie". Zu den Demokratie-konzeptionen von Ignaz Seipel', *Archiv* (Vienna), vol. 2 (1986), p. 65.

39 Staudinger, 'Austrofaschistische "Österreich"-ideologie', p. 309.

40 Gulick, *Austria from Habsburg to Hitler*, Vol. 2, p. 1425. Gulick also points out that Schuschnigg disowned the association with *Quadragesimo Anno* and that no reference was made to it in the constitution itself.

41 Wandruszka, 'Die Christlichsoziale-Konservative Lage', p. 336.

42 A. Staudinger, 'Die Christlichsoziale Partei', in Weinzierl and Skalnik, *Österreich 1918–1938*, pp. 250–3. Sections of the Austrian bourgeoisie supported the Pan-German Party, especially in Styria.

43 ibid., p. 253. The one exception was the 1924 Ramek administration: see Gulick, *Austria from Habsburg to Hitler*, Vol. 1, p. 701.

44 Staudinger, 'Die Christliche Partei', in Weinzierl and Skalnik, *Österreich 1918–1938*, pp. 250–3. Gulick, *Austria from Habsburg to Hitler*, Vol. 1, pp. 690–3.

45 ibid., p. 711.

46 I. Kerekes, *Abenddämmerung einer Demokratie: Mussolini, Gömbös und die Heimwehr* (Vienna, 1966), p. 32.

47 One-third of the country's total population of 6 million lived in Vienna. In 1929 national membership of the Social Democratic Party reached a peak of 718,056.

48 J. Lewis 'Red Vienna: socialism in one city, 1918–1927', *European Studies Review*, vol. 13, no. 3 (July 1983), pp. 335–54.

49 The Agrarian League, which was not part of the electoral pact, gained four seats.

50 Gulick, *Austria from Habsburg to Hitler*, Vol. 1, pp. 717–52. Although Social Democratic leaders called off the strike after Heimwehr leaders in Styria threatened to march against the strikers, it is doubtful, in view of their own initial lack of enthusiasm about the strike, that this was actually the cause of their decision.

51 See N. Leser, 'Austria between the wars', *Austrian History Year Book*, vol. XVII–XVIII (1981–2), p. 135.

52 J. Lewis, 'The failure of Styrian labour in the first Austrian Republic', PhD thesis, University of Lancaster, 1984, pp. 207–28.

53 Kerekes, *Abenddämmerung einer Demokratie*, p. 14. In December 1928 the British ambassador reported a speech by Seipel in Graz in which he said of the Heimwehr: 'Its object is to prevent the Social Democrats from having the sole privilege of organising processions and demonstrations in the streets for such a privilege would in the end be misused as a kind of weapon for a terrorist organization.' Public Record Office (PRO), Political, Central. Austria. FO 371 (1928), 12851, C9698, Phipps to Sir Austen Chamberlain, 19.12.1928. This was the same speech in which Seipel produced his 'True democracy' theory.

54 Carsten, *Fascist Movements in Austria*, p. 43.
55 A. Staudinger, 'Die Christlichsoziale Partei und die Heimwehr bis 1927', in *Die Ereignisse des Juli 1927* (Vienna, 1979), p. 259.
56 The strike, at Judenburg in November 1922, was political. See I. Duczynska, *Workers in Arms* (New York and London, 1978), pp. 58–9.
57 Carsten, *Fascist Movements in Austria*, p. 44.
58 Edmondson, *Heimwehr*, p. 60.
59 Carsten, *Fascist Movements in Austria*, p. 60.
60 PRO, FO 371 (1929), 13565 C8732/149/3. Phipps to Henderson, 18.11.1929.
61 ibid. When Seipel resigned as leader of the Christian Social Party in 1930 on grounds of ill health, Schober told the British ambassador that the real cause was his frustration at the dissension within the Heimwehr and the Vatican's veto of his request to become that movement's leader. PRO, FO 317, 14305 (1930), C2968, Phipps to London, 16.4.1930.
62 Gulick, *Austria from Habsburg to Hitler*, Vol. 2, p. 897. Before the 1930 election the Heimwehr tried to arrange an electoral pact with the NSDAP. When this failed the Vienna and Lower Austria Heimwehr fought a joint campaign in their areas with the Christian Social Party under the label of 'The Christian Social and Heimatwehr Party'. The remaining Heimwehr fought a separate campaign as the Heimatblock. Verwaltungsarchiv, Bundeskanzleramt, Wien Polizeidirektion, Berichte, Karton 15, Pr. Zl. IV-4602/3/30, 23 Oktober 1930.
63 E. Fischer, *An Opposing Man* (London, 1969), p. 185.
64 Goldinger (ed.), *Protokolle*, pp. 21–4 (sitting of 25 March 1933).
65 Edmondson, *Heimwehr*, p. 170.
66 K. Schuschnigg, *Im Kampf gegen Hitler* (Vienna, 1969), p. 132.
67 Goldinger (ed.), *Protokolle*, p. 212 (sitting of 25 March 1933).
68 Kerekes, *Abenddämmerung einer Demokratie*, p. 15.
69 Edmondson, *Heimwehr*, p. 41.
70 Lewis, 'The failure of Styrian labour', pp. 144–8.
71 *Unabhängige Gewerkschafter* (Leoben), 15 November 1929.
72 Lewis, 'The failure of Styrian labour', p. 151.
73 A police report on a strike in the company in 1933 concluded that the management incited a conflict in the hope that it would lead to civil strife in the area and the downfall of the government. Verwaltungsarchiv, Bundeskanzleramt 22/Stmk, Wien Polizeidirektion, Berichte, Karton 5135, Pr. Zl. IV-7416/33, September 1933.
74 Edmondson, *Heimwehr*, p. 117.
75 Staudinger, 'Die Christlichsoziale Partei', p. 135.
76 PRO, FO 371, 13565 (1929), C8732/149/3. Phipps to Henderson, 18.11.1929.
77 K. Haas, 'Industrielle Interessen Politik in Österreich zur Zeit der Weltwirtschaftskrise', *Jahrbuch für Zeitgeschichte* (1978), p. 112.
78 ibid., pp. 115–16.
79 Gulick, *Austria from Habsburg to Hitler*, Vol. 2, pp. 997–8. Dollfuss had been studying the terms of the 1917 War Economy Emergency Powers Act which provided the basis for rule by decree.

7

Conservatism, traditionalism and fascism in Spain, 1898–1937

Martin Blinkhorn

In the light of the dramatic constitutional and political changes affecting pre-civil war Spain – constitutional monarchy until 1923, dictatorship between 1923 and 1931, and republican democracy between 1931 and 1936 – discussion of the relationship between conservatism and fascism requires, first of all, recognition that *social* conservatism and *political* conservatism may not always closely coincide. When a constitutional and political system is such as to facilitate the preservation of existing social hierarchies and differences, then it is likely that those who are socially conservative will be politically conservative also; thus it was in Spain during the later nineteenth century and into the twentieth. Where a political system becomes unconvincing as a defender of established interests, the latter may begin to explore its reform or replacement, as occurred in Spain during the 1910s and 1920s. And where a regime is introduced which unambiguously threatens the position of the wealthy, privileged and otherwise conservatively inclined, then social conservatism may engender an anything but 'conservative' political stance *vis-à-vis* the newly established institutions – as was the case during the Spanish Second Republic of 1931–6.

The notion of 'fascism' is also, of course, problematical. Some individuals and movements of the interwar European, and in this case Spanish, right enthusiastically adopted the label; others assumed an ambivalent stance towards whatever they understood by 'fascism'; and others claimed hostility towards it even while being regarded as fascists by their enemies on the left. It is probably wisest, however, whatever may be our ultimate conclusion, to adopt a pragmatic approach and begin by taking fascism to be that self-consciously 'radical' strand of the right which proclaims itself as such.

The main concern of this chapter will be the political strategies of the socially conservative in Spain during the years of the Second Republic, and in particular the relationship of 'fascism' to them. First, however, it is necessary to explore Spanish 'conservatism' in the years before the coming of Republican democracy.

Writers on the subject of 'Spanish fascism', notably Stanley Payne, have laid considerable stress on Spain's lack of a 'pre-fascist tradition' such as that enjoyed by *fin-de-siècle* and early twentieth-century Italy; this, Payne asserts, helps explain the extreme weakness of self-confessed fascism in Spain before 1936.[1] And it is perfectly true that Spain did not possess, to any serious degree, the kind of widely diffused irrationalist and radical-nationalist political strands which existed in Italy from the late nineteenth century onwards and which, boosted by injections from revolutionary syndicalism and interventionism, it may be argued gave Italian fascism much of its distinctive style and tone. It follows that any Spanish political movement which too closely aped Italian fascism was therefore unlikely to strike the intellectual and popular chords necessary to attract instant mass support. As we shall see, neither during the final crisis of the Liberal Monarchy (1917–23) nor during the greater part of the Second Republic did Italian-style 'radical fascism' appeal to many Spanish conservatives dissatisfied with the political status quo.

Emphasis upon a distinctively Italian 'pre-fascist tradition', such as helped shape Italian fascism but whose absence in Spain prevented the early emergence of a successful facsimile of the Italian original, is nevertheless of limited value. It might perhaps be more fruitful to attempt to identify an indigenous, national, *counter-revolutionary* tradition capable, as was 'pre-fascism' in Italy and, more dramatically still, *völkisch* nationalism in Germany, of being harnessed in order to play a broadly similar role. Conservative Spaniards of the 1930s, even many of the more demogogically inclined, repeatedly insisted that Spain had no need of an Italianate or Germanic form of anti-liberal, anti-leftist mass movement for the simple reason that the country possessed a vigorous counter-revolutionary heritage of its own. This politico-cultural tradition, largely lacking in Italy with its very different tradition of church–state relations, might best be labelled 'Catholic traditionalism'.

Catholic traditionalism was an important political, intellectual and cultural force in Spain throughout the 1800s. During the early part of the century it became attached to, and closely associated with, Carlism, a dynastic cause born in the 1830s and which for the next century served as a vehicle for varied, fluctuating and sometimes conflicting strands of opposition to Spain's dominant liberal system. Carlism contributed to Catholic traditionalism its popular, emotional, mythic and indeed militaristic elements, while the intellectual offerings of Carlist publicists and propagandists such as Antonio Aparisi y Guijarro, Cándido Nocedal, Ramón Nocedal and Juan Vázquez de Mella were complemented by the work of non-Carlist Catholic intellectuals like Jaime Balmes, Juan Donoso Cortés, Bishop Torres y Bages and Marcelino Menéndez Pelayo.[2]

119

Although by the early twentieth century Carlism as a political movement was in poor shape, Catholic traditionalism retained a powerful influence within the Church, among both clergy and laity, and at court. By this time it had absorbed, without too much discomfort, many of the ideas of fashionable European neo-Thomist intellectuals and the social-Catholicism of Leo XIII, and had come to infuse the large and complex network of Catholic social and professional organizations which proliferated after 1900. In political terms, as most lucidly expounded by Mella, Catholic traditionalism stressed the central role of Catholic Christianity as the foundation of a corporate order which, it was fondly hoped, would restore harmony to Spain's society and polity; through 'Catholic unity', liberal individualism and parliamentarism would be superseded and the appeal of the left neutralized without recourse to centralization, bloated bureaucracies, or outright repression.[3]

Notwithstanding the declining hold of the Church and the Catholic faith upon the early twentieth-century liberal intelligentsia and working class, Catholic traditionalism also possessed what might be termed a 'constituency' – a significant section of the Spanish population, extending well beyond wealthy Catholic conservatives and intransigent clerics, which was sufficiently influenced by religious devotion and, more importantly, by the Church itself, to be attractable, should the appropriate circumstances arise, to a political party or parties espousing one or other form of Catholic corporatism. This constituency mostly consisted of the numerous small and middling peasant proprietors and tenant farmers of northern, north-central and parts of eastern Spain, together with elements of the Catholic petty bourgeoisie, *rentier* class and artisanate in most other regions. It was people such as these who provided Carlism with its admittedly contracting support as the twentieth century opened, and who during the early part of the century came to form the mass membership of Catholic interest groups, syndicates and farmers' associations; of these the most powerful and significant was the Confederación Nacional Católico-Agraria (CNCA), a sprawling organization through which wealthy Catholic landowners attempted to ensure the political passivity of smallholders and tenants. Binding such bodies together, as elsewhere in Catholic Europe, was the lay organization Catholic Action, whilst another body, the Asociación Católica Nacional de Propagandistas (ACNP), channelled the energies of the Catholic intellectual elite.[4]

During the golden age of Spain's Liberal Monarchy, from 1875 down to the end of the century, the majority of those Spaniards who deliberately or unthinkingly embraced Catholic-traditionalist ideas and values nevertheless went along more or less contentedly with the political status quo. Following the turbulent years of 1868–74, the late nineteenth-century liberal system appeared to guarantee political stability. Its two main parties, Conservative and Liberal, representing different sections of an agrarian, banking and manufacturing oligarchy, alternated politely and artificially in office, sustained by gentlemen's-club politics, clientelism and election-rigging. Crucially, and notwithstanding its 'liberal' label, the system was culturally as well as materially conservative. Thanks largely to a close church–state relationship, the Liberal Monarchy exhibited little of the institutionalized anti-clericalism which characterized its Italian counterpart. As long as the 'Alfonsine' monarchy adequately upheld the interests of religion and property, and its actual institutions functioned in doing so with relative smoothness, the power of Catholic traditionalism as the basis of a possible counter-revolutionary movement remained latent. The steady and seemingly irreversible decline of the Carlist cause, the principal repository of open traditionalist *opposition* to the system, was nevertheless deceptive as an indicator of *potential* strength, which remained considerable. For our purposes the significance of this point is twofold. In the first place, Catholic traditionalism functioned within the loose embrace of the Liberal Monarchy as a kind of 'alternative' conservatism *vis-à-vis* the 'official' conservatism of the regime; secondly, its strength not only indicated its counter-revolutionary potential but also suggested that any future mass movements of the right were likely to have to take notice of its values and constituency.

From the late 1890s, and especially following Spain's humiliation at the hands of the United States in 1898, the liberal system that had presided over a generation of political stability and relative social peace began to disintegrate. That 'oligarchic liberalism' was increasingly out of phase with a rapidly, if unevenly, changing society was clear; what remained in doubt was whether such a system was capable of maturing into a more genuinely representative liberal democracy. The disintegrative process, involving the splitting and ultimate paralysis of both major political parties, was a protracted one, gradual at first and accelerating to a climax – as in Italy – during and after the First World War. Critiques of, and challenges to, the status quo were presented by much of the Spanish intelligentsia, by the emergent forces of Catalan and Basque regionalism, and by the socialist and anarcho-syndicalist wings of a growing labour movement. These elements, together with professional discontent within the army, converged in 1917 to produce a crisis which the monarchy itself survived mainly because moderate critics drew back from the brink. The agony of the liberal system grew more, not less, acute thereafter, with the old-style party system in disarray, rural Andalusia and urban Catalonia in a state of near revolution, and Spanish arms humiliated in Morocco at the defeat of Anual (1921).[5]

The early stages of Spain's liberal crisis, between 1898 and 1917, inspired a motley range of proposals for Spain's 'regeneration'.[6] Among the first political 'regenerationists' were the Carlists, who from outside the ruling system called for its replacement by their decentralized, Catholic, 'traditional monarchy'. From within the system, some Conservatives even before 1898 had grasped the need to pre-empt total political, and possibly social, collapse through carefully controlled reform. In the wake of 1898 such hopes gradually focused on the Conservative statesman Antonio Maura. After Maura's hopes of Conservative reform were dashed, however, there emerged around his person a new and singular phenomenon, that of Maurism. Always a loose political movement, Maurism combined a Maurassian sense of the 'Pays réel' and a street element, the Young Maurists, in such a way as to suggest resemblances to Action Française, though scarcely to the European fascism of the next decade. Although Maurism achieved little and soon withered away, it was important as a forcing ground for two new forms of rightism: a politicized social-Catholicism and an authoritarian nationalism, as represented, respectively, by two of Maura's principal lieutenants, Angel Ossorio y Gallardo and Antonio Goicoechea. In its anti-parliamentarism after 1919, and in particular the behaviour of the Young Maurists, Maurism may have looked 'forward' to a new kind of authoritarianism, but what is equally striking is the extent to which it borrowed from, and indeed attempted with some success to harness, the Catholic traditionalist heritage.[7]

The more complex and profound crisis of the early 1920s did much to destroy the ambivalence which many conservative 'liberals' had earlier felt regarding the parliamentary system. Some, it is true, responded to the paralysis of old-style liberal politics and the emergence of a powerful and militant left by grasping the need for greater democratization, via either Christian Democracy or a moderate form of republicanism. Spain's first Christian Democratic party, the Partido Social Popular, founded in 1922, perished a year later when the parliamentary system itself was brought down by the *coup d'état* of General Primo de Rivera.[8] Conservative republicanism was to have its brief and illusory heyday in 1930–1. As the widespread welcome extended to Primo's *pronunciamiento* indicates, however, many other conservatives now began to abandon a liberalism which was ceasing to appear a convincing defender of their interests and of the supposed 'eternal values' of Spain.

A superficial comparison of Spain with Italy might encourage the conclusion that Spain after 1917 was fertile ground for the emergence of fascist-style movements. Important differences nevertheless dictated that the outcome of Spain's first liberal crisis would be unlike Italy's. Spain's lack of a 'pre-fascist culture' was clearly one factor, though the mixed bag of regenerationism certainly contained items susceptible to use by a radical right. Far more significant was the absence, thanks to Spain's wartime neutrality, of a postwar trauma comprised of 'mutilated victory' and a massive demobilization problem: two ingredients without which Italian fascism probably could not have existed and certainly could not have succeeded. Those middling social layers which in Italy formed most of the fascist rank and file, in Spain were at this stage either attracted to democratic republicanism or regionalist politics, or passively caught up in the Catholic-traditionalist world already referred to.[9] Spain possessed something else that Italy lacked, and that was crucially to influence the development of the Spanish right: a highly 'political' army which, while not politically monolithic, in a truly serious crisis could be expected to respond to conservative invitations to 'save' the 'essential Spain'.[10] Primo de Rivera's seizure of power may not on its own explain why no significant fascist movement appeared in Spain before the 1930s; what it does help to demonstrate is why, unlike their Italian counterparts, Spanish conservatives in the early 1920s had no need to look for protection to new and untried political forces.

The Primo de Rivera dictatorship (1923–30) occupies a distinctive place in the history of Spanish fascism, and of the conservative–fascist relationship. In the sense that it rested upon no prior mass movement and lacked a totalitarian vision, the regime was not a fascist one. Primo de Rivera himself was a benevolent and sincere paternalist, neither a radical demagogue nor a systematic hammer of the left. The nearest thing to a 'single party', Unión Patriótica, was an artificial affair designed to do little more than provide the regime with legitimacy and powers of endurance. In neither respect was it successful; when in 1928–9 the regime began to totter, any possibility of Primo's emulating Mussolini's tactic in 1924 by threatening an ungrateful establishment with the unleashing of a 'second wave' was, as he realized, utterly out of the question. Nevertheless the Dictatorship was one of the first European regimes to borrow selectively from its Italian Fascist counterpart. Although Primo himself flatly rejected the fascist label which others sought to pin on him, several of his leading political lieutenants felt very differently, admiring the Fascist regime, happily employing *fascisant* rhetoric, and attempting to introduce policies and invent institutions which offended conservative orthodoxies. It was the paternalistically reforming aspect of the dictatorship, among other things, which alienated much of Spain's oligarchy, and ultimately left Primo bereft of conservative support. In January 1930, abandoned by the Crown, the wealthy classes and his fellow officers, Primo de Rivera surrendered power.[11]

The fascist or *fascisant* elements of the Dictatorship played an important transitional role in the development of the Spanish right. Shlomo Ben-Ami has convincingly argued that the regime served as a crucible for the forging of right-wing authoritarian ideas and values and a training school for a new generation of rightist activists; it also, he suggests, via Unión Patriótica accelerated the political mobilization of the more traditional sectors of the petty bourgeoisie and peasantry. The overall result was to bequeath to the right of the 1930s a transformed value-system and a fresh leadership cadre which, whether or not they be regarded as 'fascist', were unquestionably authoritarian rather than democratic in temper.[12]

Prior to 1930, defenders of the socioeconomic status quo in Spain were never placed in the kind of situation that, elsewhere, made radical fascism an attractive proposition. The social and political crisis of 1917–23, acute as it was, in the final analysis was capable of being confronted by essentially conventional means: police and military repression and, ultimately, outright praetorianism. In April 1931, however, just over a year after the collapse of Primo de Rivera's dictatorship, the monarchy itself fell, creating an entirely novel situation. The Second Republic arrived at a time which, given the impact of the depression and the retreat of democracy abroad, could hardly have been less propitious for a new, would-be democratic regime. Although the monarchy had fallen in part through a failure of Spain's propertied classes, and the armed forces, to rally to its defence in the crisis of 1930–1, few wealthy conservatives had any genuine enthusiasm for the new regime.[13] The advent of the Republic thrust Spain, for the first time and almost overnight, into the arena of mass politics; from the start it was clear that its founders intended it to be a radically reforming regime. Between 1931 and 1933 the governing alliance of left-wing Republicans and Socialists endeavoured, by means of social, agrarian, educational, institutional and anti-clerical legislation, to transform Spanish society. In such a situation, the question was: what kind of political formations and strategies would be adopted by those anxious to resist attempts to redistribute property and reduce the influence of the Church, and how successful would they be in rallying mass support?

Since the Republic had little chance of surviving unless conservatives could be persuaded to accept it, one of its greatest tragedies must be considered to have been the political failure of Catholic republicanism.[14] Under the Republic – as under Weimar and in postwar Italy – there failed to develop a party or parties capable of providing for social and religious conservatives a political haven that would speak for their interests while cleaving sincerely and consistently to the principles and practices of parliamentary democracy. More particularly, no such party emerged that was able to embrace, and in the process republicanize, the mass of culturally traditionalist Catholics, thereby undercutting the position of their propertied and clerical patrons.

The creation of such a force was never likely to be easy, given the social and religious conflicts released by Spain's new democracy, the sheer strength of traditionalism on the Spanish right, and the authoritarian legacies of the Dictatorship. Its desirability was grasped, and the task undertaken in the early months of the Republic, by former monarchists who during the 1920s had become convinced that the monarchy was incapable of regeneration and democratization. Two members of the Provisional Government, Niceto Alcalá Zamora, an Andalusian landowner and former Liberal minister, and Miguel Maura, son of Antonio Maura, hoped to assist in the creation of a republic that would be politically democratic and cautiously reformist, yet sensitive to conservative and in particular Catholic interests and feelings. Even before the end of 1931, however, it was clear that their hopes were to be frustrated. In the first place, their participation in the Provisional Government was not sufficient to prevent the passage of a constitution, and the adoption of legislative plans, more radical, and in particular more anti-clerical, than they were able to tolerate. This drove them to resign from the government; Maura went into the political wilderness where he was to play the role of republican Cassandra, while Alcalá Zamora was elevated into the presidency of the Republic, a post important in the creation and demolition of cabinets but of little direct executive or policy-making importance. Their political party, the Liberal Republican Right, split into two smaller, highly personalist parties, Alcalá Zamora's Progressives and Maura's Conservatives; these, along with other conservative groups like the Liberal Democrats of Melquiades Álvarez, operated during the Republic as coteries of individuals, weak in genuine popular support and achieving their very limited electoral successes through a combination of clientelism and coat-tailing.

Conservative republicanism fell between two stools. On the one hand its identification with Catholicism, and even with the old regime, alienated many convinced republicans of otherwise moderate temper. On the other hand it was too identified with an anti-clerical republic, and insufficiently ostentatious in its own Catholicism, to win the loyalties either of clergy or, in large enough numbers, of Catholic laity. The root of the problem was the inability of conservative republicans to penetrate, much less take over, the complex network of organizations – Catholic Action, the CNCA, the ACNP, etc. – within which so many Catholics were enmeshed. It was this Catholic and traditionalist subculture that was to provide the more successful political parties of social conservatism with their foundations.

The rapid failure of Catholic republicanism was accompanied by the more gradual rise and fall of another possible vehicle for the republicanization of social conservatism, the Radical Party.[15] By 1931 the Radical Party, the self-styled 'historic' republican party of Spain, had already left its genuinely 'radical' past behind it. During 1931–2 it admitted as members numerous pragmatic ex-monarchists, notably in the business sector, and established itself as the main party of *republican* opposition to the governing left. In November 1933 it won an electoral success which made it the principal focus of political power for the next two years. In 1935–6, however, the Radical Party's attempt to become a cross-class, republican, conservative party collapsed in ruins. Its populist rhetoric proved insufficient to retain a once considerable working-class base as its new social constituency pushed it rightwards. At the same time, the territory of Catholic traditionalism was closed to it by virtue of its republicanism and residual anti-clericalism. It was increasingly discredited owing to the personal corruption of leading figures, and was ultimately torn apart owing to its political alliance, during 1934–5, with a new mass party of non-republican Catholicism, the Confederación Española de Derechas Autónomas (CEDA).

For a century before the coming of the Republic, the chief political standard-bearer of Catholic-traditionalist opposition to Spanish liberalism had been Carlism. The collapse of the Alfonsine monarchy and the advent of a radical and anti-clerical regime abruptly reversed Carlism's decline, and from the outset the movement constituted an important strand of right-wing, Catholic antagonism to the Republic. The growth and territorial expansion of Carlism's political organization, the Comunión Tradicionalista, from late 1931 was remarkable. With its lively youth wing and its paramilitary Requeté, the movement recruited tens of thousands of Spaniards attracted by an extreme, potentially violent alternative to the republic.[16]

Doctrinally speaking, Carlism was certainly not 'fascist' in any serious sense of the word. Carlist doctrine in the 1930s was most clearly set out by its leading ideologist, Víctor Pradera, in his book *El Estado Nuevo* ('The New State') (1935). In addition to its support for the restoration (or, more precisely, *'instauración'*) of the Carlist branch of the Spanish Bourbons, Carlism in the immediate pre-civil war years was notable for its vocal defence of the Church's role in Spanish life, and in particular in the spheres of education, culture and opinion-making, and its advocacy of administrative devolution. Since the late nineteenth century Carlism had also absorbed social-Catholic ideas, and now envisaged the setting up of a corporate state held together by unanimous but voluntary religious belief, and lacking political parties, class conflict and much of the apparatus of the modern bureaucratic state. Given the conditions then prevailing in Spain this was obviously a utopian vision; social conflict, after all, could be either rendered unnecessary or, alternatively, silenced, only through the erection and operation of a powerful coercive state of some form or other. However, anti-liberalism and increasingly, in the circumstances of the 1930s, anti-socialism were so intense in Carlist minds that a latent authoritarianism always underlay this idealized conception of a decentralized, paternalistic arcadia. At the same time it has to be recognized that the 'official' Carlism of the movement's elites was often at variance with the simpler sentiments of the rank and file, whose peasant and petty bourgeois members found it possible to combine bitter hostility to the Republic and the left with a populist hatred of excessive wealth.

Not even a hint of such contradictions troubled the rival monarchist cause, Alfonsism. Before 1923 most active supporters of the monarchy of Alfonso XII and Alfonso XIII were, naturally enough, 'liberals': that is, they accepted a pluralist society and the parliamentary system as operative in the Spain of their day. As already stated, however, the liberalism of many monarchists had always been contingent rather than passionate, and a minority had always been susceptible to the neo-traditionalism of a Menéndez Pelayo, the temptation of praetorianism, or the 'modern' authoritarian ideas associated with Maurism. Maurism proved a crossroads for many monarchists: some gravitating thereafter towards conservative republicanism, others passing via the dictatorship into the authoritarian camp.

The fall of the monarchy reinforced the latter process, not least since it could be seen as vindicating time-worn Carlist arguments that, in Spain at any rate, monarchy and liberalism were ultimately incompatible principles. Although few of the mainly well-heeled potentates of Alfonsism were likely to find the plebeian raucousness of an Italian-style fascist *movement* personally appealing, during the dictatorship and the Republic many came to be attracted to selected aspects of the Italian fascist *regime*, and to the idea of introducing an appropriately adapted version of it in Spain. If, early in the Republic, the principal influence upon the political and intellectual leaders of Alfonsism was still Catholic traditionalism, as the months passed it was increasingly blended with that of foreign authoritarian examples: Action Française, Portuguese Integralism and above all Italian fascism.

Alfonsism during the 1930s, it must be stressed, was not so much a true political party as a privileged persons' pressure group: a clique of individual politicians, intellectuals, landowners and businessmen, many of whom had traditionally been close to the centre of power and who, unlike Alcalá Zamora and Miguel Maura, had rejected the tempting embrace of republicanism when the monarchy's glow began to dim. Under the Second Republic, Alfonsism never acquired a mass following; its party, Renovación Española, founded in 1933, was, a Carlist rival sneered, a 'general staff without an army'.[17] There was therefore never much likelihood of its achieving a monarchical restoration, or the introduction of any congenial regime, through the conquest of popular opinion or the development of a mass movement. Instead, Alfonsism's leaders followed a dual strategy, consisting first of an elitist attempt at 'influencing the influencers', in particular the economic oligarchy (to which many of them belonged) and the officer corps of the Spanish army, and secondly of sponsoring anti-republican conspiracy and de-stabilization.[18]

Alfonsism's failure to attract a mass following during the Second Republic is directly attributable, like that of conservative republicanism and, as we shall see, of the radical right, to the success of what in its various guises was known as 'accidentalism'. Accidentalism involved *de facto* recognition of the Republic without acceptance of its constitution, legislation, ethos or permanence. The principle, nurtured within the ACNP and propounded in the influential Catholic daily *El Debate*, took political form until early 1932 in a right-wing umbrella organization, Acción Nacional, to which unrepentant Alfonsists, and for a time some Carlists, belonged. In 1932 the organization was renamed Acción Popular; and in March 1933, with the departure of monarchist intransigents to found Renovación Española, this in turn became the political core of the CEDA. At the moment of its birth the CEDA, with three-quarters of a million members, was the largest political party Spain had yet seen. This was because, within its confederal structure, it embraced most of the sprawling social-Catholic network referred to earlier, most notably the vast CNCA.

Under the leadership of José María Gil Robles, the CEDA's official strategy involved the use of republican democracy in order to win power, and then the use of that power to transform Spain into a corporate state. The strategy was pursued with considerable success between 1933 and 1935. In November 1933 the CEDA recorded a remarkable electoral triumph, becoming the largest single party in the Cortes. For almost a year thereafter it bolstered up a series of Radical governments, tilting the balance of Spanish politics sharply to the right. In October 1934 its pressure at last won it entry into government, provoking elements of the left into rebellion at what they considered the advance of 'fascism'. The rising, most serious in the region of Asturias, was crushed; by the spring of 1935 the CEDA appeared poised for the acquisition of 'full power'.

The tactical parallel between the CEDA and Hitler's post-1923 career is evident, but a more precise – and more openly. admitted – example was provided by the Austrian Christian Social Party and its authoritarian creations the Fatherland Front and the *Ständestaat*. The kind of corporate state envisaged by Gil Robles (the son of a prominent Carlist ideologue), the CEDA's *éminence grise*, Angel Herrera, and other thinking *cedistas* was essentially Catholic-traditionalist in inspiration. *Cedistas* claimed to distrust the all-powerful modern state, whether liberal, socialist, or fascist Italian-style; the corporate state, they hoped, would be built upon consent and would ensure general harmony without undue coercion or excessive bureaucracy. Such was the theory: yet at a time when their Austrian exemplars were having recourse to all manner of coercion and repression in pursuit of what *cedistas* admitted to being similar goals, it is hardly surprising if Spanish republicans and leftists took CEDA criticisms of 'fascism' with a pinch of salt.[19]

For the handful of Spaniards seriously interested in a radical, Italian- or German-style fascism, the political transition of 1930–1 created a somewhat contradictory climate. On the one hand, the advent of an unprecedentedly open democracy promised the appearance of sharpened political and social conflicts amid which radicalized, altogether more extreme forms of rightism might, in the European climate of the 1930s, be expected to blossom. On the other hand, the recent discrediting and collapse of a dictatorship with Italianate borrowings and fascist fringes appeared to dull the bloom of dictatorship and fascism in general. Moreover, even if a mood of nostalgia for the days of dictatorship were to seize the Spanish middle classes, it was more likely to focus on the army than on a putative fascism.

Either way, movements of the self-consciously radical right failed to flourish until the critical months of early 1936. The Partido Nacionalista Español (PNE), founded in 1930 by a bellowing Valencian neurologist, José María Albiñana, superimposed fascist trappings on a programme combining rabid nationalism with Catholic traditionalism. Despite the early publicity attracted by its paramilitary 'legionaries', the PNE never commanded mass support, or much support at all outside its home-base of Burgos. More calculatingly radical were the Juntas de Ofensiva Nacional Sindicalista (JONS), founded in October 1931 through the fusion of two smaller groups, led by Ramiro Ledesma and Onésimo Redondo and based respectively in Madrid and the Old Castilian city of Valladolid. The JONS were clearly and frankly fascist in their plebeianism, their hostility to a traditional establishment with which they had few organizational or personal ties, and their acceptance of political violence. Their 'national syndicalism', resembling that of Edmondo Rossoni and the Italian fascist 'left' and clearly intended to attract the working class and peasantry, placed them squarely on the radical right. Thanks mainly to the influence of the devout Redondo, however, they also displayed a characteristically Hispanic respect for Catholicism. Whilst prospering slightly more than the PNE, the JONS nevertheless remained irrelevant to the mainstream of Spanish politics in the early years of the Second Republic.[20]

Another strand of Spanish fascism was slower to take shape. Falange Española, founded in October 1933, was the fruit of sporadic discussions concerning the foundation of a Spanish fascist party which, almost since the Republic's birth, had been taking place in circles much closer to the old political establishment and social elite than those occupied by the JONS.[21] The Falange, leadership of which was quickly assumed by the son of the late dictator, José Antonio Primo de Rivera, adopted a 'neither right nor left' posture, hostile both to the organized left and to unrestrained capitalism, secularist and ultra-nationalistic. Together with a vague commitment to modernization and 'productivism', it also, like the rest of the right, paid homage to rural, peasant values. Although José Antonio's social connections guaranteed the Falange considerable publicity, it too failed to achieve a quick take-off, and in the spring of 1934 fused with the similarly languishing JONS to form what then became

Spain's sole significant fascist party, Falange Española de las JONS. This new version of the Falange increased its support somewhat during the politically polarized years 1934–5, yet neither to a politically significant degree nor among a particularly varied social constituency. A movement led by *señoritos* ('gents') and supported disproportionately by the sons of the wealthy, not surprisingly its radical rhetoric cut little ice with the populace at large.[22]

Radical fascism, as represented by the JONS, the Falange and FE de las JONS, had thus made little impact in Spain as 1936 opened. The explanation for this, however, lies not so much, as (say) in Britain, in the moderation and commitment to democracy of political conservatism, as in the availability of alternative channels for anti-republican, or at the very least non-republican, opinion. Some pragmatic people of property, it is true, for a considerable time looked to the Radicals to protect their interests, but often with little or no commitment to the Republic – or indeed to the party itself, which many cynically abandoned in 1935–6. A minority of Castilian landowners stuck to the Agrarian Party, a rump of pre-1923 monarchical liberalism which eventually accepted the Republic, and in Catalonia businessmen and landowners remained attached to the region's own conservative party, the Lliga Catalana. For most social conservatives, however, and in particular for the rural landlords of Castile, the latifundists of Andalusia and Extremadura, and the prosperous peasantry of Valencia, it was the CEDA which seemed to offer them what they needed: the prospect at the very least of power within the Republic, and every likelihood of the Republic's eventually being transformed into a more congenial regime in which the left would be silenced and traditional cultural and religious values restored to their proper place. Those unwilling to compromise their monarchist principles and loyalties might cling to Renovación Española or to Carlism, but out-and-out 'fascism' seemed to have little to offer.

One significant qualification does need to be entered at this point. Among the Alfonsine monarchists of Renovación Española, many of whom knew José Antonio Primo de Rivera personally, and some of whom had collaborated with him during 1930–1 in an ephemeral authoritarian-monarchist party, Unión Monárquica Española, there existed for a time a certain patronizing benevolence towards the Falange. In 1933, for example, one of Renovación Española's neo-traditionalist intellectuals, Pedro Sáinz Rodríguez, helped José Antonio develop the Falange's programme, and in 1934 the Renovación Española leader, Goicoechea, agreed to help finance the struggling Falange. In each case the understanding was that the Falange would refrain from making life difficult for the Alfonsine cause.[23] Renovación's monarchists, understandably in view of the Falange's weakness during 1933–5, saw it not as a serious competitor, much less a possible threat, but as a tool for accomplishing the paramilitary and terroristic de-stabilization of the Republic. This was a role which the Falange was indeed to play in 1935–6, although the outcome proved to be not quite the immediate restoration that its monarchist patrons had had in mind.

Parallel with Renovación Española's attempts to use the Falange for its own purposes, Alfonsine monarchism was undergoing a species of 'fascistization' itself. The first signs of such a trajectory had, of course, been visible during the Primo de Rivera dictatorship, but had then gathered momentum via organizations such as Unión Monárquica and, with the coming of the Republic, the influential intellectual 'think-tank', Acción Española.[24] Especially from 1934, as the influence of the ambitious and tough-minded José Calvo Sotelo began to tell within the monarchist ranks, Renovación Española fell prey to a frankly authoritarian, statist brand of corporatism.[25] It is in areas such as this that the quest for rigour in the use of the word 'fascism' risks becoming self-defeating. As a party or movement of opposition, neither Renovación Española nor its attempt at creating a broader base in 1934–6, the Bloque Nacional, bore much resemblance to the Italian Fascist movement of 1919–22.[26] If anything, their spirit, rhetoric and programme were much closer to those of the Italian Nationalist Association prior to its fusion with the Fascist Party in 1923. However, what inspired them was not the radicalism of Italian fascism's opposition phase, so much as what they grasped were certain essential characteristics of the Italian Fascist regime – characteristics, moreover, which owed much to the Nationalist contribution to fascism: its reverence for the state, concessions to established elites, commitment to a directed economy, etc. In other words, what the monarchist right was seeking was to achieve the 'benefits' of a fascist regime without the need for a radical-fascist mass movement.

Fascist influences were also apparent within the CEDA and the Carlist Comunión Tradicionalista, whilst taking different forms. In the former, there can be little question that authoritarian tendencies, constantly struggling with Christian Democratic ones, were both more powerful and more successful than might otherwise have been the case owing to the frank admiration for Mussolini and even Hitler that infected CEDA ranks. Most of those *cedistas* who bothered to think about it rejected Nazi racism and the extreme statism of both dictatorships, but others worried little about such details. Within the CEDA youth movement, the Juventud de Acción Popular (JAP), the influence of fascism was inescapable: representing, it is true, less a considered acceptance either of radical-rightist ideas or of the detailed realities of the Italian Fascist or Nazi regimes, than at least a partial surrender to fascist 'style', youth worship and taste for violence.[27]

To a more limited extent, something similar occurred within Carlism. Elements of the Carlist youth, especially among students, embraced socially radical ideas – or at least mouthed socially radical rhetoric – which combined violent anti-leftism with excited hostility towards the social oligarchy influential within Renovación and the CEDA. Some of the older generation, especially those with closest contacts with their Alfonsist opposite numbers, and perhaps sensing the likely impracticability of Carlist devolutionary ideas, displayed something of the Alfonsists' admiration for foreign fascist authoritarianism.[28] For all that, there nevertheless survived within Carlism a powerful resistance to centralized authority which, notwithstanding Carlist anti-leftism and acceptance of violence, on balance places the movement in a different category from fascism.

The support of so many Spanish conservatives for the CEDA represented not their rejection of an essentially authoritarian resolution of Spain's social and political conflicts, but a preference for reaching some such goal by gradual and, if possible, peaceful means. In contrast, the rest of the right offered 'catastrophism': the conviction that the Republic could be overthrown only by violence. In terms of the kind of state that it was hoped would replace the Republic in its existing form, *cedistas*, strongly influenced by Spain's Catholic-traditionalist heritage, preferred the 'Austrian' model; Carlists (officially at least) a traditional, decentralized arcadia; and Falangists and Alfonsists their respective interpretations of Italian fascism.

For the ostensibly gradualist majority of Spanish conservatives, the problem was always what course to adopt should the 'accidentalist' strategy fail and 'full power' not pass peacefully to the CEDA. In 1935–6 the nightmare came true, as the CEDA first was cast out of government and then, in February 1936, lost a general election to the Republican-Leftist Popular Front. With its strategy in ruins, the party quickly began to disintegrate from the base upwards. As it did so, both the Carlist movement and, more particularly and sensationally, the Falange expanded. This phenomenon is highly significant to the present analysis. The events of spring 1936 illustrate the relative unimportance of *ideological* nuances on the Spanish right, in comparison with strategic and stylistic ones. Much of the already *fascisant* JAP now switched to the Falange, not for doctrinal reasons but because of the latter's unambiguous acceptance of the violence that thousands of *japistas* now became convinced was necessary; some JAP sections and many individual *japistas* became Carlists for essentially the same reason, the difference in their course generally reflecting local conditions rather than a considered choice between Carlist traditionalism and Falangist fascism.[29]

Many of those conservatives, especially rich and influential ones, who still in 1936 resisted the embrace of the extreme right as embodied in the Falange and the Comunión Tradicionalista, placed their faith in the military and some not clearly identified form of authoritarian future. For them the man of the hour, until his assassination in July 1936, was no longer the has-been Gil Robles, but the ruthless 'monarcho–fascist' Calvo Sotelo. Given the growth of the extreme right in 1936, it was only in part fear of radicalism that continued to hold back many conservatives from an Italian-style accommodation with 'revolutionary' fascism. More decisive was the continued presence in the Spanish political kaleidoscope of a safer alternative: an army which, it was reasonable to hope, might carry out the *negative* task of fascism – that is, overthrow the Popular Front government and, in any recognizable form, the Republic itself – without fascism's worrying 'revolutionary' overtones. In July 1936, the hope was fulfilled.

The military rebellion of 17–18 July 1936, and the civil war which it unleashed, decisively influenced the conservative–fascist relationship in Spain. The military leadership, concentrated from the end of September 1936 in General Franco, from the start had the unquestioning support of the great majority of those influential conservatives who until recently had looked to the CEDA or even the Radicals to protect their interests. In the insurgent or Nationalist zone, normal politics were now at an end. With the CEDA reduced to shreds and Alfonsism functioning as an admittedly influential politico-military clique, two mass parties emerged, the Carlists and the Falange. Both, in the new climate, continued their recent expansion, the Falange at a phenomenal rate.[30] By the end of 1936, however, all the Falange's first-rank leaders were dead, either killed by leftist militia or, in José Antonio's case, 'legally' executed by order of the Republican authorities. With rival factions struggling for the party leadership, the Falange was in no shape to make a serious bid for power within Nationalist Spain. Indeed, it was unable to offer significant resistance when, in April 1937, Franco forcibly fused it with the Carlists and the rest of the Spanish right to form under his leadership a single political organization, Falange Española Tradicionalista y de las JONS (FET).[31]

The experience of the Falange between February 1936 and April 1937 invites comparison with that of Italian fascism during its rise to power. At the start of 1936 the Falange was still a marginal element in Spanish politics. After the February election, despite its activities for much of the time being banned and its leaders jailed, it grew as the 'established' right crumbled. From the start of the civil war its militants played an important part in physically crushing the left within the Nationalist zone, and the movement expanded still further through the recruitment mainly of conservative Spaniards won over by its ruthlessness, but also that of leftists desperate for self-preservation and organizational protection now that their own organizations had been destroyed. In April 1937 it united formally with the rest of the right – Carlist traditionalists, the

133

'monarcho–fascists' of Renovación Española and the residues of the CEDA – to form the monopolistic party of a state many would regard as 'fascist'. The parallel with Italian fascism's rise from radicalism and obscurity, via anti-leftist *squadrismo* and ideological de-radicalization, to compromise with the establishment, the acquisition of power, and fusion with Nationalism and the clerical right, is clear. In both cases there exists a coincidence between, on the one hand, numerical expansion and the achievement of power, and, on the other, a dilution of radicalism and gradual accommodation with conservative forces.

This is not to deny the existence of important differences. The relationships of Franco and Mussolini with their single parties were quite different, as were the actual processes of fusion. The role of the FET, or Movimiento as it came more loosely to be known, within Franco's Spain was designed from the outset to be instrumental and subordinate to leader and state, whereas the reduction of the Italian Fascist party to a similar role was a lengthy and less total process. As was to be expected, the influence of Catholicism within Franco's Spain was more central than it could ever be in Fascist Italy. When all is said and done, however, both regimes were alliances of the radical and the conservative right in which the latter more than held its own.

If 'fascism' is defined in terms of the highly self-conscious, not to say self-regarding, radicalism of those who founded, led and held office within interwar radical-rightist movements, then it is inescapably clear that before the spring of 1936 there were few fascists in Spain. The reasons why up to that time few social conservatives were attracted to the JONS, the Falange or the fused FE de las JONS are unsensational. Both for the wealthy and for the peasants and the provincial petty bourgeoisie, the rhetoric, values and symbols of Catholic traditionalism, employed by the CEDA and the Carlists, and more ambiguously by their youth movements and by Renovacíon Española, were simply more familiar than outright 'fascism' and bore sufficient promise of a congenial future to deter them from flirting with the unfamiliar. Moreover the CEDA, for two years at least, seemed likely to succeed. The CEDA's electoral failure in February 1936, and the coming to office of a Popular Front government, transformed this situation.

Since it cannot be disputed that the great majority of those who flocked to the Falange after February 1936 had previously been conservative in socioeconomic, religious and cultural terms, even if in many cases reactionary or 'conservative-revolutionary' politically, this development raises interesting issues concerning the relationship betwen conservatism and fascism. Why, in certain circumstances, do conservatives 'become' fascists? Stress upon the ideological and programmatic differences between conservatism and fascism suggests a process of conversion based upon acceptance of ideas previously rejected, yet it is difficult to accept such a thing in this case. It is straining credulity to imagine thousands of middle-class, mainly youngish Spaniards agonizing over the compatibility or otherwise between the social encyclicals of the papacy and the Falange's Twenty-Seven Points – or that significantly different worries preoccupied those who, rejecting the CEDA, opted not for the Falange but for the Carlists. Rather the choice was a much simpler one which suggests a stress upon style, tactics and function rather than on ideology and programmatic detail. Spanish conservatives, previously content either with the gradual road towards authoritarianism represented by the CEDA, or even with the hope of a conservative republic offered by the Radical Party, opted during the spring of 1936 for the violent route represented by the Falange, the Carlists or, of course, the military rebels of July.

This is not to say that the radicalism, totalitarianism, etc., of fascist militants is unimportant or insincere, or that the strains within enlarged fascist movements or actual regimes between 'fascist' zealots and 'conservative' *arrivistes* are insignificant either. What the Spanish case nevertheless does suggest is that to define fascism purely or primarily in terms of its ostentatiously 'radical' origins is actually to define only part and not all of a complex process involving the pursuit, and less commonly the winning and exercising, of power. Fascism does not cease to be fascism when, as in Spain in 1936–7, it broadens its base to include unabashed conservatives, or makes the compromises with established forces necessary to win and hold power. Those Spanish leftists who recognized the shallowness and contradictoriness of Falangist demagogy, who saw the various strands of the Spanish right as brothers under the skin, and who feared for the future of freedom whichever emerged dominant, knew reality when they saw it.

NOTES

1 S. G. Payne, 'Spanish fascism in comparative perspective', in H. A. Turner (ed.), *Reappraisals of Fascism* (New York, 1975), pp. 142–69.
2 For an introduction to nineteenth-century Carlism, see M. Blinkhorn, *Carlismo y contrarrevolución en España, 1931–1939* (Barcelona, 1979), pp. 15–68.
3 M. Blinkhorn, 'Ideology and schism in Spanish traditionalism, 1874–1931', *Iberian Studies*, vol. I, no. 1 (1972).
4 See Frances Lannon, *Privilege, Persecution and Prophecy. The Catholic Church in Spain, 1875–1875* (Oxford, 1987), pp. 146–69; J. J. Castillo, *Propietarios muy pobres. Sobre la subordinación política del pequeño campesino. La Confederación Nacional Católico-Agraria, 1917–1942* (Madrid, 1979); J. Cuesta Bustillo, *Sindicalismo católico agrario en España (1917–1919)* (Madrid, 1978); J. Andrés-Gallego, *Pensamiento y acción social de la Iglesia en España* (Madrid, 1984).
5 On 1917 see J. A. Lacomba, *La crisis española de 1917* (Madrid, 1970); also C. Boyd, *Praetorian Politics in Liberal Spain* (Chapel Hill, NC, 1979).
6 M. Blinkhorn, 'Spain: the "Spanish Problem" and the imperial myth', *Journal of Contemporary History*, vol. 15, no. 1 (January 1980), pp. 5–27; J. Varela Ortega,

'Aftermath of splendid disaster: Spanish politics before and after the Spanish-American War of 1898', *Journal of Contemporary History*, vol. 15, no. 2 (April 1980), pp. 317–44. The literature on 1898 and regenerationism is extensive; for a useful analysis see H. Ramsden, *The 1898 Movement in Spain. Towards a Reinterpretation* (Manchester, 1974).

7   On Maurism, see J. Tusell and J. Avilés, *La derecha española contemporánea. Sus orígenes: el maurismo* (Madrid, 1986), esp. pp. 159–218. For first-hand accounts, see J. Gutiérrez-Ravé, *Yo fuí un joven maurista*, 3rd edn (Madrid, n.d.), esp. pp. 159 ff. and A. Ossorio y Gallardo, *La España de mi vida* (Madrid, 1974), pp. 55–70.

8   Early Spanish Christian Democracy is covered in O. Alzaga Villaamil, *La primera democracia cristiana en España* (Barcelona, 1973); see also J. Tusell, *Historia de la democracia cristiana en España*, I: *Los antecedentes. La CEDA y la II República* (Madrid, 1974), pp. 104–19.

9   The traditionalist and potential fascist 'constituencies' are examined in M. Blinkhorn, 'The Iberian states', in D. Mühlberger (ed.), *The Social Basis of European Fascist Movements* (London, New York and Sydney, 1987), pp 320–48.

10 S. G. Payne, *Politics and the Military in Modern Spain* (Stanford, Calif., 1967) provides the most comprehensive general account of the Spanish army's political role in the nineteenth and early twentieth centuries.

11 For a detailed and thought-provoking analysis of the Primo de Rivera regime, see S. Ben-Ami, *Fascism from Above. The Dictatorship of Primo de Rivera in Spain, 1923–1930* (Oxford, 1983).

12 S. Ben-Ami, 'The forerunners of Spanish fascism: Unión Patriótica and Unión Monárquica', in M. Blinkhorn (ed.), *Spain in Conflict 1931–1939. Democracy and its Enemies* (London, 1986), pp. 103–32.

13 On the role of economic elites under the Republic, see especially M. Cabrera, *La patronal ante la II República. Organizaciones y estrategia 1931–1936* (Madrid, 1983).

14 Conservative republicanism lacks a satisfactory scholarly study, but see N. Alcalá-Zamora, *Memorias* (Barcelona, 1977), esp. pp. 126–202, and M. Maura, *Así cayó Alfonso XIII* (Barcelona, 1962).

15 For a recent analysis of the Radicals under the Republic, see N. Townson, 'Algunas consideraciones sobre el proyecto "republicano" del Partido Radical', in M. Tuñón de Lara (ed.), *La II República española. Bienio rectificador y Frente Popular, 1934–1936* (Madrid, 1988), pp. 53–88; also O. Ruiz Manjón, *El Partido Republicano Radical 1908–1936* (Madrid, 1976), pp. 171–600.

16 M. Blinkhorn, *Carlism and Crisis in Spain, 1931–1939* (Cambridge, 1975), provides a detailed analysis of Carlism under the Republic.

17 ibid., p. 200.

18 P. Preston, 'Alfonsine monarchism and the coming of the Spanish Civil War', in Blinkhorn (ed.), *Spain in Conflict*, pp. 160–82. The words 'influencing the influencers' are Hilaire Belloc's.

19 The most complete study of the CEDA is J. R. Montero, *La CEDA. El catolicismo social y político en la II República*, 2 vols (Madrid, 1977); see also Tusell, *Democracia cristiana*, I, pp. 139 ff. R. A. H. Robinson, *The Origins of Franco's Spain. The Right, the Republic and Revolution* (Newton Abbot, 1970), concludes that the CEDA was a potentially Christian Democratic party pushed rightward by the conduct of the left; P. Preston, *The Coming of the Spanish Civil War. Reform, Reaction and Revolution in the Second Republic 1931–1936* (London, 1978), regards the CEDA as intrinsically reactionary and authoritarian in character.

20 On the JONS and the early history of Spanish fascism, see S. G. Payne, *Falange. A History of Spanish Fascism* (Stanford, Calif. and London, 1962), pp. 10–20; S. M. Ellwood, *Prietas las filas. Historia de Falange Española, 1933–1983* (Barcelona, 1984), pp. 25–34; S. Ellwood, 'Falange Española, 1933–9: from fascism to Francoism', in Blinkhorn (ed.), *Spain in Conflict*, pp. 206–11.

21 Ellwood, *Prietas las filas*, pp. 34–7; Payne, *Falange*, pp. 21–37.

22 Blinkhorn, 'Iberian states', pp. 332–7.

23 P. Sáinz Rodríguez, *Testimonio y recuerdos* (Barcelona, 1978), pp. 220, 375–6.

24 R. Morodo, *Los orígenes ideológicos del franquismo: Acción Española* (Madrid, 1985); on *Unión Monárquica* see Ben-Ami, 'Forerunners of Spanish fascism', in Blinkhorn (ed.), *Spain in Conflict*, pp. 114–26.
25 Preston, 'Alfonsine monarchism', in Blinkhorn (ed.), *Spain in Conflict*, pp. 170–9.
26 R. A. H. Robinson, 'Calvo Sotelo's *Bloque Nacional* and its manifesto', *University of Birmingham Historical Journal*, vol. X, no. 2 (1966).
27 For divergent views on the strength of 'fascist' tendencies in the CEDA, see Robinson, *Origins of Franco's Spain*, pp. 134–5, 209–11 and Preston, *Coming of the Spanish Civil War, passim.*
28 Blinkhorn, *Carlism and Crisis*, pp. 171–82.
29 Ellwood, *Prietas las filas*, pp. 72–7; Blinkhorn, *Carlism and Crisis*, p. 235.
30 Ellwood, *Prietas las filas*, pp. 78–82; Blinkhorn, *Carlism and Crisis*, pp. 256–8.
31 On the Unification, see M. García Venero, *Historia de la Unificación. Falange y Requeté en 1937* (Madrid, 1970); M. Hedilla Larrey, *Manuel Hedilla. Testimonio* (Barcelona, 1972), pp. 219–22; and, from a Carlist point of view, J. del Burgo, *Conspiración y guerra civil* (Madrid and Barcelona, 1970), pp. 743–822.

8

Populism and parasitism: the Falange and the Spanish establishment 1939–75

Paul Preston

Threatened by the reforms of the Second Republic, the Spanish right's response was obstinate and violent. However, given the initial failure of attempts to destabilize the Republic, sponsored by the patrician right, more flexible elements confronted the possibility of mobilizing popular support in defence of rightist interests. Alongside the traditional Alfonsine and Carlist monarchists there emerged the populist Catholic authoritarian party, the CEDA, and the much smaller and overtly fascist Falange Española.[1] All of these organizations threw in their lot with the army officers who organized the uprising of July 1936. The Falange started out as the weakest of them but the circumstances of the war and the external influence of the Axis powers pushed it to prominence. The mass support of the CEDA and its youth movement, the Juventud de Acción Popular (JAP), had already started to flood into the Falange in the spring of 1936. It was further swelled by wartime recruits. For three decades thereafter, even as its own ideological edge was dulled, it was to play a central role in the regime. Indeed, it was the dictatorship's identity tag in the outside world. That was hardly surprising since it was the agency which organized mass mobilizations and controlled labour relations and was also the source of the regime's lexicon, iconography and ideological paraphernalia.

The relationship of Falange Española to the other components of the Francoist coalition was complex and constantly shifting. Both the aristocratic and the upper-middle-class right saw the primordial task as the destruction of what they perceived as the threat of disorder, anti-clericalism and communism. Ties of family and class made it natural for them to turn to the army. Thereafter, the military remained the locus of real power. The contribution of the Falange was thus of a different order. With its swaggering mimicry of Axis models and its loud egalitarian rhetoric, it was privately regarded with some distaste. It was acceptable largely because of the need for cannon fodder and for the implementation of various unpleasant tasks associated with the war, not least the repression. During the civil war and the early days of the Second World War, aristocrats and fascists coexisted well enough despite their very different social backgrounds and ideological priorities. They shared a common ground of what might be termed clerical authoritarianism and a determination to win the war. They all considered themselves part of the Movimiento, the vague generic term used to denote the Nationalist cause both during and after the civil war. After all, in April 1937 they had acquiesced more or less willingly in their unification into the regime's single party, the Falange Española Tradicionalista y de las JONS (FET). The Alfonsine monarchists had agreed to the dissolution of their organization, Renovación Española, 'with great joy and pride'. The CEDA's leader, José María Gil Robles, had similarly written to Franco of 'our willing sacrifice'.[2]

Soldiers or civilians, the Nationalists were nearly all Catholics. The Falangists aside, many were also monarchists of some kind. They certainly continued to perceive themselves as primarily Falangists, Carlists, Christian Democrats or Alfonsine monarchists and to recognize each other as such. The organizations and apparatuses of their parties had gone but the interests and commitments which they represented remained.[3] Whether they defined themselves in terms of ecclesiastical, military, monarchist, Falangist or more generally Francoist loyalties, however, depended upon a constantly changing balance of ideological commitment and sheer opportunism. Accordingly, the power balance within the coalition altered over the course of the years in response to changing domestic and international circumstances.

There were a number of constant features. Military pre-eminence was only gradually reduced, remaining constant in the three service ministries. The Ministry of the Interior was always a general until 1969, when the post passed to a military lawyer. Education remained firmly Catholic territory and the Minister of Justice was a Carlist fief until 1973. It is nevertheless possible to distinguish four periods in the evolution of the Spanish right from 1939 to 1977. They correspond roughly to the so-called 'blue era' of apparent Falangist dominance between 1939 and 1945; the period of dour Christian Democrat rule between 1946 and 1957; the burst for economic modernization presided over between 1957 and 1969 by the technocrats associated with Opus Dei; and finally the break-up of the regime coalition, the factional rivalries and the eventual transition to democracy between 1969 and 1977. Periodic adjustments of ministerial personnel were always calculated in terms of a central objective – the survival of the regime. Cabinets might be retuned according to changes in international circumstances, as was the case in 1945. Changes were sometimes Franco's response to especially fierce clashes between the *familias* or political clans, and illustrated his determination to maintain the overall balance on which the regime's stability was built. Such was the case in 1942 and 1969. Ministerial reshuffles also reflected the regime's awareness of its obligation to remain sensitive to the changing internal dynamics of Spanish capitalism; thus, economic interest was behind the Cabinet changes of 1951 and 1957.

Immediately after the civil war and during the Second World War, the regime's ideological tone was set by the Falange. Largely a reflection of the external circumstance of Axis success, this also reflected the fact that the Christian Democrats of the CEDA had still not lived down their original sin, in Franco's eyes, of their 'accidentalist' coexistence with the Second Republic. The Carlists had withdrawn to their Navarrese strongholds, the more collaborationist among them satisfied with their reward of the Ministry of Justice and preferential economic status for Navarre. The royalists of Acción Española remained on the margins, suspicious of the upstart anti-oligarchical and anti-monarchical rhetoric of the pro-Axis Movimiento. Accordingly, in the eyes of the outside world, the Falange and Francoism were consubstantial. This was illusory but understandable. Falange Española Tradicionalista y de las JONS provided the structure, the name, the vocabulary and the propaganda mechanisms of the single party. Falangism, however, was only one strand of the Movimiento.

In reality, the power of the Falange was always somewhat flimsy and never equalled that of the Nazi Party in Germany or the Fascist Party in Italy. The Falange had not conquered the state through its own efforts but had ridden to power on the back of the military uprising. It had lost any autonomous dynamism when, after the unification, it allowed itself to provide the bureaucratic structure of the new Francoist state. The Falange became the arena for place-seeking, the ever-flexible rhetoric of its leaders merely a means of currying favour and gaining promotion. The goal of national-syndicalist revolution was quietly dropped in the quest for the safe billets of state functionaries. Agrarian reform and the nationalization of the banks became part of the 'pending revolution'.[4] As the leaders aged, the party atrophied in the grip of its own 'iron law of oligarchy'. The six-month internal purge of the FET which began in November 1941 was a more protracted, bloodless version of the Night of the Long Knives whose purpose was merely to reduce competition for well-paid state jobs.[5] Paradoxically, the Falange's 'corruption' helped it survive the Axis defeat. The FET was buried too deep into the structures of local and central government to be easily rooted out, and had too little autonomy or ideological bite for a purge to be necessary.[6]

The FET fulfilled a series of useful tasks for the generals who were its real godfathers. Its mass mobilizations provided the veneer of popular support. Its bureaucratic structures stifled the aspirations of the workers and peasants. Its ideologues elaborated a Spanish version of the *Führerprinzip*, the *Teoría del Caudillaje*.[7] Ultimately, however, the fact that Franco was the party's supreme chief (*Jefe Nacional*) was a constant reminder of its unending subordination. It attained a degree of political autonomy during the days of Axis success in the World War only because Franco's ambition permitted it to do so. In the last resort, it always hastened to adjust to any political shift which he inaugurated. Nevertheless, for all its tacking and trimming, it maintained its hold on the instruments of ideological hegemony until 1975 through control of the media, of the official vertical syndicates, of the sprawling bureaucracy of central and local administration. In addition to labour relations, responsibility for housing and social security also lay with the Falange. Army officers, civil servants and trade unionists were all automatically members of the FET.

Beneath the great umbrella of the Movimiento, however, real political power depended in part on wheeling and dealing and in part on the Caudillo's view of how best the survival of his power might be secured. After 1946, the burden passed to the Francoist Christian Democrats, deriving mainly from the CEDA and associated with the Catholic pressure group, the Asociación Católica Nacional de Propagandistas (ACNP). Until supplanted by the Opus Dei technocrats in 1957, the ACNP Catholics provided the regime's public legitimacy. After 1957, the technocrats presided over a process of economic modernization and worked hard to streamline the political image of the dictatorship. Thereafter, the loss of control by an ageing and infirm Caudillo combined with growing pressure from outside to overthrow the delicate balance of regime forces and open the way to a negotiated transition to democracy. Throughout the complex evolution of the regime from 1946 to 1975, the Falange remained like a resentful and obstructive octopus, its tentacles everywhere, incapable of preventing change altogether but with its capacity for disruption unimpaired. It would have suited other elements of the Francoist coalition for the Falange to disappear, but it had entrenched itself too well in every area of national life, unwilling to let go and too powerful to be pushed.

Behind the Falange's apparent dominance of the regime, there accordingly existed a constant jostling for power, restrained always by a deep sense of the common cause. It had been precisely in the cause of eradicating liberalism, socialism and communism from Spain that many on the right had acquiesced in Franco's civil war alliances with Hitler and Mussolini, some with enthusiasm, others with a certain repugnance. Many did so with a passionate appetite for the prospect of Spain's belonging to a future fascist world order. It was these latter who set the early tone of the FET. In the main young men who had joined the party in the first months of the civil war, they were anxious for Spain to join Hitler's drive for world domination. Immediately after the civil war was won, they swamped the more conservative elements.

It was in vain that the latter looked to the Caudillo to restore the monarchy. Franco, convinced as he was of the imminence of a war to restructure the world in favour of the new, dynamic fascist powers, had other priorities. The partisans of the *ancien régime* were therefore out of fashion. Obstacles were put in the way of the restoration of their press networks.[8] Frictions between them and the dominant Falangists surfaced frequently, on one occasion in 1942 leading to a challenge to a duel issued by the Falangist Miguel Primo de Rivera, brother of the party's founder, against the monarchist President of the Royal Academy, the poet José María Pemán.[9] Dissension had surfaced much earlier as a result of Falangist resentment of the role being granted to the Church in educational matters by Franco's first Education Minister, the monarchist intellectual Pedro Sáinz Rodríguez. Repelled by the Falangist campaign against him and by the totalitarian drift of Spanish politics, he requested that he be relieved of his post on 27 April 1939.[10] The trend in favour of the Falange could also be discerned behind the replacement of the monarchist General Alfredo Kindelán as head of the air force by the Falangist General Juan Yagüe in August 1939.[11]

The Second World War brought to the surface some of the monarchists' resentment towards Franco. They had considered all along that their support was conditional on the restoration of the monarchy. The Caudillo's failure to make way for a Bourbon king inclined them to favour the Allies during the Second World War. This led to incidents such as the attempted murder by Falangists of the Carlist Minister of War, General Varela, at Begoña near Bilbao on 16 August 1942.[12] Gradually, not to say imperceptibly, a minority of the dictatorship's supporters dissociated themselves from Franco while the bulk remained: Alfonsine monarchists and Carlists, Catholics and Falangists, clerics and soldiers, happily embroiled in jockeying among themselves for power. These collaborationists were confident that the regime would preserve the social order for which they had fought the civil war. Loyal Francoists, they often called themselves monarchists only to differentiate themselves from what they saw as the lower-middle-class upstarts of the Falange, with their populist rhetoric of spurious egalitarianism. They joined in the scramble for power around Franco not in order to alter the form or content of the regime but rather to have a say in how its benefits would be distributed.

The collaborationist monarchists could salve their consciences with the thought that Franco had not yet institutionalized his regime in a way which might prove an obstacle to restoration. Moreover, they could still deceive themselves that Franco was more monarchist than Francoist. After all, he had owed his rapid promotions in the army to Alfonso XIII's personal intervention. He had been a *gentilhombre de la camera del Rey* and spoke of himself as a monarchist.[13] He had been elected Nationalist head of state in 1936 by the most monarchist of the army's generals.[14] They could also take heart from the fact that the pretender, Don Juan, keeping all his options open, was in more or less regular contact with Franco through intermediaries.

Franco treated with consideration those monarchists who could com-bine nominal allegiance to the Crown with unconditional service to his own *de facto* regency.[15] Those few who actually left the circles of the regime considered themselves to be in opposition, although clearly their position was not the same as that of the defeated Republicans, who were still being shot by the hundreds or herded into labour and concentration camps. Similarly, all those who remained were not necessarily fascists. There was wide common ground between the minority of monarchist and Catholic anti-Francoists and the majority of monarchist and Catholic Francoists. They agreed, for instance, on issues of public order, religion and anti-communism. However, the aristocrats, intellectuals and royalist army officers who dabbled with opposition believed that Franco had betrayed the monarchy by failing to restore the king after the civil war. In contrast, Francoists – even proclaimed monarchists – believed that the Bourbon monarchy should not be restored as of right but installed as a new, Francoist monarchy, only after the Caudillo had wrought necessary political changes and probably only after his death. Nevertheless, Francoists right across the spectrum were always anxious to secure for the dictatorship the legitimizing power of the monarchy. Their aim was thus to preserve links with Don Juan de Borbón and at the same time neutralize him. It was in this sense that the ultra-conservative General Juan Vigón, Yagüe's successor as head of the air force, told the pretender to 'trust in Franco like a father' and concentrate on collecting stamps or coins.[16]

Immediately after the civil war, the most serious rivalry to Falangist hegemony within the Movimiento came from ACNP Catholics, known as *propagandistas*, led by the ex-*cedista* and president of Catholic Action, Alberto Martín Artajo.[17] Relations between church and state were some-what strained until 1942. The ecclesiastical hierarchy was suspicious of the atheistic rhetoric of the Falange. The Falangists were jealous of Catholic domination of the press, education and even banking, and of the Church's political influence. Many *propagandistas* held key posts in banks and in the government holding company, the Instituto Nacional de Industria (INI). Like the Falange, the ACNP also provided a high proportion of provincial civil governors, the Spanish equivalent of French or Italian prefects.[18] They controlled seven daily newspapers and in 1939 established the influential research institute, the Consejo Superior de Investigaciones Científicas (CSIC), in collusion with the Opus Dei. The CSIC was ruled over by one of the most reliable of the Movimiento Catholics, the ex-CEDA deputy for Murcia, José Ibáñez Martín, since 1939 Franco's Minister of Education. Not surprisingly, after the crumbling of all hopes of Axis victory and the consequent decline of Falangist influence, the Catholic presence in the circles of power grew.[19]

By mid-1943, with Germany suffering reverses on the Russian front and the Allies beginning their march up the Italian peninsula, many Francoists assumed that the Caudillo would soon have to abandon power. The fall of Mussolini sent panic waves through the Francoist hierarchy. The news was kept out of the press but copies were circulated of a graphic account in a letter from the secretary to the Spanish ambassador in Rome. The ambassador, the Falangist Raimundo Fernández Cuesta, was severely rebuked by Franco for permitting an act of defeatism. The Caudillo vehemently asserted that there was no analogy between what was happening in Italy and conditions in Spain.[20] In the summer, twenty-five prominent members of Franco's Cortes, including five ex-ministers, petitioned him to restore the monarchy. More crucially, a group of senior generals, including most of those who had bestowed power upon him in Salamanca in 1936, called on him to withdraw. Franco was facing a situation similar to that which preceded Mussolini's fall. With characteristic astuteness, he spoke separately to all those involved, leading them to believe that he would soon accede to their request.[21] With Don Juan stepping up his involvement in Spanish politics, it was hardly surprising that Franco later referred to the period between late 1943 and early 1944 as 'the most grave moments that we suffered in the war'.[22]

Symptomatic of this was the fact that in October 1944 the Minister of Education, Ibáñez Martín, rejoined the ACNP in an attempt to dissociate himself from his earlier strident fascism, a significant move by a minister who had been in government for five years and was to remain there for another seven. The Caudillo's correspondence with Don Juan indicated the growing distance between them, although even the latter, in order to protect his dynastic interests, could not afford to break entirely with the Franco regime. This inhibition was reflected in his eventual reluctant decision to have his son Juan Carlos educated in Spain. Although the United States suspended oil exports to Spain in January 1944, and the fragility of the regime was manifest, the monarchist opposition had little power. Monarchist dissidents merely assumed that Franco could be forced by their pressure or, at worst, by foreign intervention to accept the restoration and abandon power. Neither the monarchists nor the left, however, were ever able to convince foreign powers that their plans for the succession to the dictator could avoid civil war and protect the West's economic interests. Franco in contrast had both a measure of popular support and control of a powerful state apparatus. These reserves of strength remained, even at the Caudillo's moments of supposedly greatest weakness. Out of fear of the return of a vengeful left, all the forces of the right clung to Franco.

The limits of monarchist opposition to the regime were exposed by the publication of Don Juan's address to the nation, the so-called 'Lausanne

'Manifesto', on 19 March 1945. Inspired by the Allies' restoration of the Italian king, it called on Franco to abandon power. Monarchists sat tight, waiting to see if Franco would leave. Although certainly concerned, Franco kept his head, following the advice of his *éminence grise*, Luis Carrero Blanco, to 'hang on for dear life'. He was heard to comment that 'those of us who play no part in politics are worried about the international offensive against Spain'.[23] In the postwar government reshuffle of 18 July 1945, Franco recognized, as always on Carrero Blanco's advice, changes in the configuration of both international and domestic forces. By inviting the ACNP leader, Martín Artajo, to join the government as Minister of Foreign Affairs, he hoped to present a Christian Democratic image more in tune with developments elsewhere in Europe. Although a monarchist, Martín Artajo was a typically pragmatic accidentalist, less concerned with a monarchical restoration than with reducing the Falangist influence within the regime and advancing Catholic interests.[24]

Catholic readiness to move away from fascism represented a desire to cast off the burdens of Falangism while retaining the regime's essential authoritarianism in a more acceptable guise. Again, as with the monarchists, a truly progressive tendency would emerge among the regime Catholics only decades later and after a painful political evolution which would culminate in open opposition. After 1945, the pragmatic rightists who, despite their discomfort at the Falange's anti-oligarchical fascist rhetoric, had been content to be part of the Movimiento in its most pro-Axis phase, proclaimed themselves monarchist, Carlist, Christian Democrat or just plain Catholic. To their relief, the regime made serious efforts after 1945 to sever its links with a fascist past. A pseudo-constitution was elaborated, in the form of the 1947 *Ley de Sucesión*. Through the device of plebiscites, the dictatorship was dressed up as 'organic democracy'. The 'fascist' elements were firmly played down and openly embraced only by groups of zealots who kept their opinions discreetly behind the walls of the Falange.[25]

The feebleness of the ACNP Catholics' commitment to change was illustrated by the fate of Martín Artajo's extremely conservative political plans. These proposed a 'traditional monarchy'; representative bodies of economic and moral interests and a special freedom of expression, limited to 'diffusion of the truth and certainly not of error'. However, at the Cabinet meeting at which his ideas were to be discussed, a hostile atmosphere ensured his silence.[26] Franco nevertheless used this 'progressive' tendency to promote his regime abroad, particularly in Rome. Martín Artajo as Foreign Minister could project a positive image of Francoist Spain. In September 1946, the youthful and urbane Catholic Joaquín Ruiz Giménez was appointed Director of the Instituto de Cultura Hispánica, a post involving much foreign travel. The 'Catholic' family was indefatigable in its proselytizing for the regime at home and abroad.

Their collaboration was to bear eventual fruit in 1953, in the shape of the Concordat with the Vatican and the Bases agreement with the United States.

In fact, the moment of greatest danger for Franco had passed by the end of 1946. Don Juan had to choose. He could emphasize his democratic credentials at the expense of dialogue with the regime, in order to facilitate joint action with the moderate left. Any rapprochement with the left, however, carried with it the certainty that, even if Franco were to go, the monarchy would still have to be subjected to a plebiscite. Aware of King Umberto's unpleasant experience in the Italian referendum of June 1946, Don Juan was reluctant to commit himself to such an option. Moreover, with the Cold War turning Franco's anti-communism into an asset, he was tempted to maintain good relations with the Caudillo for the short-term benefits that might accrue to his family and his supporters.

Don Juan's tactical indecisiveness at this time was actually a reflection of his essential political weakness. The introduction of Franco's Ley de Sucesión on 30 March 1947 brutally exposed the Caudillo's perception of Don Juan's impotence. Inspired by Martín Artajo, the law represented the apogee of the Catholic attempt to de-Falangize and legitimize the Movimiento. It proclaimed Spain to be a kingdom, whose head of state for life was Francisco Franco. He could nominate to the Cortes at any moment a king or a regent to succeed himself. Don Juan was warned by Carrero Blanco of the imminent announcement, but only in the afternoon of the day on which it was made on Spanish radio.[27] Incensed by this discourtesy and the indefinite postponement of a restoration, he issued on 7 April 1947 the so-called Estoril Manifesto, rejecting the law as a 'constitutional fiction' contrary to the principles of monarchy.[28] It was an empty gesture. Once the regime's propaganda machinery went into operation, the referendum on the law provided a massive popular endorsement.

The *Juanistas* were in disarray. Collaborationist monarchists, outside the Falange but none the less part of the Movimiento, were beginning to prosper and therefore had less and less reason to risk the dangers of opposition. The law gave them the excuse they needed to relinquish even token opposition. *Juanista* opposition was being neutralized and the embarrassment of Falangism shoved into a corner. With the Church and the army remaining loyal, the Francoist coalition was intact. The hour of the loyalist Catholics had struck. Even Falangists hung on docilely, reluctant to relinquish access to the spoils system. The only cloud on the horizon was the regime's inability to resolve the growing economic and social problems which it faced. That would soon oblige Franco to make further changes which would in turn lead eventually to the break-up of his regime. Otherwise, for the present all seemed well.

The United States had already begun the process of bringing Franco's Spain into the Western sphere of influence. Moreover, Don Juan had effectively acknowledged the way things were moving in the Caudillo's favour. While the more anti-Francoist members of his privy council were negotiating with the Socialists, the pretender was holding talks on the dictator's yacht, *Azor*. On 25 August 1948 he agreed to his son Juan Carlos being educated in Spain. Don Juan did not want his dynasty to be for ever separated from its homeland like some of the forlorn Balkan royalty who frequented the casino at Estoril.[29] Franco had drawn the sting of the monarchist opposition. Inside Spain, however, the collaborationist monarchists and Catholics were delighted. They happily jumped to the fanciful conclusion that Franco had promised an early restoration and thereby absolved themselves from any obligation even to toy with opposition.

Don Juan knew that their confidence was baseless. Whatever else he did, he had to counter Falangist pressure for Franco to slam the door definitively on a future restoration. Had this happened it might have been difficult, even after Franco's death, to get the monarchy back on the political agenda. The pretender's caution was justified by the solidity of the Francoist coalition and by Franco's ability to tack to the prevailing winds. Army officers, collaborationist Carlists, monarchists, Falangists and Catholics as loyal to the Vatican as Martín Artajo and Ruiz Giménez continued to work in harmony with hard-line Francoists like the ever-present Carrero Blanco and the Minister of Information, Gabriel Arias Salgado. Moreover, there seemed to be movement from the regime side. When the government was exposed as incapable of a creative response to the strike wave of 1951, Franco reshuffled the Cabinet. Long-serving ministers associated with the Falange, like Juan Antonio Suanzes and Ibáñez Martín, were dropped. The Carlist Antonio Iturmendi returned as Minister of Justice and the Conde de Vallellano came in as Minister of Public Works. Ruiz Giménez became Minister of Education. With the regime presenting a more acceptable face, the possibility of removing it altogether seemed to be drifting away. The return of ambassadors in 1950, Spanish entry into UNESCO in 1952, and the Concordat and the treaty with the United States in 1953 were harsh blows both to the democratic opposition and to those monarchists who had hoped for an early restoration.

The 1951 reshuffle also heralded a major crisis for the Falange, into which the strengthening of the regime monarchists drove a wedge. Henceforth, the FET was to be divided between a collaborationist majority prepared to swallow the regime's creeping monarchism, and a minority of hard-line purists committed to a totalitarian republic. The collaborationists were prepared to compromise their ideological principles rather than relinquish the fruits of power. The various liberalizing initiatives of Ruiz Giménez exacerbated tensions within the Movimiento. Indeed, at the

November 1955 rally at El Escorial to commemorate the anniversary of the death of the Falange's founder, José Antonio Primo de Rivera, Franco was called a traitor.[30]

The regime Catholics began to press home their advantage. Rather as Martín Artajo had done in the mid-1940s, they began to seek ways of contributing to the regime's stability by modifying its dictatorial features. A curious amalgam of collaborationist followers of Don Juan and Opus Dei intellectuals emerged, known collectively as the Tercera Fuerza: a 'third force' against both the Falange and the conservative Catholics, or self-proclaimed Christian Democrats, of Martín Artajo. Some but not all the leading lights were figures connected with the Opus Dei, for example, Rafael Calvo Serer, Florentino Pérez Embid and Gonzalo Fernández de la Mora. Others, like the industrialist Joaquín Satrústegui, were liberal supporters of Don Juan. They were committed to the eventual restoration of a traditional monarchy under Don Juan, albeit within the context of the ideals of the Movimiento. In an article published in Paris in September 1953, and widely circulated within the Francoist establishment, Calvo Serer claimed that the Falangists and the old regime Catholics had lost their way. For suggesting that only a team from the new group could modernize the regime, Calvo Serer was dismissed from his posts in the CSIC.[31]

The Tercera Fuerza was put to the test in the municipal elections held in Madrid on 25 November 1954, the first since the civil war. Sponsored by the monarchist newspaper *ABC*, its candidates were subjected to intimidation by Falangist thugs and by the police. Nevertheless, although official results gave a substantial victory to Falangist candidates, the monarchists claimed to have received over 60 per cent of the vote.[32] Revealingly, Martín Artajo wrote to Franco: 'What is the point of allowing an opposition candidate and an independent candidate? I fear that with this we have fallen into the old game of political parties.'[33] In attempting to curry favour thus, Martín Artajo achieved the near-impossible and made the dictator appear more liberal than his own Cabinet. More realistic than his minion, Franco concluded that the strength of a critical right-wing force called for some action. Accordingly, he met Don Juan at the Extremaduran estate of the Conde de Ruiseñada on 30 December 1954. He made no concessions concerning a restoration, but his gesture drew the sting of the monarchists. Shortly afterwards, in interviews in the Falangist *Arriba* on 23 and 27 January 1955, Franco talked of his successor and declared that he must be someone 'completely identified with the Movimiento'. Within six months, Don Juan stated that the monarchy had always been 'in agreement with the spirit of the Movimiento and the Falange'.[34]

This apparent rapprochement between the dictator and the pretender caused further disquiet in Falangist circles. Indeed, throughout the Francoist establishment, battle lines were already being drawn up for a future power struggle. Falangists, Francoist Catholics and Tercera Fuerza, realizing that outside the Movimiento little could be done, all hoped to mould the Movimiento in their own image. Tensions came to a head in early February 1956, when Falangists clashed with progressive Catholics and left-wingers in the University of Madrid Law Faculty. In a typical judgement of Solomon, Franco sacked both Ruiz Giménez and the most senior Falangist in his cabinet, Raimundo Fernández Cuesta. As Minister Secretary General of the Movimiento, Fernández Cuesta had been unrestrained in his criticism of the Tercera Fuerza. He was replaced by José Luis de Arrese.[35] Throughout 1956, Arrese made serious efforts to alter the fundamental laws in order to give the National Council of the Movimiento the ultimate right to dismiss Franco's successor and thereby perpetuate the Falange's pre-eminence. Arrese's scheme so resembled the pseudo-constitutions of the Soviet bloc that regime monarchists, Carlists and the Church joined in opposing it.[36] The balance of power was tipping ever further away from the Falange. Some of the brighter young stars in its Frente de Juventudes and Sindicato Español Universitario, such as Rodolfo Martín Villa and Juan José Rosón, were already coming to terms with this and turning themselves into 'apolitical' administrators deeply entrenched in the regime's structures. Other, slightly more senior, figures were working on creating an altogether more anodyne and 'progressive' variant of developmental Falangism. Two such figures were Manuel Fraga Iribarne, who became director of the Instituto de Estudios Políticos, and Torcuato Fernández Miranda, who was made Director-General of Universities.[37] These Movimiento apparatchiks, and others like them, would eventually play a crucial role in the transition away from dictatorship after 1975.

Franco, however, still faced the problems of tension between Falangists and monarchists and of the growing stagnation of the Spanish economy. After lengthy consultations with Carrero Blanco, he turned in February 1957 to the so-called 'technocrats'. A thoroughgoing remodelling of the Cabinet brought in the experts who were to control the levers of economic power. Alberto Ullastres became Minister of Commerce and Mariano Navarro Rubio Minister of Finance. In various ministries, technocrats such as Gregorio López Bravo, José María López de Letona and José Luis Villar Pallasí became under-secretaries and departmental heads. Laureano López Rodó was given overall responsibility for major administrative reform as Technical Secretary General of the Presidencia del Gobierno (Cabinet Office). The Falangists who remained in the Cabinet were of the domesticated variety: Arias Salgado, Arrese and José Solís Ruiz. Like the Tercera Fuerza group, the 'technocrats' were closely associated with the Opus Dei but were keener on modernizing than on liberalizing the regime. They were neo-Francoists concerned above all with the regime's and their own survival. In that sense, the technocrats became accomplices to Franco's immobilism by providing the means to close the door on political reform and substituting for it economic and administrative reform.[38] Monarchists but not *Juanistas*, they believed, under the influence of Carrero Blanco, that the future lay with a Francoist monarchy under Juan Carlos resting on the authoritarian foundations of the dictatorship.[39]

To a certain extent, the rise of the technocrats signified Franco's acceptance of a muted Tercera Fuerza option. However, it did mean that the hopes of the genuinely liberal supporters of Don Juan were dashed, forcing them into a form of internal opposition. The monarchists were divided between those who were still committed to a constitutional monarchy under Don Juan and those within the regime who had become identified with the plans of Carrero Blanco for a Francoist monarchy under Juan Carlos. Increasingly, the more perspicacious elements in the regime came to recognize a need to create a broad extra-Francoist platform in readiness for the eventual demise of the Caudillo and the Falange. Admittedly, at the end of the 1950s, the regime was gradually starting to solve its economic problems without political reform as it had its diplomatic ones in the 1940s. Nevertheless, Spanish liberals of right and left had reason to feel that the tide was turning. They hoped that the new US president, Kennedy, would reverse Eisenhower's pro-Franco policies, and believed that Spain's need to enter the European Economic Community (EEC) could only favour their cause. The focusing of attention on Europe proved doubly effective as a result of the regime's growing interest in international acceptance and, in particular, its petition to join the EEC on 9 February 1962. The European activities of the opposition and their good reception contrasted starkly with the reaction to the regime's abortive overtures to the European Community. Indeed, the appeal of Europe was broad enough to provide a meeting ground for the tolerated conservative opposition within Spain and the exiled opposition. Between 5 and 8 June 1962, monarchists, Catholics and renegade Falangists met Socialists and Basque and Catalan nationalists at the IV Congress of the European Movement in Munich.

The reaction of the Francoist press to the Munich meeting was hysterical. This was understandable. As a result of the strike wave in the spring of 1962, the first signs of conflict between the regime and the Catholic Church were becoming visible. There was suddenly a plausibility about communist claims that their policy of national reconciliation was about to bear fruit in a wide front of anti-Franco forces. Respectable Catholics and monarchists had consorted with exiled democrats. The signs that the Francoist coalition was breaking up were immensely disturbing. Many of the Spanish delegates were arrested and exiled for their part in what came to be known as the 'filthy Munich plot'.[40] Significantly, on 10 July Franco introduced more 'progressive' Opus Dei elements like López Bravo, as Minister of Industry, and Manuel Lora Tamayo, as Minister of Education, into his Cabinet. The regime was being forced to change. When that change was eventually exposed as inadequate, a gradual process would begin whereby its more far-sighted servants would embark on the slow path to the democratic opposition. The democratic right-wingers at Munich had provided them with a bridge of respectability. The congress revealed the growing strength of non-Francoist groups within Spain and their greater willingness to act in public and in unison. The regime's false European pretensions had béen exposed in international terms. More importantly, a moderate democratic right had publicly emerged, to which the left could relate and with which it could establish a dialogue. Munich had underlined a moment of crisis and had shown a way out without bloodshed.

Inevitably then, from the mid-1960s, concern over the future dominated the attitude of the right both inside and outside the regime. It was this preoccupation which largely underlay a resurgence of interest in the monarchy. Now, however, the monarchists' options were widened by the presence of Juan Carlos in Spain, and his apparently close relationship with the Caudillo. The more sophisticated Francoist politicians placed themselves squarely in the Juan Carlos camp, seeing this as the most plausible way to ensure a continuation of the regime after Franco's death. These *continuistas* embarked upon '*operación príncipe*' to get Juan Carlos named Franco's successor. This goal was pursued with especial enthusiasm by Opus Dei and was brought to a successful conclusion in 1969.[41] The Francoist advocates of Juan Carlos hoped that he would preside over a limited reform. They had little idea, however, that he would turn out to be the paladin of full-scale democratic change.

For their part, the Falangists hoped to perpetuate a Movimiento in which they would continue to control the great institutions, the vertical syndicates, the social security system and local administration. The non-Falangist elements, however, while paying lip-service to the idea and ideals of the Movimiento, preferred to see it as a great ideological umbrella over all loyal Francoists. This broad interpretation of the Movimiento tended to gain ever greater sway as Franco himself came to acknowledge that his regime had to adjust to the changing circumstances of the world in the 1960s: a position symbolized by the rise of Carrero Blanco, López Rodó and the Opus Dei technocrats. The job of modernizing the Movimiento was entrusted to the least dogmatic of the senior Falangists, José Solís Ruiz, a political conjuror.[42] Together, these figures spread the rhetoric of 'political development', 'liberalization' and 'modernization'. They nevertheless did so with an air of desperation after the application for EEC membership was rejected in February 1962. While the 'technocrats' tried to gain democratic credibility for the regime, both the EEC and the Munich meeting effectively denied it. However, the desperate efforts of the technocrats were to open cracks within the Francoist establishment from which would eventually sprout some democratic growths.

There was now talk of setting up 'political associations', limited of course to those who were unequivocally committed to the principles of Francoism and to their survival. Political associations would effectively systematize what had previously been random jockeying for power between informal pressure groups, and in a way which would allow the regime to derive some moral legitimacy. The idea was never fully implemented until 1974. However, together with the Press Law introduced in 1966 by Manuel Fraga, the idea exposed some of the divisions within the Francoist elite. The Press Law was cautious and restrictive, yet did allow an element of debate at the moment when preparations for the future were on the agenda both of regime elements and of the opposition.[43] Three broad tendencies could be discerned within the regime. On the far right were those Falangists committed to what was known as *inmovilismo*; in the centre were the so-called *continuistas*, led by Carrero Blanco, who hoped to perpetuate the regime under the closely invigilated monarchy of Juan Carlos; and on the left, straddling regime and opposition, were the so-called *aperturistas* who hoped for a limited democratic solution under Don Juan. Out of this last group's ability to maintain dialogue both with the genuinely democratic left and with the *continuistas* was eventually to emerge the negotiated and bloodless transition to democracy between 1975 and 1977.

Anxiety about the future also played a large part in the development of non-Francoist conservatism. There was an awareness that the right as a whole was in serious danger of being inextricably linked in the popular mind with the regime. Fears consequently existed of a total conservative eclipse in a post-dictatorial regime created under the aegis of Communist- or Socialist-dominated democratic forces. The result was a general agreement that the non-Francoist right should aim to be a source of dialogue and gradual change and that this set it apart from the other, increasingly confrontational, opposition forces. This underlined the ambivalence in the conservative ranks throughout the Franco period. Christian Democracy, as had been the case previously with *Juanista* monarchism, tended to become a political refuge for those conservatives who, having benefited from and tacitly approved of Francoism, now saw that political change was on the horizon.[44] This was to be increasingly the case as the regime began to disintegrate in the late 1960s and particularly as the Church evolved into a stern critic of the dictatorship.

In July 1967 Carrero Blanco assumed the vice-presidency with the express intention of preparing the ground for a Francoist monarchy in the person of Juan Carlos. Such a monarchy was to be irrevocably committed to the continued exclusion from Spain of Communists, Socialists and liberals. The irrelevance of such a project was vividly exposed by the fact that, until his assassination in 1973, Carrero's governments reeled under the combined assaults of working-class unrest, student dissent and Basque terrorism. That in itself made many erstwhile Francoists consider their futures. What tipped the balance for many was the fact that, under threat, the regime *continuistas* were forced to resort to unrestrained brutality against their opponents. Moreover, they found themselves increasingly in alliance with the *inmovilistas* who came to be known as the 'bunker'.[45] Its starkest manifestation consisted of ultra-rightist terror squads which subjected left-wing students and professors, clandestine union leaders and liberal priests to sporadic violence.

The squads were merely the most visible symptom of Falangist anxieties about Franco's increasing frailty and the dangers of a succession to Juan Carlos. Disturbed by the increasing scale of working-class and student unrest and by the emergence of Euskadi Ta Askatasuna (ETA), an organization capable of penetrating the regime's image of invulnerability, the Falangist right of the regime felt itself to be under siege. The slogans, pamphlets and wall-daubings of its young activists used a nostalgic civil war rhetoric which reflected their feelings that history was turning against them. The Falange had adapted to disagreeable change for over thirty years in order to enjoy the fruits of the civil war victory. That the party seemed to be over was reflected in Hitlerian talk of withdrawing to a bunker and fighting in the rubble of the chancellery. At best, neo-Nazi groups played a useful role in the tactics of beleaguered Francoism, terrorizing the opposition without stigma for the regime itself. More sophisticated was the propaganda effect of blurring the government's adoption of an increasingly hard line against all forms of dissent, because the invention of a fanatical extreme right put the regime as if by magic in a centre position. Yet even in 1973 it was already too late. Within six months Carrero Blanco would be dead.

The more the ultra-right lashed out at enemies of the regime the more the Church tended to identify itself with regional and working-class protest. At first implicitly and later explicitly, the Church withdrew its stamp of moral legitimacy from the regime.[46] At the same time, the regime was revealing its incapacity to respond to the social discontent consequent upon economic development. Many in the business community were led to hanker after a more modern political context for their activities. The technocrats' scenario had assumed that rises in per capita income would obviate the need for political change. The wave of strikes, demonstrations and terrorist attacks which marked the 1969–73 period undermined that assumption. Hardline Francoists in the army and the Falange muttered that development had been a mistake and that survival demanded a return to the ethos of 1939. With Franco descending into senility and closeted with an ultra-rightist clique in his El Pardo residence, these were the regime forces most likely to influence him.[47] Even one-time collaborationist monarchists and Catholics were forced to the conclusion that a democratic *apertura* (opening) was necessary to avoid the entire edifice being swept away. Their attitude was revealed in the increasingly critical line adopted by the principal monarchist and Catholic newspapers, *ABC* and *Ya*. In consequence, many young and perceptive Francoist functionaries began to toy with the idea of a dialogue with the opposition. Their natural interlocutors were the monarchists of Satrústegui and Areilza and the left Christian Democrats of Gil Robles and Ruiz Giménez.

In Catalonia, Madrid and Seville, liberal *Juanista* monarchists began to join broad opposition fronts with Socialists, Communists and other leftists. The most influential conservatives, like Gil Robles, Satrústegui and Areilza, hoped for some kind of bloodless transition to a democratic monarchy under Don Juan. However, with the regime more and more in the hands of those prepared to go down fighting, the progressive right was concerned about the left-wing opposition's belief that mass pressure would overthrow the dictatorship. A search began for a middle way. Monarchist thinkers and academic theorists began to comb the pseudo-democratic rhetoric of the Francoist constitution to see if it could be exploited to permit real democratization. At the same time, many liberal *Juanistas* came to the conclusion that to have any opportunity of bringing about a 'legal' evolution to democracy, they must recapture Juan Carlos from the technocrats. Given that the prince was less committed to the perpetuation of Francoism than the regime's propaganda had made out, that was to prove easier than they expected. The legalist and evolutionary project was to come into its own in 1976.

Conservatives and 'apolitical' Movimiento functionaries played a significant role in the peaceful transition to democracy after Franco's death in November 1975. Their willingness to accept and participate in the process of change undermined the diehard reactionaries of the regime. A forum for debate was established, involving both right and left and based on a mutual need for democracy. The progressive right's ability to recognize the need for pragmatism and flexibility in the face of Spain's changed social and economic structure made a considerable contribution to the bloodless nature of the transition to democracy. The appearance of a recognizable contemporary Spanish conservatism was not, however, the culmination of a gradual and inexorable political development. It owed more to the peculiarities of the Franco regime and its incompatibility with the demands of a modern industrialized nation. The monarchists and the Falangist zealots of the 1940s bore little resemblance to the conservatives and the Movimiento apparatchiks of the mid-1970s. Their capacity to evolve was greater than that of a regime which had lost its main asset, its pragmatism. The activities of the ultra-rightist bunker had the inadvertent effect of advertising the fact that the regime's obsolescence would admit of no further tinkering. The patricians in whose interests the civil war had been fought were not threatened by the change. The only victim of the transition was the Falange, and it had been well paid over forty years for its services rendered.

NOTES

1 P. Preston, *Las derechas españolas en el siglo XX: autoritarismo, fascismo y golpismo* (Madrid, 1986); M. Blinkhorn, *Carlism and Crisis in Spain, 1931–1939* (Cambridge, 1975); R. de la Cierva, *La derecha sin remedio* (Barcelona, 1986); P. Preston, *The Coming of the Spanish Civil War* (London, 1978).

2 *Sur* (Malaga), 25, 28 April 1937; M. García Venero, *Historia de la Unificación (Falange y Requeté en 1937)* (Madrid, 1970), pp. 216–19; M. García Venero, *Falange en la guerra de España: la Unificación y Hedilla* (Paris, 1967), pp. 391–427. For a critical account of Falangist dissidence, see the much censored A. Alcázar de Velasco, *Siete días de Salamanca* (Madrid, 1976).

3 S. M. Ellwood, *Spanish Fascism in the Franco Era* (London, 1987), pp. 58–9.

4 A. de Miguel, *Sociología del Franquismo: análisis ideológico de los ministros del régimen* (Barcelona, 1976), pp. 43–8.

5 Ellwood, *Spanish Fascism*, pp. 69–70.

6 R. L. Chueca, 'FET y de las JONS: la paradójica víctima de un fascismo fracasado', in J. Fontana (ed.), *España bajo el franquismo* (Barcelona, 1986), pp. 60–77.

7 F. J. Conde, *Contribución a la doctrina del Caudillaje* (Madrid, 1942).

8 J. I. Escobar, *Así empezó . . .* (Madrid, 1974), pp. 325–30.

9 J. Ma. Pemán, *Mis almuerzos con gente importante* (Barcelona, 1970), pp. 239–43. The relatively innocuous published text of his speech, 'Calvo Sotelo, precursor del movimiento nacional', may be seen in *Homenaje de la Real Academia de Jurisprudencia y Legislación a José Calvo Sotelo* (Madrid, 1942), pp. 255–72.

10 Report of German ambassador, Von Stohrer, to the Wilhelmstrasse, 19 November 1938, *Documents on German Foreign Policy*, Series D, Vol. III (London, 1951), p. 797; X. Tusell, *La oposición democrática al franquismo* (Barcelona, 1977), p. 34. In his memoirs, Sáinz Rodríguez fails to explain his 'resignation'; see P. Sáinz Rodríguez, *Testimonio y recuerdos* (Barcelona, 1978), pp. 254–74. He is slightly more explicit in his contribution to A. Bayod (ed.), *Franco visto por sus ministros* (Barcelona, 1981), pp. 26–8.

11 Yagüe's promotion was also an attempt to neutralize him by removing him from command of the powerful Foreign Legion; see R. Garriga, *El general Juan Yagüe* (Barcelona, 1985), pp. 171–4. Kindelán's dismissal was not unconnected to the involvement of his son in a plot to bring Don Juan to Spain; see A. Kindelán, *La verdad de mis relaciones con Franco* (Barcelona, 1981), pp. 16–17.

12 J. Ma. Gil Robles, *La monarquía por la que yo luché (1941–1954)* (Madrid, 1976), pp. 20–4; L. López Rodó, *La larga marcha hacia la monarquía* (Barcelona, 1977), pp. 503–7; Ellwood, *Spanish Fascism*, pp. 84–8.

13 J. A. Ansaldo, *¿Para qué . . . ? De Alfonso XIII a Juan III* (Buenos Aires, 1951), p. 51; López Rodó, *Larga marcha*, pp. 13, 17; H. Thomas, *The Spanish Civil War*, 3rd edn (London, 1977), p. 414.

14 A. Kindelán, *Mis cuadernos de guerra* (Barcelona, 1982), pp. 101–11. For a much more critical account, see G. Cabanellas, *La guerra de los mil días*, Vol. I (Buenos Aires, 1973), pp. 640–61.

15 N. Jones, 'Monarchism in Spain', MA thesis, University of Reading, 1973, p. 7.

16 R. Calvo Serer, *Franco frente al rey* (Paris, 1971), p. 21.

17 See the remarks made in 1940 and 1943 by Fernando Martín-Sánchez Juliá in J. Ynfante, *La prodigiosa aventura del Opus Dei: Génesis y desarrollo de la santa mafia* (Paris, 1970), pp. 29–30.

18 A. Saez Alba, *La otra 'Cosa Nostra', la Asociación Católica Nacional de Propagandistas y el caso de 'El Correo' de Andalucía* (Paris, 1974), pp. XXXIII–XXXV.

19 J. Tusell, *Franco y los católicos: la política interior española entre 1945 y 1957* (Madrid, 1984), p. 24.

20 X. Tusell and G. García Queipo de Llano, *Franco y Mussolini: la política española durante la segunda guerra mundial* (Barcelona, 1985), pp. 208–9: R. Fernández Cuesta, *Testimonio, recuerdos y reflexiones* (Madrid, 1985), pp. 221–2; Sir Samuel Hoare, *Ambassador on Special Mission* (London, 1946), pp. 211–12.

21 López Rodó, *Larga marcha*, pp. 36–44; Tusell and García, *Franco y Mussolini*, pp. 222–5; Calvo Serer, *Franco frente al rey*, p. 12.

22 Tusell, *Oposicion*, p. 76.

23 *Textò auténtico del manifiesto de S. M. el Rey* (Lausanne, 19 de marzo de 1945); López Rodó, *Larga marcha*, pp. 88–9; Tusell, *Franco y los católicos*, p. 55.

24 S. G. Payne, *The Franco Regime 1936–1975* (Madison, Wis., 1986), pp. 350–1; Tusell, *Franco y los católicos*, pp. 52–79.

25 López Rodó, *Larga marcha*, pp. 75–104.

26 Tusell, *Franco y los católicos*, p. 110.

27 López Rodó, *Larga marcha*, pp. 88–9.

28 Gil Robles, *La monarquía*, p. 209; Tusell, *Oposición*, pp. 162–9.

29 Gil Robles, *La monarquía*, pp. 267–73.

30 Calvo Serer, *Franco frente al rey*, p. 14.

31 ibid., pp. 29–30.

32 ibid., pp. 31–2.

33 Tusell, *Franco y los católicos*, p. 294.

34 Tusell, *Oposición*, pp. 235–7.

35 For a dense and elliptical account of the intra-regime tensions accompanying the university disturbances, see R. de la Cierva, *Historia del franquismo: aislamiento, transformación, agonía* (Barcelona, 1978), pp. 136–43.

36 J. L. de Arrese, *Un etapa constituyente* (Barcelona, 1982), *passim*; Fernández Cuesta, *Testimonio*, pp. 243–4; Ellwood, *Spanish Fascism*, pp. 118–21.

37 M. Fraga Iribarne, *Memoria breve de una vida pública* (Barcelona, 1980), pp. 25–6; M. Durán, *Martín Villa* (San Sebastián, 1979), pp. 39–55; P. Lizcano, *La generación del 56: la universidad contra Franco* (Barcelona, 1981), pp. 231–4.

38 L. Suárez Fernández, *Francisco Franco y su tiempo*, Vol. V (Madrid, 1984), pp. 320–6; Calvo Serer, *Franco frente al rey*, pp. 14–15.

39 López Rodó, *Larga marcha,* pp. 136 ff.

40 D. Ridruejo, *Ibérica*, July 1962, quoted in D. Ridruejo, *Casi unas memorias* (Barcelona, 1976), pp.391–2; P. Preston, *Salvador de Madariaga and the Quest for Liberty in Spain* (Oxford, 1987), pp. 28–9.

41 Payne, *Franco Regime*, pp. 536–42; López Rodó, *Larga marcha*, pp. 222–386.

42 Ellwood, *Spanish Fascism*, pp. 121–6.

43 A fascinating account of this period from inside the regime is provided by R. Calvo Serer, *La dictadura de los franquistas. 1. El 'affaire' del 'Madrid' y el futuro político* (Paris, 1973), *passim*.

44 F. Alvárez de Miranda, *Del 'contubernio' al consenso* (Barcelona, 1985), pp. 88–9; P. Preston, *The Triumph of Democracy in Spain* (London, 1986), pp. 8–30.

45 Preston, *Las derechas*, pp. 135–42; Luis Ramírez, 'Morir en el búnker', in *Horizonte español 1972*, Vol. I (Paris, 1972), pp. 3–20.

46 N. Cooper, *Catholicism and the Franco Regime* (Beverley Hills, Calif., 1975), pp. 37–43; J. Chao Rego, *La Iglesia en el franquismo* (Madrid, 1976), pp. 150–231; G. Hermet, *Les Catholiques dans l'Espagne Franquiste*, Vol. II (Paris, 1981), pp. 398–421; R. Díaz Salazar, *Iglesia, dictadura y democracia* (Madrid, 1981), pp. 227–83.

47 Preston, *Triumph of Democracy*, pp. 36, 51, 63; A. Izquierdo, *Yo, testigo de cargo* (Barcelona, 1981), p. 37; V. Gil, *Cuarenta años junto a Franco* (Barcelona, 1981), pp. 139–202.

9

Conservatism, dictatorship and fascism in Portugal, 1914–45

Tom Gallagher

Portugal was one of the first European countries to experience a strong backlash against liberal democracy. By the end of the First World War a reaction against bourgeois liberalism had already gripped many politically aware Portuguese. Inevitably, the country's rural character, geographical isolation from the rest of Europe, and freedom from pressing territorial grievances meant that the counter-revolutionary challenge followed its own local course. The right in Portugal offered nothing original in the realm of thought or action that could be taken up by fascists elsewhere. Much of its own inspiration derived from France, hardly surprising since modern Portugal has been more profoundly influenced by French cultural norms than any other European country.

When the Lusitanian Integralist movement was founded in 1914, it borrowed heavily from the ideas of Charles Maurras and Action Française. The Integralists were ultra-nationalists who eulogized rural values and promoted monarchy, unencumbered by parliament but with provision for local autonomy, as a solution to Portugal's political needs. The chaos and mismanagement that disfigured the parliamentary republic, installed following the monarchy's overthrow in 1910, gave this coterie of mainly upper-class intellectuals an audience for which otherwise it could not have hoped. So turbulent were politics in a 16-year era which witnessed forty-four governments and an average of two attempted coups per year that in 1918 the Integralists were even able to participate in the shortlived military dictatorship of Major Sidónio Pais which, at their instigation, drew up a constitution allowing for representation on corporatist lines. Action Française would have to wait more than another twenty years to enjoy an influence such as that deployed in 1918 by its Portuguese disciples; nevertheless the brief regime of Sidónio Pais proved to be the pinnacle of their achievement. The Integralists were unable to turn growing disgust with the corrupt and rudderless parliamentary system into support for a revamped monarchy, since even before its removal the House of Bragança had forfeited the backing of the Portuguese elite and of Lisbon public opinion. During the 1920s the Integralists were weakened by schism over the issue of the monarchy, and were too abstract and dreamy to create a popular movement or produce a workable alternative to the republican regime.

The Catholic right started from an even weaker position, but avoided some of the Integralists' basic mistakes and was accordingly much better placed to exercise influence when in 1926 the floundering rule of mediocre café politicians was finally ended by full-scale military intervention. The Catholic Church's identification with the most reactionary elements in the monarchy had earned it the persistent hostility of republicans, which after 1910 turned into open victimization. With the Church in disarray and many religious leaders in exile, there emerged in 1912 a lay Catholic movement which, most unusually, was not under clerical tutelage. In emergency conditions, with the very existence of the Portuguese Church seemingly in jeopardy, members of the revived Academic Centre for Christian Democracy (CADC) formed a political party, the Portuguese Catholic Centre (CCP), achieving some success in giving Catholicism a less hidebound and more modern image. The CCP avoided dabbling in coups and conspiracies, participated in republican elections and regularly won seats in the rural north where religious devotion was still strong at most levels of society.

In 1922 the CCP declared itself neutral on the question of the monarchy. This was largely the achievement of the normally self-effacing Dr António de Oliveira Salazar, professor of economics at Coimbra University and a rising star in Catholic political circles. A monarchist himself, Salazar believed that preoccupation with external forms of government was a wasteful distraction when what was needed was a programme of action to cure Portugal's dire economic and political problems. Salazar, who since his youth had been strongly influenced by Maurras, emphasized the latter's watchwords of Nation, Family, Authority and Hierarchy as the best means of securing the common good, while rejecting his belief in 'Politique d'abord' and the ideas flowing from it.[1] Other influences were papal social doctrine and the writings of French conservative sociologists like Le Play.

It was Salazar's reputation as a financial expert rather than his wider political philosophy which, in 1928, prompted Portugal's inexperienced military rulers to appoint him Minister of Finance with extraordinary powers to stave off national bankruptcy. By means of centralized economic controls, cuts in state expenditure, and some internal borrowing he was able in 1930 to proclaim his financial 'miracle'.[2] As the rest of Europe slid into depression, there grew up around Salazar's achievement a mystique which by 1932 had earned him the premiership of Portugal and mastery of an authoritarian regime which he increasingly civilianized. Less stress was placed upon the fact that Portugal contrasted with most of Europe in not being locked into the world economy; it did not depend altogether on the export of primary products; and, for all its faults, the republic left no major foreign debts: all of which makes Salazar's achievement more prosaic.

The confirmation in office of a retiring, scholarly intellectual over the heads of frustrated men on horseback, and this in an age when the prevailing style of European dictators was loud and aggressive, makes the Portuguese authoritarian experience appear incongruous. Of course, behind Salazar's meek exterior lay an ambitious and proud man with a Machiavellian mind and great self-discipline. It is less often recognized that, by the end of the parliamentary era, Portugal was more receptive to a low-key type of right-wing solution than to a bolder, more flamboyant approach involving demagogy and the mobilization, rather than the calming, of opinion. It was this, as much as traditional Portuguese aloofness towards Spain, that accounted for the limited impact upon Portugal of the flamboyant dictatorship of General Miguel Primo de Rivera (1923–30), and explains why Mussolini's most avid Portuguese disciple, Homem Cristo Filho, 'the first authentic and indisputable Portuguese fascist', died in Rome in 1928 almost unnoticed back home.[3]

By 1926 there reigned, even among previously engaged Portuguese, a profound and all-embracing political weariness. Nearly all political ideals had been devalued by the overblown rhetoric and misrule of the outgoing regime, even the right being tarnished through having during its brief periods of power abundantly revealed its own failings. Anti-political impulses were strong among students, the lower middle class, and those other groups which were already providing the basis for fascist movements elsewhere in Europe. Owing to the slow tempo of change in an overwhelmingly rural country where the family remained strong and which was in general insulated from many of the shocks currently transforming European politics, there existed relatively few rootless or *déclassé* elements from which the leadership of mass counter-revolutionary movements could be drawn.[4] Simply because economic crisis was such a recurring feature of Portuguese history, this had a less electrifying effect on the Lisbon and Oporto middle classes than it did on their counterparts in more industrialized countries. Perhaps had there been a prolonged struggle for power in 1926 rather than a bloodless takeover, it might have provided the climate for the emergence of a more sharply defined and full-blooded brand of authoritarian rule. Instead a politically exhausted nation was placed in the hands of a thoroughgoing conservative who, rejecting the belief that authority resided in the people, was determined to ensure that his *Estado Novo* ('New State') did not need them for its survival.

The structure of the *Estado Novo* fully reflected Salazar's elitist designs. In 1933 a cosmetic referendum endorsed a new constitution which declared

Portugal a corporative republic. The death of ex-King Manuel II in 1932 removed much of the heat from the monarchical question and most monarchists were prepared to recognize General Oscar Carmona as head of state. The constitution gave him the power to dismiss the Prime Minister and the Cabinet, demonstrating the degree of Salazar's confidence in the pliable staff officer who had facilitated his rise to power. Real power, of course, existed outside the various constitutional instruments. A national assembly was created, but it was a decorative body whose members were virtually hand-picked by Salazar and then endorsed by a mere 7 per cent of the adult public in 'elections' wherein no opposition candidate was ever successful. Even so, Salazar took no chances – the assembly possessed no binding powers and remained a consultative body whose president in the 1940s received an advance summary of every proposed speech.[5]

Even more of a façade were the corporative institutions which emerged in the 1930s following the abolition of trade unions, strikes and employers' associations. The new associations of class and professional interest groups did not become autonomous centres of power as the official ideology suggested should happen.[6] Corporatism was a theoretical showpiece that quickly proved a practical illusion. Behind the rhetoric was created a crude form of state-sponsored capitalism which oversaw an internal distribution of resources in favour of the already privileged. Salazar was not bluffing in 1930 when he declared: 'Let us protect the state before we look after the poor and the weak.'[7] The proletariat lost its tenuous bargaining power in the new economic order, but so did small-scale producers who watched helplessly as corporative regulations encouraged the growth of large monopolies in different sectors of manufacturing and commerce.

An economy dominated by a small number of powerful units was far easier for Salazar to control than a more diverse aggregation of economic interests. The corporative machinery also enabled him to regulate the pace of economic change to suit his regime's traditionalist values. Economic change for its own sake did not appeal to him; in 1933 he openly declared that 'all achievement is not progress and ... backwardness may simply mean that we have not departed too much from the principles of rational economy'.[8]

Opposition from the business community to Salazar's centralizing economic measures appears to have been localized, sporadic and hence easily overcome. Salazar's corporative drive was not altogether inconsistent with long-term trends in the history of Portugal, whose business sectors have always been strongly dependent upon the state and have only rarely sought to demonstrate their autonomy or even affirm a separate identity by creating large employer associations. In time, perhaps most came to terms with the highly regulatory edifice created by Salazar: a process more painful for some of the chief architects of the corporate state such as Teotónio Pereira. Those younger former Integralists who had

160

hoped to see à new dynamic order emerge from the corporate state which they had been hired to construct were rapidly shifted sideways into administrative or diplomatic posts once the necessary preparatory work was completed. Those who accepted Salazar's formula of 'a strong state, an organized political nation, and a controlled political economy' could expect to rise high in the New State hierarchy. Salazar also looked to the familiar university world for colleagues and to well-off groups in the provinces to staff the regime's political and ceremonial posts.[9] Unlike the more cosmopolitan, secular and slightly more progressive members of the Lisbon and Oporto bourgeoisie, they had few qualms about accepting that the majority even of literate people should be excluded from political decision-making; to much of the provincial bourgeoisie, especially in the north, Salazar was a symbol of continuity who shared their traditional views and would protect their vital interests while also giving them opportunities for enrichment.

Salazar's famous 1928 statement that 'I know quite well what I want and where I am going', and his marathon stay in office, lend credence to the belief that he was adhering to some carefully arranged master-plan. In reality, however, his intentions may have been more open-ended.[10] Several inconsistencies in his early speeches suggest that he was not altogether clear in his own mind about which type of political arrangement would be the most appropriate vehicle for his conservative ideas. In 1930 he had warned that 'dictatorship ... is a delicate instrument which ... one can easily abuse. For this reason it is as well that it should not aspire to eternity.'[11] Yet by 1934 he was ready to affirm that 'dictatorships today do not seem to be any longer parentheses between regimes'.[12] Similarly, with regard to the corporate state he may originally have entertained hopes of devising a system with elements of genuine economic participation, before eventually concluding that even among his own supporters the talent and commitment necessary to pioneer new institutions were not readily available. Addressing them in 1930, he revealed his scepticism about their qualifications to stand alongside him in his mission to regenerate Portugal:

> I wonder if in the hearts of those who say they support me there is that devotion to our country which is capable of sacrifice; that desire to serve and will to obey ... a consciousness of order, of justice, and of honest work.[13]

As Salazar steadily consolidated an informal personal dictatorship, the narcissistic side of his personality became more evident. Such statements as 'Unfortunately there are a lot of things that seemingly only I can do' revealed a superior, talented individual who regarded himself as uniquely qualified to rule Portugal.[14] Inevitably there were vocal elements in the counter-revolutionary camp who disagreed and who advanced programmes that were radically different from Salazar's in content and, especially, style. In the early 1930s, even as Salazar was putting the finishing touches to his *Estado Novo*, conditions briefly proved favourable for the emergence of a noisy movement of the radical right. In their different ways, sporadic opposition revolts, the advance of fascism in the heart of Europe and the spectre of a left-wing Spanish republic galvanized elements who felt that full-blooded authoritarian rule, making no concessions to liberal democracy, was the best means to safeguard the new order. The União Nacional (UN), an official political movement launched in 1930, held few attractions for radicals who searched for a more dynamic vehicle to realize their aspirations. Eventually, in 1932, a more purposeful substitute appeared with the launching of the blue-shirted National Syndicalist movement.

The blueshirts attracted support, particularly among the urban middle classes, that had eluded earlier, stillborn authoritarian parties. By the early 1930s, sections of the petty bourgeoisie may have been rediscovering their taste for political involvement as the benefits of Salazar's financial dictatorship began to seem increasingly illusory. Deflationary policies that restricted credit and reduced purchasing power were proving unpopular with small businessmen, not a few of whom went to the wall. In 1933, after two-thirds of Lisbon's voters abstained in the constitutional referendum, the British embassy commented that 'Lisbon is not yet won over to the Estado Novo'.[15]

National Syndicalism's greatest impact was on young people in universities and schools. They, together with young officers unhappy at the army's relegation to the political sidelines by a bashful professor, were conspicuous at the series of well-attended rallies and banquets held to promote the movement's leader, an early Integralist, Rolão Preto. The movement gathered momentum despite Rolão Preto's lack of real charisma and his use of 'bourgeois' and 'capitalism' as negative symbols. Sorel, Proudhon and Marx, or so he claimed in old age, were the chief influences on his thought.[16] 'It is necessary that the rich be less rich so that the poor be less poor' was a typical blueshirt slogan.[17] In *Revolucão Nacional*, the daily that he edited, Rolão Preto applauded the rise of Hitler and extolled the cult of violence, although in 1933 he conceded that unlike the more 'materialistic' and 'cruel' fascist movements in Italy and Germany he was also moved by Christian impulses.[18]

The blueshirts could make only limited headway in the absence of a national crisis and with the vacuum in right-wing politics having been all but filled in favour of orthodox conservatism. Their mainly urban appeal was demonstrated in 1933 when they took their campaign to the rural north and met physical opposition from local elements of the União Nacional.[19] Eventually in July 1934, soon after the assassination by

162

Nazis of Dollfuss, the Austrian dictator whose Catholic corporatist regime was probably the European authoritarian system most closely aligned with Salazar's, the National Syndicalist movement was dissolved and its leader exiled. Salazar had already thrown down the gauntlet to the blueshirts at a well-publicized meeting in May 1934 where he attacked the 'totalitarian state' and speculated about whether

> it might not bring about an absolutism worse than that which preceded the liberal regimes ... Such a state would be essentially pagan, incompatible by its nature with the character of our Christian civilization and leading sooner or later to revolution.[20]

The radical right was tamed in Portugal far more smoothly than in, for example, Spain, Romania, Brazil and Japan where not dissimilar political movements posed headaches for authoritarian regimes mistrustful of mass mobilization. Many middle-ranking National Syndicalists crossed over to the União Nacional and received jobs as regime propagandists and state functionaries. Patronage was a tool which Salazar always wielded with consummate skill to win over more radical spirits inspired by foreign models and disappointed in the evolution of the New State.

The blueshirt episode helped convince Salazar that youth needed a political outlet which his regime had hitherto not provided. Opportunistically he appropriated several blueshirt symbols and approved the creation of a voluntary youth movement, the Accão Escolar Vanguarda, which quickly suffocated under official patronage. In May 1936 it was replaced by the Mocidade Portuguesa, in which all schoolchildren were required to enrol. The eruption of the Spanish Civil War in July 1936 encouraged the regime to borrow some of the trappings of an Italian and German fascism that now appeared firmly in the ascendant. Salazar gave his blessing to the Portuguese Legion, a pro-regime militia with access to weapons, membership of which became compulsory for many lower-ranking bureaucrats. Activists showed what they were capable of in 1936 by publicly beating up members of a Lisbon crowd who had had the temerity to cheer the arrival of the British navy.[21] Far grimmer was the reputation of the secret police, the Polícia de Vigilancia e Defesa do Estado (PVDE), who carefully watched the poor of the towns and cities and whose commander, Agostinho Lourenço, was the only state official to whom the money-conscious Salazar granted unlimited funds.[22]

Although the army was one of the few institutions the secret police were not encouraged to penetrate, by 1938 Salazar had greatly curtailed its autonomy. New procedures laid down that promotion was by selection rather than seniority, and Salazar appointed himself Minister of War with a junior officer, Captain Fernando dos Santos Costa, as his deputy. The fact that a captain dedicated to the *Estado Novo* was able to give orders to generals showed how the army had evolved from being a guarantor of the regime to an increasingly pliant instrument of authoritarian control. While his subordinate gave fellow 'nationalist' officers second jobs in the corporative bureaucracy, Salazar was even able to enforce a law curtailing officers from engaging in business, hitherto a necessity for many in this poorly paid profession.[23]

How far did Salazar's conservative police state evolve during the 1930s in the direction of a totalitarian dictatorship comparable in style, methods and ideology with the radical fascist regimes of Italy and Germany? A general answer will be attempted by examining the similarities which brought the *Estado Novo* and mid-European fascism closer together and the differences which, in key respects, nevertheless separated them.

Possibly the most striking similarity between Salazar and his Axis contemporaries was the degree of his personal control over the regime's activities. Of course, personal identification over affairs of state is not confined to fascist systems, and in the *Estado Novo* it took its own highly individual form. The informal power structure fashioned by Salazar reflected his own retiring and calculating personality. Afraid of crowds and reluctant to make speeches, if he sponsored a cult of personality it was very different from those on display in Rome and Berlin. Reading between the lines of speeches referring to Hitler and Mussolini, one sometimes gains the impression that he regarded the former as dangerous and irrational and the latter as a vulgar upstart.[24] Salazar never described himself as a dictator and his publicity machine scrapped the term 'dictatorship' after he became premier in 1932. On the eve of important decisions being announced in Lisbon, he often buried himself in his native northern village, and he preferred to leave public occasions to the dignified President Carmona who was depicted in propaganda as a national grandfather. Occasionally he talked of resignation, encouraging factions within the *Estado Novo* to believe that the succession was not a closed issue. But while the *Estado Novo* had a more impersonal image than the Italian and German regimes, Salazar's grip on power was just as firm as, or even firmer than, Hitler's or Mussolini's. In 1936 a US diplomat reported that Salazar 'can make any decision without necessity for consultation with any other individual in Portugal';[25] four years later another member of the US legation commented that he 'oversees practically everything' down to planning state exhibitions, editing military guides and controlling the most trivial forms of expenditure.[26]

Nationalism was the main source of Salazar's doctrine as it was of Mussolini's and Hitler's. Each saw the advantage of utilizing a cultural agent which permeated society and was classless. However, *Estado Novo* nationalism was broadly based and, at least where Europe was concerned, unwarlike. Salazar stated categorically in 1934 that 'Portugal has no need of wars, usurpations or conquests'.[27] His nationalism was 'sane and non-aggressive' and stemmed from Portugal's long historical existence and relatively secure sense of national identity.[28]

Salazar agreed with all European fascist leaders that democracy was an obstacle to national greatness. His propagandists accordingly pilloried liberalism in general and particularly the disastrous local variant which Portugal had endured before 1926. But whereas democracy was condemned in Portugal for failing to honour its virtues of freedom, honest government, accountability of rule, etc., in fascist propaganda these selfsame virtues were scorned in favour of revolutionary substitutes which Salazar could not bring himself to accept. Perhaps he would not have disagreed with his young assistant and eventual successor, Marcelo Caetano, who declared in 1934 that 'we will save everything in liberalism that is good and human'.[29] The 'pagan' caesarism of Mussolini 'which recognizes ... no moral or legal order' moved a critical Salazar to wonder whether the Italian and German regimes were compatible with Christian civilization.[30] In 1936 he spoke openly of similarities between fascism and Nazism on the one hand and communism on the other, these relating mainly to their common promotion of the totalitarian state 'to whose ends all the activities of the citizen are subject and men exist only for its greatness and glory'.[31]

Anti-communism nevertheless remained one of the driving impulses behind the rise of fascism, and the priority given to it helped blur the differences within the authoritarian right during the 1930s. In Portugal during the initial seizure of power, there had not existed that fear of proletarian revolution which had served as a catalyst in mobilizing the right in Italy and Germany. Up to the outbreak of the Spanish Civil War, members of the Portuguese Communist Party were treated less harshly than were their comrades under other right-wing dictatorships. In 1936 Álvaro Cunhal, a rising young Communist, was even able to sit his law finals in prison and receive brilliant marks, thanks to the intervention of Santos Costa, Salazar's normally hardline deputy in the War Ministry.[32] The fact that they hailed from the same area and had family ties still counted for more than ideological scruples. Spanish communism's advance, from tiny sect to player of a central role within Republican Spain during the civil war, nevertheless appeared a fearful portent to the Portuguese right, and thereafter communism became a major negative symbol in *Estado Novo* propaganda. Regarding Hitler as an unreliable barrier against the spread of communism from the east, Salazar stayed aloof from the Anti-Comintern Pact signed before the Second World War by Germany, Italy, Spain and Japan: a right-wing international whose brittleness was exposed by the Nazi-Soviet pact.

The course of the Second World War served only to increase the Portuguese leader's dread of communism. The British ambassador reported in 1942 Salazar's belief that, unless the *Wehrmacht* succeeded in smashing the Soviets that summer, 'Europe will be engulfed in a wave of communism such as no power of earth can stop'.[33] At home the secret police, the PVDE, had for some time been treating local Communists as their most dangerous enemy. By the early 1940s a resourceful Communist Party was already proving to be the price for a harsh exploitation of the working class. Salazar may not have been completely dismayed by this development, since the presence of the red menace gave bite to his anti-communist propaganda, kept his own political waverers in line and weakened the credibility of the domestic opposition.

Reliance on force was another common trait shared by the dynamic fascist states and more traditionalist counterparts like the *Estado Novo*. The apparatus of internal repression constructed by Salazar was possibly even more omniscient and effective than anything developed in the Axis states. In one interview Salazar even excused the use of torture, but indiscriminate mass terror was not a feature of his rule.[34] Opponents could continue to reside in Portugal and keep their property – provided they abstained from politics and lived as private citizens. Harsh penalties awaited persistent infringers of the 'no politics' rule, especially if they were Communists. However, the death penalty was never restored and Salazar rejected a 1937 bill, proposed by the ultra-right deputy José Cabral, to make crimes against the safety of the state punishable by death or life imprisonment.[35] In 1935 he had bowed to the wishes of radical rightists by passing a law outlawing secret societies and specifically aimed against freemasons.[36] However, it was never rigorously enforced; bankers and army officers were able to maintain their masonic affiliations and a handful of Salazar's later ministers were even enrolled into the banned movement.

Ultra-rightists moulded by Action Française or keen to emulate the latest trends from Nazi Germany ventilated anti-Semitic sentiments which sometimes even crept into government organs. Yet these were random outbursts which the government did not encourage. Although the treatment of Africans in the Portuguese colonies bears comparison with the Nazi use of forced labour in occupied Europe, Salazar did not go in for systematic persecution of social minorities. As persecution of the German Jews was stepped up during the late 1930s, he publicly dissociated himself from anti-Semitism. In 1938 the press was allowed to criticize Nazi persecution of the Jews and, in a small but telling gesture, the government bought a disused synagogue in Tomar, not far from the famous Catholic shrine of Fatima, and turned it into a Jewish museum.[37] Samuel Schwarz, the Polish Jew who had restored the building, was given Portuguese citizenship in 1939, one year before many Jewish refugees fleeing the Nazi terror were warmly welcomed in Lisbon. One member of Portugal's small Jewish community, the eminent academic economist

Dr Moses Bensabat Amzalak, was a longstanding friend of Salazar's and served on many public committees during the *Estado Novo* era.

An attempt has been made to show that the similarities of style and method which linked the Portuguese New State with Fascist Italy and Nazi Germany, for example their nationalism, anti-communism, anti-democratic outlook, reliance on force and belief in the leader principle, masked subtle but important differences that made it hard to define them as uniform political systems. More clear-cut differences in policy and organization show how Salazar's Portugal deviated in even more fundamental ways from the model of a fascist state.

At no time did Salazar show any willingness to create a party to take over the machinery of state and thus give rise to a party-state wielding totalitarian power at every level of society. He was, indeed, hostile to the whole party concept, and when in 1930 he formed the União Nacional it was on the strict understanding that it was a civil association or 'non-party'. The UN was designed to restrain public opinion rather than mobilize it, and by the time Salazar decided in the 1940s to allow 'slightly free elections' it had become too decrepit to do anything other than stuff the ballot boxes with pro-regime voting slips. Ministers, diplomats and senior civil servants were never compelled to join it; in the system of personal absolutism which Salazar had constructed to suit modern conditions, there was really no place for a mass party: the agencies which mediated between government and people were administrative and technical, not political.[38]

Although Salazar, like Mussolini and Hitler, set about creating a strong state to fulfil his goals, it was not required to be as drastic as theirs in its regulatory or coercive methods; the aim was merely to strengthen existing social values and modes of behaviour rather than pioneer a radically new social order. Education was viewed as a key aspect of social control that could reaffirm traditional values. After 1936, Minister of Education Carneiro Pacheco politicized the school curriculum and made it a prime source of *Estado Novo* propaganda.[39] In the countryside especially, great care was taken to inculcate the values of nationhood, family and love for one's locality. The school was deliberately used to keep the rural population where it was and discourage emigration to the city. In speeches and interviews Salazar frequently referred to the social dangers posed by a growing population which between 1920 and 1940 increased by one-quarter to 7 million.

One political tendency represented in Parliament argued that mass literacy was a luxury Portugal could not afford since it only encouraged individualism, ambitions that could not be satisfied in society, and hence anti-social behaviour. Extremists who wished to close schools that catered for the poor did not get their way, but the high illiteracy rate which continued throughout the *Estado Novo* testified to their influence in ruling circles. Several of those who took a reactionary position in the education debates of the 1930s also identified readily with Nazi Germany and were partisans of the Axis during the Second World War. However, in domestic politics they did not, as a rule, campaign for the emulation of National Socialist policies in the economic and social spheres, since this would have forced them to abandon large parts of their backward-looking strategy. To copy Italy or Germany by developing industry, building up a modern, well-equipped army and indoctrinating public opinion would have required a social upheaval – and a full-scale literacy drive. So, in practice, those ultras inside the *Estado Novo* who did not shrink from describing themselves as fascists gave only selective endorsement to Nazi-Fascist ideals as practised in Germany and Italy. They applauded Hitler's anti-communist and anti-liberal stance, wished Salazar to emulate him by launching an even more ruthless drive against his enemies and wanted to see less emphasis on Portugal's alliance with Britain. But, in the final analysis, they were content to back a strategy of depoliticization in which religious campaigns like the cult of Fatima had greater salience than propaganda of the kind master-minded by Goebbels.

Salazar's economic strategy differed markedly from that of the fascist powers. Admittedly he used the machinery of the corporate state to curb the autonomy of private business associations, centralize economic controls and sponsor economic growth in limited directions, but the state did not itself heavily invest in economic enterprises or launch its own. In 1933 Salazar expressed doubt about state intervention in the economy as practised in Hitler's Germany:

> I fear he may go too far in the economic and social spheres . . . Were the word Communism to disappear from Germany, but the idea to remain under another name, the danger would be the same. It is usually risky to adopt the same weapons as your adversary, for they are apt to be turned on you.[40]

It was only near the end of the *Estado Novo* that the regime went in for ambitious capital projects, like the building of the Cabora Bassa dam in Mozambique or the Sines energy complex, comparable with some of the grandiose economic schemes of Hitler and Mussolini. A balanced budget and a stable currency were the relatively mundane symbols which Salazar deliberately used in his heyday to characterize the *Estado Novo* and underline its unhurried tempo and style.

The defining characteristic of the fascist economy in the 1930s was a policy of strict protectionism allied to rapid industrial expansion. Salazar's traditionalist prejudices ruled out the latter while the preconditions for pursuing a policy of strict autarky did not exist in Portugal. High tariff barriers would have been an unrealistic policy for a country dependent on foreign trade for the sale of its primary products and for the purchase of capital equipment. Portugal lacked the raw materials and above all the large internal market which would have allowed it to pursue a nationalist strategy of economic self-sufficiency. So Salazar was making a virtue of necessity when he proclaimed in 1936 that 'Portugal may be numbered among those which are least protectionist. We believe that the extreme protectionism which we see spreading everywhere is a serious mistake.'[41]

Only in agriculture did Salazar borrow some of the autarkic measures introduced in the fascist economy. Mussolini's Italy provided the inspiration for a 'wheat campaign' designed to stimulate domestic production and reduce dependence on costly imports at a time of high prices on the world market. Salazar was anxious to avoid bread shortages and a rise in the price of the staple element in the diet of the poor, being mindful of how, in the past, these developments had led to outbreaks of lower-class unrest. However, his minions sometimes enforced the policy in a highly arbitrary manner; for instance, in 1939 the US legation reported that in the north peasants had gone hungry during the previous winter after they had been forced to uproot their vines and plant wheat.[42]

If economic isolation was impractical, Salazar had no qualms about pursuing a policy of political isolation. He kept his distance from Hitler and Mussolini, with whom he avoided all treaty obligations for fear that Portugal might become trapped in the fascist orbit and be sacrificed to their political expediency. As a land power, Germany had nothing to offer Portugal and the alliance with Britain was maintained even as the British international position weakened in the 1930s. During the early stages of the Spanish Civil War, fears were expressed in the Foreign Office that Portugal might drift into the Nazi orbit.[43] This was at a time when some fascist symbols were being adopted in Portugal, but control of foreign policy remained in the hands of permanent officials like Luiz Sampayo – overseen of course by Salazar.

Salazar strove for a Nationalist victory in Spain because he believed it offered the best hope for an end to direct foreign intervention in the Iberian peninsula. In the event of a Republican victory he feared that the peninsula would be Balkanized and Portugal absorbed and sovietized. Nor was he blind to the threat from within the other camp, from Falangist elements eager to unite Portugal and Spain in one Iberian state.[44] In order to neutralize this threat, Salazar sought to win Franco's friendship and gratitude by providing whatever diplomatic, military and economic help Portugal could afford in order to ensure his victory.

In 1939, with a new European war looming as the Spanish conflict finally ended, Salazar persuaded the victorious Franco to adhere to a policy of neutrality or at least non-belligerence. This policy was enshrined in the 1939 Iberian Pact in which the two peninsular states promised to respect and protect each other's territory and to enter into no pact or alliance involving aggression against the other. In Spain, the policy of disengagement from the European war had its critics among fascist Falangists who identified with the Axis cause; in formulating his foreign policy, however, Salazar faced few difficulties from their Portuguese counterparts, who represented a much weaker element within his power structure. No Portuguese counterpart to the Spanish Falange had been allowed to advance its claims, and Salazar brooked no intervention in the formulation of foreign policy from the various Catholic, monarchist, nationalist and conservative interests who made up the elite.

Although Salazar felt the European war to be largely the consequence of errors committed by the democracies since 1918, he maintained the ancient pact with Britain not least because Portugal's maritime and African interests were still dependent on British control of the sea-lanes. Had Britain chosen to invoke the Anglo-Portuguese alliance early in the war, the outcome could have been a definite split in the regime between those who identified with Portugal's ancient treaty partner and others whose political philosophy made them warm to the idea of a new, German-led, European order. Portugal's importance as an unoccupied and accessible European neutral meant that diplomatic missions and foreign intelligence services displayed inordinate concern about the political complexion and foreign sympathies of Portuguese ruling circles. British and American diplomatic services, along with their clandestine adjuncts, gathered vast quantities of information which, despite the doubtful accuracy of much of it, nevertheless demonstrated that pro-German feelings were very common among political functionaries, regime supporters and even close members of Salazar's entourage; as late as 1943 the Foreign Office was reliably informed that a majority of the cabinet were 'known Germanophils'.[45]

Widely differing factors influenced the alignment of *Estado Novo* personnel with one side or the other. Some were undoubtedly motivated by ideological sympathy. They included senior officers like Colonel Alfredo Sintra, head of the air force,[46] as well as Ministry of Propaganda functionaries like the deputy head, Antonio Eça de Queiroz, and journalists in the state-supervised press. Despite rigid censorship, a paper's sympathies could be readily discerned according to the prominence given to Allied or German dispatches or whether any were carried from the Soviet side.[47] An intelligence source reckoned that in 1942 the semi-official *Diário de Manhã* was '70 per cent pro-Nazi', and it was only after the Normandy landings of June 1944 that it began to modify its pro-German stance.[48] Until late in the war, *Alerta*, a fascist weekly, was 'published with the knowledge and support of the government'.[49] Salazar did not place too many restrictions on the extreme right because he may have felt that

170

the effect of its propaganda work was relatively harmless. While alarmed at the prospect of a Nazi-dominated Europe, he hoped in the first half of the war that a negotiated peace might leave Germany in a strong enough position to act as a bulwark against communism, and he may have been temperamentally reluctant to check those zealots whose anti-communism took the form of admiration for Hitler.

Some, especially in the army, gained a pro-German reputation because they admired the fighting qualities of the *Wehrmacht*; Santos Costa, Salazar's deputy in the War Ministry, perhaps fell into this category, though he claimed shortly before his death that any position he adopted towards the combatants was motivated solely by a desire to safeguard Portuguese interests.[50] In 1943, after Britain had invoked the alliance to gain military facilities in the Azores, he admitted that in Cabinet he had opposed Salazar's decision to accede.[51] Perhaps Britain's refusal to sell Portugal arms in 1937 still rankled with him, or he may have felt the need to affirm his position as head of the 'nationalist' faction in the Portuguese government.

The faction's hard core comprised monarchists and Catholics, but during the war the broader Catholic faction began subtly to redefine its political position and move away from the ultra-right. The lead was taken by the head of the Church, Cardinal Cerejeira, whose longstanding friendship with Salazar made him politically important. Influenced by the Nazi seizure of Catholic Poland and by reports of religious persecution there and within Germany itself, he took a pro-Allied position early in the war. Other Catholics disagreed. Especially noteworthy was the writer Dr Alfredo Pimenta, 'head of a small ultra-nationalist coterie of intellectuals who make no secret of their pro-German and anti-British views'.[52] A confrontation occurred in 1943 after Pimenta had 'sneered ... at the Pope's injunction to pray for the return of the Russian people to the fold of the church'.[53] Cerejeira then responded by depriving Pimenta of the title 'Catholic writer' in an official statement which referred to his influence having 'become the cause of scandal among the faithful'.[54]

Diplomatic sources reckoned that the majority of notables who could be classified as pro-Axis were more likely to be motivated by political or economic self-interest than by ideological considerations. As the Axis cause waned, a number of officials gravitated to the sidelines or opportunistically supported the Allies. Some played both sides, among them the Espirito Santo brothers, rich bankers of Jewish origin who despite lucrative dealings in occupied Europe still enjoyed the protection of the British embassy and of Salazar, who rescued one of them from the clutches of the Gestapo in Paris.[55]

'As long as Salazar continues to make all the important decisions, the opinions of his ministers are relatively unimportant' was the view of a US embassy official in 1944.[56] It was prompted by an important Cabinet reshuffle in which Salazar actually promoted figures like Santos Costa, Julio Botelho Moniz and Costa Leite who, not long before, had been identified with the Axis cause. In this and in other ways, Salazar sought to demonstrate to the Allies that he was master of his own house and was disinclined to soften the character of his regime because of the impending collapse of the European far right outside the Iberian peninsula.

In 1942, the British ambassador had talked frankly to Salazar about 'the Gestapo methods of his own police and the maltreatment of his own people', but afterwards no pressure was put on him to lighten his rule.[57] Portugal avoided the ostracism which Franco's Spain received at the hands of the Western nations in the early postwar years. Britain and the United States had been convinced by Salazar's tenacious defence of Portuguese neutrality that he was 'a very hard nut to crack'.[58] Others mindful of his Cassandra-like warnings, made in the early part of the war, about the recuperative powers of Soviet communism were ready, in the climate of cold war Europe, to fall for propaganda which depicted him as a pillar of Christian civilization. There were few official protests when the *Estado Novo* chose the moment of European fascism's defeat to tighten its grip on the country. New laws expanded the powers of the secret police (renamed the Polícia Internacional e de Defesa do Estado [PIDE]), laid down harsher sentences for anti-government activity, and allowed for the dismissal of civil servants, teachers and professors for political offences. They were more expressive of Salazar's intentions than his widely heralded decision in 1945 to allow opposition candidates to stand for the first time in legislative elections and have the *Estado Novo* rechristened an 'organic democracy'. If the PIDE had been avowedly pro-Axis during the war, its growing salience after 1945 might have produced more of an outcry abroad; however, a thorough analysis by US Naval Intelligence in 1942 contended that its German links had been exaggerated. The report, based on information from police officers, Portuguese businessmen and British agents, argued that 'one is probably closer to the truth in saying that officers are chosen because they are fanatically in favour of the Salazar regime and that what pro-Axis sympathies they may have, result from the affinities of that regime to the totalitarian states'.[59]

No evidence has emerged that moderates in the Lisbon power structure pressed during the closing stages of the war for the offsetting of Allied hostility through controlled liberalization, or contemplated ditching Salazar for a more conciliatory figure. Members of the power elite were motivated by the feeling that they must hang together or would surely hang separately. The degree of popular opposition to the regime had been demonstrated by major disturbances in 1943 and 1944, triggered off by chronic food shortages and accurate rumours of war profiteering and corruption in government circles.

Salazar did not believe that the army could be indefinitely relied upon to contain disorders that had been orchestrated by the Communist Party. Officers and men were badly paid and shabbily treated, and in 1944 there were cases of soldiers refusing to go into action against protesters.[60] After 1943, servicemen were forbidden to attend Allied or Axis propaganda meetings, the authorities fearing the spread of dangerous ideas, especially from the Allied side.[61] Important commissions were given to reactionary and even unbalanced officers because it was felt that they could be relied upon to stop at nothing if a major uprising against the government occurred.[62] The new 1944 Cabinet was described by an American source as a 'ministry of fear' which betrayed Salazar's 'apprehension of the future'.[63] Apparent pro-German loyalties did not dissuade him from staffing his Cabinet with 'nationalists' in order to fortify the regime against revolution. It was reported that contingency plans were drawn up in 1944 for the creation of an SS-type body, drawn from the most reliable sectors of the army, the National Republican Guard and the secret police, that 'would repress all popular movements'.[64] The impetus for this drastic departure came from ultra-right officers in the ministries responsible for law and order. The plan was never activated because existing forms of repression proved able to scatter militant opposition in 1944–5.

At moments of crisis and uncertainty such as 1936 or 1945, 'ultras' within the power structure became more visible than 'moderates'. Salazar always drew most of his advisers and longest-serving ministers from the more right-wing groups in his entourage. They were far more dependent on him, and hence more loyal, than 'moderates' who could envisage a political existence for themselves in a post-*Estado Novo* regime (as indeed has proved to be the case for some ex-ministers now active in democratic politics). Whilst the far right managed to colonize and monopolize loyalist fronts like the Legion, the Mocidade and the UN, the influence it thereby wielded was mainly negative: it was usually able to act as a counterweight against reform and renewal from within, but was incapable of turning these agencies into autonomous sources of power which even Salazar had to heed. The far right lacked the political skills and the dedication necessary to breathe life into stillborn bodies which Salazar had incapacitated at birth. It was bereft of some of the most energetic and visionary nationalists who, after Salazar had neutralized the blueshirts and isolated the Integralists, found a new home in the democratic opposition. Only, perhaps, if the radical right had built up a powerful military following in the years of transition after 1926 might an effective and potentially successful challenge to his restrictive brand of right-wing politics have emerged – but by then the dominant military elites were tired of political experimentation. Thereafter, Salazar offered the most reactionary factions of the *Estado Novo* abundant opportunities for self-enrichment, together with the shadow, but never the substance, of power.

NOTES

Research on which this chapter is based was made possible with the help of an award in 1984 from the Twenty-Seven Foundation of the Institute of Historical Research.

1 F. Nogueira, *Salazar*, Vol. I, *A Mocidade e os Principios* (Coimbra, 1977), p. 71.
2 P. C. Schmitter, 'The "Regime d'Exception" that became the rule: forty-eight years of authoritarian domination in Portugal', in L. Graham and H. Makler, *Contemporary Portugal: the Revolution and its Antecedents* (Austin, Tex., 1979), p. 33.
3 J. Medina, 'Os primeiros fascistas portuguesas', *Vértice*, nos 400–1 (September–October 1977), p. 604. Cf. C. Barreira, 'Homem Cristo Filho: algumas considerações em torno do seu percurso ideologico-politico', in *O fascismo em Portugal* (Lisbon, 1982), pp. 175–86.
4 H. Martins, 'Portugal', in S. J. Woolf (ed.), *European Fascism* (London, 1968), p. 307.
5 Public Record Office (PRO), FO 371 (1943), 34632, John Balfour to Sir Anthony Eden, Foreign Secretary.
6 B. Kohler, *Political Forces in Spain, Greece and Portugal* (London, 1982), p. 171.
7 A. de Oliveira Salazar, *Doctrine and Action. Internal and Foreign Policy of the New Portugal*, trans. R. E. Broughton (London, 1939), p. 107.
8 ibid., p. 168.
9 Schmitter, 'Regime d'Exception', p. 44.
10 Salazar, *Doctrine and Action*, p. 45.
11 ibid., p. 84.
12 ibid., p. 238.
13 ibid., p. 109.
14 This statement was included in an official note issued in 1935 and quoted by A. H. de Oliveira Marques, *A History of Portugal*, Vol. 2, *From Empire to Corporative State* (New York, 1973), p. 215.
15 PRO, FO 371 (1933), annual report from Portugal.
16 J. Medina, *Salazar e os Fascistas. Salazarismo e Nacionalsindicalismo: a historia dum conflito 1932–5* (Lisbon, 1978), p. 187.
17 M. Caetano, *Minhas memórias de Salazar* (Lisbon, 1977), p. 70.
18 Quoted in Medina, *Salazar e os Fascistas*, pp. 128–9.
19 ibid., pp. 30–4.
20 Salazar, *Doctrine and Action*, p. 231.
21 United States National Archives, Washington DC (USNA), Record Group 853.00/966, 'Report on conditions in Portugal', by Herbert C. Pell of the US Legation, 5 August 1938.
22 USNA, 18172, Intelligence Division, Chief of Naval Operations, US Navy Department, 'Portugal, political forces', 29 May 1942.
23 USNA, 99526, Intelligence Division, Chief of Naval Operations, US Navy Department, 'Portugal: government, foreign relations, political forces, organization of government and personality sketches of leaders', 26 September 1944.
24 A. Ferro, *Salazar. Portugal and her Leader*, trans. H. de Barros Gomes and John Gibbons (London, 1939), p. 176.
25 USNA, Record Group 853.00/933, 'Recent trends in Portuguese politics', by R. G. G. Caldwell, US Legation, 3 December 1936.
26 USNA, Record Group 853.00/1014, 'Brief summary of the political situation in Portugal', by Bert Fish, Minister of the US Legation, 1940.
27 Salazar, *Doctrine and Action*, p. 223.
28 ibid., p. 37.

29 Caetano, *Minhas memórias*, p. 69.
30 Salazar, *Doctrine and Action*, p. 231; Ferro, *Salazar*, p. 176.
31 Salazar, *Doctrine and Action*, p. 54.
32 Interview with General Fernando dos Santos Costa, Lisbon, July 1981.
33 PRO, 954/21, papers of Lord Avon, formerly Sir Anthony Eden. Sir Ronald Campbell, British ambassador in Lisbon, to Mr Anthony Eden, Foreign Secretary, 15 April 1942.
34 Ferro, *Salazar*, p. 138.
35 PRO, FO 371 (1937), annual report from Portugal.
36 A. H. de Oliveira Marques, *A Maconeria Portuguesa e o Estado Novo*, 2nd edn (Lisbon, 1983), pp. 61–3.
37 Details are provided in J. M. Santos Simões, *Tomar e a sua Judaria* (Tomar, 1943).
38 W. Opello, 'Portugal's administrative elite: social origins and political attitudes', *West European Politics*, vol. 6, no. 1 (1983), p. 64.
39 USNA, Record Group 853.00/933, 'Recent trends in Portuguese politics', by R. G. G. Caldwell, US Legation, 3 December 1936.
40 Ferro, *Salazar*, p. 350.
41 Salazar, *Doctrine and Action*, p. 26.
42 USNA, Record group 853.00/987, 'Political and general conditions in Portugal', by Herbert C. Pell, US Legation, 24 July 1939.
43 G. A. Stone, 'The official British attitude to the Anglo-Portuguese alliance, 1910–45', *Journal of Contemporary History*, vol. 10, no. 4 (October 1975), p. 738.
44 I. Delgado, *Portugal e a Guerra Civil de Espanha* (Lisbon, 1980).
45 PRO, FO 371 (1943), C692/66/36, 27 July 1943.
46 USNA, Office of Strategic Services Collection (OSS), 11997, 'Attitude of Portuguese general officers', Lt Col. W. E. Shipp, US Military Attaché to OSS, 27 January 1942.
47 USNA, OSS, 19710, 'The Portuguese press', August 1942.
48 ibid.; USNA, OSS, 243594, 'Public opinion in Portugal', 13 July 1944.
49 USNA, OSS, 10379, 31 October 1944.
50 USNA, 99526, Intelligence Division, Chief of Naval Operations, US Navy Department, 'Portugal: government, foreign relations, political forces, organisation of government and personality sketches of leaders', 26 September 1944; interview with General Fernando dos Santos Costa, Lisbon, July 1981.
51 ibid.
52 PRO, FO, 371 (1943), 34644, 4 August 1944.
53 ibid.
54 ibid.
55 USNA, OSS, 26546, 'Personal background of individuals in the government or closely associated therewith', 22 October 1942.
56 USNA, Record Group 853.00/9–2844, 'Changes in the Portuguese Cabinet', by Edward Crocker, US Embassy, 28 September 1944.
57 PRO, 954/21, Avon papers, Sir Ronald Campbell, British ambassador in Lisbon, to Mr Anthony Eden, Foreign Secretary, 15 April 1942.
58 PRO, 954/21, Avon papers, Sir Ronald Campbell, British ambassador in Lisbon, to Mr Anthony Eden, Foreign Secretary, 18 April 1942.
59 USNA, 18172, Intelligence Division, Chief of Naval Operations, US Navy Department, 'Portugal, political forces', 29 May 1942.
60 USNA, OSS, 10265, report based on information from 'a source who is Republican in his sympathies', 14 October 1944.
61 USNA, OSS, 60317, report of new decree Law no. 32: 745, 30 April 1943.
62 USNA, 40939, Intelligence Division, Chief of Naval Operations, US Navy Department, 22 July 1943.
63 USNA, 99526, Intelligence Division, Chief of Naval Operations, US Navy Department, 'Portugal: government, foreign relations, political forces, organisation of government and personality sketches of leaders', 26 September 1944.
64 USNA, OSS, 10265, report based on information from 'a source who is Republican in his sympathies', 14 October 1944.

10

The conservative right and the far right in France: the search for power, 1934–44

Roger Austin

Although considerable research has been conducted into the ideology, organization and sociological background of various groups of the interwar French right,[1] understanding of the relationship between the conservative and the far right has been obstructed by a shortage of empirical evidence and a preoccupation with a specific issue: that of the degree of penetration achieved by fascist ideology in the France of the 1930s. Faced with an almost total dearth of relevant archival material in the Archives Nationales for the period 1936–40, historians of the French right have been obliged to rely heavily upon newspapers and other printed sources. In departmental archives, however, there does exist valuable documentary evidence which throws light on the relationship between the conservative right and some of the more important groups on the far right. In particular, the detailed and highly perceptive monthly reports from the 'political' police, the *Commissaires Spéciaux*, to local prefects provide an analysis of political movements, industrial unrest and public opinion at local level. Quite apart from what they reveal about popular *mentalité* on the right, these sources suggest that ideological differences between the far right and the conservative right were often buried, especially between 1934 and 1938 when conservatives and extremists shared a common commitment to recapturing political power.

France in 1934 was feeling the effects both of long-term social and technological changes, set in motion by urbanization and the First World War, and of the more immediate consequences of the world depression. In both town and country the experience of change was often bewildering or painful. Even though France had won the war, changes in morality and technology created a profound sense of confusion. From abroad, too, were now coming disquieting signs of change. The French public was clearly unsure about the best way to face up to the perceived threat from Hitler. In December 1933, for example, the *Commissaire Spécial* in Nice wrote to the prefect:

The public feels that we are at a turning point in history. The diplomatic activity of Hitler's government is overturning the established order of things in Europe. Should we come to an understanding with him or should we be firm and resolute towards him?[2]

The sense of domestic and foreign crisis fuelled doubts about the ability of the parliamentary system to defend the nation and what were seen as the legitimate interests of different sections of society. It is against this background that we must interpret the increasing extra-parliamentary activity that was to provide an important link in relations between the conservative and the far right. Crucial to these developments were the events of February 1934, triggered by a financial scandal involving the banker Stavisky and his connections with influential figures in the ruling centrist Radical Party. Police reports throughout France during January 1934 conveyed the depth of public anger provoked by the affair: anger which, at its most extreme, indicated the immense symbolic value attached to the scandal as an illustration of everything that was wrong with the parliamentary system. The *Commissaire Spécial* in Cannes described in this way the mood of the mainly bourgeois public in his area:

In previous reports I have underlined the wave of anti-parliamentary feeling which was sweeping the area and the danger this represented for the Republican regime. Now after the Stavisky affair, the public can scarcely be held back from their elected representatives. It is they, it is said, who are responsible for the state of moral and material anarchy in which the country finds itself . . . Nothing good will ever be achieved while universal suffrage continues. The public believe in the Republic but only on condition that it reforms and cleans itself up.[3]

The extent to which the Republic itself was under attack became more apparent on the night of 6 February 1934 when some 25,000 right-wingers assembled in Paris for what most historians now agree was a 'Boulangist' demonstration against a centre-left government rather than a fascist putsch.[4] Although the three main groups who took part – the Jeunesses Patriotes, the Croix de Feu and the Union Nationale des Combattants – did not attempt to seize power, the police opened fire on the demonstrators and there were fatal casualties on both sides. Within a day the Radical Socialist premier Daladier had resigned and been replaced by the old right-wing conservative Gaston Doumergue at the head of a government of national union.

Reaction to these momentous events was to shape the political alliance which began to emerge on the right. Reports from many areas[5] suggest that the popular response was made up of three main elements. The first was the sheer intensity of feeling aroused, even in quiet areas like the Ariège where 'you would have to go back to the sombre days of July 1914 to find a moment to compare with the mood of the population since the events of February'.[6] This sensitizing of public opinion was crucial in creating conditions for mass involvement without which the extra-parliamentary right could never have developed.

Secondly, public opinion was politically polarized. In Lyon, the *Commissaire Spécial* noted with alarm that the normally moderate populace had, for the first time, shown sympathy towards the demonstrators,[7] whereas reports from Montpellier revealed that the mobilization of public opinion was in the opposite direction, in defence of the Republic:

> The events of 6 February are seen not as a movement against parliamentary morality, which is generally condemned, but against the regime, the Republic and its freedom ... all the republicans joined together in a common front for its defence and at least 4,000 of them, a number without precedent here, took part in a demonstration of solidarity on 12 February.[8]

At Rennes the prefect noted that there were now two totally antagonistic blocs. On the right stood the Action Française, Solidarité Française, the Jeunesses Patriotes and the Ligue des Contribuables, while on the left were 'workers, civil servants and artisans, the mass of the people determined to defend hard-won rights and profoundly attached to republican institutions'.[9] In Saint-Nazaire, the public had never been so divided, according to the *Commissaire Spécial*.[10] The effect of this polarization of public opinion was to push the conservative right into a closer alliance with the far right. February 1934 marks a decisive point in this developing relationship.

No less important was the third characteristic of public reaction to February 1934: the evident approval extended by some sections of the population towards the use of extra-parliamentary pressure to remove the government of the day, which greatly boosted the employment of organized violence as part of the political process. For example, in Montluçon (Allier) it was reported that the readiness of the war veterans to take power 'and put things back in their natural place' was 'very favourably welcomed'.[11] This predisposition towards direct action amongst hitherto politically dormant groups provides a key to understanding relationships on the right between 1934 and 1936.

THE EXTRA-PARLIAMENTARY RIGHT
AND THE CONSERVATIVE RIGHT, 1934–6

From February 1934 the police noticed a marked increase in the activities of far right groups and their intention of forming a 'National Front' to oppose the common front of the left. What was it that held together Action Française, the Croix de Feu and the Union Nationale des Combattants? All of them shared a view of France that owed much to integral nationalism and found expression in violent anti-communism, varying degrees of xenophobia, and a belief in vaguely corporatist solutions to French economic problems. They favoured authoritarian forms of government which would strengthen the powers of the executive over parliament. Above all, however, they nursed a common commitment to the use of political methods involving direct action. In particular they showed a willingness to match the growing strength of left-wing street demonstrations and to mobilize support through noisy meetings, cavalcades and provocative posters.

These tactics served one major function: they provided a growing number of men who felt cheated by parliament's failures with an outlet for their patriotic idealism. For many Frenchmen the most formative experience of their lives had been the trench warfare of 1914–18, when the use of violent action within a disciplined framework had been put to the service of their country. Since the end of the war there had been few opportunities for waving the tricolour or recapturing the *frisson* of action against the enemy – until the crisis of 1934. Faced with the internal threat of communism and the dangers outside France, many ex-servicemen enrolled in the ranks of the extra-parliamentary right in the belief that a call to arms was imminent.

As numbers in these paramilitary groups began to increase during 1934, their organizers had to deal with the question of how they were to be financed. As subscriptions to newspapers or voluntary contributions were proving inadequate for their growing ambitions, each group began looking for outside aid, the importance of which was starkly underlined in a police report in May 1934:

> There are rumours about a meeting between representatives of the Neo-Socialist party and Solidarité Française. In conservative right circles, there is scepticism about whether a close understanding can be reached since both are short of money and are looking for financial support.[12]

The need of radical right-wing groups for money and their penchant for the methods of direct action formed the basis of their links with the conservative right. The two shared enough common ground ideologically to make an alliance possible. What they both wanted was the destruction of communism, for schools to be patriotic and for parliamentary democracy to be reformed in such a way as to provide a guarantee of order in the country. The two issues on which they occasionally appeared to diverge – attitudes to capitalism and the far right's demands for radical change –

were never, at least before mid-1935, seriously divisive. Like the perfume magnate François Coty, many industrialists were prepared to subscribe to the view that there was 'good capitalism', founded on work, and 'bad capitalism', based on speculation. In spite of all the rhetoric on the far right about the evils of capitalism, this owed much more to the need to attract the petty bourgeoisie and disaffected employees than to any real concern for weakening the primacy of profits or property. Similarly, conservatives could afford to tolerate the far right's veiled attacks on their unwillingness to break with the past, if these populist clichés succeeded in rallying sections of the centre to the cause of order and a united stand against their left-wing enemies.

The two groups nevertheless agreed to employ different methods in pursuit of these common goals. This understanding was a crucial element in the relationship. It was articulated most clearly by parliamentary representatives of the Fédération Républicaine, the largest group on the conservative right in the Chamber of Deputies. Philippe Henriot, for example, saw these extra-parliamentary allies as 'a useful barrier of resolute men against the threatening violence of revolutionary forces'.[13] The two groups could work together if they accepted 'their parallel but different and autonomous tasks'.[14] Henriot wanted to restrict the paramilitary groups like the Croix de Feu to assembling large numbers of people for achieving temporary goals in the 'defence of order', but by mid-1935, when the Croix de Feu claimed to have 350,000 members,[15] it was no longer willing to play what it perceived to be a subordinate role.

The importance of the Croix de Feu numerically, tensions within the movement and the ambitions of its leader, La Rocque, led to a new relationship with the conservative right. In the immediate aftermath of February 1934, La Rocque was already under attack from some sections of his movement for his alleged indecisiveness and failure to take advantage of the situation. In the following months the movement's organizers had to work hard to maintain the sense of energy and action that was most likely to attract new members. La Rocque's technique was to insist that a state of crisis existed throughout the country and that his followers must be ready for 'H' hour and 'D' day. In June 1935 the prefect in the Moselle reported that La Rocque was telling the Croix de Feu that 'the end of the parliamentary regime is in sight, probably in October or November when parliament will be unable to balance the budget':

That's when the hour of the Croix de Feu will sound and our Association with its ideas in power will go into action to reorganize the country!

As with any oppositional faction with pretensions towards becoming a mass movement, La Rocque needed to keep his rank and file in a constant state of alert and to widen the appeal of the movement by attracting the victims of the economic slump. Evidence from police informers who had infiltrated the Croix de Feu now suggests what the effect of this was. Industrialists like Mercier and Wendel who were sympathetic to the movement began to have serious doubts about continuing to support it when La Rocque persistently denounced banking interests.[16] The threat of losing their backing led La Rocque to divert his followers' attention away from the causes of economic discomfort and towards its symptoms. From mid-1935 he thus encouraged the Croix de Feu to set up soup kitchens and dispensaries, and to become involved in a range of welfare activities.[17] These initiatives carried the additional advantage of providing a good public relations platform to complement street violence with the Communists. But to satisfy his followers' taste for action and to stem the trickle of resignations from inveterate street fighters, La Rocque allowed the Croix de Feu to organize hugely impressive motorcades. In September 1935, for example, the *Commissaire Spécial* in the Nord reported that no fewer than 560 vehicles were used for a private Croix de Feu meeting.[18] Other reports referred to 'motorized columns' being 'ambushed' by Communists who smashed the windscreens with volleys of well-aimed stones.[19] What mattered for La Rocque was permitting a level of violence which would provide a clear demonstration of the movement's dynamism without allowing it to tarnish his image of defending order. By the autumn of 1935, whatever La Rocque told his followers about seizing power, he was not prepared to overthrow the government and may already have begun to question whether he was likely to benefit from the polarization of public opinion.

As each month went by there were unmistakable signs that La Rocque was being portrayed by the left as the embodiment of fascism. Giant posters accused him of fomenting violent civil war in France.[20] In short, La Rocque and the Croix de Feu were being used not only to strengthen links between the Communists and Socialists but also to woo the centre, the voters who traditionally supported the Radical Socialist Party, into an anti-fascist Popular Front. La Rocque's eagerness to appeal to the centre explains why so much Croix de Feu propaganda denied that its members were fascists and claimed that it was the Communists who were 'red fascists'. La Rocque was already beginning to realize that the problem of the extra-parliamentary right was that its tactics unified the opposition. Furthermore, it was not clear what advantages the Croix de Feu would gain if it helped the conservative right win the elections scheduled for 1936. These considerations provide the key to understanding what is otherwise a complete mystery. When, in 1936, legislation was passed banning 'combat groups and private militia', the Croix de Feu was dissolved with virtually no word of protest. The most convincing explanation for this was that La Rocque had already decided that he had a far better chance of achieving power through creating a new political party which would represent the whole of the right. The first signs, then, of rivalry between the 'old right' and the 'new' were beginning to appear.

VICTORY ON THE LEFT
AND REACTION ON THE RIGHT, 1936–8

As France's political and economic crisis deepened in 1935, the government of Pierre Laval attempted to survive by pursuing a rigorous deflationary policy which was put into effect through a series of decree laws. The cuts in public expenditure, coupled with the means by which they were enforced, were perceived by the left not only as an attack on basic liberties but also as further proof that the extra-parliamentary right had been thrown into action to defend the capitalist right. In Lyon, for example, the public services union denounced deflationary tactics as a sign of 'the intolerable domination of a handful of *affairistes* whose scandalous privileges and insatiable appetite are the cause of the misery and privations of those who have only their jobs for survival'.[21] The railwaymen's union saw the decree laws as social repression masking fascism, and with a keen sense of history claimed that 'The feudalists are ruining the country to save their privileges'.[22]

If we can believe contemporary political commentators, this feeling was not confined to a minority of trade union activists. Even journalists writing for the moderate Catholic press, such as A. Michelin, explained the victory of the left in the legislative elections of 1936 by saying that not only was the left united and the right divided but

> the mass of our people is strongly attached to the Republic and believed the Republic to be in danger: its liberties, which they hold so vital, were seen to be threatened.[23]

These perceptions are important in understanding the explosion of joy which, on the left, greeted victory in the late spring of 1936 and, in turn, the sense of utter alienation and desperation that gripped the bourgeoisie. The noisy victory demonstrations throughout France, the provocative singing of the 'Internationale', and the waving of the Red Flag in public places accompanied by shouts of 'La Rocque au poteau' were the visible signs that power had fallen into the hands of the Socialist, Communist and Radical Socialist alliance. Worse was to come. The wave of strikes and factory-occupations in support of improved wages and a shorter working week succeeded in forcing employers to agree to the workers' demands. But the employers' surrender in the shape of the Matignon agreement, signed on 12 June 1936, was accepted in many cases with extreme reluctance. From this point, evidence from two very different departments, the Ardèche and the Rhône, suggests that the relationship of the conservative to the far right was primarily determined by the need to stem what were seen as the 'catastrophic financial and political consequences'[24] of the Popular Front's social legislation.

The first line of defence open to the conservative right was opposition within the parliamentary framework. Having lost control of the Chamber of Deputies, they looked increasingly to the Senate where, as early as May 1936, hopes were being pinned for a showdown with the Chamber.[25] The composition of the Senate was such that a certain 'social and economic conservatism'[26] could be played upon as the strikes persisted and as their character began to alter. Certainly in Lyon, where 71,000 workers were out on strike by July,[27] police reports noted that the public was now worried by the 'revolutionary nature of the strikes' and by the 'continuation of the strike movement'.[28] When the Senate expressed its reservations about some of the aspects of the new social laws, the *Commissaire Spécial* in Lyon reported that this 'had certainly encouraged the employers to resist the workers' demands more strongly'.[29] The role of the Senate as an obstacle to social change under the Third Republic has been outlined elsewhere,[30] but its ability to delay or water down legislation favourable to employees' interests was restricted by parliamentary convention. Nevertheless, the conservative right, once it had recovered from the shock of defeat, now began to mobilize its energies to use whatever weapons it could to limit the damage. In the Chamber itself, although the moderate right played the role of loyal opposition, the Fédération Républicaine was intransigent,[31] mixing political filibustering with ferocious personal attacks on the Jewish members of the government.[32] Such personal invective, which became increasingly characteristic of the right, succeeded in driving the Minister of the Interior, Roger Sallengro, to suicide.

Although Sallengro's death may have afforded a grim sense of revenge to the second-rate newspaper hacks who had hounded him, such tactics offered no practical help to hard-pressed employers. Indeed, as they were forced to raise wages to agreed national levels and to accept compulsory collective bargaining and paid holidays, employers looked increasingly outside parliament for help. With their factories or workshops occupied, and faced with the certainty of higher production costs, many adopted a series of measures designed to sabotage government legislation. They began by refusing to negotiate while factories were occupied or in some cases by clearing the factory by force.[33] This was frequently followed by the sacking of workers and the threatened or actual closure of the factory. Others, in smaller businesses, belonged to a more paternalist tradition and simply raised prices by 10 per cent to avoid confrontation with their workers. The number of instances where employers in either rural Ardèche or industrial Lyon adopted these means of protecting their

own authority and resisting the effects of Popular Front legislation, testifies
to a blunt refusal to accept the popular will. And it certainly led some of
them to look for means of undermining the solidarity of their workers.

The dramatic increase in membership of the Communist trade union,
the Confédération Générale du Travail (CGT), from 50,000 to 775,000
between June 1935 and March 1937 was an unmistakable sign of the
extent to which large sections of the working class had become politicized.
To counter their pressure for the full implementation of the 40-hour week
and the other measures agreed at Matignon, employers stepped up their
discreet support for unions which were openly hostile to the CGT. In
the Ardèche cement factories, situated on the west bank of the Rhône
and the only industrialized area of the department, a group constituting
about a quarter of the workforce and calling itself the 'corporatist defence
union' complained to the prefect that they had been forced into an illegal
strike. The Ministry of Works inspector reported to the prefect that the
group had been set up 'with the support of the employer'.[34] Apart from
these Syndicats Professionels Français[35] employers attempted to use the
Christian trade union, the Confédération Française des Syndicats Chrétiens
(CFTC), to divide the workforce.[36] Membership of the CFTC had also
increased, from 8,000 to 20,000 between mid-June 1936 and spring
1937,[37] but its numbers fell so far short of matching those of the CGT
that employers turned elsewhere: first to La Rocque and then to Jacques
Doriot.

LA ROCQUE, DORIOT AND
THE CONSERVATIVE RIGHT

Within months of the Croix de Feu being dissolved, La Rocque had formed
a new political party, the Parti Social Français (PSF). At meetings from
July 1936 onwards the PSF played upon latent fears of communism and
warned that the strike movement was an attack on property and a cause
of social disorder. One of its posters in Lyon typified the PSF's appeal to
the conservative centre and right:

> France is in peril!
> Your liberties are compromised
> Individual property is swept aside
> The family is under threat
> Communism, controlled from Moscow,
> Wants to set up a bloody dictatorship![38]

To small-scale industrialists, traders and shopkeepers La Rocque offered
not merely words of comfort in their darkest hour but the promise of actual
help. From September 1936 the PSF began to set up 'professional unions'

of a distinctly corporatist character. The message of anti-communism and social order which had worked so effectively for the Croix de Feu before 1936 was even more successful now. On 3 October 1936, for example, 422 cars and buses brought a total of between 3,000 and 4,000 supporters to Annonay in the Ardèche from five neighbouring departments.[39] Even so, by the end of November 1936 the PSF in the Rhône and the Ardèche had not yet succeeded in attracting much support from the political centre, which was still reported to be generally loyal to the Popular Front government.[40]

During the next four or five months, however, there was a discernible shift in public opinion towards the right, which those experienced observers of political behaviour, the *Commissaires Spéciaux*, ascribed to three factors. The first was inflation, which was attributed by some to employees' excessive demands for salary increases and by others to the cupidity of employers. Whatever the cause, its effects were clearly visible; even those whose wages had been increased now claimed to be no better off. It was among this group of employees, 'those who regret having voted for the Popular Front',[41] that the PSF began trying to recruit from January 1937. The second issue was the government ban on opposition meetings, which was seen not as 'a desire for maintaining order'[42] but as a rather arbitrary way of silencing criticism, particularly since Communist demonstrations were not included in the ban. Indeed, when the prefect in the Ardèche banned a private PSF meeting planned for February 1937 on the grounds that a threatened counter-demonstration from the left would provoke violence, it made the government appear to be acting illegally, to defend Communist interests. Posters went up asking

Are we still in a Republic?
Under the threat of Moscow's servants,
the prefect bans our private meetings . . .
Legality is on holiday.[43]

This line of attack on the Popular Front government was coupled with a growing sense of unease about the extent to which it was subject to Communist control. By the spring of 1937, reports in Lyon on local reaction to the violent incidents at Clichy, near Paris, where a riotous clash between the PSF and the Communists had produced serious casualties, showed that the Communists were blamed by not only the right but also the centre. The *Commissaire Spécial* reported that

A large number of republicans, Radicals and even some Socialists, while accepting that the PSF provokes the left, assign responsibility to the Communists who are trying to create difficulties for the Popular Front with the hope of getting exclusive authority over the working class.[44]

Finally, it was the continual and successful denigration of the government's policies and exploitation of fears regarding devaluation and the creation of a National Corn Office which caused the centre to drift rightwards. In Lyon, with its solid attachment to the Radical Socialist Party, the police commented specifically on this shift in April 1937, noting that although the middle classes were still, in general, attached to the idea of social progress without revolution and 'deaf to the appeal of extremists',

> the consequences of certain reforms, particularly relating to the legis-
> lation for the 40-hour week, are attracting a certain number of small
> shopkeepers to the PSF, who exploit their difficulties.[45]

By mid-1937, therefore, a tide of opinion was beginning to flow towards the PSF, whose membership was now as high as 600,000–700,000. This did not, at first, unduly alarm the conservative right, since PSF support was coming not from their own ranks but from disaffected Radical or Radical Socialist voters. Indeed, whenever they could, leaders of the conservative Fédération Républicaine made a point of appearing on the same platform as far rightists in the hope, police said, of 'benefiting electorally'.[46]

But La Rocque's independence and ambition were already apparent. In the Chamber of Deputies he had tried to persuade a group of Fédération Républicaine members to form a PSF block,[47] provoking the anger of both the industrialist François de Wendel and the federation's leader, Louis Marin. What revealed the gulf which was beginning to appear between the 'new right' of the PSF and the conservative right was La Rocque's determination to compete electorally. This became apparent in April 1937 in what historians now refer to as 'the Mortain affair'.[48] At a by-election in this conservative area of La Manche in western Normandy, La Rocque put up a PSF candidate against that of the Fédération Républicaine. Open hostility erupted in the form of polemical articles in the two groups' newspapers, the conservative *La Nation* and the PSF's *Le Flambeau*. It was not that there were any serious ideological differences between them – on the contrary, they had now become electoral rivals for an overlapping clientèle.

In addition to La Rocque's decision to compete for power constitution-ally within the republican framework, which was a serious enough threat to the traditional conservative interests represented in the Fédération Républicaine, he was also refusing to join a coalition of rightist groups launched in the spring of 1937, under the banner of the Front de la Liberté, by Jacques Doriot. The Fédération Républicaine, which rallied to this new alliance, did so not only to 'use [it] for its own electoral ends',[49] as one police report put it, but also, according to political commentators, to strengthen its own hand against La Rocque.[50] La Rocque refused to join the Front de la Liberté, partly in order to preserve a certain freedom of movement but also because he did not want to get trapped into a union of the right held together only by hatred of communism. His experience between 1934 and 1936 had shown him the dangers of being caught in a situation where public opinion was polarized and his movement was made use of by both the left and the conservative right. This time, La Rocque was determined to hold on to some of the centre ground, a tactical calculation which led him from mid-1937 to the outbreak of war to distance himself from Doriot and the Fédération Républicaine, and to present his party as both attached to republican institutions and in favour of firm government. In effect, as the Popular Front alliance began to break up during 1938, La Rocque's PSF began to attract more and more support from disenchanted Radicals.[51]

To those on the conservative right, the loss of La Rocque was a blow, particularly given his enormous success in attracting a mass following which could have been of value to them. Moreover, the support which the PSF had been providing for employers' morale, a conspicuous feature of its activity in the Ardèche and elsewhere, was no longer quite so evident. In their search for a new ally who without being an electoral rival would be able to sustain resistance to the left, the Fédération Républicaine believed it had the ideal solution in Jacques Doriot's Parti Populaire Français. Doriot's working-class origins, his career as a Communist deputy until 1934 and his subsequent aversion to Moscow placed him in a unique position when, in 1936, he launched the Parti Populaire Français. This was the only movement on the far right to have a genuinely working-class base and supporters on the shop floor who were violently anti-communist. Although Doriot, like La Rocque, denounced the abuses of capitalism along with communism, even the most recent analysis of the party's paper-thin ideology shows that Doriot accepted profit as an essential motor in the economy.[52] When Doriot launched his Front de la Liberté he was delighted that Marin, Vallat and others from the Fédération Républicaine had joined since this would probably 'bring him regular subsidies from the Comité des Forges', the steel industrialists' organization.[53] In return for these financial considerations, employers were almost certainly hoping that Doriot's followers would act as strike-breakers. This was becoming a matter of urgency as the initial wave of strikes over wages and paid holidays gave way during 1937 to industrial action aimed at forcing recalcitrant employers to implement the changes. In short, as François de Wendel put it, Doriot's men could be of interest to the Fédération 'to the extent that their methods differ from ours'.[54]

It was upon this understanding, much more than upon a common commitment to modernizing industry, that Doriot's alliance with big business hinged.[55] The Communist Party was correct in its claim that the PPF newspaper, *L'Émancipation Nationale*, 'is printed and sold under the control of French big business in order to dislocate the Popular Front and the CGT'.[56] Detailed reports on strikes, the activities of political parties and analysis of public opinion in the Ardèche and the Rhône reveal the nature of the alliance between the Fédération Républicaine, the employers and Doriot's PPF. From March 1937 the PPF succeeded in establishing rival unions to the CGT in the weaving, clothing and chemical product industries in Lyon. According to the police, the PPF 'Professional Sections' invariably sided with 'the employers' organizations'[57] during industrial disputes. The same process was even more dramatically illustrated in the Ardèche: in the industrialized Rhône valley, the CGT was already claiming in July 1937 that since the government's 'pause' in its economic reforms, 'the working class has been subjected to violent attacks from bourgeois capitalists'.[58] Police reports later in the year on trouble in the Lafarge cement factories near Le Teil confirm this impression. In November 1937 the *Commissaire Spécial* reported to the prefect that 'The unexpected dismissal of 12 workers at the Lafarge factory is seen by most of the workers as an offensive by the employer'.[59] By the end of December all 600 workers were called out on strike in defence of 'their union rights, against unjustified dismissals of union militants and the non-renewal of their collective contract'.[60] When the owners shut down the factory the PPF intervened, calling for a mass rally in Le Teil on 6 February 1938 to protest against 'the illegal strike' and to support the 'Independent Group for a return to work' led by a PPF activist.[61] In spite of the prefect's ban on the PPF demonstration, seen by both the police and the Radical Socialist mayor of Le Teil as a humiliating climbdown in the face of threatened violence from the Communist Party,[62] Doriot made a brief appearance, protected by PPF militants and the police.

The *dénouement* of this incident is extremely revealing of the mutually beneficial relationship between the PPF and the employers. In April 1938 inflation and material hardship forced the workers to return on what were substantially the employers' terms. For its part, the PPF attracted new recruits and in January 1939 was holding its departmental congress in Le Teil. The prefect reported to the Minister of the Interior that this was not only the biggest meeting of the right in the department but that the absence of opposition to it was 'a clear demonstration that since the chalk and cement strikes from 1937 to April 1938, the PPF has won a firm foothold in Le Teil'.[63]

Two other aspects of the strike deserve comment. The first was Doriot's careful use of language which played down the extent of his support for the factory owners. He was variously reported by eyewitnesses at Le Teil as saying 'Social conservatism is as detestable as bolshevism. Between the 200 families and communism there is still room [for us]'.[64] Or again: 'We are totally for the worker and against the boss if he doesn't respect the laws.'[65] These statements, which could be taken as evidence of Doriot's anti-capitalism and as part of the ideological scaffolding of a fascist party, need to be interpreted in the context in which they were delivered. Contemporary commentators had no doubt that they were mere rhetoric which concealed 'the close union which exists between the employers and the PPF, an unacknowledged union perhaps, but nevertheless real'.[66] The second noteworthy feature of the strike, and more specifically of the ban on Doriot's planned meeting in February 1938, was the way in which the prefect, the official representative of the republican government, was once again forced to deny basic political rights to a political party. Just as the left's threats of disorder had made the prefect cancel La Rocque's PSF meeting in Annonay in February 1937, so the same tactic was used successfully a year later against the PPF. In 1938, however, the consequences were extremely damaging to the left since the episode both threw discredit on the regime's official representative and provoked a sense of solidarity on the right. The depth of anger was reflected in letters sent to the prefect, one of which announced

> I've always voted left but as a result of the injustice directed against Doriot, it's him I'll vote for next time.[67]

In fact, Doriot's lack of interest in electoral politics as against strike-breaking actions and dramatic appearances at illegal party meetings meant that he never really capitalized on potential support. Although the PPF's membership increased to some 300,000 in 1938,[68] it never achieved mass appeal of the kind enjoyed by La Rocque's PSF.

What conclusions can be drawn about the conservative right and the far right between 1936 and 1939? Whatever benefits the PPF provided for employers in its strike-breaking capacity, or for the Fédération Républicaine in providing strong-arm protection for its meetings, the party did not enjoy widespread support in either the Ardèche or the Rhône. In Lyon, for example, police reports were quite categorical that the PPF had made little impact: its regional congress, held in July 1937, attracted only 1,200 members out of 60,000 who had been invited. In October 1937 the party was said to be 'in complete decline'; by early 1939 it still had not made up lost ground and was 'viewed with suspicion by public opinion'.[69] On the other side of the Rhône, although the PPF made some inroads in Le Teil, this was the only town where it appears to have enjoyed much success. It is difficult to avoid the conclusion, therefore, that Doriot's willingness to allow his party to be linked to the conservative right benefited the latter far more than his own supporters.

Analysis of La Rocque's Parti Social Français highlights two further important elements in the relationship of the 'old' and the 'new' right. Where Doriot had sought an alliance with the conservative right and had been effectively manipulated by it, La Rocque's decision to compete with the conservatives on the same ground provoked their outright hostility. In the Ardèche he came up against a formidable array of conservative interests represented in parliament by Xavier Vallat and two other deputies. Their exceptionally close ties with business, the Catholic Church, the peasantry and military veterans' associations left very little room for the PSF to make headway. It was a measure of the conservative right's strength that when PSF militants decided to compete in the 1937 local elections they had to present themselves as conservative candidates. At the same time, the Radical Socialist centre was sufficiently aware of the temptations some of its followers might have for the PSF to warn them openly of PSF infiltration.[70]

Hostility between the conservative right and the PSF was even more evident in the Rhône where Philippe Henriot, addressing a private meeting of the Fédération Républicaine in Lyon, was prevented from speaking by PSF demonstrators and was only able to address his supporters with the protection of PPF strongmen.[71] The immediate cause of the hostility was the role played by Henriot and Vallat over allegations that La Rocque had received secret subsidies from the Ministry of the Interior in the 1930s. Although the attempt to discredit the PSF leader damaged both La Rocque and the conservative right, by December 1937 the PSF congress brought together 25,000 members and local party leaders felt sufficiently strong to force their followers into choosing between the Fédération Républicaine and themselves. It was a highly successful tactic. By clearly distinguishing themselves from the conservative right, the PSF continued to recruit a growing number of shopkeepers and small business owners,[72] as well as former supporters of the Radical Party and even skilled workers.[73] Although it may in general be true that the Radical Party, by keeping the middle classes firmly attached to democratic values, contributed significantly to the failure of interwar fascism in France, the PSF's ability to erode Radical support indicates a perceptible shift towards Bonapartism within a republican framework. This tendency of the French middle classes to turn in moments of crisis to authoritarian republicanism rather than fascist disorder has been usefully stressed by Philippe Machefer.[74]

At the same time it is necessary to underline the rapidity of the conservative right's recovery following the election setback of 1936, its strength being attested by its use of parliamentary and extra-parliamentary means to weaken and then, by 1938, bring down the Popular Front government. It was the conservative right's resilience and financial power that enabled its members to dominate the partnership with Doriot[75] and, according to René Girault, to 'use and abuse their financial power in an overwhelming concern to achieve a definitive political victory.'[76] Furthermore, evidence concerning groups which included a substantial conservative element like the army,[77] the ex-servicemen's organizations,[78] the Church,[79] and the peasantry[80] indicates that although each contained

190

a current which was sympathetic to the far right, the majority invariably rejected *fascisant* solutions to the crisis of the 1930s.

Antoine Prost's conclusions on the role of the war veterans' associations are extremely significant here. The importance of these associations lay not merely in their representation of some 3 million people, but also in the role of their Italian and German counterparts as vital ingredients in the growth of fascism and national socialism. In France, however, Prost has demonstrated that in spite of the rhetoric of one of the largest war veterans' groups, the Union Nationale des Combattants, 'the opinion of the servicemen, which was also mainly that of the middle classes, worked in favour of moderation and good sense in the confrontation between workers and bourgeoisie'.[81] Among the peasantry, where the average drop in revenue between 1929 and 1935 was 50 per cent,[82] the agricultural crisis did throw up 'peasant defence committees' under Henri Dorgères which had 400,000 members in 1939 and made a virtue of direct action. But, just as the PPF's members were used as strike-breakers by urban employers, Dorgères' 'greenshirts' were manipulated by agricultural employers against striking farmworkers and pickets.[83] Although Dorgères' movement confirms the existence of a strong current in French society which nursed a taste for uniforms and a willingness to use violence, there was, as Allen Douglas has recently concluded, nothing uniquely fascist about this.[84] It was rather that the conservative right, unsure about how far it could count on the army in the event of a showdown with the left, needed 'shock troops' both as strike-breakers and to mount counter-demonstrations to those of the Communists.

The role of the French army in internal politics during the 1930s suggests that although some officers were attracted to the Croix de Feu,[85] read extreme right-wing newspapers,[86] and were often extremely hostile to Parliament, they were not willing, as were so many of their Spanish equivalents, to bring down a republican government. Whatever reservations they may have expressed about the French government's pact with Soviet Russia in 1935, the only evidence of sedition in the army relates to the so-called *Cagoule*, in which during 1937 a minority of officers allowed an anti-communist network in the army to extend its operations into civilian Paris. On balance, historians have concluded that, despite this clear disaffection within the officer corps, there existed no large-scale, organized conspiracy,[87] and that although the Chief of Staff, Weygand, had brought civil–military relations 'near to collapse',[88] his replacement in 1935 by General Gamelin helped to ensure the loyalty of the army to the Republic. However, the enthusiasm with which the army embraced the Vichy regime in 1940 and its willingness to support Philippe Pétain, the hero of Verdun, suggests that loyalty to the Republic was a matter of duty rather than conviction.

A similar perspective was shared by many in the Catholic Church, though here the divisions between conservative Catholicism and Christian Social democracy make generalization more difficult. What can be said is that from 1935 the Church hierarchy was warning its followers against abandoning organizations attached to Catholic Action in favour of secular 'leagues' which might weaken state authority.[89] Simultaneously, it was discouraging Catholic workers from joining the CGT and ordering priests to play no active role in the Croix de Feu.[90] This 'middle line' between the temptations of left and right was interpreted locally according to the prevailing sociopolitical forces. In the Ardèche, for example, the hostility of the Catholic Church to the Popular Front and its open support for conservative politicians was partly due to the influence of Xavier Vallat, local deputy and president of the Fédération Nationale Catholique. The Church's staunchly conservative position in the Ardèche embraced an anti-Semitic current, due partly to Vallat's influence and partly to the persistence of catechism lessons which stressed Jewish responsibility for the crucifixion. The existence of anti-Semitic ideas on the conservative right and in a department where there were no Jewish refugees deserves comment in the context both of debates over the penetration of fascist ideology in French society and of the relationship between fascists and conservatives.

Although there is an impressive body of evidence for the existence of anti-Semitic ideas and activities, either in specific areas like Paris and Alsace[91] or in right-wing movements like Solidarité Française[92] and Action Française, anti-Semitism was clearly shunned by other right-wing groups like the PSF and, until 1940, most of the PPF. Furthermore despite recent claims, based on newspaper analysis, regarding the extent to which anti-Semitism possessed a widespread currency in the 1930s, police reports from different places and at different times fail to provide corroborative evidence. As early as March 1933 the mainly conservative area around Nice was said to be 'outraged by German persecution of Jews' and regarded these measures as 'a crime against humanity'.[93] Later, in November 1938, at a time when French policy was designed to limit Jewish immigration as part of the government's appeasement of Nazi Germany,[94] the public of Lyon were equally incensed by the persecution of *Kristallnacht*. Even if they disliked their country's being used for political assassinations, they were not, according to the police, at all interested in 'a few isolated sections of the extreme right who, attempted to exploit the incident for their anti-Semitic cause'.[95] Anti-Semitism was not therefore as widespread or as deep-seated as some secondary sources have implied,[96] nor was it a phenomenon which differentiated the conservative right from the far right. This conclusion adds further weight to the argument that it was not ideology that marked the old right from the new, but the methods employed in the pursuit of power.

In most cases the conservative right was sufficiently strong simply to hold its ground and bend the far right's activism to its own will. Nothing illustrates the success of this tactic better than developments in 1940 when, following military defeat at the hands of the Germans, it was the conservative right which came to occupy the positions of power in the new government at Vichy, while the far right, even with the support of the German authorities, remained isolated, and denied any real influence, in Paris.

VICHY 1940–4

Debate on the nature of the Vichy regime – whether it was fascist or merely authoritarian and conservative – has generally been based upon analysis of ideology. However, the most recent contribution to this discussion from Zeev Sternhell[97] has shifted the argument away from ideology to forms of government and control. Sternhell claims that the difference between the men of Vichy and the Paris *collaborationistes* was very slight, since Vichy was a totalitarian enterprise with the same essential nature as fascism. The evidence for this assertion deserves careful scrutiny.

The reforms of French society enacted between 1940 and 1942 under the description of a 'National Revolution' were conservative rather than modernizing. The important roles given to the Church and the army in reshaping education and youth policy, for example, suggest the influence of traditional rather than fascist values. The conservative character of educational changes is illustrated not only by the regime's readiness to allow the existence of both confessional and secular youth movements but also by the manner in which it clipped the wings of the most promising youth movement, the Compagnons de la France, when it seemed to be developing fascist leanings in 1940–1.[98] Research into the political surveillance of teachers shows, again, that the teaching corps were being mobilized not for a fascist crusade but, in effect, for a conservative counter-revolution.[99] Nevertheless the means employed to ensure political uniformity among both teachers and public at large oblige us to consider carefully whether Vichy might not properly be defined as fascist, by virtue not of its ideology but of the repressive and coercive character of its enforcing agencies.

As evidence of Vichy's strongly executive character, historians have already drawn attention to the exceptional powers wielded by Pétain as *Chef de l'État*, the removal of all freely elected groups at national and local level, and the abolition of trade unions. Yet Vichy's ability to impose an ideological blueprint throughout the country depended not only on local officials but also on its success in mobilizing mass support. Its chosen vehicle, and its eyes and ears in every village and town, was the Légion des Anciens Combattants. This organization, which welded together the various ex-servicemen's associations into a single party with uniform, fascist-style salute and powers to exert populist pressure on the administration, has been identified as a key element by Roger Bourderon in his description of Vichy as a fascist state.[100] Although the success of the Légion was uneven, it clearly did play an important role up to 1942 in satisfying a taste for political activism and in encouraging the sort of climate of fear and suspicion in which the denunciation of 'suspect' individuals was legitimized as a patriotic duty.[101] It was from the ranks of the Légion, furthermore, that recruits were drawn in 1942 to the more overtly paramilitary Service d'Ordre Légionnaire and in 1943 to the Milice. Although there was no inexorable progression from one to the other, reports based on intercepted letters from members of the Milice suggest that this was without question a fascist movement.[102] Its founder, Joseph Darnand, clearly intended the Milice to be in France what the Fascist Party was in Italy and the Nazi Party in Germany. Until November 1943 it attracted those who had 'a degree of patriotic enthusiasm mixed with religious fervour' and 'the conviction of serving an ideal, willingly consenting to the necessary sacrifices'.[103] From this point, although there were many resignations from Miliciens who believed that their idealism had been subverted by Laval, some went a step further in the service of their anti-communist ideals by joining the Waffen SS and fighting on the Eastern Front against the Russians. One of them wrote to a friend in Nice in January 1944:

> If we are victors in this war ... it's we SS who will liquidate all the present rubbish to make another France, National Socialist, clean and healthy. That revolution will be different from Pétain's and it's not with kid gloves that we'll sort out the fiddlers and the Jews.[104]

The unequivocally fascist character of these sentiments needs to be seen in context: although the Milice had a core of committed idealists who, along with opportunists and fugitives from the law, were thrown into extremely repressive military action against the Resistance, they were ostracized not only by the Vichy administration and public opinion[105] but also by other branches of the police. The Groupes Mobiles de Reserve, La Garde and the Gendarmerie were all openly hostile, often (according to reports drawn up in 1945) refusing to co-operate with any action that the Milice undertook.[106] However totalitarian the police structure may have *appeared* between 1942 and 1944, the evidence so far does not suggest that it was truly totalitarian in practice.

The other major instruments through which Vichy attempted both to identify dissent and, later, to shape public opinion were the joint services of surveillance, censorship and propaganda. We now know[107] that Vichy's massive and secret interception of letters and phone calls, co-ordinated by the Service du Contrôle Technique (SCT) was designed both to throw light on public opinion and to reveal criminal activities and political opposition. Until Laval's return to power in April 1942, the targets of surveillance were just as likely to be members of Doriot's Parti Populaire Français as people who were on the left or who simply listened to the BBC. Dissent was therefore defined by the SCT officials as dissent from Pétainism, whether it came from the left or further to the right. The control of this exceedingly powerful weapon by a politico-military clique until mid-1942, therefore, set up the possibility of a permanent intrusion into individual privacy in the service of a conservative counter-revolution.

The totalitarian potential of this service was blunted by a degree of public knowledge of its operation[108] and the inability of police or judicial authorities to use incriminating correspondence to enforce confessions. To have done so would have rendered public what the then premier, Darlan, wished to keep totally secret. Even though the level of convictions from intercepted communications remained low, there is no doubt that the clandestine operation of the SCT fuelled suspicion and doubt, which in turn provoked a terrifying level of denunciations.[109] Laval's reorganization of the SCT after 1942 was aimed at manipulating public opinion towards supporting the more overtly fascist policies of his administration. In particular we can now see that the remarkably successful propaganda messages of Philippe Henriot, which were extremely damaging to the Resistance and robbed it of popular support in many areas,[110] were shaped by SCT knowledge of public opinion's private fears. Although the power of the SCT as a means of totalitarian social control had by this stage been weakened by widespread access to Resistance information sources which contradicted Vichy's controlled media, it contributed in a very telling way to neutralizing public opinion.

The SCT, therefore, probably constituted the strongest piece of evidence in support of Sternhell's claim that Vichy was fascist by virtue of its totalitarian character. Having argued that the main difference between the old right and the new during the 1930s lay in the means of seeking power rather than ideology, we must now ask whether it can convincingly be claimed that the old right, having achieved power in 1940, was prepared to employ methods of retaining power that were, at least in part, fascist. The weakness of any such case is twofold. First, without a detailed study of the police under Vichy – and especially the *police judiciaire* – it is difficult to measure how far the *potentially* totalitarian character of the SCT became a reality through police prosecution. Secondly, it is by no means obvious that the state's arbitrary intrusion into private correspondence throughout French society should be regarded as *fascist* simply because it had a *totalitarian* character.

However, given the composition of Laval's governments from 1942 to 1944 and the unmistakably manipulative use made of the SCT there are good grounds for suggesting that the regime's *intentions* were both ideologically and politically fascist even if, in reality, it was often unable to enforce them. In contrast, between 1940 and 1942, Vichy's repression was directed towards settling old scores in the interests of a self-consciously peasant and rural society. To describe this period as fascist is so reductionist as ultimately to empty the word of meaning.

The relationship between French conservatives and the far right from 1934 to 1944, as discussed in this chapter, has placed stress upon the need to examine *Realpolitik* as well as ideology. It represents a deliberate attempt to shift the discussion away from the realm of ideas, where conflicting definitions of fascism are unlikely to be resolved, towards an examination of the means by which different groups on the right competed for power through a combination of parliamentary and extra-parliamentary methods. While the far right tried to make use of tactical alliances, first with the conservatives in 1936–40 and then with the Germans in 1940–4, it is difficult to avoid the conclusion that the appeal of their methods to the French public was extremely limited and that when they achieved a measure of power between 1942 and 1944 it was with sullen acquiescence rather than popular acclaim. Although a section of the conservative right blocked them from effective power, the conservatives' own victory in 1940, when they were able to obtain revenge for the 1936 electoral defeat, turned out to be a pyrrhic one which placed upon them the stain of collaboration. Only the willingness of right-wing groups to constitute such resistance movements as the Organisation Civil et Militaire and to demonstrate their commitment to the Republic by military action saved them from a prolonged spell in the political and social wilderness. Ultimately, in 1943, the experience of what 'Better Hitler than Blum' actually meant turned the conservative right decisively towards the centre. And, significantly, just as the First World War had legitimized methods of direct political action in defence of integral nationalism, so the left's and the right's shared experience of clandestine warfare between 1940 and 1944 allowed a new consensus to emerge.

NOTES

I should like to thank the University of Ulster for providing financial support for this resarch and my colleague, Dr Ian Connor, for his comments on a draft of this chapter.

1   The best account is R. Rémond, *Les Droites en France* (Aubier, 1982), which contains a good bibliography; see also Z. Sternhell, *Ni Droite ni Gauche. L'Idéologie Fasciste en France* (Paris, 1983); S. Berstein, 'La France des Années Trente Allergique au Fascisme', *Vingtième Siècle*, no. 2 (April 1984); and P. Bernard and H. Dubieff, *The Decline of the Third Republic, 1914–1938* (Cambridge, 1985), p. 242.

2 Archives Nationales (AN), F7 13030.
3 ibid.
4 S. Berstein, *Le 6 février 1934* (Paris, 1975).
5 I have examined reports for sixteen departments in different regions of France.
6 AN, F7 13030. Commissaire Spécial to prefect.
7 AN, F7 13040. Reports on 23 February 1934.
8 AN, F7 13034. Report on 28 February 1934.
9 AN, F7 13034. Reports on 3 March and 3 May 1934.
10 AN, F7 13035. Reports on 6 March 1934.
11 AN, F7 13238. Police note of May 1934.
12 AN, F7 13238. Police note of 25 May 1934. The Neo-Socialists were a small right-wing group led by an ex-leftist, Marcel Déat.
13 Quoted by W. D. Irvine, 'French conservatives and the "New Right" during the 1930s', *French Historical Studies*, vol. VIII, no. 4 (Fall 1974), p. 542.
14 ibid. Irvine is here quoting Baudouin, president of the Fédération Républicaine in the Seine Inférieur, in *La Nation*, 6 July 1935.
15 *Le Flambeau*, no. 15, 8 June 1935.
16 AN, F7 13241. Note on 20 July 1935.
17 AN, F7 13241. Note on 29 June 1935.
18 AN, F7 13241.
19 ibid.
20 Archives Départementales de l'Ardèche (ADA), 292 Z.
21 Archives Départementales du Rhône (ADR), 4M 269. Tract from Fonctionnaires et agents des services publics du Rhône, Lyon, 4 July 1935.
22 ADR, 4M 269.
23 A. Micheline in *Politique*, May 1936, quoted in R. Rémond, *Les Catholiques, le communisme et les crises 1929–1939* (Paris, 1960), p. 148.
24 ADA, 292 Z. Report from Commissaire Spécial, 20 June 1936.
25 ADR, 4M 236. Report from Commissaire Spécial, 22 May 1936.
26 *Léon Blum, Chef du Gouvernement 1936–7. Actes de Colloque* (Paris, 1967), pp. 168–72.
27 ADR, 4M 236. Note on 10 July 1936.
28 ADR, 4M 236. Notes on 22 June and 23 July 1936.
29 ADR, 4M 236. Note on 22 June 1936.
30 Bernard and Dubieff, *Decline of the Third Republic*, p. 289.
31 *Léon Blum, Chef du Gouvernement*, p. 142.
32 J. Touchard and L. Bodin, *Le Front Populaire, 1936* (Paris, 1972), p. 185.
33 ADA, CAB 15M17. Cases reported on 13 July 1936.
34 ADA, CAB 15M31. Reports on 22 June and 16 July 1936.
35 Félix Ponteil, *Les Bourgeois et la démocratie sociale* (Paris, 1931), p. 279.
36 ADA, 292 Z.
37 Ponteil, *Les Bourgeois et la démocratie sociale*, p. 280.
38 ADR, 4M 236.
39 ADA, 292 Z. Police report, October 1936.
40 ADR, 4M236. Commissaire Spécial to prefect, 24 November 1936.
41 ADR, 4M236. Commissaire Spécial to prefect, 23 January 1937.
42 ADR, 4M236. Commissaire Spécial to prefect, December 1936.
43 ADA, 292 Z.
44 ADR, 4M236. Commissaire Spécial to prefect, March 1937.
45 ADR, 4M236. Commissaire Spécial to prefect, April 1937.
46 ADR, 4M236. Commissaire Spécial to prefect, February 1937.
47 J. N. Jeanneney, *François de Wendel en République: l'argent et le pouvoir, 1914–40* (Paris, 1976), p. 5.
48 P. Machefer, 'Le PSF et le Front de la Liberté, 1936–1937', *Revue d'Histoire Moderne et Contemporaine* (January–March 1970), p. 116.
49 ADR, 4M236. Report on 24 June 1937.
50 Irvine, 'French conservatives', p. 557.
51 ADR, 4M236. Report on 1 July 1938.

52   Jean-Paul Brunet, 'Un fascisme Français: le Parti Populaire de Doriot (1936–1939)', *Revue Française de Science Politique*, vol. 33, no. 2 (April 1983), pp. 260, 275–6; Dieter Wolf, *Doriot, du Communisme à la Collaboration* (Paris, 1969), pp. 212–13.
53   Jeanneney, *François de Wendel*, p. 569.
54   ibid.
55   K.-J. Müller, 'French fascism and modernization', *Journal of Contemporary History*, vol. 11, no. 4 (October 1976), pp. 75–108.
56   ADA, 292 Z, 2 July 1937.
57   ADA, 4M236. Reports on March 1937, July 1938 and January 1939.
58   ADA, 292 Z. CGT tract, July 1937.
59   ADA, 292 Z. Report on 19 November 1937.
60   *Le Petit Valentinois*, Journal Républicain de la Drôme et de l'Ardèche, 12 February 1938, ADA 55 Z.
61   ADA, 55 Z. Police report from Le Teil to prefect, 4 February 1938.
62   ADA, 552. Letter from Mayor of Le Teil to Prefect of Ardèche, 5 February 1938.
63   ADA, 68Z. Prefect to Minister of the Interior, 6 February 1939.
64   *Le Petit Dauphinois*, 7 February 1938.
65   ADA, 55Z. Police Chief, Le Teil, to prefect, 7 February 1938.
66   *Le Petit Valentinois*, 12 February 1938.
67   ADA, 55Z.
68   Berstein, 'La France des Années Trente', p. 92.
69   ADR, 4M236. Reports from Commissaire Spécial to prefect.
70   ADA, 55Z. Prefect to Minister to the Interior, 16 February 1938.
71   ADR, 4M236. Reports, February and March 1938.
72   ADR, 4M236. Reports on 18 December 1937.
73   ADR, 4M236. Report, July 1938.
74   P. Machefer, *Ligues et fascismes en France, 1919–1939* (Paris, 1974), p. 32; S. Berstein, *Histoire du Parti Radical: Crise du Radicalisme, 1926–1939* (Paris, 1982).
75   Irvine, 'French conservatives', p. 559.
76   R. Girault, 'La trahison des possédants', *L'Histoire*, no. 58 (July-August 1983).
77   A. Horne, *The French Army and Politics* (London, 1984).
78   A. Prost, *Les Anciens Combattants et la Société Française, 1914–1939*, 3 vols (Paris, 1977).
79   Rémond, *Les Catholiques*.
80   M. Gervais, M. Jollivet and Y. Tavernier, *Histoire de la France Rurale*, Vol. 4 (Paris, 1976), pp. 425–42.
81   Prost, *Anciens Combattants*, Vol. 1, p. 189. A good local example of UNC attitudes can be found in the monthly *Le Poilu*, published in the Ardèche.
82   Gervais, Jollivet and Tavernier, *France Rurale*, p. 433.
83   ibid., p. 437.
84   See also Allen Douglas, 'Violence and fascism: the case of the Faisceau', *Journal of Contemporary History*, vol. 19, no. 4 (October 1984), pp. 689–712.
85   AN, F7 13241. Police note on 18 June 1935.
86   Henri Guillemin, *Nationalistes et Nationaux, 1870–1914* (Paris, 1974), p. 348.
87   M. Anderson, *Conservative Politics in France* (London, 1974), pp. 225–9.
88   Horne, *French Army and Politics*, p. 58, quoting from P. C. F. Bankwitz, *Maxime Weygand and Civil-Military Relations in Modern France* (Cambridge, Mass., 1967).
89   Rémond, *Les Catholiques*, p. 129.
90   ADA, 293 Z. Report on 24 October 1937; also Anderson, *Conservative Politics*, p. 207.
91   P. Kingston, *Anti-Semitism in France during the 1930s* (Hull, 1983); AN, F7 13040. Reports from Colmar, 1935.
92   AN, F7 13034. Reports in 1935.
93   AN, F7 13030. Commissaire Spécial to prefect, 3 March 1933.
94   V. Caron, 'Prelude to Vichy: France and the Jewish refugees in the era of appeasement', *Journal of Contemporary History*, vol. 20, no. 1 (January 1985), pp. 157–76.
95   ADR, 4M 236. Report on 5 December 1938.
96   R. Paxton and M. Marrus, *Vichy France and the Jews* (New York, 1981), pp. 45–71.

97 Z. Sternhell, 'Sur le fascisme et sa variante française', *Le Débat*, no. 32 (November 1984).
98 R. Austin, 'The educational and youth policies of the Vichy government in the department of Hérault', PhD thesis, University of Manchester, 1981, ch. 5.
99 R. Austin, 'Political surveillance and ideological control: teachers in the Midi', in R. Kedward and R. Austin (eds), *Vichy France and the Resistance: Ideology and Culture* (London, 1985), pp, 13–35.
100 R. Bourderon, 'Le Régime de Vichy, était-il fasciste?', *Revue d'Histoire de la Deuxième Guerre Mondiale*, no. 91 (July 1973).
101 Austin, 'Political surveillance and ideological control'.
102 AN, F7 14937. Report on the Milice, 23 November 1945, based on the archives of Vichy's Service du Contrôle Technique.
103 ibid.
104 AN, F1A 3744. Letter intercepted on 16 January 1944.
105 Roderick Kedward, *Occupied France. Collaboration and Resistance 1940–1944* (London, 1985), p. 66.
106 AN, F7 14937. Report, November 1945.
107 R. Austin, 'Intelligence and surveillance under the Vichy regime: the role of the Service du Contrôle Technique', *Intelligence and National Security*, vol. 1, no. 1 (Spring 1986).
108 Marcel Ruby, *La Contre Résistance à Lyon, 1940–1944* (Paris, 1981), p. 10.
109 Austin, 'Intelligence and surveillance'.
110 ibid.

11

Conservatism, authoritarianism and fascism in Greece, 1915–45

David Close

'Of the formation of genuine political parties of Right and Left there is as yet no sign' reported the British ambassador to Greece, Oliver Harvey, in 1931.[1] This view has been shared by subsequent commentators because of the haziness of ideological divisions in Greece, and the importance of political patronage and personal loyalties in determining party alignments. Yet by 1931 ideological differences had in fact appeared between Greece's two dominant camps: the Venizelists, followers of the country's leading liberal statesman, Elevtherios Venizelos, and consisting largely of the Liberal Party; and the Antivenizelists, consisting largely of the Populist Party. Of the two the former had shown themselves in various ways to be the more democratic, populist (notwithstanding their opponents' label) and progressive.

The division of Greek politics into two camps, the 'National Schism', dated from 1915 and was precipitated by bitter differences between Venizelos and King Constantine I concerning Greece's wartime role and the respective prerogatives of Crown and premier. The Antivenizelists were characterized by attachment to the monarchy and the interests of old Greece, which consisted of the western islands and southern mainland. The Venizelists were moulded by their experience in 1916 of rebellion against the monarchy, and were identified with the nationalist cause in the new lands – added between 1912 and 1918 – of Crete, Epirus, Macedonia and Thrace. The last two provinces were settled by most of the refugees who left Asia Minor following the 'disaster' – Greece's defeat by Turkey – of 1922. These refugees, who formed one-fifth of the total population of Greece, tended to be poor and radical. In the public reaction against the 1922 disaster, the Venizelists surged to power and in 1924 abolished the monarchy.

During this period the Venizelists went some way towards adopting a democratic organization based on local associations (which flourished more in areas of refugee settlement), whereas the Populists remained unashamedly a party of notables, relegating their local organizations to a menial role. Largely for the benefit of the refugees the Venizelists brought about sweeping land reforms in the 1920s, which the Antivenizelists tried to obstruct on behalf of large landowners. The Venizelists also did much to expand primary education and promoted the status of the popular form of the language (*demotic*), while the Antivenizelists defended the status of the elite form (*katharevousa*) and the bloated system of classical secondary education which nurtured it.

The Venizelist camp embraced a wide range of political positions. It contained a radical wing with which Venizelist leaders enjoyed a close but troubled relationship, rather like that of Liberals and Labour in pre-1914 Britain. Right-wing Venizelists received the support of Antivenizelists against the Venizelist left in debates on the Idionym Law of 1929, which was designed to outlaw communist activities outside the parliamentary and electoral spheres. The law left the police free to interpret as 'communist' most forms of industrial agitation, and was essentially a response by employers, and the propertied and official classes allied with them, to the social problems created by the rapid industrialization of the interwar period and exacerbated in the 1930s by the depression. Antivenizelists and right-wing Venizelists thenceforth tended to be distinguished by ruthlessness in persecuting alleged communists and unwillingness to remedy the grievances to which communists appealed.[2] When Antivenizelists returned to power, from 1932 onwards, they ran the police, while industrial unrest happened to be more widespread in Venizelist areas.

The Antivenizelist comeback revived the earlier ferocity of the National Schism, and in the process strengthened the opponents of parliamentary rule in both camps. Because it destroyed consensus over the legitimacy of the political system and politicized the army, the National Schism had led to the appearance in the 1920s of would-be dictators with military backgrounds and clienteles. The most important of these military strongmen were, in the Venizelist camp, Theodore Pangalos and Nicholas Plastiras and, in the Antivenizelist camp, George Kondylis and John Metaxas. (Metaxas, however, had been a professional politician since 1921 and had few or no clients left in active service.) In the international atmosphere of the 1930s such figures naturally found some of the style and slogans of fascism attractive.

They found pretext for their ambitions in the inability of the political system to remedy the social problems that arose after the First World War as a result of industrialization, the refugee influx and the rapid growth of cities. Another problem, that of defence, became acute in 1935, when Mussolini's foreign policy became more aggressive, and Greece found itself exposed to risk of simultaneous attack by Italy and a constantly revisionist Bulgaria, thirsting to recover access to the Aegean. A further argument for dictatorship was the communist presence. Although the Communist Party had only about 2,000 members until 1932, it alarmed most politicians, who habitually exaggerated its influence and sensed its potential in a country with weak trade unions, puny social democratic groups and scarcely any provision for social welfare.[3]

Greek parliamentary politics exhibited defects widespread in Europe after the First World War: unstable governments, and politicians pre-occupied with gaining office and dispensing patronage – the last an especially time-consuming activity in Greece. The civil service, swollen by politicians' need for patronage, tended to be inefficient and corrupt, so that voters depended on politicians to intercede with it on their behalf. Effective government at national level depended on the leadership of an extraordinary personality, and there was a particularly serious hiatus of such leadership between Venizelos' downfall in 1932 and Metaxas' accession in 1936. The press was characterized by scandal-mongering and polemical savagery. Much of the electorate, more than a quarter of which was illiterate, was apathetic and venal, voters tending to be bound – especially in old Greece – by personal loyalty and patronage to local notables who operated through oppressive *kommatarchs* (the Greek counterpart to Spanish *caciques*).[4] Most politicians recognized these faults to some extent, but preferred, through principle and self-interest, to tackle them by democratic means. The danger was that their demoralization in the face of national problems might make them acquiesce in the ambitions of a would-be dictator. This had already happened once, in 1925, but the dictatorship in question – that of Pangalos – had been short-lived and had provoked a revulsion of opinion in favour of parliamentarism.[5]

A genuinely fascist response to these problems was negligible. Several fascist groups appeared in the 1930s, but their membership was minute and their leaders of low calibre. To explain these facts both German and British observers thought it worth stressing national character. Apart from the Communist Party, voluntary organizations of any sort were weak in Greece, and given the Greeks' proverbial individualism and love of political argument for its own sake, it seemed inconceivable to these observers that any fascist movement could flourish.[6] International factors were also important. While the appeal of Nazism was limited, as generally in eastern Europe, by its violence and irreligion, that of Italian fascism was limited by the fact that, since Mussolini's bombardment of Corfu in 1923, Italy had been seen as the main national enemy. During the invasion of Ethiopia, for example, prayers for that country were offered in Greek churches.[7]

The main reason for the fascists' weakness, however, was a lack of exploitable issues. Anti-communism was already being overworked by others; and in the brutal suppression of strikers the police needed no help. It was scarcely possible for a Greek to be an aggressive nationalist in the aftermath of the Asia Minor disaster of 1922; and Greece's vulnerable position thereafter made irredentism obviously suicidal. The exchanges of populations between Greece and Turkey after 1922 left Greece relatively homogeneous, with ethnic minorities that were small and confined to the new lands in the north. The most important were the Slavo-Macedonians (forming about 2 per cent of the national population), the Muslims and the Jews (each forming 1 per cent), all chiefly inhabiting Macedonia and Thrace. The National Schism virtually precluded a national racist movement, since it was based to a considerable extent on tension between Greek refugees and Greek natives. The refugees, and the Venizelists representing them, were identified with the policy of assimilating the new lands, and so incurred the electoral antagonism of the ethnic minorities, whose support the Antivenizelists consequently secured. The Jewish community, centred in Thessaloniki, was especially vulnerable to Venizelist persecution, since its wealthier section attracted economic jealousy while its poorer section made a small but much-publicized contribution to the Communist vote.[8]

Anti-Semitism and anti-communism, together with militarist nationalism, characterized the most important of the fascist groups, the National Union of Greece (EEE), founded in 1927. Apparently confined to Macedonia, it had 7,000 members in 1931, and included a large proportion of refugees, and also of ex-soldiers and former members of anti-Slav bands of the pre-1912 era. Although active in parades and violent against Jews, it had little electoral influence. Most of its members voted for Venizelist candidates, and it shattered when trying to turn itself into a political party in 1933.[9] It was the only fascist group to field candidates in a general election – that of January 1936 – when its seven candidates received only 505 votes. A General Student Association was also formed, offering a significant counterweight to Communists among students in the University of Athens. Other allegedly fascist groups seem to have consisted merely of loosely organized followers of minor politicians, who relied heavily on the support of ex-officers. They included the Greek National Socialist Party under the former royalist George Merkouris, who published *The Corporate State* in 1936, and the Organization of the National Sovereign State under an ex-officer, Theodore Skilakakis, which was based in Thessaloniki and published the newspaper *Kratos* ('The State').[10]

During 1935, in response to an abortive Venizelist revolt on 1 March and the expansion of the Communist Party, the right-wing character of the Antivenizelists became increasingly evident and their anti-parliamentary wing strengthened. The revolt provoked a purge of Venizelists from the armed forces and public service, and a prolonged persecution of their political sympathizers. The Venizelist left was thus driven, by shared persecution, into rapprochement with the Communist Party. The latter, strengthened by its adoption of a Popular Front strategy, exploited the polarization caused by Antivenizelist repression and the unprecedented manifestations of economic discontent, especially strikes, in the years 1935–6. In July 1936 the Communists concluded an alliance with the

203

Agrarian Party which promised them a breakthrough in rural areas. At this time their membership seems to have risen to something over 10,000, although most non-communists assumed that it was much greater and saw the Communists' hand everywhere in industrial unrest. The result was to hasten the drift of wealthier businessmen, which had been started by the depression, from the Venizelist to the Antivenizelist camp.[11]

It was presumably in order to appeal to recruits such as these that Panayotes Tsaldaris, the Populist premier, tried in mid-1935 to maintain a moderate stance against the clamour of his supporters for reprisals against Venizelists and a restoration of the monarchy. During this period Tsaldaris and moderate elements within his party developed a reformist policy which offered political peace by supporting constitutional processes and asserting that the National Schism was outdated. They recognized the new importance of social questions, to which they responded with promises to implement provisions for social insurance (which had long been in preparation by successive governments), and to introduce minimum wages, the arbitration of industrial disputes, a housing programme, and reforms to make taxation more equitable.[12]

Although his programme seems to have had strong electoral appeal, Tsaldaris was ousted by extremists in his own party, led by Kondylis, with the decisive backing of the leaders of the armed forces, especially the Commander-in-Chief of the army, Alexander Papagos. Kondylis established a military-based dictatorship in October 1935 as a prelude to restoration of the monarchy the next month. The conspirators' chief aim was no doubt to safeguard their partisan hegemony in the army and state, but they also had other motives. The army leaders – like police officers and other state officials – were alarmed by the apparent danger that Communists might infiltrate the armed forces via national servicemen, and were anxious to see the reimposition of social order and efficient government, neither of which the ineffectual Tsaldaris had proved able to offer since 1932. Efficient government would, they hoped, end a long-standing neglect of their professional interests.[13] Kondylis ostentatiously admired Mussolini's style of leadership and included the National Socialist Merkouris among his supporters. His programme consisted largely of a promise of 'national regeneration', an appeal to military glory, and vague socialist proposals to reform the tax system and remedy the abuses of capitalism.[14]

When the king, George II, arrived, he nevertheless broke with Kondylis and appointed a caretaker administration to organize a fair general election. Admiring the institutions of Britain, where he had spent his exile, he professed to loathe the brutality and demagoguery of fascism. But he lacked the will-power, or perhaps the opportunity, to free himself from dependence on the right. When the election of January 1936 produced a deadlock between the camps he found himself unable to construct a parliamentary government without making concessions to the Venizelists, who for him were tainted by association with the recent revolt. Meanwhile the apparent possibility of concessions to Venizelists or Communists threatened to provoke a revolt by the leaders of the armed forces and police.[15]

The king now began to discover his own distaste for political responsibility, and turned for help to Metaxas, who had been a firm friend of his father, King Constantine. Although he had only six supporters in Parliament, Metaxas had the necessary decisiveness and prestige to keep the army out of politics. On becoming premier he took advantage of a widespread decline of faith in parliamentary rule resulting from the political deadlock and the intensification of long-term problems. Among the wealthier classes, in the centre and on the right of the spectrum, there was growing readiness to consent to the establishment of an authoritarian government which it was hoped would provide effective administration and maintain order. It was in particular because of the alleged – and imaginary – danger of communist revolution arising out of the current spate of strikes that Metaxas secured the king's consent to the suspension of Parliament and civil liberties on 4 August 1936.[16]

Metaxas' regime can be aptly described as a 'royal bureaucratic dictatorship'.[17] This label could also be applied to the regimes that had recently appeared in Bulgaria, Yugoslavia and Romania, but in important ways Metaxas' regime was more original than its neighbours. For much of his life Metaxas had been a fervent monarchist, and he never became able or, it seems, inclined to undermine the authority of the king, who remained genuinely free to dismiss him and kept the allegiance of the army officers.[18] Metaxas dissolved his own party, and showed no serious intention of establishing another. Several of the most powerful positions in the state were held by personal followers, most of whom came from outside the sociopolitical establishment and had little previous weight. Nevertheless most of the ministers, subministers, governors and nomarchs (the equivalent of French or Italian prefects) under Metaxas were socially elite figures of a type commonly appointed by previous heads of government: especially army officers and civil servants, but also academics, bankers, lawyers and businessmen. Professional politicians, however (other than Metaxas' few personal followers), were almost completely excluded. The most marked feature of the regime was its exaltation of the state machinery, something that came naturally to Metaxas, who belonged to a civil service family and had risen in the army with the help of influential connections to the head of the General Staff. He now strove, with success, to make all branches of the state more efficient and respected (even though he failed to prevent corruption among his hangers-on). The increase in the administration's energy and accessibility to the public was remarked on by foreign observers. Metaxas consequently earned the respect of state functionaries in general, including especially army and police officers.[19]

Metaxas viewed the Orthodox Church as the moral branch of the state and went to even greater lengths than previous governments to enforce loyalty to it. Although himself a deist, he attached vital importance to the Church as both a national institution and a basis of morality. He saw as one of the functions of his regime's official youth movement, the Neolaia, the enforcement of church attendance on all children. His regime dismissed many teachers for alleged irreligion, and compelled primary teachers to take their children to church on Sundays. The police extended their former role in enforcing religious observance and conventional morality. They imposed, for example, new restrictions on gambling dens, night-clubs and places selling drink, with the aims of restricting crime and of forcing fathers to spend more time with their families.[20]

The general effect of Metaxas' policies was to give the state machinery even wider powers and patronage than before. Vast numbers of local councils were suppressed and replaced by government nominees, on the grounds that they were inefficient. The councils' control over the agrarian constabulary – the last vestige of local power over police – was transferred to the nomarchs. Trade unions and agricultural co-operatives were brought under state direction, allegedly as a step towards organizing the whole economy on corporatist lines – a goal that was repeatedly stressed but which always remained remote.[21] State control was also tightened over all levels of the educational system, professors being more tightly supervised and school textbooks redrafted with ideological considerations in mind.[22] The Neolaia was exhorted to serve as an auxiliary arm of the state, especially of the police, who acquired unprecedented powers to spy, arrest and torture, on the pretext of combating communism.[23]

Metaxas set himself the aim – which he knew to be audacious – of curing his countrymen of their attachment to political liberty. As a target for the regime's propaganda, parliamentary politicians soon loomed still larger than communists, and the faults of the superseded parliamentary system were constantly stressed. The country's history from ancient times was reinterpreted so as to discredit its democratic phases, and the 'Third Greek Civilization' of the current regime was presented as this history's logical culmination. Yet in trying to give his countrymen the sense of discipline, respect for hierarchy and devotion to the state that they notoriously lacked, Metaxas was influenced less by Greece's past than by what he had seen of imperial Germany when he studied at the War Academy as a young man.[24]

The vehicle chosen by Metaxas for the realization of these dreams was his youth movement, the Neolaia. To this he became devoted as the one hope that his ideas might survive his death, which he sensed to be approaching.[25] The movement eventually enrolled most children of school age, and offered them moral, cultural, physical and, for boys, military training. He took pride in the fact that children of different social backgrounds mingled within it. Clearly he intended to give children a sense of national community overriding old status distinctions, and to provide recruits to the regime. Should we then regard the Neolaia as the beginning of a revolution by cultural means? No, for two reasons. Take for example the contents of its magazine. Apart from political lectures, which were nebulous and trite, the items were morally conventional: extracts from the Bible, features on the monarchy, descriptions of children's games, episodes from ancient Greek history and announcements of sporting events. One can see why Metaxas characterized the movement, to one of his supporters, as an attempt to adapt boy-scouting to Greek circumstances.[26]

The other reason is the Neolaia's lack of idealistic attraction to youth. It is clear that the meteoric growth in its membership was due to official coercion and patronage. Metaxas impressed on state employees, including police and schoolteachers, that he attached supreme importance to the organization. Children who refused to join were consequently faced with severe sanctions – even expulsion from school and subsequent difficulty in finding work. The enthusiasm which many children displayed, for example at official parades, could be explained by the sense of excitement and importance which they derived from such events, as well as by the recreational activities which the Neolaia provided. For the cadres there were more solid attractions in the form of pay, allowances, the use of cars and access to official patronage. We have evidence that many of the officials thus recruited were corrupt and thuggish.[27]

As in other right-wing dictatorships of the time, nationalism was basic to the ideology of Metaxas' regime. Metaxas was patriotic in a deeply emotional way, and preoccupied with the problem of national identity, which was especially acute in a relatively new state where institutions were derived from foreign models and much of the culture was imported. He maintained that his countrymen shared certain values that together formed a distinctive ideology which his regime was dedicated to promote. The corollary, for Metaxas, was that Greeks should be insulated from foreign influences. He told a foreign representative of the YMCA that he deprecated contact between Greek members of the organization and its foreign counterparts – as he did 'all forms of international intercourse' except between specialists – on the grounds that it would weaken their readiness to fight in defence of their country.[28]

In no real sense, however, was Metaxas a militarist, a fact which can be explained partly by Greece's vulnerable position, mentioned earlier, and partly by the character of the man himself, who had been cautiously realistic about the dreams of expansion which had captivated most of his countrymen before 1922. The respect which he inculcated for military values was only such as would have been approved by orthodox conservatives everywhere. More surprisingly, perhaps, he did not allow any ideologically based campaign against alien minorities, such as characterized integral nationalists in, for example, France. The conditions of Jews are said to have improved under his regime and he forbade discrimination against them in recruitment to the Neolaia, although they may nevertheless have been excluded unofficially. The newspaper *Elevtheron Vēma* (which like all the national press was strictly censored, especially on foreign matters) attacked Vichy's xenophobia and anti-Semitism as ignoring history, mentioning that many famous Frenchmen had been of foreign origin. Slavophones in northern Greece were, admittedly, harassed by the police, but on the pragmatic grounds that they were a potential fifth column for Bulgarian aggression. The racial tolerance of the regime was perhaps due to its leader's previous career. Metaxas had grown to maturity in the old lands, where ethnic discord was negligible or absent, and as an Antivenizelist he became accustomed to regarding the ethnic minorities of northern Greece as potential supporters. We can conclude that Metaxas' nationalism was essentially a pacific and therefore conservative force.[29]

Ostentatious concern for the conditions of the poor was another trait which Metaxas shared with other right-wing leaders of the time; but his was of long standing and seems to have had more real content than was often the case. His apparent motives were a desire to undercut the appeal of communism, and a paternalistic morality which led him to note in his diary 'my joy lies with the poor and with children'. He proclaimed his fellow-feeling with peasants and workers, and denounced plutocrats and the idle rich in terms which caused them alarm. His government imposed minimum wage-rates and limits to working hours which were a real burden to many employers, who generally resented them. It did much to implement the long-deferred scheme of social security, and greatly expanded health facilities and expenditure on social welfare. Conventionally for the extreme right in Europe, he revered the peasant way of life as conducive to patriotic feeling, and claimed to have made it more viable by debt relief and other measures. He tried in various ways to make the taxation system more equitable. For a number of reasons – chiefly the high rate of inflation, as well as the increased burden of taxation on all classes – it is doubtful whether the standard of living of the poor did improve, but informed observers believed that Metaxas wanted to achieve that result.[30] Unconventionally for the far right in Greece he worked to raise the status of *demotic*, which he represented as part of the national heritage.[31]

Metaxas' attitude to the existing social hierarchy was basically conservative, although he was more far-sighted than most of the right in trying to give this hierarchy moral validity and to remedy lower-class grievances. He claimed to base his policies on the *astike* class (the nearest English word being 'bourgeois'), by whom he meant the majority of the population who were independent property-owners, urban and rural, most of them small-scale and not clearly differentiated by social distinctions. In general this appeal to small property-owners resembled that of the former Populist Party. His attempts to alleviate social discontent were motivated in part by desire to safeguard property rights, and to enable workers to join the ranks of property-owners. Despite his attempts to make taxation more equitable, he showed no interest in redistributing wealth between social groups, and almost completely suppressed strikes and other forms of economic protest. He promised vaguely to create a new ruling class, which, unlike the old class of politicians, would represent all social groups and all regions. In practice he governed, as we have seen, through existing elites, and seems to have done little to make them more accessible to those without wealth. For example, entrance to universities and senior secondary schools was restricted. Given the character of the Neolaia, his talk of a classless hierarchy to be achieved through it should be dismissed as a pipe-dream. But, in the light of the disgusted remarks made by foreign observers about the Neolaia cadres, it seems likely that they were drawn to some degree from the poor and uneducated.

The character of the Metaxas regime is made clearer by its attitude to foreign counterparts, as well as to the rest of the right within Greece. Like right-wing leaders in other countries, Metaxas insisted that his regime was a unique product of national tradition, and in fact showed jealousy of foreign influence to an extent that seems unusual for Greek politicians of the early twentieth century. Nevertheless there is reason to believe that he was substantially influenced by foreign thinkers and models. His library shows that he had for many years been interested in modern political thought, and that he read widely in French, German and to a lesser extent Italian. After he made himself dictator, his private mention of foreign regimes indicates that he had them much in mind. According to well-informed observers, he and his supporters studied the regimes of Hitler, Mussolini and Salazar when considering such matters as a political constitution, the corporative economy, an official party and the youth movement. In these and other matters Metaxas and his followers had at first no clear sense of direction. However Metaxas repeatedly drew attention, in private, to the similarity between his regime and Salazar's, a similarity which seems to have been widely recognized in official circles. Among the items which suggest its influence are the legislation to organize the agricultural population into 'peasants' houses', and the projected constitution, with its provision for a corporative assembly alongside a political one.[32] Another regime which was seen as especially similar was Pétain's in its initial phase, in 1940. *Eleutheron Vēma* described its policies sympathetically and at length, praising Vichy's promotion of athletics among youth, its strengthening of traditional family ties, attempts to stop the drift of peasants to the cities and restrictions on the sale of alcohol, and above all its vendetta against leftist politicians of the Third Republic.[33]

Metaxas' regime probably shared with those of Salazar and Pétain the influence of Charles Maurras and his school of integral nationalism. Maurras' influence is known to have been widespread among Greek monarchists in the early twentieth century, and seems reflected in the fact that a copy of his works is among the most-thumbed books in Metaxas' library. Metaxas' ideas also resemble closely those of a former political associate, Ion Dragoumis, a Greek representative of integral nationalism and a disciple of Maurice Barrès.[34]

With the fascist movements of eastern Europe generally, Metaxas' regime shared its conventional religiosity and its attractiveness to state officials. It nevertheless differed from them in two vital respects. The first was the non-militant character of its nationalism, and the second the fact that it was a *regime*, based on the prevailing establishment, which tried unsuccessfully to create a *movement*, whereas the others were movements at odds with their prevailing political systems.[35] Hitler's regime – and Mussolini's by 1938 – were still further removed from that of Metaxas, because of their distrust of conventional religion, their militarism, racism and cult of violence, and their intimate relationships with totalitarian movements originating outside the establishment. The differences were accentuated by the fact that the Axis increasingly threatened Greece's security, whereas liberal Britain became Greece's guarantor. These considerations seem to explain why Metaxas delivered to a *Times* correspondent in 1939 'a peroration on the iniquities of the Nazi mentality which ... he found ... a violent contrast with that of the Germany he had known' before 1914. Of the US ambassador in 1940 he asked, rhetorically, 'how to get rid of Hitler?', volunteering the comment that '[the Nazis] are practically communists – began as socialists, you know'.[36] The regime displayed basically conservative features which differentiate it from fascism and which it shared with the contemporary regimes of Salazar, Pétain – and, one can add, Franco, after the decline of the Falange from around 1943. These regimes correspond closely both to the 'rightist authoritarian' category of Stanley Payne and to the 'nationalist' category of Anthony Smith, each of whom shows how his respective category differs from fascism.[37]

There nevertheless remained important features which Metaxas' 'Fourth of August' regime, like its contemporary counterparts, shared with the Axis dictatorships. Metaxas privately noted that the latter resembled his own regime in being totalitarian, anti-liberal, anti-communist, having a 'peasant and worker base' and so being anti-plutocratic.[38] After all, they too were police states, with vigorous leader cults, which had destroyed parliaments and free trade unions. His two most powerful lieutenants, Constantine Kotzias, governor of Athens, and Constantine Maniadakis, minister for the police, openly admired aspects of the Nazi regime. It seems likely that many Neolaia cadres would have felt at home, if not in Nazi Germany, then at least in Fascist Italy. Indeed some Greek fascists contributed to the establishment of the dictatorship, even though Metaxas' attitude to them was purely instrumental and he dissolved fascist organizations together with all others. The General Student Association and the EEE provided some of the original nuclei of the Neolaia in its early phase when it was languishing for lack of voluntary support. Theodore Skilakakis, leader of the Organization of the National Sovereign State, was a confidential supporter in May 1936 when he took the post of Minister of the Interior and prepared the ground for dictatorship by appointing supporters to nomarchies and governorships. Admittedly he seems to have been valued not for his fascism – which may indeed have been an embarrassment at this delicate stage – but for his connections with fellow-participants of Metaxas and himself in the Antivenizelist military revolt of 1923. He was in fact soon to be dismissed for plotting against the regime.[39] Metaxas also recruited to his government respected figures who were independent of parties and noted for their anti-democratic ideas: Constantine Zavitsianos and Alexander Korizis (both prominent proponents of authoritarianism and corporatism), as well as the eminent manufacturer Andreas Hadjikiriakos. It seems significant that they, like Skilakakis, at some stage left the government, which from the start was dominated by Metaxas himself and came to consist almost entirely of his adherents or of neutral figures. It was mainly because of the exclusiveness of the regime, combined with harsh suppression of dissent in all quarters, that many conservatives came to dislike it.[40]

When Italy attacked Greece in October 1940, the Metaxas regime found itself facing a dilemma similiar to that which afflicted the French extreme right in its attitude towards the Axis. Metaxas' government directed the war with determination and success, yet forbade attacks on fascism as such because these would have given dissident journalists and intellectuals a long-awaited opportunity to attack the government by implication. For most of the population, who had come to detest the regime and associate it ideologically with the Axis, it was impossible to distinguish between Italy and fascism. Left-wing Venizelists and Communists were by conviction the most wholehearted advocates of war against the Axis. Maniadakis resisted the pleas of Communist political prisoners to be released to fight the Italians. But in order to meet the needs of the war effort, and to appease the public as well as Britain, the government had to recall to active service many Venizelist officers who had been cashiered on political grounds, and release most of the politicians who had been suffering 'internal exile'. In so far as these people could not continue to be denied political expression in the event of victory against Italy, it was clear that the regime in its existing form could not survive the war.[41]

The growing likelihood of war with Germany posed a different sort of dilemma. The army leaders saw that Greece had little chance of resisting a German attack, and several were for this reason disposed to follow the example of Greece's northern neighbours in seeking some sort of accommodation with Germany. Many state officials who, like Metaxas, had been Antivenizelist and therefore pro-German in the First World War, were similarly disposed to acquiesce in Germany's domination of the Balkans. However, Metaxas imposed on the General Staff a 'Polish' policy of defending Greece's sovereignty and territorial integrity, a policy supported by the Anglophile king as well as by most of the population. The authority of Metaxas (who died nine weeks before the German invasion) and of the king (who had to find a successor to Metaxas) kept all of the Metaxist ministers and most of the army leaders loyal to this policy until after the invasion started. As a result Metaxas' most powerful followers were obliged to flee overseas to evade the conquerors.[42]

The German invasion shattered the forces of the right. Some chose to join the king's government and army in Egypt, where they found much opportunity for futile intrigue. Some chose collaboration with the Germans who, however, made this course unattractive by their contemptuous and exploitative attitude towards Greece. Some joined the organized resistance, which acquired immense popular prestige but tended to repel right-wingers because it was dominated by Venizelists and Communists – for whom it was a natural continuation of their struggle against Metaxas. In these circumstances the majority of the right preferred to remain quiescent, and in the case of army officers were encouraged in doing so by the king's orders to avoid political activity. Political associates of Metaxas were now repugnant to the Germans as well as to their fellow-countrymen, and in an attempt to win favour in both areas the collaborationist government persecuted them.[43]

Fascist organizations promptly revived in order to collaborate with the Axis. They were so insignificant, however, that they made a negligible contribution to the quisling administrations, and relatively little even to the Greek forces later raised by the Germans to fight the resistance. Because Greek fascists were so uninfluential, the Germans gave them little political backing. Thus although several veteran fascists such as John Iannaros sought German patronage, the only one to receive a prominent political post was George Merkouris, as governor of the National Bank. In addition, two quisling ministers, Sotirios Gotzamanis, a politician, and George Bakos, a Metaxist general, adhered to fascist groups. The Germans made little attempt to attract able collaborators.

In fact they almost destroyed their chances of doing so by their harsh exploitation of Greece and by letting their Italian and Bulgarian allies arm ethnic minorities in their respective zones of occupation.

The fascist groups thus attracted few members. Of those whom they did attract, many seem to have been drawn by the hope of food rations or other privileges. Relatively many fascist supporters were located in Macedonia, drawing on the native anti-Semitism and including for a time a resurrected EEE. A number of groups merged, apparently under pressure from the authorities, into the National Socialist Political Organization (ESPO), led by Dr Speros Sterodemas, including Merkouris and Iannaros, and supported by Gotzamanis. According to a good British source ESPO attracted 2,000 members, making it much the largest fascist group. It issued grandiose declarations of principle, linking conservative values with 'socialism' and ancient Greek traditions. It established a youth organization, supervised by the quisling Ministry of Education, and received aid from the Germans, whom it repaid by betraying resisters and attacking Jewish property. Like other such groups, it was vulnerable to attacks by resisters, who bombed its headquarters and thus killed Sterodemas in September 1942.

The quisling ministers were of low calibre and had little authority even over the police. Most were strongly right-wing in the Greek sense: the ideas of order, security, family, religion and country had the same resonance for them as for Metaxas, and now seemed more than ever threatened by the left. The first administration, which consisted largely of Metaxist generals under George Tsolakoglou, shared Metaxas' identification with state officials and aversion to politicians. Both Tsolakoglou and the third of the three quisling premiers, the veteran politician John Rallis, had distinguished themselves before Metaxas' dictatorship by their readiness to take unconstitutional action to secure the king's return. Most quisling ministers were not strongly inspired by faith in German victory or in Nazism. Tsolakoglou and Rallis later claimed, convincingly, that they had always thought that Germany would lose the war. They seem to have been motivated both by opportunistic ambition and by conservative principles, which, by the time that Rallis became premier in May 1943, led to a panicky obsession with the communist menace.

The cause of the panic was the growing domination of the country by the resistance organization EAM/ELAS, which was openly left-wing and covertly directed by the Communist Party. Rallis tried to rally all its opponents, and established the Security Battalions to act as their spearhead. These were recruited from rival resistance groups harassed by EAM/ELAS, from former officers who included Venizelists but eventually consisted in the main of Antivenizelists, from well-to-do people fearful for their property, and – among the rank and file – from people who were merely desperate for food and pay. They, together with other collaborationist forces, reached a strength of over 16,000, including about 1,000 army officers, and in fighting resisters, whom they viewed as communist bandits, incurred heavy casualties on the Germans' behalf. A small group operating in Macedonia under Colonel George Poulos was genuinely pro-Nazi, but the bulk of the collaborationist forces felt no special enthusiasm for Nazism and wished to keep open the chance of reconciliation with the British, who were obviously destined soon to liberate the country and were upholding the king's authority over the armed forces in exile.[44]

After the Germans' withdrawal from Greece, a tacit alliance ranging from right-wing terrorists to conservative Venizelists formed under British protection to resist the apparent threat of a Communist coup. Then, in conditions of growing civil war, the British reconstructed the security forces from right-wing materials, while preparing both for the restoration of parliamentary government and for the reinstatement of the king. While trying to place centrist (which tended to mean Venizelist) politicians in prominent positions, the British – and still more their successors the Americans from 1947 – relied mainly on Antivenizelists to man the new political system, since it was they who were the most vehemently anti-communist. In these circumstances fascism was forgotten and the old division between the authoritarian and the constitutionalist right lost much of its significance. Many of the former Security Battalionists could soon resume their battle against the left under official auspices, and all but the most prominent of former collaborators secured rehabilitation. Eventually, in the late 1940s and early 1950s, even Metaxists were able to re-enter politics with success, profiting from their reputation as experienced opponents of communism. During the civil war, which ended with the defeat of the left in 1949, the diverse strands of the right could share the label 'Nationalist' (*ethnikofron*) which, having apparently entered into use during the occupation, signified devotion to the traditional institutions of monarchy, Church, family and private property, together with opposition to communism with its alien ideas and Slav affiliations.[45] Thus the Greek right achieved unprecedented unity.

In the development of the Greek right in this period, two themes are of special relevance. One is the persistent tendency of reactionaries to gain ground at the expense of conservatives, not only in the conditions of national independence up to 1941, but also in those of Axis occupation (1941–4) and subsequently of British-American hegemony (1944–9). The tendency existed despite the fact that by Balkan standards Greek conservatives were unusually vigorous, owing to the attachment to political liberties of a range of influential elites comprising most professional politicians and their supporters, together with their allies among intellectuals and journalists. Reactionaries were distinguished by their readiness to take dictatorial and violent measures to suppress the left and safeguard their own positions. After the purge of 1935 they prevailed in the army and police, and until 1944 were supported by small but active fascist groups. The reactionaries' advance was made possible by a prolonged crisis of legitimacy in the political system, and was stimulated by the militancy of the left, which was itself fed by the severity of the economic problems facing conservative governments.

The second theme is the degree to which foreign powers shaped the extent and nature of the reactionaries' gains. For example, the Italian threat to Greece up to 1941, and Greece's dependence on Britain which was in large part a consequence of this threat, weakened the fascist overtones of Metaxas' dictatorship. Had Greece been in the Axis camp, these overtones would probably have been at least as strong as in Franco's emergent regime during the same period. Metaxas might for example have appealed to Greek chauvinism by laying claim with Axis support to Cyprus. During 1941–4, collaborationism and fascism were crippled by the harshness of the Axis powers, and their partiality to Bulgaria and ethnic minorities. Three major prerequisites of fascism – ethnic competition, a conspicuous Jewish population and a threat from the left – existed in Macedonia and Thrace, and these might, given Axis encouragement, have produced a much stronger fascist movement than they did. After 1944, the victory of the reactionaries was first made possible by British backing, but then limited by the insistence of the British and their American successors that the reactionaries must respect the forms of parliamentarism. Eventually, in 1967, the reactionaries asserted their independence by establishing a dictatorship with quasi-fascist features that by then were markedly anachronistic. When this dictatorship collapsed in 1974, it effectively brought to an end a coalition of forces whose origins have been examined in this chapter.

NOTES

1 Public Record Office (PRO), Foreign Office Records (FO), 371/15232/190–1, C6557.
2 G. T. Mavrogordatos, *Stillborn Republic. Social Coalitions and Party Strategies in Greece, 1922–1936* (Berkeley and Los Angeles, Calif., 1983), pp. 81–93, 146, 161; N. C. Alivizatos, *Les institutions politiques de la Grèce a travers les crises, 1922–1977* (Paris, 1979), pp. 274, 299–300.
3 Mavrogordatos, *Stillborn Republic*, p. 93; FO, 371/15232/190–1, C6557.
4 PRO, FO, 370/314/110, L6862; 371/15966/99, C4423; 371/15966/236–9, no doc. no.; 371/20390/299, no doc. no.; 371/2390/270, R6606; 371/20392/74, R1436; Mavrogordatos, *Stillborn Republic*, p. 67; E. Kalandzēs, *Saranda Chronia Anamneses* (Athens, 1969), pp. 10–11.
5 T. Veremis, 'The Greek state and economy during the Pangalos regime, 1925–6', *Journal of the Hellenic Diaspora*, vol. VIII, no. 2 (Summer 1980), p. 44.
6 PRO, FO 371/13658/24, C7798; 371/19506/308, R2288; 371/20390/198, R4920; Y. Andricopoulos (ed.), *Ē Rizes tou Ellinikou Fasismou* [documents] (Athens, 1977), pp. 56–7.
7 J. W. Borejsza, 'East European perceptions of Italian fascism', in S. U. Larsen, B. Hagtvet and J. P. Myklebust (eds), *Who Were the Fascists? Social Roots of European Fascism*

(Bergen, Oslo and Tromsø, 1980), pp. 362, 364; C. Sarandis, 'The emergence of the right in Greece, 1920–40', DPhil thesis, University of Oxford, 1979, p. 296; PRO, FO 371/20389/10.

8   Mavrogordatos, *Stillborn Republic*, pp. 227, 237–41, 247.
9   ibid., pp. 209, 255, 259; Y. Andricopoulos, 'The power base of Greek authoritarianism', in Larsen *et al.* (eds), *Who Were the Fascists?*, p. 571; PRO, FO 371/10772/42–3, no doc. no.; 371/15232/190, C6551; 370/16771/129, no doc. no.; Andricopoulos, *Ē Rizes*, pp. 56–7.
10 ibid.; *Eleutheron Vēma*, 25 February 1933, p. 3; Sarandis, 'Emergence of the right', pp. 405, 408; S. Linardatos, *Pos Eftasame stēn Tesserēs Avgoustou* (Athens, 1965), p. 223.
11 Mavrogordatos, *Stillborn Republic*, pp. 93, 135–6, 345–8; B. Birtles, *Exiles in the Aegean* (London, 1938), pp. 52, 304, 338, 360; L. Archer, *Balkan Journal* (New York, 1944), p. 23; PRO, FO 371/19507/86–7, R3174; 371/18393/22, R1162.
12 Sarandis, 'Emergence of the right', pp. 330–2, 360–3.
13 ibid., p. 133; N. Charalambēdēs *et al.*, 'To Mystikon Archeion tou Maniadakē', *Ethnikos Kyrix*, 2 November 1949, pp. 1, 3; ibid., 3 November 1949, p. 1; Metaxas Papers (General State Archives, Athens), 103, memo. by A. Papagos, 28 January 1939.
14 Sarandis, 'Emergence of the right', pp. 365–9; PRO, FO 371/19509/152, R6250; 371/19509/162, R6289; 371/19509/192, R630; 371/19509/225, R6554; 371/19509/254, R6703; 371/19509/274, R6717; 371/19509/349, R7361.
15 Archer, *Balkan Journal*, pp. 40–2; P. M. Pipinelis, *Georgios B* (Athens, 1951), pp. 85–6, 93–5; PRO, FO 371/19509/373, R7428; 371/21147/96, R347.
16 A. Papagos, *O Ellinikos Stratos ke ē Pro Polemou Proparaskevē tou* (Athens, 1945), p. 107; J. Iatrides (ed.), *Ambassador MacVeagh Reports. Greece 1933–47*, (Princeton, NJ, 1980), pp. 84–5; PRO, FO 371/19506/139, R19504; 371/19508/45, no doc. no.; 371/19508/64, R5781; 371/20386/195, R2124; 371/20389/291, R541; 371/20390/160, R4662; 371/20390/198, R4920; 371/20390/270, R6606; G. Dafnēs, *Ē Ellas metaxē dēo Polemon 1923–40*, Vol. B (Athens, 1974), pp. 428–9; Sarandis, 'Emergence of the right', pp. 342, 418–26; J. Metaxas, *To Prosopiko tou Ēmeroloyio* [Diary], ed. P. Vranas (Athens, 1951–64), Vol. D1, p. 242.
17 A phrase of J. L. Hondros in his *Occupation and Resistance. The Greek Agony, 1941–4* (New York, 1983), p. 26.
18 Metaxas, *Ēmeroloyio*, Vol. D2, p. 488.
19 ibid., Vol. A2, pp. 448, 542; Kalandzēs, *Saranda Chronia Anamnēses*, p. 52; D. H. Close, 'The police in the 4th August regime', unpublished paper delivered to International Historical Congress, 'Dictatorship and Occupation', Athens, April 1984.
20 Metaxas, *Ēmeroloyio*, Vol. A2, p. 586; ibid., Vol. C2, p. 603; PRO, FO 371/21150/47, R2469; 371/24909/220, R4248; K. S. Antoniou, *Istoria tēs Ellinikēs Vasilikēs Chorofilakēs*, Vol. 3 (Athens, 1965), p. 1481.
21 E.g. *Efimerēda tēs Kivernēseos*, series A, 24 October 1939, p. 3056; 7 November 1939, pp. 3055–6; Close, 'Police'; PRO, FO 371/22361/392, R9966; 371/23770/331–2, R7655; 371/20390/323, R7014.
22 *Tessera Chronia Diakivernēseos I. Metaxa* (Subministry of Press and Tourism, Athens, 1940), Vol. 3, p. 194; PRO, FO 371/23777/193, p. 7, R886.
23 Linardatos, *Tesserēs Avgoustou*, pp. 181–2; Close, 'Police'.
24 FO 371/20390/323, p. 2, R7014; Metaxas, *Ēmeroloyio*, Vol. B2, p. 452; ibid., Vol. D2, p. 743; Metaxas papers, file 17, 'Summary of conversation between J. Metaxas and H. P. Lansdale, 13 December 1938'; *Messager d'Athènes*, 10 January 1939.
25 Metaxas, *Ēmeroloyio*, Vol. D2, pp. 458, 467, 470.
26 Issues of *Neolaia* for summer and autumn 1939; Kalandzēs, *Saranda Chronia Anamnēses*, p. 54; cf. E. R. Tannenbaum's view that 'the pervasive spirit' of the Italian fascist youth movement was 'like that of the Boy Scouts' (*Fascism in Italy. Society and Culture, 1922–45* [London, 1972], p. 141). I owe this reference to Ms V. A. Holbrook.
27 PRO, FO 371/22360/6, R3532; 371/22371/192–3, R10301. The organization's papers (General State Archives, Athens, file 16) contain evidence of numerous scandals.

28 Anon., *Ai Ideai tou I. Metaxa dia tēn Ellada kai ton Ellinismon* (Athens, *c.* 1952), pp. 34, 47, 59; Metaxas, *Ēmeroloyio*, Vol. C2, p. 651; PRO, FO 371/20390/270, R6606; Metaxas Papers, Metaxas-Lansdale conversation, 13 December 1938.

29 *Eleutheron Vēma*, 2 September 1940, p. 4; PRO, FO 371/23760/13, 16, R330; Mavrogordatos, *Stillborn Republic*, pp. 246–7, 252, 255.

30 Sarandis, 'Emergence of the right', p. 418; PRO, FO 371/23770/356, R11677; 371/22359/289, p. 19, R5726; 371/22370/355–6; 371/24909/134, R3682; Metaxas, *Ēmeroloyio*, Vol. D1, p. 382; ibid., Vol. D2, p. 459.

31 Anon., *Ai Ideai tou I. Metaxa*, p. 94.

32 PRO, FO 371/21148/142; 371/23780/231–2, R1907; Metaxas, *Ēmeroloyio*, Vol. D2, pp. 654, 862–6; Linardatos, *Tesserēs Avgoustou*, p. 38.

33 *Eleutheron Vēma*, 29 July 1940, pp. 1–2; ibid., 6 August 1940, p. 4; ibid., 9 August 1940, p. 1; ibid., 7 October 1940, p. 4.

34 C. Maurras, *Enquête sur la Monarchie* (Paris, 1925), in the Benaki Library, Athens. See also G. Serefis, *Cheirografo tou Septemvriou 1941* (Athens, 1972), p. 17; Sarandis, 'Emergence of the right', p. 25; G. Augustinos, *Consciousness and History. Nationalist Critics of Greek Society 1892–1914* (New York, 1977), ch. 5.

35 See P. F. Sugar (ed.), *Native Fascism in the Successor States* (Santa Barbara, Calif., 1971), pp. 130–8, 148–54; N. Oren, *Revolution Administered. Agrarianism and Communism in Bulgaria* (Baltimore, Md, 1973), pp. 18–20, 31–2, 51.

36 PRO, FO 371/24909/157, R322; Iatrides (ed.), *Ambassador MacVeagh Reports*, pp. 81–2; Archer, *Balkan Journal*, p. 78.

37 S. G. Payne, 'The concept of fascism', in Larsen *et al.*, *Who Were the Fascists?*, pp. 20–3; A. D. Smith, *Nationalism in the Twentieth Century* (Canberra, 1979), pp. 56–7, 63–4, 78–82.

38 Metaxas, *Ēmeroloyio*, Vol. D2, p. 553, 2 January 1941.

39 Linardatos, *Pos Eftasame*, pp. 223, 226, 242; *Tesserēs Avgoustou*, pp. 42–3, 153–4; *Katheriminē*, 14 July 1936, p. 4.

40 PRO, FO 371/22371/92, p. 5, R10301; Archer, *Balkan Journal*, p. 57; Iatrides (ed.), *Ambassador MacVeagh Reports*, p. 112.

41 Seferis, *Septemvriou 1941*, p. 53; PRO, FO 371/24910/102, 114, 128, R8218; 371/23781/318, R5586; Metaxas, *Ēmeroloyio*, Vol. D2, pp. 544–54.

42 PRO, FO 371/24914/2, R7582; 371/23782/141; G. K. E. Tsolakoglou, *Apomnēmonevmata* (Athens, 1959), pp. 12–13; J. Koliopoulos, 'Unwanted ally: Greece and the great powers, 1939–41', *Balkan Studies*, vol. 23, no. 1 (1982), pp. 13–14; I Documenti Diplomatici Italiani (Ministro degli Affari Esteri), 9th series, Vol. 5, 1939–43, p. 268; Andricopoulos (ed.), *Ē Rizes*, pp. 102–7.

43 See especially N. A. Stavrou, *Allied Politics and Military Interventions* (Athens, 1977), pp. 33–43; L. Baerentzen (ed.), *British Reports on Greece* (Copenhagen, 1982), p. 26; Archer, *Balkan Journal*, p. 213.

44 US National Archives (Washington, DC), State department, RG59, R & A, 872, 'Greek Quisling and pro-Axis organizations, 26 April 1943'; A. Gerolymmatos, 'The Security Battalions and the civil war', *Journal of the Hellenic Diaspora*, vol. XII, no. 1 (Spring 1985), pp. 22–3; Hondros, *Occupation and Resistance*, pp. 78–85; H. Fleischer, 'Contacts between German occupation authorities and the major Greek resistance organizations: sound tactics or collaboration?' and L. Baerentzen, 'The liberation of the Peloponnese, September 1944', both in J. O. Iatrides (ed.), *Greece in the 1940s. A Nation in Crisis* (Hanover, NH, and London, 1981), pp. 52, 134, 350, n. 33; H. Fleischer, 'Nea stēchēa yia tē schesē Yermanikon archon katochēs ke tagmaton asfaleias', *Mnēmon*, vol. 8 (1980–2), pp. 191–201; Tsolakoglou, *Apomnēmonevmata*, pp. 159–74; G. Rallis (ed.), *O Rallis Omilei ek tou Tafou* (Athens, 1947), pp. 42–4, 56–64. I have been generously helped by advice from Dr H. Fleischer concerning Greek fascism during the occupation.

45 G. Alexander, *The Prelude to the Truman Doctrine. British Policy in Greece 1944–7* (Oxford, 1982), pp. 96–8, 118–20, 160–1, 173–8, 195, 205; L. Wittner, *American Intervention in Greece, 1943–9* (New York, 1982), pp. 41, 109–16, 240–1; G. Chandler, *The Divided Land. An Anglo-Greek Tragedy* (London, 1959), pp. 57, 65–6, 128, 134, 165; H. Richter, 'The Varkiza Agreement and the origins of the civil war', in Iatrides (ed.), *Greece in the 1940s*, p. 174; Stavrou, *Allied Politics*, pp. 91–2.

12

Fascists and conservatives in Romania: two generations of nationalists

Irina Livezeanu

The relationship between fascist and conservative tendencies in interwar Romania was a dynamic and complex one. On the one hand, the ideological line between the two was blurred by a common nationalism which received an enormous impetus from Romania's territorial expansion in the aftermath of the First World War. On the other hand, the two tendencies engaged in bitter conflicts which also contributed to the radicalization of nationalist discourse. The fascists – and their precursors in the nationalist student movement, with whom this chapter is largely concerned – used terrorist methods against mainstream politicians whom they charged with corruption and insufficient nationalism. While the National Liberal authorities arrested, tortured and, in the late 1930s, executed right-wing nationalist radicals, the latter emerged from their literal and figurative trials as popular heroes, legitimized by the nationalism which they and the Liberals shared. Radical nationalist goals, such as the limitation of national minorities in professional elites and educational institutions, paralleled those of mainstream nationalists preoccupied with completing Greater Romania's national consolidation. Electoral alliances between fascist and mainstream parties, such as that in 1937 involving the Iron Guard and the National Peasants, and the migration across the conservative–radical divide of leading political personalities like Octavian Goga or Alexandru Vaida-Voevod, further indicate the fluid and dynamic nature of the fascist–conservative relationship.

The strictly political and organizational turning-points in the life of Romanian fascism have been recorded in standard treatments of the Iron Guard.[1] Little attempt has been made, however, to understand either the precise relationship between the fascist movement and mainstream Romanian politics, society and sociopolitical thought, or the attractiveness of radical-nationalist, and increasingly fascist, ideas to so much of the post-1919 young generation. Much of the standard literature deals summarily with the 1920s, concentrating instead on the mid- and late 1930s when, in the form of the Iron Guard and other extremist parties, fascism became electorally significant. Even the best studies barely touch

218

on the issues of nationalism and national consolidation which form the crucial context within which Romanian fascism developed. Eugen Weber, for example, dismisses the possibility that nationalism might have played a part in fascist organizing efforts, arguing that in Romania 'nationalism was not an issue of party politics but part of the general consensus' and that therefore 'a radical nationalist political movement could not succeed . . . by recruiting nationalists against anti-nationalists'.[2] Although the existence of that nationalist consensus is indisputable, Weber ignores an important point: that Romanian fascists did not so much prosper by organizing against anti-nationalists, as gain popularity and legitimacy by defining themselves as the best and the purest nationalists within that consensus.

To understand Romanian fascism a study of its origins and context is necessary. These lie in the period immediately following the war, when Romania's expanded borders still awaited international sanction and were therefore still fragile; when Old Kingdom Romanians were busy exploring ways of coping with the large minority populations which lived alongside Romanians in the new territories; and when Corneliu Zelea Codreanu, the future leader of the Iron Guard, was a law student at Jassy University and a disciple of A. C. Cuza, the 'father' of twentieth-century Romanian anti-Semitism. Without attempting an exhaustive treatment of the Romanian fascist phenomenon, this chapter will seek to locate it within the postwar nation-building agenda and, in the context of the nationalist rhetoric engendered by state- and nation-building policies, to explain both its appeal to the young and the legitimacy it received from their elders.

Given the problematic of this volume, it is important to stress that, whilst interwar Romania possessed perhaps the most important fascist movement outside Italy and Germany, the country's Conservative Party barely survived the First World War. Before 1914 the Conservative Party had been one of two 'governmental' parties, rotating in office with the National Liberals; its postwar demise was the result of internal factionalism (exacerbated by wartime events), the wartime pro-German sympathies of one of its factions and the radical agrarian reform of 1918 which almost entirely destroyed the large estates whose owners had been the party's backbone.[3]

The lack of a party actually calling itself 'Conservative' during the interwar period did not, however, signify an absence of conservative political forces. Of the mainstream parties, the oldest surviving and most powerful throughout the 1920s and 1930s was the National Liberal Party. The National Peasant Party, fruit of a merger in 1926 of the Peasant and the Transylvanian National Parties, stood to the left of the National Liberals, but also effectively declared itself of the establishment by abandoning the Peasantists' class struggle thesis in favour of the principle of national solidarity.[4] General Alexandru Averescu's People's League, later the People's Party, enjoyed brief popularity after 1918 thanks to Averescu's prestige as a war hero; its early promise of developing into a serious rival to National Liberalism was soon dashed, however, as it became apparent that only the Liberals' approval and self-interested manipulation could give it access to power.[5]

What adds complexity to any analysis of Romanian centrist and right-wing politics, whether conservative or radical, is that the postwar 'status quo' represented a profoundly revolutionized state of affairs, 'conservation' of which demanded more than traditional conservative measures.[6] The 'mechanism of [Old Romania's] political life which had been so clear and so simple'[7] before the war became a lot more complex and less stable as a result of territorial expansion and democratic reforms. The establishment of a new political equilibrium required any party in power to work towards the construction of a unified cultural and institutional framework by mobilizing hitherto untapped national forces. The transformation of the Romanian kingdom into Greater Romania should thus be regarded as a national – no less disruptive than a social – revolution.

Romania's postwar territorial expansion involved the annexation of Bessarabia from Russia, Bukovina from Austria and Transylvania from Hungary. In 1914 the area of the Old Kingdom was 137,903 sq. km; that of Greater Romania in 1919 was 295,049 sq. km. In the same period, Romania's population increased from 7,771,341 to 14,669,841. In 1930, according to the first postwar census, it stood at 18,057,028.[8] To the revolutionary effects of such massive and sudden expansion were added those of fundamental social and political reforms: universal manhood suffrage, a sweeping land reform and the emancipation of the Jews. The significance of these measures was vast: first, they brought into the political arena the two antipodes of Romanian social, ethnic and cultural symbolism, the Jew and the peasant; secondly, the land reform, by partially satisfying peasant land-hunger, made it possible for the social question to take second place to the national question. Through these reforms the Old Kingdom's reactions to the annexation and assimilation of the new provinces were mediated.

The Romanian state and nationalist elites faced a multitude of problems concerning both national and state consolidation: institutional and legal centralization; the struggle against regionalism; recruitment and expansion of national elites to replace foreign ones; the implantation or nurturing of national consciousness among uneducated and educated strata that, having lived for as long as anyone could remember under foreign rule, either remained illiterate or were socialized into a foreign culture; and the assimilation of newly enfranchised voters into a national political process. In order to assimilate the new provinces with their substantial minority populations and regionalized Romanian-speaking populations, policies were initiated which intensified processes of national mobilization. The resulting populist-nationalist discourse came to dominate political, social and cultural life, while integral nationalism became widely accepted as a framework for most current ideologies.

Greater Romania was predominantly rural and agricultural, only 20.2 per cent of its population living in urban areas.[9] Ethnically and religiously, the newly enlarged country was quite diverse, with most of the non-Romanian, non-Orthodox minorities living in the new provinces. While in the Old Kingdom minorities had comprised less than 8 per cent of the population,[10] in the new Romania the figure was close to 30 per cent.[11] Romanians constituted a little over two-thirds of the country's population, with an important Hungarian (and Szekler) minority in Transylvania and lesser but sizeable German, Ukrainian and Russian populations in the new provinces. The Jews – the only substantial minority in the Old Kingdom – now constituted a significant minority element in both the old and the new territories.

Not only were Romanians ethnically 'diminished' with the addition of the new provinces but, with Romania becoming proportionately less urban than before the war, the urban–rural demographic balance also shifted to the disadvantage of ethnic Romanians; in 1930 they represented only 58.6 per cent of the urban population. In the Old Kingdom, Romanians had constituted three-quarters of the urban population, but in each of the new provinces they represented just over or just under one-third.[12] In general the Romanians were the peasants of the new provinces and in large measure also of the old. Demographic factors such as these combined to create an inescapably volatile situation.

In the underdeveloped world of newly united Romania the challenges of nation-building involved a confrontation between peasant and townsman. The peasant, the nation's common denominator in both the old and new provinces, now became the symbol of the nation and the ally of the state. He was invited to take steps which would raise his personal status and that of the nation: to become educated, to enter the middle class, to move to town, to join the bureaucracy, to take an industrial or, more often, a commercial job. For peasants with little or no urban experience or previous education, with no business or friendship networks beyond the village, such moves were nevertheless problematic, necessitating competition with members of much more experienced 'foreign' elites who were not easily dislodged from their prior positions in the professions, the cities and the schools.[13] Because the networks supporting them in these positions were not automatically swept away with the change of boundaries and state power, there ensued between peasant and urbanite, village and town, Romanian and 'foreigner' a bitter and protracted struggle in which it seemed that the Greater Romanian state itself was at stake.

221

Greater Romania's ethnic and social structure meant that between the wars Romanian national identity was defined, by the state and by nationalists of all shades, as fundamentally rural. Massive educational expansion was justified with reference to the 'awakening' of the peasants and the consequent strengthening of the nation. The peasantry was to contribute its ethnic essence to the state and the schools were to train the peasants for their public – and national – role. In nationalist discourse, indeed, the terms 'Romanian' and 'peasant' became almost interchangeable. While the educated elites of non-Romanian communities were viewed circumspectly – their priests, teachers and intellectuals being frowned upon for resisting the nationalization of minority schools and other institutions, for entertaining agitation and for unwillingness to accommodate themselves to the new structure of the state – Romanian authorities believed that lower-class, rural 'foreigners' could be assimilated to Romanian culture and citizenship without posing a threat to the nation.

Romanians differentiated among the various minorities according to their assimilability. Predominantly rural ethnic groups such as the Ukrainians were considered more assimilable than the Magyars and Germans, who were more urban than the Romanians. Least assimilable were the most urban community of all, the Jews. In prewar Romania the Jews, as non-Christians, had been excluded from citizenship and from acquiring rural property; partly – and increasingly – as a result of such legal constraints their communities had even then been 'overwhelmingly urban, commercial and industrial' in character.[14] Although emancipation in 1919 brought a legal solution to the much-belaboured 'Jewish question',[15] many Romanians regarded this imposed measure as itself the problem, and the Jews' new civil and political rights as illegitimate.

To those who embraced a 'ruralist' definition of the Romanian nation, towns and their inhabitants were foreign and therefore suspect. The Bucharest-based state may have held political and coercive power, but in the new provinces it had difficulty penetrating the civil society represented by urban milieux, culture and elites. Cultural institutions and urban elites surviving from earlier political and social structures blocked the progress of young, aspiring Romanian elites just out of the village. The state encouraged the expansion of the latter element through educational channels not only because it had a serious interest in changing the ethnic character of the country's elites but also because with the offspring of Romanian peasants it could conquer the towns and the cultural strongholds. Through education the Romanian peasant might attain higher social status, a bureaucratic white-collar job, and more personal power; by thus advancing into the urban, high-cultural world previously dominated by foreign elites, the transformed peasant would make Romania a true nation-state. Romanians, especially the young, regarded this conquest of the towns and of elite positions as a national mission, all the more appealing in terms of their own self-interest. By displacing the foreign urban elites, of which the Jews were both a part and, more importantly, a symbol, the influx of educated peasants would bring to bear an ancestral culture elevated by the state educational system; in the urban context, this peasant culture writ large would become the essence of the modern Romanian nation.

The populist nationalism so prevalent within interwar Romanian politics, society and culture was thus a by-product of nation-building activity. Following the doubling of Romania's territory and population, the Romanian state and elites worked towards the assimilation of all that could be considered assimilable. Given the overwhelmingly rural character of the Romanians, the foreignness of the towns in the new provinces, the need to expand Romanian elites within the new territories and to establish a Romanian presence in the nationally crucial cultural and urban spheres, the nation- and state-building processes were accompanied by a growing anti-urban, populist, xenophobic and anti-Semitic discourse. This nationalistic climate favoured the growth of a fascist movement.

The ideological and political lineage of Romanian fascism can be traced back to its beginnings as a student movement in the early 1920s. Radical nationalist protest erupted on campuses as an expression of dissatisfaction with overcrowding and competition in higher education. Within a few years campus nationalists succeeded in reducing a set of complex problems to a general complaint against the large number of minority students with whom they were obliged to compete for resources and, looking ahead, also for jobs in the bureaucratic and professional elite. Attacks against minority students were aimed particularly at Jews, who constituted the largest minority group within the university population. While focused primarily on university issues, student nationalism also represented a backlash against the left, whose organizing efforts enjoyed some success immediately after the war. This left-wing upsurge was widely identified with possible Russian (and, briefly, Hungarian) designs on Romania's new territories; with the large refugee Jewish population fleeing into Bessarabia from the Ukraine; and with the large number of Jewish students, especially from Bessarabia, at the University of Jassy and at the new Romanian campuses, Cernăuţi and Cluj. The nationalist student movement gained national attention, not only because of its considerable dimensions and violence but also because it reflected, in raw and exaggerated form, the preoccupations of Romanian state-builders and mainstream nationalists: in particular that with fashioning a truly Romanian elite to replace still powerful minorities in the new provinces.

University politics represents an ideal locus for studying the convergence and conflict between mainstream and extreme nationalism, since it was here that the goals of conservative politicians attempting to achieve equilibrium in a still loosely integrated state, and those of a younger generation eager to assure its place in the new state, dovetailed in such a way as to foster the beginnings of a fascist movement. The 'new generation' of young radical nationalists came to be recognized as spokesmen not only of their own generation but also, by extension, of the nation.[16] This was possible because the younger and older generations of educated Romanians possessed overlapping perceptions and goals. In particular they shared a common identification of the day's burning problems: on one side they saw the foreign cities and elites, and on the other the underprivileged and uneducated Romanian peasantry. Differences between the generations are equally important, however, for the fanaticism and intransigence of the young were directed not only at the foreign cultural and urban enclaves with which they and their elders were equally uncomfortable, but also at the 'soft', compromising older generation of politicians itself. The young generation accordingly condemned the Liberal constitution of 1923 because it 'sold out' to the Great Powers by complying with the St Germain treaty and guaranteeing the civil and political rights of the national minorities. Although the Liberals also considered the Great Powers to be interfering in Romania's internal affairs, they at the same time understood the international treaties to be, all in all, a not unreasonable price to pay for Greater Romania's very existence.

A frequent condition of right-wing radicalization is the real or widely imagined existence of a powerful left. In the immediate aftermath of the war the Romanian left, besides making a show of force in strikes and street demonstrations, was widely perceived as strong owing to the communist victories in Russia and Hungary, neighbouring states from which Romania had acquired, respectively, Bessarabia and Transylvania. Fear of Bolshevism, which came to be identified with threats to greater Romania's territorial integrity, accordingly swept the country at all levels of society. Although, as their Russian counterparts turned from war to desertion and revolution, Romanian troops maintained military discipline,[17] Bolshevik propaganda was nevertheless effective when it addressed the Romanians as peasants. In 1917, during the infectious first stages of the Russian revolution, King Ferdinand was accordingly moved to promise extensive land and electoral reforms.[18]

The impression of a Bolshevik threat in Romania, and especially in the new provinces, in the form both of possible armed hostility from the neighbouring states and of Soviet-inspired domestic radicalism, is on balance confirmed by French diplomatic and military sources.[19] While outside agitation is almost always assumed in these reports, local postwar conditions were themselves propitious to the organizing efforts of the left. Romanian authorities were deeply concerned about communist organizations uncovered in Bessarabia, which they believed were made up mostly of Russian Jews,[20] and also feared the spread of Bolshevism to Transylvania. In the fall of 1919 anti-Bolshevik propaganda calling for a fight to the end against 'the red beasts' was published by the state printing works and distributed widely by police agents. Government propaganda made the explicit connection between Jewishness and Bolshevism, asserting that only Jews were Bolsheviks and identifying the leaders of the recently evicted Bela Kun regime in Hungary as mostly Jews and deserters from the Romanian army.[21]

Independently of these overlapping territorial and ideological struggles, domestic lower-class unrest provided the authorities with further cause for worry. The war had produced massive dislocation and, in many enterprises, the militarization of labour.[22] In the aftermath of war and German occupation, peasant and working-class living standards had fallen. The outcome of these conditions was a wave of working-class militancy between 1918 and 1921, manifested in work stoppages, strikes and demonstrations: phenomena seen by conservatives like Nicolae Iorga as 'revolutionary'.[23] 'Anti-Bolshevist' responses to such developments in the early postwar period encompassed not only state repression of labour unrest but also cultural propaganda projects. These, propelled by local initiative but appealing to the state for support, tended to arise in industrial regions where socialist and labour activity was concentrated. Local notables opened patriotic cultural centres ('hearths'), and published and distributed to artisans, workers and peasants anti-Bolshevik brochures designed to combat the spread of socialism.[24]

A general left-wing upsurge, albeit one shortlived and ultimately easily contained, was compounded in the public mind by the influx of Jewish refugees into Bessarabia: an estimated 30,000 to 60,000 by the end of 1921 according to Jewish sources.[25] This transient population alarmed the Romanian authorities; the Ministry of the Interior's General Under-Inspectorate of Security for Bessarabia wrote in a report to the Ministry of Education that

the avalanche of refugees from across the Dniester is the most powerful current of the danger of communist anarchy, which is trying to undermine our whole State organization. Their multiple organizations and their methods of struggle – just by virtue of the fact that they do not express themselves openly and loyally, but in the shade, spreading clandestinely-printed leaflets, using couriers, spies, coded correspondence etc. ... brought here by these refugees who are the expression of the apostolate of communist ideas – are that much more dangerous, for even if these refugees were not directly in the service of the Soviets, even then, imbued and possessed by the need for destruction, they propagate in every way the germ of anarchy.[26]

225

In addition to their alarm at the refugees' suspected political sympathies, the authorities feared that Bessarabia's cultural and ethnic heterogeneity, considered great enough already, would be increased by these non-Romanian speakers,[27] and that the problem might spread from Bessarabia to neighbouring Moldavia, where much of the Old Kingdom Jewish population was concentrated.

There thus emerged in interwar Romania, and particularly in Bessarabia and Moldavia, an identification between Jewishness and Bolshevism. Since for Romanian nationalism both these terms held non- and anti-national connotations, anti-Semitism and anti-communism became signposts of an extremist version of the national ideology.

Reaction to Romania's 'red years' was an important element within the ideology of the future leader of Romanian fascism, Corneliu Zelea Codreanu,[28] who in September 1919 became a law student at the University of Jassy.[29] While this reaction represented an amplification of that concern for their country's social and territorial security which was nursed by many Romanians, including the authorities, it was Codreanu's feeling that the latter were not responding vigorously enough to the leftist and Jewish danger.[30] On arriving in Jassy from a provincial town in Moldavia, Codreanu was struck by the left's ascendancy, not only in working-class milieux but also at the university. Mirroring official fears about Jewish refugees from Bessarabia, Codreanu saw himself and other campus nationalists as 'smothered by the immense mass of Jewish students from Bessarabia, all agents of communist propaganda'.[31]

Proclaiming the universities' 'national duty to open wide the gates to the youth of Bessarabia which longed for Romanian culture', Ministry of Education officials and some university professors had initially favoured a generous admissions policy towards Bessarabian students; if not admitted, the argument ran, they would end up at Russian universities.[32] The provision of state-subsidized cafeterias and dormitories for students from the new territories aroused among Old Kingdom youth an animosity which was intensified by ethnic and political considerations.[33] Of the 4,062 Bessarabians enrolled at Jassy University between 1918 and 1930, only 1,306 (32.2 per cent) were ethnic Romanians; 1,794 (44.2 per cent) were Jews, with Russians making up 11.3 per cent, Bulgarians 4.5 per cent and Ukrainians 4 per cent.[34] The university was in general marked by the large number of students from the newly annexed territories: in 1921-2 over half of its students were from Bessarabia, Transylvania and Bukovina.[35] The Bessarabians were largely under leftist influence.[36]

In response to the university's leftist atmosphere, Codreanu's first organized political experience was in a shortlived nationalist-syndicalist workers' group, the Guard of National Consciousness. The counter-socialist strike-breaking activity of this organization reached its peak in the spring of 1920, only to lose its *raison d'être* soon thereafter owing to the Averescu government's own labour-repressive measures.[37] In 1920-1 Codreanu turned his attention to student politics. With no more than forty nationalist students confronting 'the great majority of the others, dominated by the Communist organizations',[38] he faced an uphill struggle. He wrote later that

> The progress of these anti-Romanian ideas, maintained by the mass of professors and students, and encouraged by all the enemies of enlarged Romania, no longer found in our student world the least nationalist resistence. There were only a few of us ... who tried still to remain firm on our positions, but we found ourselves surrounded by an atmosphere of contempt and hostility. Our colleagues who had as their motto 'freedom of conscience', and [who] preached all the other freedoms, spat after us when we passed in the streets and in the school corridors. They had become ... more and more aggressive. Meeting upon meeting attended by thousands of students propagated Bolshevism [and] attacked the Army, Justice, the Church [and] the Crown.[39]

Unable to rally massive support for the nationalist cause, Codreanu resorted to lonely, 'heroic' actions. Alone, or occasionally with a few others, he attempted to block the official return to classes in protest against the dropping of the traditional religious ceremony, interfered with the production of Jewish plays, vandalized Jewish and democratic press offices and scuffled with liberal Jewish journalists whom he held responsible for favouring the nation's enemies.[40] These and other actions were repudiated by the official student society; in May of 1921 Codreanu's behaviour was still seen as no more than a nuisance which the university's main student organization felt sure it could contain with the help of the administration.[41] The latter proved obliging, expelling Codreanu on 2 June 1921.[42] The move had no practical effect, however, since Codreanu received the full support of the Jassy Law School in which he was enrolled and the dean of which was the well-known anti-Semite A. C. Cuza.[43]

During the academic year 1921–2, Codreanu established himself firmly as a nationalist student leader. Capitalizing on the notoriety surrounding his expulsion from the university and reinstatement within the Law School, he was elected president of the Law Students' Association.[44] Since the Law School was the best-attended branch of the university, this was a strategic position; Codreanu was able to use it in order, for example, to introduce a weekly study group, which attracted many students from within and even outside the Law School, on aspects 'of the Jewish question considered from a scientific point of view'.[45] Such extra-curricular discussions did not occur in a vacuum but built upon the anti-Semitic content of Cuza's highly popular lectures on political economy.[46] The official General Association of Jassy Students, hitherto dominated by the left, now began to lose influence to Codreanu's organization. On 21 May 1922 Codreanu declared the dissolution of the association, and in its place founded the Association of Christian Students.[47] This body, by virtue of its title, automatically excluded Jews and thus many leftists, isolating both elements and reducing the spread of communist influence among Jassy students.[48]

There was nothing new about the anti-Semitic theories which Cuza, partly in association with Nicolae Iorga, had developed at the turn of the century and which were now taken up wholesale by Codreanu. In the early aftermath of the war, however, Codreanu and Cuza stood on the fringes of the university political establishment. The re-actualization of anti-Semitic theories, with difficulty at first, as the credo behind the students' mass protests and as the motto of the new generation, was related to a broader legitimacy indirectly offered by the policies of nation-building.

The formative experience of the nationalist student movement – and by extension of the fascist movement into which it developed – occurred in 1922, when mass protests erupted on all Romanian campuses demanding the exclusion from university of Jewish students, or at least the application of a *numerus clausus*. The nationalists were concerned with the ethnic balance not only of the universities but also of society at large, and particularly of the leadership stratum.[49] But, as the forge of the country's professional and intellectual elite, the universities – seen as both the root and a symbol of the whole problem – were of most immediate and special concern to the nationalist students. It was there that the lawyers, doctors, journalists, pharmacists, engineers and academics of the future were concentrated – all at a volatile age and exhibiting the mostly rural backgrounds of the Romanians as opposed to the more urban profiles of the minorities – and that accordingly the tensions of Romanian and non-Romanian, rural and urban elites were most acute.

Anti-Semitic demonstrations were occurring more and more frequently in November 1922,[50] and by early December the rightist student movement had become an uncontrollable threat to peace and order.[51] By virtue both of its intensity and its spontaneity, this first great outburst of nationalist student protest has been described by its veterans as a 'spontaneous explosion', a 'volcanic eruption' and a 'spasm of the sick nation'.[52] The particular incident which sparked off the nation-wide student protests took place at the Cluj medical school. The demand of ethnic Romanian medical students that dissection of Jewish cadavers be carried out only by their Jewish colleagues quickly came to symbolize the sense of national wrong that pervaded the ethnic

228

Romanian student body.[53] Evoking the atmosphere and events of that time, Ion Moţa, a student spokesman from Cluj and a future Iron Guard leader, wrote:

> Misery, dampness, a housing shortage, overcrowded dormitories for the Romanians. Carefree leisure, terrible increase, lack of worries for the foreigners, who had become defiant. On street corners one heard that that year, in the first year of medical school, Kikes were four times as numerous as Romanians .. [News of a female Romanian student's suicide sparked off protests, and after these were received by the university administration] with irony, the tremor of the first news shook us all: the medical students broke the chain that was choking us, they chased the Kike students out of the dissecting room.[54]

On 10 December 1922 student delegates from all four Romanian campuses gathered in Bucharest, where a joint list of demands, focusing upon the *numerus clausus*, was formulated and a general university strike declared to press them home.[55] Throughout the interwar period this date was to be celebrated, often violently, by nationalist students as a symbol of the generation of 1922's continued struggle for its original goals.[56]

Codreanu's writings indicate the ideological work that was required to make the Jewish question a focal point and unifying element of the nation-wide student movement. While a large urban Jewish population and a tradition of anti-Semitism existed in north-eastern Romania – in Moldavia, where Cuza and Codreanu were based, in Bessarabia and in Bukovina – in the other provinces the proportion of Jews was lower and political anti-Semitism less important. In the 1920s close associates of Codreanu from Jassy had to visit Bucharest and Cluj to 'educate' their colleagues on the Jewish question.[57] This suggests that in those regions where anti-Semitic traditions were superficial, students were attracted less by anti-Semitism for its own sake than by fascist promises of economic security in a fully nationalized society – especially when fascists also gained control of university cafeterias and dormitories.[58]

In March 1923 the new Romanian constitution was signed, including the Jewish emancipation provisions imposed by the Treaty of St Germain. Despite this immediate setback, in time the generation of 1922's broader goals of mobilizing mass support behind an integral nationalist, anti-Semitic and anti-democratic programme succeeded quite well. Much of mainstream public opinion proved to be broadly behind the new generation, whose struggle was commonly perceived as justified and righteous in view of the 'unfair' and 'overwhelming' proportion of Jews in higher education and the professions. Support came not only from veterans' organizations such as the National Union of Former Combatants,[59] but also from academics and intellectuals. Professors opposed to violent forms of the student struggle were nevertheless able to sympathize with its motivations and programme, while the rights of expression of the incendiary student movement – which the government occasionally tried to control and censor – were often defended by the mainstream nationalist press.[60]

In March 1923, in the Cluj newspaper *Conştiinţa Românească*, Sextil Puşcariu, professor of philology and former rector of Cluj University, applauded the 15,000 youths of the student movement; united in a single cause, unaffected by regionalism and manifesting a cohesion rare for Romania, the movement was, he declared, 'a healthy and spontaneous reaction of the national preservation instinct'.[61] Addressing the Circle of Bukovinian Students, Puşcariu pronounced the *numerus clausus* to be of interest to all those who wished the country well, for 'In our country [which we] gained with so many sacrifices, we no longer have air to breathe; the invasion of the foreign element stifles us, chokes us'.[62] The *Cuvântul Nostru* obituary for Dimitrie Onciul, dean of the School of Letters in Bucharest and president of the Romanian Academy, praised Onciul's ardent support for the student movement. He had told the students:

> You are like *turburelul*, like new, fermenting wine, and your enthusiasm is natural. You are fermenting great ideals, of which we approve, and if need be we will approve you even more.[63]

A similar position was taken up by one of Romania's greatest living poets, the Transylvanian Octavian Goga. Although best remembered politically for his collaboration with Cuza in the 44-day 'Goga–Cuza government' of December 1937–February 1938, during the preceding two decades Goga's political career had spanned the National Party of Transylvania, Averescu's People's Party, the National Agrarian Party and the National Christian Party. According to Paul Shapiro it was only after 1932 that Goga 'turned increasingly to extreme nationalism and anti-Semitism, toward the "immovable" Professor Cuza'.[64] It is interesting, therefore, to look at Goga's views of the student movement in the 1920s when, as a leading member of Averescu's People's Party he stood well within the range of mainstream nationalism.

From 1922 Goga was director of, and a frequent contributor to, the Cluj magazine *Ţara Noastră*, from which in 1927 he published a collection of essays under the title *Mustul care fierbe* ('The Fermenting Must').[65] The volume opens with a dedication to the younger generation in which Romania's 'disjointed society' is likened to a 'fermenting must' and the 'dogma' of the national idea identified as the only hope for the future:

> It is proof of the people's health that the new intellectual generation professes this dogma and embarks upon its course with these slogans.

This is a guarantee that out of the present ferment our organic truths will emerge victorious, and that the scum will sink to the bottom. With hope for the great renewal, I dedicate my book to the young generation.[66]

Goga's dedication was appropriate since he shared many of the young generation's obsessions, among them the danger of losing Romanian culture, art, literature and the press to an invading, implicitly or explicitly Jewish, intellect, and the already acknowledged loss of Romania's cities to the same foreign spirit. The students, he commented, had instinctively 'noticed a threat, and had put themselves in its way':

I see you not as narrow spirits resistant to ideas of progress, but rather as an ingenuous expression of a whole people. Ten thousand boys torn from among the people, representing all social classes ... cannot amount to a case of collective madness. That you may also have incorrect slogans is possible, but your inspiration is from the normal course of our past, you are the national idea on the march, the new halting place for tomorrow.[67]

While ostensibly more liberal *politically* than Cuza, Codreanu and their followers, Goga nevertheless defended his nation's 'prerogatives of blood' and deplored 'any inopportune infiltration' into Romanian culture.[68] Like the spokesmen of student nationalism, he also referred to an actual foreign invasion, almost certainly an allusion to the Jewish inhabitants of, and refugees into, Romania's new territories:

We give the impression that we are a sick body, and on sick bodies ... parasites usually appear. Look around you, as, in some new California, from all parts of the globe fortune-seekers are descending upon this blessed land, with which they have nothing in common but its exploitation. From all sides, our frontiers are invaded by guests ... who sow corruption and execration, making grow the doubtful froth of cities and awakening a trail of awkward discouragement in the pure soul of our peasants. This wave of foreigners grows ceaselessly, like a column of conquerors.[69]

While Goga's support for the stance of the new generation was enhanced by his impeccable literary prestige, the significance of one man's opinions, even if he was Romania's poet laureate, might be questioned. The evidence for much broader social support for the student movement, however, includes a fairly long list of judicial acquittals for crimes committed by fanatically dedicated young nationalists, members either of Cuza's League of National Defence or, after 1927, of Codreanu's Legion of the Archangel Michael, later known as the Iron Guard.

The first of these judicial victories came in the wake of a radical-nationalist conspiracy, uncovered in 1923, to assassinate Liberal politicians and Jewish bankers.[70] The plot was Ion Moţa's idea for keeping alive student resistance after a discouraging stalemate in the *numerus clausus* agitation. In prison, on the eve of the trial, Moţa assassinated the 'traitor' whose actions had resulted in the discovery of the plot. Even so, the accused were acquitted. The verdict may have been based ultimately on a technicality, but the atmosphere created around the trial was undoubtedly important to the outcome. Horia Sima, a later leader of the Iron Guard, describes the pressure exerted by student supporters who had gathered in Bucharest from all the Romanian universities in late March 1924:

The thousands of students . . . maintained the capital in a continuous effervescence, and succeeded in winning public opinion to their cause. The day of the trial [29 March 1924], the Court was guarded by powerful cordons of gendarmes, themselves encircled by tens of thousands of men who intoned patriotic songs and demanded the students' acquittal. The trial took place in an atmosphere which managed to disconcert governmental circles. The roles had been reversed: it was no longer a question of trying the students, but rather the ruling class. THE ACCUSED STUDENTS HAD BECOME THE ACCUSERS OF THE GOVERNMENT, THE TRUSTEES OF THE NATIONAL CONSCIENCE. Public opinion had identified the true culprits in the ranks of the government. The pressure of public opinion nullified the government's apparatus of intimidation, [and] the influence of the Jewish-controlled press. The jury gave an acquittal verdict, to the applause of the whole audience.[71]

On 25 October 1924 Codreanu assassinated the Jassy police prefect C. G. Manciu, a feared and hated enemy of the student movement who had used harsh means, torture included, to try to repress it. Codreanu also wounded two other police officers.[72] His trial opened in March 1925 in Focşani, a town with a substantial Jewish population on the Moldavian–Wallachian border. It soon became clear, however, that the anti-Semitic atmosphere in Focşani would influence the jury toward a favourable verdict for the assassin and on 17 March the trial was accordingly adjourned.[73] Riots immediately erupted which local officials described as 'twenty-four hours of terror'.[74] Dinu Dumbravă, a Bucharest journalist who visited Focşani to investigate the story, reported that the town looked as though it had been 'devastated by an enemy army' or struck by 'an insane revolution';[75] the damage had been inflicted by some 100 students and another 200–300 'vagabonds', but the ground had been prepared by anti-Semitic propaganda in the local schools.[76]

Nationalist spirit ran high in Focşani. After the riots, despite orders for the confiscation of inflammatory leaflets, a local bookstore displayed a portrait of Codreanu 'mounted and framed in a place of honour' in its window, alongside a special edition of the nationalist student newspaper *Cuvântul Studenţesc* which 'was point-blank inciting to crime in the name of the Romanian people, stating that the "entire student body was in solidarity with Manciu's punishment"'.[77] A local resident interviewed by Dumbravă referred to the riots and to Codreanu's trial (which was to reconvene in May) in menacing metaphors: 'What [happened] was only a rehearsal, a lesson to be remembered. It was only the betrothal: the wedding will be in May! All the Jews must be hanged or chased with rocks!'[78]

Dumbravă found that the local police, apparently acting under orders, had failed to intervene effectively to control the disturbances.[79] This is curious. The same National Liberal government which, lacking confidence in its ability to control potential violence and obtain a guilty verdict against Codreanu, had adjourned the trial in order to move it to a calmer setting where an indictment might be brought successfully, had then ordered the police to close their eyes to the pro-fascist sympathizers who rioted in frustration at the adjournment. The Liberals, it appears, were unwilling openly to use force to suppress the pro-Codreanu crowds lest this tarnish their own nationalist credentials. The consequent paralysis of the forces of public order therefore seems to indicate a public opinion victory for the radical-nationalist camp.

Turnu Severin, the town chosen to host the reconvened trial, had, like its whole region, a small Jewish population – 500 out of a population of 25,000. It had no experience of outright anti-Semitic agitation, although there were certainly some anti-Semites there – a few young merchants and commercial clerks, 'naturally a group of students', and some teachers – and, while the Liberal-affiliated weekly newspaper gave vent to occasional anti-Semitic attacks, the anti-Semitic movement had not taken root among the population at large.[80] The police prefect for the district of Mehedinţi and the local Liberal Party chief promised to collaborate in maintaining order before and during the trial, and local authorities 'guaranteed' the government the accused's condemnation.[81] Local and judicial authorities were proved wrong in their confident prognoses, however, for even at Turnu Severin radical nationalists were successful in mobilizing public opinion and creating an atmosphere sympathetic to Codreanu.

In his memoir of the Turnu Severin trial, on which the following account is based, Sabetay Sabetay, a former resident of the town, describes the change in its mood and the jury's consequent acquittal verdict.[82] The transformation in Turnu Severin's atmosphere owed much to the pilgrimage there of hundreds, later thousands, of Codreanu's supporters, especially students. The newcomers influenced local anti-Semitic merchants to put Codreanu's portrait in their windows, and, under various pretexts, organized daily meetings involving ever larger groups of the local population. The town was thus turned into a 'general headquarters of anti-Semitism'. Although local Jews did not ultimately suffer much violence, this was due to increased patrols and defensive measures. To the Jewish community this felt more and more like a state of siege. Jews restricted their outings to a minimum; Jewish shops kept their shutters lowered and closed earlier in the evenings; in synagogues prayers were whispered; and in synagogues and Jewish homes lights were kept dim. As the trial approached, tensions rose: 'Everything seemed to forecast a pogrom.' On the eve of the trial the whole town was wearing national colours, people sported swastikas and walls were covered with inflammatory manifestos. Postcards of Codreanu in national folk costume had been sent by the thousand to the provinces, and the route he was expected to travel to the courtroom was strewn with flowers.[83]

The trial, held in the theatre in the centre of town, lasted a week. The local weekly, *Tribuna*, appeared daily and sometimes twice daily to cover the event. On the day when sentencing was due, Jewish merchants agreed to keep their shops closed to avoid devastation. The Romanian Bar Association had resolved that no member should agree to represent Manciu's widow. According to Sabetay 'This decision made quite an impression not only in Turnu Severin, but in the whole country. It was undoubtedly an advertisement, and an indication for the jury members.'[84]

Codreanu commanded considerable support nation-wide by the time of the trial, including campaigns in some of the wide-circulation newspapers like the Bucharest daily *Universul*. Although the prosecution did manage to obtain its own lawyer, the prejudicial atmosphere amid which the trial proceeded cannot be doubted. The prosecutor's demeanour and statement to the jury are telling: 'With a tear of regret in his eye', Titu Constantinescu, arguing that no one had the right to take justice into his own hands, asked for a verdict of guilty. He nevertheless qualified his request by identifying extenuating circumstances: 'Anarchy had penetrated the university because of the large number of foreigners.' 'Like everyone', he added, 'I too say: Romania for the Romanians first of all.'[85] The acquittal, by a jury all of whose members wore swastikas on their lapels, came as a surprise to nobody.[86]

Marxist historians have generally argued that in Romania bourgeois politicians were the accomplices of fascist criminals and, conversely, that the nationalism and anti-Semitism of the fascists were instigated by the capitalist class, in collusion with the government, to divert the lower classes from developing class consciousness.[87] Ioan Scurtu, for example, writes that after the First World War, as social conflict sharpened, the dominant classes tried to 'find new methods and forms of action, intended to channel the dissatisfaction of the masses on a diversionary path. Such a role was fulfilled by the right-wing and extreme right-wing organizations which appeared after 1918.'[88] Such arguments are meant to explain the leniency of the police and the judicial system towards fascist crimes.[89] While at first glance the Manciu assassination trial seems to be a case in point, on closer scrutiny the 'bourgeois complicity' argument at best describes only the effect of the Liberals' insufficient intransigence in this instance, and not the mechanics or possible motivations of Liberal strategy.

Clearly, if the government had actually wanted to acquit Codreanu it would not have bothered to move the trial. In fact the Liberals were unhappy at having lost control of the trial proceedings in Focşani. Their principal motive may have been fear of the threat to social peace posed by rioting and violence, but their desire to try to convict Codreanu appears to have been genuine. They therefore switched the trial from Focşani, where an acquittal was imminent, to Turnu Severin where they hoped – in vain – for a neutral atmosphere and a conviction. .

The leniency of the police – under the guidance of the higher authorities – in Focşani during the March riots, as well as the subsequent position of the prosecution, were thus the outcome not of voluntary Liberal complicity but of intense pressure from public opinion in favour of radical nationalism. Given the widespread – and largely favourable – recognition of Codreanu as a spokesman for Romanian nationalism, the Liberals could not take a totally intransigent stance against him without risking serious political damage. In other words, rather than the Liberals manipulating the radicals, the Liberals were the manipulated ones. This type of mechanism explains the nationalist political capital that Codreanu and the organizations to which he belonged – the League of National Christian Defence and later the Legion of the Archangel Michael – were able to employ in their recruitment efforts and in gaining broader support within Romanian society for crimes committed 'in the name of the nation'.[90]

The dynamics of the conservatism–fascism relationship in Romania were largely a function of the political agenda established by the Great Union of 1918. While fulfilling the historic national goals of Romanian patriots, the union brought with it the demographic dilution of the Romanian nation, the ruralization of the Romanians *vis-à-vis* newly incorporated minority nationalities, and thus a painful consciousness of the thinness of Romanian elites. Conservative nation- and state-building strategies were aimed at rectifying the balance in the Romanians' favour and thereby securing the integrity of the expanded state. The student spokesmen of the 'generation of 1922', who were to become the first leaders of Romanian fascism, articulated – initially in the context of university life – a radicalized version of the conservatives' own political goals.

235

In the winter of 1923–4 several government ministries exchanged letters about a rumour that teachers and priests, especially in Transylvania, were propagating fascism.[91] The Metropolitan and primate of the Orthodox Church in Bucharest, responding to an enquiry from the Ministry of Education, expressed the Church's puzzlement about fascism:

> Some speak well of it, others show it to be an anarchic organization. The former say that fascism works for the salvation of the Romanian organism against corrupt and corrupting foreignism; thus [according to them] . . . [fascism] would defend the interests of our people. The others say that . . . [fascism] is an organ of destruction of order and legality in our state, and that it uses revolutionary means; thus [according to them it would be] an organization harmful to our people.[92]

This document represents one of the most naïve contemporary perspectives on the history of fascism in Romania, but, perhaps by virtue of this very naïveté, it expresses essential features of the fascist paradox in the Romanian context. The young generation and the fascist ideology which it espoused possessed a fundamental legitimacy in interwar Romania, precisely because their radical nationalism was so well suited to the nation-building project which was the declared goal of most mainstream politicians and of naïve conservatives such as the Orthodox prelate. Establishment nationalism and radical fascism had a great deal in common. Although the one was basically conservative and stood for political stability and autarkic modernization, while the other was visionary, violent, revolutionary and lacking in economic strategy, the two shared a desire to limit the nation to 'true' Romanians, the idea of using the state for the Romanian nation (not for a society of equal citizens), and a commitment to creating an ethnic Romanian elite large enough to administer the expanded state. In addition they shared an idiom: one which for establishment nationalists was sometimes demagogic – a short-cut in election campaigns – but for the fascists always represented a sincerely-held credo. For all these reasons the establishment could ill afford to suppress the fascists, at least openly.

The terms of this paradox had been set by the tasks incumbent upon the Romanian state and its patriotic elites after the doubling of its territories in 1918. This revolutionary expansion required energetic nation-building policies which could come directly from the state itself but also from autonomous national-revolutionary groups. Although the young generation's radical-nationalist leadership, which was also the vanguard of Romanian fascism, was often critical – and violently so – of the country's political establishment for its compromises, corruption and laxness, not only did it view itself as the vanguard of the nation but it also won recognition as such from its more conservative elders whose primary goal was the full political integration of Greater Romania. It was this young leadership, with its radical ideology, that in the 1930s mobilized broad strata of the population, suffering the effects of the depression, in a politically significant fascist movement.

NOTES

Research for this chapter was supported in part by a grant from the International Research and Exchanges Board with funds provided by the United States Information Agency and by the Memorial Foundation for Jewish Culture. I wish to thank Geoff Eley for his comments on an earlier draft.

1   E. Weber, 'Romania', in H. Rogger and E. Weber (eds), *The European Right* (London, 1965), pp. 501–74; M. Fătu and I. Spălățelu, *Garda de Fier: Organizație teroristă de tip fascist* (Bucharest, 1971); F. L. Carsten, *The Rise of Fascism* (London, 1971), pp. 181–93; Z. Barbu, 'Rumania', in S. J. Woolf (ed.), *Fascism in Europe* (London and New York, 1981), pp. 151–70.
2   E. Weber, 'The men of the Archangel', *Journal of Contemporary History*, vol. I, no. 1 (1966), p. 104.
3   H. L. Roberts, *Rumania: Political Problems of an Agrarian State* (New Haven, Conn., 1951), p. 91; M. Mușat and I. Ardeleanu, *Political Life in Romania 1918–1921* (Bucharest, 1982), pp. 47–8, 62, 66–7; P. Shapiro, 'Romania's past as challenge for the future: a developmental approach to interwar politics', in D. N. Nelson (ed.), *Romania in the 1980s* (Boulder, Colo., 1981), p. 21.
4   I. Scurtu, *Viața politică din România 1918–1944* (Bucharest, 1982), p. 62.
5   Mușat and Ardeleanu, *Political Life in Romania*, p. 188; Scurtu, Viața politică pp. 50–3.
6   See Shapiro, 'Romania's past', p. 20.
7   Ș. Zeletin, *Burghezia română, origina și rolul ei istoric* (Bucharest, 1925), p. 165.
8   Institutul Central de Statistică (ICS), *Anuarul Statistic al României 1937 și 1938* (Bucharest, 1939), pp. 41–5.
9   ibid., p. 44; J. Rothschild, *East Central Europe between the Two World Wars* (Seattle, Wash., and London, 1977), p. 285.
10 ibid., p. 284.
11 ICS, *Anuarul Statistic 1937/8*, pp. 58–61.
12 See D. Sandru, *Populația rurală a României între cele două războaie mondiale* (Jassy, 1980), pp. 51–2; ICS, *Anuarul Statistic 1937/8*, pp. 58–61.
13 On the use of the term 'foreign' to refer to national minorities in the Balkans and Eastern Europe, see B. Jelavich, *History of the Balkans: Twentieth Century*, Vol. 2 (Cambridge, 1983), pp. 135–6.
14 A. Janos, 'Modernization and decay in historical perspective: the case of Romania', in K. Jowitt (ed.), *Social Change in Romania, 1860–1940: A Debate on Development in a European Nation* (Berkeley, Calif., 1978), p. 91; see also Jelavich, *Balkans*, p. 26.
15 On the Jewish emancipation see C. Iancu, *Les Juifs en Roumanie (1866–1919): de l'exclusion a l'émancipation* (Aix-en-Provence, 1978), pp. 270–4.
16 On the 'new generation' see Z. Ornea, *Traditionalism și modernitate în deceniul al treilea* (Bucharest, 1980), pp. 454–64; G. Călinescu, 'Noua generație. Momentul 1933', in *Istoria literaturii române de la origini pînă la prezent* (second edn, Bucharest, 1982), pp. 947–91; and I. Livezeanu, 'Excerpts from a troubled book: an episode in Romanian literature', *Cross Currents: A Yearbook of Central European Culture*, 3 (1984), p. 298.
17 See General Winogradsky, *La Guerre sur le front oriental* (Paris, 1926), p. 316, and N. Iorga, *Histoire des Roumains et de la romanité orientale*, Vol. X: *Les Réalisateurs de l'unité nationale* (Bucharest, 1945), p. 543.
18 Iorga, *Histoire des Roumains*, p. 543; see also K. Verdery, *Transylvanian Villagers:*

Three Centuries of Political, Economic, and Ethnic Change (Los Angeles, Calif., and London, 1983), p. 278.

19 Ministère de la Guerre, Direction de l'Armée de Terre, Vincennes (V) 7N 1459/3; V 7N 1458/1,2; Ministère des Affaires Étrangères, Archives diplomatiques, Quai d'Orsay (QD), 55/3–4RV, 5R; QD, Z10 27/165, 1 February 1920; QD, 29/47 RV48, 29 August 1924. Some French military reports, however, disclaim the existence of any true Bolshevik danger in Romania. For instance General Berthelot, in a telegram of 23 February 1919 (QD, Z6 27/67), flatly denied that uprisings or strikes were a problem in Romania.

20 QD, Z22 27/250R, 15 December 1920.

21 Alliance Israélite Universelle (AIU) Roumanie VIII/C 53.

22 Muşat and Ardeleanu, *Political Life in Romania*, pp. 25–6.

23 ibid., pp. 248–9; Iorga, *Histoire des Roumains*, p. 543.

24 See Arhivele Statului, Bucureşti, Fond Casa Şcoalelor (CŞ)/1920/7/106; CŞ/1920/7/124; and CŞ/1920/6/274–276.

25 Central Archives for the History of the Jewish People (CA)/RM 133/2, 22 October 1921; *Paix et Droit*, vol. I, no. 8, (October 1921); AIU Roumanie VIII/C56. The Romanian government at one point believed that there were 100,000 refugees, an inflated figure which seems to be proof of the alarm with which the government regarded the refugees.

26 Arhivele Statului Bucureşti, Fond Ministerul Instrucţiunii şi Cultelor (MIC)/1921/273/11–12, 30 May 1921.

27 AIU Roumanie VIII/B77, 10 November 1921.

28 See also Carsten, *Rise of Fascism*, pp. 182–3.

29 C. Z. Codreanu, *La Garde de Fer* (Grenoble, 1972), pp. 9, 11.

30 H. Sima, *Histoire du mouvement légionnaire* (Rio de Janeiro, 1972), p. 18.

31 Codreanu, *Garde de Fer*, p. 11.

32 MIC/1918/193/11, 22 August 1918; and MIC/1918/193/15.

33 MIC/1918/188/2.

34 Calculated from O. Ghibu, *Basarabia în statistica Universităţii din Iaşi* (Bucharest: Extras din *Arhiva pentru Ştiinţa şi Reforma Socialǎ*, Vol. X, nos. 1–4, 1932), p. 22.

35 Arhiva Universitǎţii 'Alexandru Ioan Cuza', 2/1922/539–540, cited in M. C. Stǎnescu, *Depun mǎrturie în faţa istoriei: Timotei Marin militant şi publicist comunist (1897–1937)* (Jassy, 1977), p. 14.

36 Stǎnescu, *Depun mǎrturie*, p. 15.

37 Codreanu, *Garde de Fer*, pp. 14–19; Fǎtu and Spǎlǎţelu, *Garda de Fier*, p. 35; Sima, *Mouvement légionnaire*, pp. 19–20.

38 Sima, *Mouvement légionnaire*, p. 21; Codreanu, *Garde de Fer*, p. 38.

39 Codreanu, *Garde de Fer*, p. 12.

40 Codreanu, *Garde de Fer*, pp. 26–39; MIC/1921/176/6–9; S. Neagoe, *Triumful raţiunii împotriva violenţei (Viaţa universitarǎ ieşeanǎ interbelicǎ)* (Jassy, 1977), pp. 93–101.

41 MIC/1921/176/7.

42 Neagoe, *Triumful raţiunii*, pp. 100–1; MIC/1921/176/8,9.

43 MIC/1921/176/1, 3–5, 10–14; Sima, *Mouvement légionnaire*, p. 21.

44 Neagoe, *Triumful raţiunii*, p. 110.

45 Codreanu, *Garde de Fer*, p. 42.

46 Sima, *Mouvement légionnaire*, p. 24; Codreanu, *Garde de Fer*, pp. 42–4.

47 Neagoe, *Triumful raţiunii*, p. 113. See also Codreanu, *Garde de Fer*, p. 51, where the date given is actually 20 May.

48 Sima, *Mouvement légionnaire*, p. 21.

49 Sima, *Mouvement légionnaire*, pp. 21–3; and 'Situaţia la Cernǎuţi' ('The situation in Cernǎuţi'), *Cuvântul Studenţesc*, I/16 (30 May 1923). The nationalist elements in Cernǎuţi said that they wanted '*numerus proportionalis*' not only in the university but in all branches of social activity.

50 MIC/1922/479/57. See also Neagoe, *Triumful raţiunii*, p. 171, and Z. de Szasz, *The Minorities in Roumanian Transylvania* (London, 1927), p. 336.

51 Neagoe, *Triumful raţiunii*, p. 178.

52 Sima, *Mouvement légionnaire*, p. 22; Codreanu, *Garde de Fer*, pp. 63–4; I. Moţa, *Cranii de Lemn Articole* (Munich, 1970) pp. 230–1.

53 Szasz, *Minorities*, p. 290.
54 Moţa, *Cranii de Lemn*, pp. 228–9.
55 Codreanu, *Garde de Fer*, p. 64.
56 Fl. Dragne and C. Petculescu, *Frontul Studenţesc Democrat: Pagini dim lupta antifascistă a studenţimii române* (Bucharest, 1977), p. 16. The National Peasant newspaper *România* dubbed the annual celebration of 10 December the 'holiday of broken windows' because of the damage regularly perpetrated in Jewish neighbourhoods. *Paix et Droit*, vol. 6, no. 10, (December 1926).
57 Weber, 'The men of the Archangel', pp. 115–16; Codreanu, *Garde de Fer*, pp. 116–17.
58 L. Pătrăşcanu, *Sub trei dictaturi* (Bucharest, 1944), pp. 203–6.
59 *Cuvântul Nostru*, I/4, 25 March 1923.
60 The Peasant Party, for example, protested the suppression of student newspapers, gatherings and demonstrations in the spring of 1923. *Cuvântul Nostru*, I/1 (18 February 1923).
61 *Cuvântul Nostru*, I/4 (25 March 1923).
62 ibid.
63 ibid. *'Turburelul'* is the idiomatic expression for must or new wine which is still in fermentation, thick and murky with unsettled sediment.
64 P. Shapiro, 'Prelude to dictatorship in Romania: the National Christian Party in power, December 1937–February 1938', *Canadian-American Slavic Studies*, vol. 8 (Spring 1974), p. 49.
65 O. Goga, *Mustul care fierbe* (Bucharest, 1927).
66 ibid., p. 7.
67 'Ideia Naţională: Conferinţă în faţa studenţilor universitari din Cluj' ('The National Idea: Lecture [held] before the students of Cluj University'), in ibid., pp. 38–9.
68 ibid., pp. 37–8.
69 ibid., pp. 29–30.
70 The account that follows is from Sima, *Mouvement légionnaire*, pp. 28–32.
71 ibid., pp. 31–2.
72 Fătu and Spălăţelu, *Garda de Fier*, p. 52; Sima, *Mouvement légionnaire*, pp. 35–7.
73 *Paix et Droit*, vol. 5, no. 4, (April 1925).
74 D. Dumbravă, *Fără ură! Pregătirea şi dezlănţuirea evenimentelor din Focşani în zilele de 17 şi 18 martie 1925. Cercetări. Documente. Mărturisiri.* Ancheta întreprinsă după evenimente ca trimes special al ziarelor, *Dimineaţa* şi *Adevărul*, p. 6.
75 ibid., p. 7.
76 ibid., p. 6. Choirmasters, for example, had taught their pupils the anti-Semitic 'Students' Hymn'.
77 Dumbravă, *Fără ură!*, p. 8.
78 ibid., p. 22.
79 ibid., p. 6. See also *Paix et Droit*, vol. 5, no. 4, (April 1925).
80 S. S. Sabetay, 'Procesul Codreanu la Turnu Severin' ('The Codreanu Trial in Turnu Severin'), *Toladot*, 4/9 (March 1975), pp. 17–18.
81 ibid., p. 17; Sima, *Mouvement légionnaire*, p. 38.
82 Sabetay, 'Procesul Codreanu', *passim*.
83 *Paix et Droit*, vol. 5, no. 6, (June 1925).
84 Sabetay, 'Procesul Codreanu', p. 19.
85 *Paix et Droit*, vol. 5, no. 6, (June 1925); see also Fătu and Spălăţelu, *Garda de Fier*, pp. 52–3.
86 ibid.; Sabetay, 'Procesul Codreanu', p. 20.
87 See Patrăşcanu, *Sub trei dictaturi*; Fătu and Spălăţelu, *Garda de Fier*; and Scurtu, *Viaţa politică*: all *passim*.
88 Scurtu, *Viaţa politică*, p. 68.
89 See, for example, Fătu and Spălăţelu, *Garda de Fier*, pp. 52–3.
90 Fascist assassins were repeatedly acquitted in interwar Romania: see *Paix et Droit*, vol. 6, no. 9 (November 1926), and Fătu and Spălăţelu, *Garda de Fier*, pp. 66–8, 98, 104–5.
91 MIC/1924/211/51–54.
92 MIC/1924/211/53. The Romanian word *'neam'*, here translated as 'our people', has strong connotations of family and racial kinship.

13

Conservatives and fascists in the Nordic countries: Norway, Sweden, Denmark and Finland, 1918–45

Stein U. Larsen

During the Second World War, the final phase of their existence, the four main Nordic variants of fascism found themselves in very different situations. Norwegian Nazism, in the form of Nasjonal Samling (National Unity) was distinguished by its deliberate co-operation with the Germans, who placed at the head of a Nazi government its leader, the notorious and eponymous Vidkun Quisling. The Danish 'führer', Fritz Claussen, and his Danmarks Nationalsocialistiske Arbeider Parti (National Socialist Workers Party of Denmark) achieved lesser prominence; demanding of the occupying Germans the same status as their Norwegian counterparts, they were unceremoniously rebuffed. In neutral Sweden there existed a number of small far-right groups, the largest being Sven Olof Lindholm's Svensk-Socialistisk Samling (Swedish-Socialist Unity); although their prewar impact had been meagre, during the war some of their leading personalities were occasionally questioned by the police when attempting to serve German interests and agitating in favour of Sweden's entry into the war on Germany's side. Finland's experience was shaped by the Soviet Union's surprise attack in November 1939. In the ensuing atmosphere of national unity, even the fascist Isanmaalinen Kansanliike (People's Patriotic Movement) (ILK) was tolerated: indeed, during the so-called 'war of continuation', when Finland was allied with Germany, its leader, Dr Vilho Annala, was actually a minister in the first coalition government.

Even before the war, the fascist parties' positions in relation to their respective political opponents and rivals had varied widely. The purpose of this chapter will be to examine the differing relationships between fascism and the Conservative political parties in the four Nordic countries, together with any fascist leanings displayed by other groups broadly definable as conservative. In the final section an attempt will be made to bring together this necessarily general picture and present a brief theoretical explanation of Nordic fascism's failure to 'capture' conservatism.

WHAT WAS NORDIC FASCISM?

Nowadays, the concept of 'fascism' is generally used to refer to parties and movements resembling, as far as their principal components are concerned, the Italian and German paradigms. Analytically speaking, the purpose here is to mount empirical hypotheses testable in relation to movements which can be held to have features in common. In the constitutional and political environment of the Nordic countries, fascism, however much its militants resented the fact, took the form of political parties obliged to fight electoral campaigns. In examining Nordic fascism, we shall accordingly begin by focusing upon fascist and national socialist political parties.

Finland

Finland's most important fascist party, the Isanmaalinen Kansanliike (ILK), was launched on 10 April 1932 and survived until 19 September 1944 when it was dissolved as the direct result of armistice negotiations between Finland, the Soviet Union and Great Britain. The party was created as a direct continuation of Lapua, a *fascisant* movement founded on 1 December 1929 and outlawed in 1932 by President Swinhufvud. As such, the IKL was clearly intended to provide a legal basis for pursuing Lapua policies and maintaining organizations which supported past Lapua actions. The essentials of the party's programme can be reduced to the following six points: (1) vehement anti-communism; (2) emphasis on corporatism as a substitute for a parliamentary republic; (3) intense nationalism and hostility to the Soviet Union; (4) 'Finnification' in the language question, implying non-toleration of Swedish as a minority language; (5) application of the 'leadership principle' in organization; and (6) emphasis on Protestant, conservative religiosity. In many important respects, therefore, the IKL conformed to a fascist stereotype: indeed, it was quite frank concerning its resemblance to foreign models.

At first the IKL found conservative allies. In the 1933 parliamentary election it co-operated with the conservative Kansallinen Kokoomus (National Coalition Party), their joint list obtaining a total of thirty-two representatives (fourteen IKL and eighteen Conservatives). In 1936, however, the Conservatives broke the electoral alliance; the IKL fought separately and again obtained fourteen representatives, with 97,891 votes (8.2 per cent). Although in 1938 the Minister of the Interior, Urho Kekkonen, issued a ban on the IKL on grounds of its revolutionary character, the courts declared the ban unconstitutional, thereby enabling the party to pursue its political goals openly until the Soviet invasion. In the 1939 election, nevertheless, the number of IKL representatives shrank from fourteen to four, and its votes to a mere 6.6 per cent, clear evidence that

241

Finnish fascism was on the wane. As the party became more and more politically isolated, it began to exhibit increasing concern for ideological purity and unwillingness to compromise: classic characteristics of a party in decline.

Norway

Nasjonal Samling was born on 17 May 1933. Although the decision to found a fascist party was taken following Quisling's departure from the post of Minister of Defence in the minority Agrarian cabinet, the idea had been circulating for some time. In the 1933 parliamentary elections Nasjonal Samling nevertheless performed poorly, attracting only 27,850 votes (2.2 per cent) and failing to elect a single representative to the Storting. This disappointment proved destructive to the party's future development; it fared no better in local elections, whilst in the last prewar parliamentary election, that of 1936, it obtained still fewer votes (26,577) than in 1933 and again failed to elect a representative. A major split in the party in 1936 also weakened its internal structure. Before the German invasion on 9 April 1940, Norwegian fascism was therefore of only minor importance. During the war Nasjonal Samling's membership grew to more than twice the level of its electoral support in the 1930s, i.e. more than 50,000. Considering the great enthusiasm with which the party was originally welcomed in 1933 and its wartime membership, its meagre electoral support is at first sight puzzling.

The programme of Nasjonal Samling, published in detail in 1934, contains many of the elements most typical of fascist/national socialist ideology: (1) a corporatist conception of society; (2) strong emphasis upon nationalism and Christianity; (3) paternalistic attitudes towards education and family life; and (4) an economic policy based upon the principle of autarky, and laying particular stress on the primary sectors of the economy.

Denmark

Of the four Nordic countries, Denmark presents perhaps the most bewildering picture: one of numerous small groups or factions, all aspiring towards becoming a major fascist party. Numerous such groups appeared and disappeared, both before and after the founding of the Danmarks Nationalsocialistiske Arbeider Parti (DNSAP) on 19 November 1930, illustrating the ideological disagreements present on the Danish extreme right. These disagreements surfaced over many aspects of fascist/national socialist ideology, but more particularly demonstrated the peculiar difficulty facing fascism in Denmark: the proximity of Germany and the problems associated with the presence of a German minority in Denmark and vice versa.

Before the war DNSAP membership never exceeded the paltry figure of 5,000, but under the German occupation the influx of new members raised the total membership for the whole period to 39,000. The DNSAP's electoral record resembled that of Norway's Nasjonal Samling. In 1932 it polled 1 per cent (mainly in South Jutland), in 1935 0.99 per cent and in 1939 1.8 per cent; in 1943, when Denmark, as the only occupied country which held elections during the war, voted, the DNSAP obtained 2.1 per cent (43,309 votes). In both 1939 and 1943 the DNSAP elected three representatives to Parliament, but like their Finnish counterparts they found themselves completely isolated politically, and failed to attract any support for their policies. DNSAP motions were either ignored or reformulated by the other parties in such a way as to ensure that Parliament could never be said to be supporting Nazi proposals.

Sweden

Sweden's long history of small-scale fascist movements dates from the foundation in 1924 of the Svenska Nationalsocialistika Frihetsførbundet (Swedish National Socialist Freedom League). Despite a succession of splits and newly formed movements, an essential continuity of ideals and personnel persisted, so that in 1938, when the Nationalsocialistiska Arbetarpartiet became Svensk Socialistisk Samling, the party could claim to represent Swedish fascism's mainstream tradition. Svensk Socialistisk Samling was finally dissolved in 1945.

The various Swedish fascist groups were deeply divided on such issues as economic policy, where every attitude from left to right was visible; tolerance of religous freedom as against a policy of *Gleichschaltung*; and the desired degree of distinctiveness from foreign models. The dominant approach before 1939 appears to have embraced an independent, anti-capitalist fascism based on a strong, anti-parliamentary, corporate state, together with a belief that the Swedish people should be protected from foreign immigration, and that the proud heritage of the Gustav Vasa era in the sixteenth century should serve as the inspiration for a new period of greatness.

Like its Norwegian and Danish counterparts, Swedish fascism obtained little electoral support. In the 1932 parliamentary election the Nysvenska Nationalsocialistiska Førbundet (New-Swedish National Socialist League) obtained 15,170 votes in the few constituencies it contested: a mere 0.6 per cent of the total vote. In the 1936 election, two competing groups, the Nationalsocialistiska Arbetarpartiet and the Sveriges Nationalsocialistiska Partiet, fractions of the previously united movement of Birger Furugård and Sven O. Lindholm, won 20,408 votes (0.7 per cent) between them.

While not contesting the 1940 election, at a time when Denmark and Norway were under German occupation, Svensk Socialistisk Samling did participate in that of 1944 but obtained only 4,204 votes (0.1 per cent). Even by the standards of the other Nordic movements, therefore, Swedish fascism was electorally weak. Nevertheless, in view of the apparent strength of related groups and factions in interwar Sweden, it would be wrong to state that the impact of fascism was as weak as the simple number of votes would seem to suggest.

THE DEVELOPMENT OF
NORDIC FASCISM

The relative strength of Finnish fascism is directly relatable to the legacy of the 1918 civil war. This 'incomplete' victory inspired an intense antagonism towards Marxism and communism which, in the years before the formation of the IKL, was incorporated in the Lapua movement and, in 1930, threatened the Republic itself. The most important countervailing force appears to have been the Finns' inherited attachment to constitutionalism and a widespread fear of a rightist coup.

Anti-communism, feeding upon the sustained radicalism of the country's large Socialist party, the Norske Arbeiderparti (Norwegian Workers Party), also served as the principal stimulus for Norwegian fascism. However the Norske Arbeiderparti's shift to a social-democratic position in 1933, combined with a rapid decline in the strength of communism and an easing in the effects of the depression, left fascism with little 'political space' in which to flourish. Only with German help was it able to achieve strength and power.

Perhaps the most adequate explanation for the weakness of fascism in Denmark resides in the 'theory of circumpolarity'. As in Switzerland, Belgium, the Netherlands, Czechoslovakia, and perhaps Poland and even France, nationalism in Denmark was inspired by feelings directed against a larger neighbour. Patriotic nationalism, which in essentials differs little from the nationalist component within fascism, always emphasizes the concept of 'greatness' in terms of people and territory. All the small nations just mentioned, and even the two larger ones, if thinking in expansionist terms would be bound to do so at the expense of Germany; alternatively, they would be obliged to acknowledge that the expansion of the Third Reich inevitably involved their own interests. A large fascist movement within their own borders would therefore constitute a risky venture. At the same time the patriotic nationalism of such small fascist parties as the DNSAP suffered from the inherent logical inconsistency of imitating a more powerful examplar whom they simultaneously feared.

Swedish fascism's greatest difficulty involved the unifying of numerous small forces into a single and more powerful political movement. The conflict between nationalism and a susceptibility to German inspiration; the problems of anti-capitalism and the incorporation of farmers and merchants; the difficulty of supporting a strong Church whilst tolerating free-church groups – not to mention such religious minorities as Jews: these and other obstacles made the unification of Swedish fascism impossible. And unity, of course, is precisely the most important prerequisite of a successful fascist organization and the development of the *führerprinzip*. Beyond this, the question of why Sweden did not experience a more successful fascist movement is hard to answer. Whilst it may simply be necessary to conclude that Sweden lacked the conditions that elsewhere promoted fascism, that is not to say very much.

THE CONSERVATIVE PARTIES
BETWEEN THE WARS

An important obstacle to fascist success in the Nordic countries was the ability of Conservative parties to counter the challenge of fascism and contribute to its political isolation. If, as tends to be argued, it is among those who 'normally' support Conservative parties that the greatest susceptibility to a fascist appeal lies, then their immunity from fascism in the 1930s is of particular interest for our analysis.

The challenge of electoral defeat

When the general trend of Conservative electoral performance is studied (see fig. 13.1) the overall impression, notwithstanding the recovery and greater stability of Danish conservatism, is one of gradual and even drastic decline throughout the Nordic region.

The sudden drop in the Conservative vote, occurring either shortly before or in the wake of the depression which began in late 1929, presented a distinct opportunity to new parties capable of offering, and attracting support for, new solutions to the acute economic problems of the time and, in their own way, of promising to revitalize traditional conservative values and ideology. Since the Conservatives either lacked radical solutions to the crisis or else favoured broadly similar measures to those advocated by the fascists – i.e. some mild form of corporativism and autarky – they had the choice of two tactics: to combine with the fascists or to isolate them.

In Finland and Norway elections between the wars were conducted on the basis of the 'list' system of proportional representation. Electoral alliances involving two or more parties could be announced on the ballot paper or the voting list; nevertheless the votes for each party were also

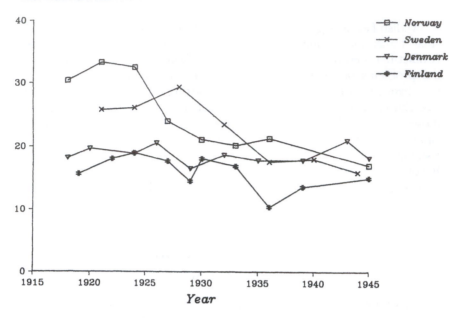

Figure 13.1   Percent Votes for Conservatives, 1918–45

counted separately, making it possible to establish which candidates and which parties actually won a given seat. The system offered an inducement to form electoral alliances which was absent in Sweden and Denmark, whose electoral arrangements lacked provision for 'list co-operation'.

Given the prevailing political climate in Finland, the conservative Kansallinen Kokoomus (National Coalition Party) opted to fight the 1933 election in alliance with the IKL. This was not, however, a mere electoral coalition, for the National Coalition Party came close to being overtaken by the IKL leaders, much as Hitler 'captured' the bourgeois nationalists in Germany. The IKL tactic of presenting itself as 'above parties' enabled it to influence the central committee of the National Coalition Party and obtain the approval of an overwhelming majority of its members for the IKL's general programme. Such a 'surrender' of an independent party to a coalition partner which was also a new and radical opponent is rare in western democracies. The danger in this situation was clearly recognized, however, by J. K. Paasikivi, the Conservative leader during the early years of the Republic, who at this point returned to national politics. Once elected National Coalition Party chairman, Paasikivi succeeded in severing the party's connection with the IKL by declaring the latter's ideology a foreign import incompatible with the republican constitution. As a result no electoral alliance was formed in either the 1936 or the 1939 election.

In Norway, Nasjonal Samling also sought a Conservative electoral ally, in this case the Høire (Right) party. The Høire's central committee rejected the offer and ordered local constituency organizations to refuse all co-operation with the fascists. However in Bergen, Norway's second city, the central committee's will was flouted and an electoral alliance created; in the third largest city, Trondheim, a majority in favour of an alliance was close to achievement. The Høire's chairman, C. J. Hambro, fought determinedly against Nasjonal Samling, clearly perceiving the dangers inherent in any involvement with Quisling's unpredictable machinations.

Fascism and Conservative youth

Depression, combined with major electoral losses, presented the Nordic Conservative parties with an acute problem. The gradual recovery, or at least the stabilization, of the Conservative vote in Denmark, Sweden and Norway made any renewal of efforts at electoral co-operation with the fascists unlikely. None the less, following weak Conservative electoral performances in Denmark (1928), Norway (1928 and 1933), Finland (1929) and Sweden (1933 and 1936) there existed within traditional Conservative circles tensions conducive to experiments with fascist alternatives. This was particularly the case within the youth sections of the Nordic Conservative parties, which proved to be very fertile soil for fascism. Generally mistrustful of their 'mother' parties and believing them insufficiently adaptable to new thinking and dynamic initiatives, the Swedish, Danish and Norwegian Conservative youth organizations showed themselves to be ready to opt for many of the novel ideas contained within the fascist credo. The exception was the youth wing of the Finnish Coalition Party, which largely resisted the temptation to embrace fascism.

In Sweden the Sveriges Nationella Ungdomsførbund (National Youth League of Sweden) (SNU) was founded in 1915; although not deliberately intended as the youth organization of the mother party, the Almänna Valmansførbundet (General Election League), it nevertheless came to be generally accepted as such. A salient characteristic of the conservative wing within the early Swedish parliamentary system was its members' reluctance to form themselves into a national party, in part due to the bicameral nature of Sweden's parliamentary system in which the indirectly appointed upper chamber enjoyed the power to veto bills and budgets coming from the lower house. This enabled the Conservative majority, made up of a varied blend of interests, to govern and share power with the king's Cabinet without the need to form a national party organization for fighting elections. It was not until 1935 that the two Conservative parties, one for each chamber, were merged into a single national organization.

This decentralized structure made it difficult for the Conservative leadership to control developments within the various party branches. In 1934 a crucial test of party unity was provoked by the strength of pro-Nazi attitudes among the new SNU leadership, elected after the fall of the 1928–30 Conservative government. The latter was in office when the depression struck Sweden, and as a minority government had no chance of success with a genuine Conservative platform. The SNU, regarding it therefore as a failure, began to advocate corporativism, a planned economy, a new nationalism and a distrust of democracy extending to Sweden's own parliamentary system. In 1933 the Conservatives, concerned at the SNU threat, attempted to form a 'Conservative Front', involving a 'campaign of vitalization', conservative nationalism and 'non-fascism'; the idea was to absorb the conservative elements in the SNU, isolate the remainder, and thereby prevent the organization from pursuing its independent course. The campaign failed, however, and a break became increasingly likely. SNU members began to wear grey shirts (shortly afterwards forbidden by Parliament) and negotiations with the Conservatives broke down. When, early in 1934, the party at last organized its own youth section, the SNU proclaimed itself a separate party and began to compete electorally with the Conservatives.

From 1934 Sweden thus possessed another semi-fascist party besides the aforementioned Swedish Socialist Unity party and its splinter groups. The SNU attracted little support, however, receiving in 1936 only 26,750 votes nationally; moreover, even if its programme and organizational style conformed to the model of a fascist organization, it did not co-operate with Swedish Socialist Unity. The latter, indeed, regarded the SNU (renamed the Youth League and National League of Sweden in 1936) with suspicion, dismissing its members as 'covert Jews' who would 'lead the fresh new spirit into reactionary sidelines'. Nevertheless, the SNU was driven towards an increasingly pro-Nazi ideological position which it was never to abandon. For its part, the new Conservative Youth organization appears to have remained within the party's guidelines and not to have been tempted by the ultra-nationalist path pre-empted by the SNU.

The novel and radical ideas of fascism exercised a similarly strong influence upon Konservativ Ungdom (the Danish Conservative Youth Organization) (KU), which from the early 1930s succumbed to new impulses which opponents saw as emanating directly from the German NSDAP. The Conservative Youth began to don uniforms, renamed their most active units 'Stormtroopers', adopted the raised-arm salute, and provided their members with paramilitary training during intensive summer-camps which often ended in mass parades. Fascism also influenced their ideas and programme, which embraced corporativism, anti-parliamentarism, a planned, state-regulated economy, fervent nationalism and emphasis on higher military budgets, etc. The Conservative Party leadership was incensed at this tactical and ideological turn, and strenuously resisted the importation of ideas from Denmark's powerful German neighbour.

This situation took on particular delicacy when viewed as a new turn in the constitutional debate which had affected Denmark, and not least Danish Conservatives, since the beginning of the century. The Konservative Folkeparti (Conservative People's Party) had for years resisted any revision of the bicameral and partially indirect structure of the Danish Parliament; during the previous decade, however, under the chairmanship of Christmas Møller, the majority of the party had changed their position. Since conflict between the majority and the Conservative right, led by Victor Purschel, continued to rage throughout the 1930s, it was profoundly uncomfortable for the party when the Konservativ Ungdom began to advocate a 'revolutionary' constitutional change clearly influenced by fascist models: a corporativist, anti-democratic structure and a recourse to 'above party', plebiscitary solutions to crucial issues.

During these hectic years, under the chairmanship of Jack G. Westergaard (1932–6), Konservativ Ungdom achieved a membership of some 30,000 and a degree of popularity sufficient to restrain many Young Conservatives from joining the DNSAP or other extremist organizations. When Westergaard resigned, however, Møller was able to co-operate so closely with his successor as to achieve a decline in extremist tendencies within the KU and its return to Conservative orthodoxies. Møller's success, in this and in generally steering his party in a moderate, reformist direction, was much assisted by the fact that the two opposition forces facing him – Purschel's right-wing party faction and the KU – were prevented by their respective ultra-conservatism and radical rightism from combining to offer a real challenge to the party leadership. All in all, therefore, and especially in comparison with Sweden, the eventual outcome in Denmark of struggles between the Conservative leadership and the more radical youth was a successful mending of political fences.

In Norway the issue of fascist influence among Conservative youth reared its head in relation to both the Unge Høire (Young Conservatives) and the Konservative Studentforening (Conservative Student Association). As in Denmark and Sweden, the Young Conservatives demanded from their party a new and more radical strategy for solving the economic and political crisis of the day. In addition they proposed a tougher approach towards Marxism in general and the leftist Norwegian Workers Party in particular. The Young Conservatives and the Conservative students were impressed by events in Germany and viewed fascist ideas as blending 'genuine' conservatism with refreshing new alternatives. The authority of the state, they argued, must as a matter of the utmost necessity be strengthened and the economic liberalism which formed so prevalent a part in the Conservative platform be played down; heightened emphasis upon nationalism was vital in order to bind Norwegians together in a closer unity; patriotism and nationalism should constitute the Conservative alternative to Socialist agitation and stress upon class conflict.

Although Young Conservatives spoke and wrote harsh words concerning the mother party's inability to renew itself and face the future aggressively, the conflict never reached a true climax. At the Høire's 1934 National Convention the Young Conservatives were successful in persuading the party to establish two joint committees for the formulation of new programmes: one for the strengthening of the state in a more authoritarian, yet plebiscitary, direction; the other for replacing the Høire's liberal economic principles with a stress upon state planning and corporativism. Little in the way of practical policies emerged from these initiatives, however, and from 1935 tensions among the Young Conservatives arising out of fascist-inspired right-radicalism subsided. An important factor in this was the internal development of Nasjonal Samling. After the breakdown in 1934 of negotiations with the non-socialist parties on a joint electoral list, there began within Nasjonal Samling a process of voluntary political isolationism. When the party moved, however uncertainly, in favour of anti-Semitism, and then in 1936–7 became bitterly divided over the issue of applying the *führerprinzip*, the danger of fascist influence among Conservative youth dwindled to almost nothing.

The position of the youth organization of the Finnish National Coalition Party was very different from that of its counterparts in the rest of the Nordic region. After the foundation in 1922 of the patriotic Akateeminen Karjala-Seūra (Academic Karelia Society), which based its membership on students and the educated young, other Conservative youth organizations found themselves largely deprived of potential 'space' in which radical fascism could develop. The Academic Karelia Society effectively monopolized the seeds which in the other Nordic countries germinated within the youth organizations of conservatism.

Fascism and the threat of Conservative schism

Fascist leanings were apparent not only within the youth organizations of Nordic conservatism but also within the parties themselves and among Conservative voters impressed by news of Nazi successes in Germany. In fighting their internal battles the party leaders – Møller (Denmark), Paasikivi (Finland), Hambro (Norway) and Lindman (Sweden) – highlighted two main factors: the danger of socialist takeover and the threatening nature of fascist ideology. Repeatedly demanding unity in the ranks, they argued that if Conservative voters flirted with fascist alternatives the effect would be to weaken conservatism, divide the non-socialist vote, and probably increase socialist parliamentary representation, perhaps to the point at which socialist majorities and even socialist states might become likely. In any case, they warned opponents within their parties, fascist notions of 'leadership' were unacceptable; even if Conservatives did desire a stronger state and more 'responsible' leadership, this must not be implemented through a German- or Italian-inspired dictatorship which would involve the destruction of *all* parties, the Conservative parties included, and a total end to free political discourse. The two lines of argument thus merged into a prediction of the destruction of democracy and the imposition of dictatorship – either socialist or fascist.

On the whole the Conservative leaders were successful in their efforts to prevent losses on the far right of their parties. Only a few examples occurred of Conservative deputies leaving to form their own groups or join the fascist/national socialist parties, and it was equally rare for leading non-parliamentary Conservatives to embrace fascism. One important exception was the departure of Victor Purschel from the Danish Conservative People's Party in 1938 to form his own Nationelt Samvirke. His schism should nevertheless be seen as the outcome of a protracted personal conflict between the party's old and new leaders, rather than as directly reflecting the issue of fascism. Purschel failed to attract much support for his new party and never became a true supporter of the Danish fascists. He later co-operated with Dansk Samling (Danish Unity) and Arne Sørensen, and remained a bitter opponent of modern Danish conservatism.

In Finland, the borderline between conservatism and fascism was particularly unclear in the case of the fascist Lapua movement (1929–32). Although P. E. Swinhufvud, the Conservative President of the Republic elected in 1931, had received Lapua support, he was fully alive to the danger represented by the movement, co-operated in erecting barriers against it and, as already mentioned, in 1932 banned Lapua outright. Swinhufvud's own intransigent conservatism remained undiluted, as did his hostility towards the Social Democratic Party which he refused to allow into any coalition government. Only after his term was over was Finland's characteristically all-encompassing type of coalition politics able to develop.

A strong ultra-conservative wing also existed during the 1930s within the party of Finland's Swedish minority, the Swedish People's Party, with the Swedish Independence League providing the Swedish-speaking counterpart to the Academic Karelia Society. Perhaps owing to the Swedes' minority position, however, a schism on the part of Swedish ultra-conservatives was always unlikely. In general terms it may be suggested that between them the Academic Karelia Society, the Lapua movement and IKL embraced so many conservative and patriotically minded Finns that little space remained for other organizations.

251

Statements such as the last one make possible the following, tentative, theoretical generalization: it was the overall strength of fascism in a particular country which determined the degree of factionalism within Conservative parties and of semi-fascist tendencies within Conservative youth organizations. Where, as in Finland, there existed a strong fascist movement, this acted as a magnet to all ultra-conservatives and freed those Conservatives who remained from splintering tendencies. In the other three Nordic countries, where fascist strength was much less, experimentation and confrontation with fascist ideology abounded, ensuring that the Conservative leaders faced a difficult task in putting their houses in order.

CONSERVATIVES, SEMI-FASCISTS AND OTHERS

Besides outright fascist and national socialist parties, and the appearance of fascist/national socialist tendencies within Conservative parties and their youth movements, all four Nordic countries witnessed during the interwar period the emergence of numerous other groups of broadly rightist, if not strictly fascist, tendency.

A significant Danish example was the German-speaking Slesvig Party. Founded in 1919 and at first relatively moderate, during the Anschluss and Czech crises of 1938–9 the Slesvig Party became thoroughly Nazified and anti-Danish, and began to look towards a German Anschluss of North Slesvig. The party was effectively marginalized, however, by a unitary 'Danish Front' and crushed at the general election of 3 April 1939. During the 1920s and 1930s numerous other conservative and nationalist groups emerged in Denmark, some of which provide further examples of moderation shifting towards semi-fascism. Among these were Dansk Samling (Danish Unity), created by Arne Sørensen as a 'Third Alternative' to liberal-capitalism and socialism. Stressing 'social control over property, productivism, and respect for Christian morality', Dansk Samling enjoyed little success until joined by Victor Purschel in 1939, when it became more openly conservative and patriotic. Whilst extremely critical of Danish democracy and prone to use Hitlerian language, with the Occupation in 1940 many of its leaders joined the Danish resistance.

A similar search for a 'third way', involving the idealization of a new society based neither on class nor on free market enterprise, was the Danmarks Retsforbund (Danish League of Rights, i.e. Single Tax Party), founded in 1922. While the party itself never flirted directly with fascists or Nazis, its ideology appears to have attracted people who later did move in such a direction. During 1939–40 its only deputy proceeded to found a new party, the Nationale Genrejserparti (National Resurrection Party); in April 1940, after having been joined by other, more Nazi-oriented groups, the party was renamed the Dansk Folkeparti (Danish People's Party).

Other, more purely 'idealistic' groups which formed during the 1930s – for example, the JAK (Jord, Arbeid, Kapital – 'Land, Work, Capital'), and more religiously oriented bodies such as Tidehverv ('Changing Tide') and the Oxford Movement – were indicative of a certain ferment among conservative Danes, without, however, being in any serious sense fascist in character.

Several 'alternative movements' also appeared in Norway. One small party, the Frisinnede Venstre ('moderate liberals'), provides an excellent example of 'slippage' from conventional conservatism towards fascism. The Frisinnede Venstre was founded in 1909 as a conservative breakaway from the radical-liberal Venstre party, and from then until 1926 worked closely with the Høire. In the late 1920s it began to operate more independently and adopt a more stridently nationalistic posture. Election results proved disappointing, however, and by 1936 it was evident that the new strategy had been a dire miscalculation. Electoral collaboration with Nasjonal Samling in 1933, and support in the party press for Quisling's ideas, discredited the party, drove away many of its previous supporters, and put off other Conservative voters. From 1933, as the Frisinnede Venstre, its name changed in 1931 to the Frisinnede Folkeparti (Liberal People's Party), became increasingly gnawed by frustration and despair, it fell commensurately prey to semi-fascist ideas. The Frisinnede Venstre's decline, when seen in relation to its conservative rivals' relative success, might thus be held to contain a lesson for Conservative leaders in dealing with fascism. The moral seemed to be: do not, in times of crisis and electoral setback, flirt with the fascists; attempt instead to defeat them at the polls and to isolate their ideas when these reach your own organization.

The closest Norwegian analogue to Dansk Samling, not least in being built around its leader's world-view, was B. Dybwad Brochman's Samfunnspartiet (Commonwealth Party). The Samfunnspartiet stood for a moral reconstruction of Norwegian society and a radical, anti-'big money' economic philosophy. It never won more than one deputy in the Storting, and its long-term future was doomed when, after the war, Brochman was accused of collaboration.

By far the most important 'semi-fascist' movement in interwar Norway, however, was the Fedrelandslaget (Patriotic League). Although treated by some writers as an unambiguously fascist organization, and although some of its members did move over to Nasjonal Samling, the Fedrelandslaget is more correctly regarded as a generally patriotic, charismatic organization than a strictly fascist one. Founded in 1925 with the aim of invigorating the country's non-socialist parties and bridging 'minor' differences among them, the Fedrelandslaget numbered among its members and supporters such 'big names' as Fridthof Nansen, Christian Michelsen, Jens Bratlie and Joackim Lemkuhl. Moderately conservative but vehemently anti-Marxist and nationalistic, it also formulated a radical economic programme involving a planned but non-socialist economy. As a non-party organization, whilst not presenting candidates at elections it instead strove to ensure that 'good' candidates appeared on all the non-socialist lists. Its numbers grew quickly until by 1930 it claimed a membership of 100,000: far in excess of anything that could be claimed by any one non-socialist party in Norway, and comparable with the strength of IKL in Finland at its peak in 1936. The political and organizational potential of the Fedrelandslaget was very great, and particularly alarming to the Høire. From 1930 onwards, however, the Høire succeeded in rechannelling into its own coffers financial support from sources which had previously assisted the Fedrelandslaget, and in pinning upon the latter the label of 'irresponsibility'. In acting thus, the Høire was concerned less with the alleged semi-fascist tendencies within the Fedrelandslaget than with its own sense of slackening control over those of its supporters who admired the energetic newcomer.

The Fedrelandslaget had planned to steer the non-socialists from behind the scenes into a single 'bloc'. When these tactics failed its leaders finally decided to launch themselves as a separate political party. By the time this decision was taken, however, after the 1933 election, most of the early enthusiasm had subsided; in 1936 the Fedrelandslaget received only 11,111 votes and elected no deputies. From 1934 the Fedrelandslaget began negotiations with Nasjonal Samling, thereby demonstrating the typical pattern of 'rightist radicalization' in the context of frustration and decline.

A similar proliferation of semi-fascist and 'alternative' rightist groups was apparent in interwar Sweden. As Eric Warenstam's work has shown, these included appeals for 'new, far-right coalitions', associated with well-placed individuals such as Count Erik von Rosen, Colonels E. Grafstrøm and Martin Ekstrøm and the lawyer Sven Hallstrøm; new organizations like the 'New Swedes' and 'Swedish Opposition', which stressed anti-Semitism, corporatism and eventually the full gamut of Hitlerian ideas; and other shortlived radical-right organizations such as Captain Ebbe Almqvist's Svenska Folkpartiet (Swedish People's Party), the Fosterländska Førbundet (Fatherland Association), and the closest Swedish equivalent to the Norwegian Samfunnspartiet and the Dansk Samling, C. S. Dahlin's National-Radikala Samlingspartiet (National Radical Unity Party).

The 'space' between more-or-less 'pure' fascism and other non-socialist alternatives was occupied by the Kyrkliga Folkpartiet (Religious People's Party), founded in 1930 by a group led by the parish priest Ivar Rhedin and centred around the newspaper *Gøteborgs Stiftstidning*. 'We are not in general conservative', the Kyrkliga Folkpartiet declared, 'but in relation to matters of Church, religion and our country we may be forced to be so.' The Kyrkliga Folkpartiet also desired a reconstruction of political life along authoritarian lines consistent with fascist ideology. Visits to Germany convinced Rhedin that Hitler had solved many of the problems on the party's agenda, and both before and during the Second World War he became one of Nazism's leading Swedish spokesmen. Nevertheless the Kyrkliga Folkpartiet, like the other groups just referred to, enjoyed no electoral success, and became increasingly isolated.

Finland appears to present a rather different, and much less clear, picture. One reason for the lower visibility of conservative 'alternatives' may well be the considerable integrative effect of the Lapua movement which, from the very beginning in 1929, provided the opportunity for a wide variety of world-views to come together within a single organization. In particular the special role of clergymen like K. R. Kares and Elias Simojoki, and lay preachers such as O.Vihantola, made Lapua a vehicle for religious interests which elsewhere in Nordic required discrete organizations. The Lapua movement, and later the IKL, may also have absorbed much of the impetus for non-Christian 'alternatives', but hard evidence on this is lacking.

VOLUNTARY WEAPON ORGANIZATIONS: CONSERVATIVE PRECURSORS OF FASCISM?

A characteristic feature of the post-1918 period in the Nordic region – as in much of Europe – was the growth of armed organizations of middle- and upper-class males. In Denmark, Norway and Sweden these organizations were founded in direct response to working-class radicalization following the Bolshevik revolution, the intention being to protect hired strike-breakers, to back up the police in the face of labour unrest and civil strife, and even to supplement the regular armed forces in the event of a 'red' upheaval or other extraordinary political situations.

The Nordic 'volunteer corps' varied widely in strength and significance, from the small and ephemeral to those able to command considerable manpower. Owing to the Nordic countries' wartime neutrality, however, the 'world war veteran' element so prevalent within most European volunteer organizations was absent. Often bearing titles emphasizing the notion of 'shelter' (e.g. Skyddskår, Samfunnsvern, Forsvarsliga, Leidang, Stockholms Luftforsvars Frivilliga Beredskapsforening [1929–33]: also known as Munck's Corps, the Danske Nationalkorps, the Unge Grænsevern, etc.), the volunteer corps were often linked to so-called 'aid' associations such as Samfunnshjelp (Aid to Society) which emerged during 1919–21 in all four Nordic·countries. The initiative for the creation of these bodies came from private enterprise interests, with both financial and indirect support coming from the national employers' federations. Particularly important was the Finnish Yhtymä-Vientiraūha (Export Peace).

Several examples exist of the 'aid associations' and the volunteer corps preventing and even totally aborting serious strikes during the early 1920s. However as the tensions between labour and employers gradually subsided, through the acceptance of negotiating machinery and mutually binding, long-term agreements, the attraction of such organizations withered. Weapon-licensing was tightened up, uniforms were banned, and all voluntary military training was linked directly to the armed forces. The exception was Finland, where no long-term agreement between employers' and employees' organizations materialized, so that Export Peace remained active down to the late 1930s.

The role of voluntary military organizations was very different in Finland, where the regular army had been dissolved by the Tsar in 1901 and victory in the civil war in 1918 had been achieved by a mainly volunteer army. The new, regular Finnish army was established after the war at a time when the 'white', volunteer Civil Guard was the real instrument of power in the country. The question as to how far Finland's vigorous fascist and *fascisant* movements were dependent upon the existence of the Civic Guard has been much debated. Evidence abounds that Civic Guard members participated in the various activities of the Lapua movement which, significantly, was organized on the same district pattern as the Guard, and that Civic Guard backing was crucial to Lapua's recruitment of mass support. The existence of these voluntary, well-armed and well-trained battalions thus made links between conservative, 'white' Finland and Lapua-type fascism possible. When put to the test, however, during Lapua's Mäntsälä rebellion in 1932, a great majority of Civic Guards proved their independence of fascist control, remaining loyal to the conservative president, Swinhufvud – a civic guardist *par excellence* himself. It was the Mäntsälä episode which provoked Swinhufvud's dissolution of Lapua.

The numerical strength of the Civic Guard – around 100,000 in 1920, a figure that was generally maintained thereafter – was only one measure of armed conservative potential. Many Jaegers, German-trained officers in the Finnish regular army, were known to sympathize with rightist ideas, whilst prominent associations such as the League of War Veterans and the Defence League were ultra-conservative bodies which laboured to unite the Civic Guard, elements of the army and the mass organization of Lapua into a broad anti-communist and fascist-like wave. Why, then, did Finland not experience a fascist takeover in the early 1930s? The mass organization of Lapua may have been ready, while sufficient voluntary armed personnel, outnumbering the army three-to-one, seemed available and ideologically prepared. Swinhufvud, elected president in 1931, was a zealous right-winger and a member of the conspiratorially inclined Defence League, who had been been elected with active Lapua support. The question is as difficult as that of why Finland experienced no Communist coup in mid-March 1948, but the answer must lie largely in the ultimate reluctance of Finnish Conservatives, following the resolution of the constitutional crisis of 1930 in favour of the democratic republic, to abandon constitutionalism.

CONSERVATISM, FASCISM AND THE FARMERS

Since it is generally accepted that the rural population leans more strongly towards conservatism than the population as a whole, it is obviously necessary, in discussing Nordic conservatism, to examine those organizations and parties identified with farmers' interests. The Nordic countries were unusual in interwar Europe in possessing well-defined 'Farmers'' parties, founded just before or just after the First World War: in Denmark the Venstre (agrarian 'liberal' party); in Finland the Maaslaisliitto (Agrarian Party); in Norway the Bondepartiet (Farmers' Party); and in Sweden the Bonde Førbundet (Farmers' League). The platforms of these parties, whilst dominated by the material concerns of farmers, also projected the general world-view of traditionally minded rural areas. Often, as in eastern Europe, such perspectives were not merely conservative but downright anti-modern and also nationalistic, while the mobilization of farmers could easily assume the character of a mass populist movement.

The depression affected farmers in the Nordic countries differently according to their main economic activities. Farmers and farm-labourers involved in the exporting sector – for example forest owners and workers in Norway and Finland, large and middling meat and bacon producers in Denmark – were badly hit by the declining export market. Many small farmers, especially on recently created smallholdings with high indebtedness, found themselves facing bankruptcy and foreclosure owing to the effect of internal devaluation policies. Such variations in regional circumstances meant that the farmers' parties faced somewhat differing challenges.

Like the Conservative parties, all the farmers' parties were losing votes during the 1930s, votes which in the cases of Norway, Denmark and Finland seem likely to have switched to the extreme right. The farmers' parties were thus up against the same problems as their Conservative 'neighbours'. Only in Norway, however, did the Farmers' Party, some of whose leaders thought of Nasjonal Samling as their urban counterpart, enter into direct negotiation with the fascists over a possible National

Bloc: an approach conditioned by election losses and the Bondepartiet's lack of urban impact. In this context it must be borne in mind that between 1931 and 1933 Quisling served as Minister of Defence in a Bondepartiet cabinet, and that of all the Nordic farmers' parties the Norwegian was probably the most nationalistic.

The position of the Finnish Agrarian Party in relation to Lapua and the IKL was rather more complex. Although the party co-operated with Lapua in electing Svinhufvud to the presidency, it was an association about which the Agrarians felt uneasy. After the dissolution of Lapua they completely dissociated themselves from its reincarnation, the IKL – and it was an Agrarian Minister of the Interior, Kekkonen, who unsuccessfully attempted in 1938 to ban the IKL.

In Denmark the Venstre experienced a right-wing schism when three deputies were forced out of the party for belonging also to the Landbrugnes Sammenslutning (Farmers' Association). The three became the basis of the Frie Folkeparti (Liberal People's Party), initiated by the Landbrugnes Sammenslutning in May 1934. In 1938 the new party's five deputies were joined by another from the Venstre. The Frie Folkeparti and the Landbrugnes Sammenslutning occasionally appeared together with the Danish Nazis at public rallies, and in some areas lasting contacts were established. Both the Frie Folkeparti and the Landbrugnes Sammenslutning became seriously discredited when, following the German invasion on 9 April 1940, they initated negotiations with the occupiers on behalf of farmers' interests.

The Danish Landbrugnes Sammenslutning, membership of which exceeded 100,000, may be regarded as a populist crisis organization (in 1935 it organized a mass march on Amalienborg Castle, the king's residence, to express farmers' grievances), similar examples of which surfaced in Norway, Sweden and Finland. The Bygdefolkets Krisehjelp (Rural People's Crisis Organization) was established in Norway to counter the foreclosures which commenced in eastern Norway in 1931. By employing novel, direct methods against the representatives of banks and proprietors who turned up to evict bankrupt farming families, Bygdefolkets Krisehjelp was able in a relatively short time to build up a strong organization and claim numerous successful actions. From the start the Bondepartiet and the Social Democrats campaigned against the Bygdefolkets Krisehjelp, and the ensuing isolation probably explains the latter's willingness to join with Nasjonal Samling in the 1933 elections. This alliance proved fatal for Bygdefolkets Krisehjelp, however; the populist organization found itself discredited and labelled as 'fascist', its organization disintegrated, and its members and voters returned to the Bondepartiet and the Social Democrats. At no time did its membership exceed 12,000.

A similar organization was created in Sweden in 1929. The Riksförbundet Landsbygdens Folk (Swedish National Rural Union) aimed at organizing farmers on a broadly trade union basis, and rejected the direct action strategy of the Bygdefolkets Krisehjelp. In contrast to the latter's sudden decline, the Riksførbundet's membership continued to expand throughout the 1930s, reaching a maximum of around 52,000. The 'fascistization' of the organization went less far than was the case with its Norwegian counterpart, although some local unions provided exceptions and reports do exist concerning flirtation between local Riksførbundet organizations and national socialist groups.

Finnish agrarian populism was above all evident in the mass mobilization achieved by Lapua. Nevertheless Lapua was always a political movement rather than a farmers' union or economic pressure group. Its farming support, moreover, seems to have more closely resembled that of the Landbrugernes Riksførbund than that of the Bygdefolkets Krisehjelp and the Riksførbundet. A further complication was the appearance in Finland of two left-wing splinters from the Agrarian Party, representing a variety of expressions of localized rural-agrarian protest. The Smallholders' Party, formed in 1929, and the Rural People's Party, founded in 1933, fused in 1936 into the Smallholders and Rural People's Party, obtaining 3.1 per cent of the vote and electing five deputies. At the next election most of their support reverted to the Agrarians, but their activities continued until 1954.

THEORETICAL SUMMARY

This broad account of the relationships between Conservative parties, and conservatism in general, and fascism in the Nordic countries produces the following picture. In the four countries examined, the Conservative parties were able to resist the pressures of fascism with respect both to the prevention of 'fascistization' within the youth sections and to fractionalization on the party right. Nor did they witness any large-scale loss of membership or voters to the radical right. After the serious electoral losses in the elections of the late 1920s and early 1930s, the Conservative parties' voting strength stabilized; in any case, there is little evidence that Conservative losses were ever converted into fascist gains. Indeed, the precise sources of fascist electoral support remain unclear. Agrarian parties and interest groups also faced and successfully resisted fascist challenges, even if from time to time in the 1930s the situation was confused by the activities of *ad hoc* organizations and isolated individuals. The 'new alternatives' in the political arena, and the various volunteer, semi-military, protection and 'aid' organizations, most of which belonged in the conservative camp, proved susceptible to fascist influence; nevertheless, even if on occasions these organizations did co-operate with, support or even briefly ally with the fascist parties, it would on the whole be untrue to suggest that they actually 'went fascist'. These conclusions, obviously with some exceptions of detail, are valid for all the Nordic countries: conservatism was challenged by, and tasted the flavour of, fascism/national socialism, but was only marginally revitalized or renewed by it.

Why was Nordic conservatism able to resist fascism? Two categories of condition, the underlying and the contingent, are relevant to any explanation. The former, accounting for the general level of each country's sociopolitical stability, help to explain the overall potential for fascism and should be regarded as already fixed at the outset of the 'fascist period' in 1918–20. The stronger 'fascist potential' present in Finland when compared with the other three countries must therefore be related to a unique – for the Nordic region – set of underlying conditions: the experience of civil war in 1918, Finnish territorial claims against the Soviet Union, the distinctive radicalization of the Finnish Communist Party, etc.

'Contingent' conditions themselves fall into two subcategories, which may be termed the 'external' and the 'internal'. The former are those impulses, favourable or unfavourable to the development of fascism, which originated abroad: the depression, the impact of news from Germany, the involvements of German Nazis in Danish North Slesvig, Soviet expansionism, etc. The internal conditions are those mainly discussed in this chapter; that is to say the politics, economics and cultural developments within the Nordic countries themselves. In order to understand the manner in which these contingent, internal conditions shaped the conservative–fascist relationship it is necessary to focus upon the concepts of isolation and diffusion, the main thesis of this chapter being that the Conservatives' resistance towards fascism depended upon their ability – and that of the political system of which they were a part – to isolate, and at the same time diffuse, the impulse and ideas of fascism.

Given their decline around 1930, Nordic Conservatives were vulnerable to novel ideas concerning ideology, organization and leadership. Young Conservatives absorbed some of these novelties within their own ranks, but few actually deserted to the fascists. Many on the far right of the Conservative parties employed the aesthetics of fascism in their attacks on the party leaderships, but again few left to join fascism. The farmers' and agrarian parties for a time looked towards 'national blocs', hoping to link up with the fascists, but then pulled back even after having introduced semi-fascist elements into their own programmes. Other broadly conservative groups and parties, whilst the true originators of what would often be considered fascist or national socialist ideas, found themselves in competition with those whose fascism was unambiguous. In the course of this complex process of adaptation, however, conservatives of various kinds came to assume strongly anti-fascist postures, stressing their differences with fascism and attempting to isolate the fascist and national socialist parties through labelling them as irresponsible, as extremists, as imitators of Hitler, etc. In this they may actually have been more effective than the Social Democrats and Communists, who often claimed the credit for isolating the fascists through the outspokenness of their anti-fascist propaganda.

The fascist and national socialist parties faced precisely the opposite dilemma. On the one hand they were anxious to be 'pure' fascists or national socialists and thus monopolize the new, vital message that was enjoying such success in Germany; on the other, they needed followers and hence essayed a variety of forms of alliances and 'blocs'. The process of 'isolation and diffusion' of Nordic fascism took place in three stages. In the first stage the fascist message was diffused widely throughout the conservative camp; in the second, both the conservatives and the fascists, for very different reasons, worked towards the isolation of fascism; in the third, the diffusion of fascism was brought to an end when the fascist and national socialist parties were isolated through the stigmatization of their extremist position.

This process, whereby the 'establishment' successfully negotiates the diffusion and isolation of radical impulses, is not limited to the 'fascist period' in Europe, something very similar having at one time or another happened with social democracy, the 'green' movement and the present-day far right. The strength and dynamism of new political impulses, and their adaptation or isolation, are surely reflections of the political system itself and of its distinctive characteristics. Thus, in the Nordic countries, fascism failed to prosper between the wars because the underlying conditions were unpropitious and because contingent, internal conditions offered fascism insufficient additional opportunity. Although Finland, with the most favourable underlying conditions, was most affected by fascism and the radical right, following the resolution of the 1930 constitutional crisis the country's political situation converged with those of its Nordic partners. The transformation wrought by the Soviet invasion of November 1939 came too late, and in too unhelpful a manner, to give the Finnish fascists another chance. Even the circumstances of 1941–4, when Finland was allied with Germany and German military forces were present in the country, failed to provide the IKL with the opportunity for power presented to its Norwegian and Danish counterparts.

BIBLIOGRAPHY

1 Comparative study of Nordic fascism:

Larsen, S. U., Hagtvet, B. and Myklebust, J. P. (eds) , *Who Were the Fascists? Social Roots of European Fascism* (Oslo, Bergen and Tromsø, 1980), pp. 586–750. Lindström, U., *Fascism in Scandinavia* (Stockholm, 1985). Larsen, S. U. and Montgomery, I., *Kirken, Krisen og Krigen* (Bergen, 1982), pp. 259–311. Nilsson, S., Hildebrand, K.-G., and Øhngren, B., *Kriser och Krispolitik i Norden under mellankrigstiden* (Uppsala, 1974), pp. 71–104.

2 Denmark

The DNSAP:
Paulsen, H., *Besættelsemagten og de danske nazister* (Aarhus, 1970). Djursaa, M., *NSAP. Danske nazister 1930–1945* (Copenhagen, 1981). Lohmann, H. P., *Dansk folkefællesskap 1936–42* (Odense, 1984). Eigaard, S., *'Frø av ugræs...', Denmarks National Socialistiske Parti 1930–34* (Odense, 1981).

Danish conservatism:
Winther, J., *Fra Krise til Krig 1929–1940. Det Konservative folkespartis historie*, Vol. II (Copenhagen, 1966). Kraft, O. B., *En konservativ politikers erindringer 1926–1945* (Copenhagen, 1971) Quaade, A. and Ravn, O., *Høire om! Temaer og tendenser i den anti-parlamentariske debat* (Copenhagen, 1979).

Denmark in the 1930s, general analyses:
Rasmussen, E., *Vælferdstaten på vej 1913–1939* (Copenhagen, 1965). Andersen, R., *Damnark i 30'rne. En historisk mosaik* (Copenhagen, 1968).

3 Norway

Nasjonal Samling:
Brevig, O., *'Fra parti til sekt'* (Oslo, 1969). Loock. H.-D., *Quisling, Rosenberg und Therboven - Zur Vorgeschichte und Geschichte der nationalsozialstischen Revolution in Norwegen* (Stuttgart, 1970). Skodvin, M., *Striden om okkupasjonsstyret i Norge frem til 25 september 1940* (Oslo, 1957). Danielsen, R. and Larsen, S. U., *'Fra ide til Dom'* (Bergen, 1976). Dahl, H. F. , Hagtvet, B., and Hjeltnes, G., *Den Norske nasjonalsocialismen. Nasjonal Samling 1933–1945 i tekst og bilder*; Frøland, K., *Krise og kamp* (Oslo, 1962). Gabrielsen, B. V., *Menn og Politikk* (Oslo, 1970). Blom, I., 'Bønder og blokkforhandlinger 1933–1936', *Historisk Tidsskrift*, 4 (1972). Bull, E., 'Kriseforliket mellom Bondepartiet og det norske Arbeiderparti i 1935', *Historisk Tidsskrift*, 2 (1959).

On the Conservatives and the Fedrelandslaget:
Danielsen, R., *Borgerlig oppdemmingspolitikk 1918–1940* (Oslo, 1984); Nordland, A., *Hårde Tider. Fedrelandslaget i norsk politikk* (Oslo, 1973).

Norway from 1919 to 1945, general analyses:
Bull, E., *Klassekamp og Fellesskap 1920–1945* (Oslo, 1979). Bull, E., *Norge i den rike verden. Tiden etter 1945* (Oslo, 1979). Furre, B., *Norsk Historie 1905–1940* (Oslo, 1972). Dahl, H. F., *Norge mellom krigene. Det norske samfunn i krise og konflikt 1918–1940* (Oslo, 1971).

4 Sweden

On Swedish fascism and right-radicalism:
Warenstam, E., *Fascismen och nazismen i Sverige 1920–1940* (Stockholm, 1970). Warenstam, E., *Sveriges Nationalle Ungdomsførbund och Høgern 1928–1934* (Stockholm, 1965). Sastamoinen, A., *Hitlers svenska førtrupper* (Stockholm, 1947). Carlson, H., *Nazismen i Sverige. Et varningsord* (Stockholm, 1942).

On conservatism, farmers' organizations, etc.:
Tortstendahl, R., *Mellan nykonservatism och liberalism* (Uppsala, 1969). Thullberg, P., *Bønder går sammen* (Stockholm, 1977).

Sweden from 1919 to 1945, general analyses:
Carlson, S., *Den svenska historien 10. Vår egen tid från 1920 til 1960-talet* (Stockholm, 1968). Birgerson, B. O. (ed.) , *Sverige efter 1900. En modern politisk historia* (Stockholm, 1984).

5 Finland (works in English and Swedish)

The Finnish right, general analyses:
Rintala, M., *Three Generations: the Extreme Right in Finnish Politics* (Bloomington, Ind., 1962). Rintala, M., 'Finland', in Rogger, H. and Weber, E. (eds), *The European Right. A Historical Profile* (London, 1965), pp. 408–42. Rintala, M., 'An image of European politics: the People's Patriotic Movement', *Journal of Central European Affairs*, 21 (1963).

Lapua and the IKL:
Djupsund, G. and Karvonen, L., *Fascismen i Finland. Høgerextremismens førankring hos valjarkåren 1929–1939* (Åbo, 1984). Rosengren, C., *Lapporørelsens utomparlamentariske verksamhet och påtrykningspolitik gentemot stasmakten til och med presidentvalet år 1931* (Åbo, 1973); Alapuro, R., 'Students and national politics: a comparative study of the Finnish Student Movement in the interwar period', *Scandinavian Political Studies*, 8 (1973). Alapuro, R. and Allardt, E., 'The Lapua movement: the threat of a rightist takeover in Finland, 1930–1932', in Linz, J. and Stephan, A. (eds), *The Breakdown of Democratic Regimes* (London, 1978); Kalela, J., 'Right-wing radicalism in Finland during the interwar period', *Scandinavian Journal of History*, 1 (1976). Athi, M., 'Det blåsvarta brødraskapet', *Historisk Tidsskrift før Finland*, 2 (1983). Athi, M., 'Konspiration - massrørelse - partibildning', *Kritisk fascismeforskning* (Nordisk Sommer-universitet no. 13, Copenhagen, 1982). Karvonen, L., 'Det blåsvarta brødraskapet', *Finsk Tidsskrift*, 5 (1983).

The Conservative Party:
Bonsdorff, G. von, *Samlingspartiet* (Lovisa, 1947).

General analyses:
Wahlback, K, *Från Mannerheim til Kekkonen* (Stockholm, 1967). Puntila, L. A., *Finlands Politiska Historia 1809–1966* (Helsinki, 1972).

Conservatism and the failure of fascism in interwar Britain

John Stevenson

British fascism was among the weakest manifestations of fascism in interwar Europe. During the 1920s and in the years immediately following the Wall Street Crash, it was represented by a number of minority parties, highly marginalized in terms of contemporary politics, lacking influence within the existing political system and scarcely capable of achieving significant political impact outside it. Even the British Union of Fascists (BUF), whose formation in 1932 inaugurated a new, more expansive phase under a more effective leader, Sir Oswald Mosley, failed to make a decisive impact upon British politics. Electorally, the BUF failed to elect a single MP or even a single local councillor. As an extra-parliamentary movement it failed to mobilize sufficient support or find a suitable occasion to exercise a major influence on domestic politics during the 1930s. The BUF thus represents an important example of a European fascist movement 'squeezed out' as a significant force in both conventional and extra-parliamentary politics.

Why did British interwar fascism fail? Context was of major importance, for fascism in Britain had to operate in a climate which both politically and economically offered far less promising terrain than existed in other parts of Europe. Britain emerged from the First World War with a relatively stable parliamentary monarchy in which the principal traditions of liberal democracy were both longstanding and highly regarded. It had a relatively mature and well-entrenched system of political representation which had withstood the upheavals of industrialization and urbanization, had absorbed the huge sacrifices and challenges of the First World War, and had already shown itself capable of adapting its political structure to an at least nominal acceptance of mass democracy. The Representation of the People Act of 1918 virtually completed the process of conferring on the adult population as a whole – with the notable exception of women under 30 – full democratic rights. Already the political system had proved itself capable of representing major interests and a mass electorate without the destructive clash between propertied and propertyless which had been the nightmare of so many nineteenth-century thinkers. As Sidney Low was able to write in 1904:

The great peril, so constantly present to the minds of the philosophical opponents of democracy, in ancient and modern times, has been averted; and even under a wide popular franchise we have not as yet found ourselves in the presence of two political parties, the one including all those who own property, and the other of those who possess little but their hands and their votes.[1]

In spite of the tensions of the Edwardian era when the Irish Question, the suffragette campaign and the rise of trade union militancy seemed to threaten many of the assumptions of 'Liberal England', there was little evidence that they had done so in the aftermath of the First World War. The coming of war itself had shelved the immediate issue of Irish Home Rule and the threat of the 'Ulsterization of British politics'. The re-emergence of open conflict in Ireland after 1916 and the protracted guerrilla war which led to the partition of Ireland in 1921 remained somewhat isolated from the mainstream of British politics. Bitter as the guerrilla war in Ireland was, it failed to affect the British polity as a whole. The creation of an independent southern Ireland and of a self-governing province in the north worked remarkably well on a short-term political level in removing the 'Irish Question' from British politics.[2] The action of the Irish Free State in suppressing its own nationalist extremists during the civil war with the Irish Republican Army which followed upon partition, and the willingness of Westminster politicians to let Stormont run Ulster on its own terms, effectively defused a potentially explosive situation. Northern Ireland was not destined to become, in this period at least, the source of nationalist, right-wing recrimination against interwar governments. Ulster was not to be Britain's Sudetenland or Belfast its Fiume.

The suffragette challenge was politically less serious in its threat to liberal democracy. Although the resort to methods of violent outrage demonstrated the fragility of the assumptions which governed the conduct of domestic politics before 1914, they were not sufficiently serious in consequence to produce major changes in the way politicians comported themselves or to tear apart the fabric of Edwardian society. If anything violence and outrage alienated more opinion than it gained and, initially, the women's suffrage movement was overtaken by the outbreak of the war, when patriotic enthusiasm took a leading place alongside the fight for women's rights.[3] The war was to prove immensely helpful to the women's cause, however. Their claim for a share in formal democratic rights was accepted in 1918, though on terms which remained discriminatory until 1928. For women in the interwar years the political system had yielded just sufficiently to satisfy some basic aspirations and to accommodate them within conventional politics.

In the case of trade unionism a potentially much more formidable challenge presented itself. With over 4 million members in 1914, almost a quarter of the workforce, many of them heavily represented in vital areas of production, fuel and transport, the trade unions were clearly a power in the land. The immediate prewar years had witnessed a mounting toll of strike activity and the spread of socialist and syndicalist ideas was widely recognized as raising major issues in British politics. Negotiations for the formation of the 'Triple Alliance' of railwaymen, transport workers and miners in the summer of 1914 seemed to presage a new era of industrial and political conflict, in which talk of a general strike became increasingly common. Right up to the outbreak of war levels of strike activity remained high, with a five-month lock-out in the London building trades during the early part of 1914 and widespread stoppages in other industries. But the war, as elsewhere, introduced a completely new dimension. Although strong internationalist and pacifist sentiment was maintained by a minority, the trade union movement was swept along by the same tidal wave of patriotism which affected the country as a whole. A 'strike truce' called by the General Federation of Trade Unions and the Trade Union Parliamentary Committee at the end of August 1914 reduced the number of days lost in strikes to a fraction of that in the prewar months. In retrospect, it is possible to argue that there was some exaggeration of the nature of the challenge which the trade unions appeared to offer in the years before the First World War. Organized labour was certainly flexing its muscles, but its strength was usually employed to obtain negotiation or the successful resolution of negotiations rather than to subvert the state. Already leading trade unionists were finding themselves being brought to accommodation with employers through the intervention of leading politicians and other third parties. Successful industrial action, concessions in the field of social reform, and the formation of a Labour Party to pursue the interests of organized labour at Westminster brought advances which helped to incorporate the unions in the existing political order. Enunciated famously as 'gradualism', the dominant British brand of socialism was already showing itself more interested in reform than revolution.

The First World War enormously enhanced the influence of organized labour. Membership of the trade unions rapidly increased and their consent was seen as vital to war production – indeed, to the continuance of the war itself. Labour and trade union representatives were brought into the highest levels of government and acquired much-needed experience at ministerial levels. Although a growing number of labour disputes in the latter years of the war and the influence of the Russian Revolution added powerful stimuli to the left-wing socialism and syndicalism represented in 'Red Clydeside' and the Shop Stewards' Movement, the forces of accommodation remained strong. The prospect of a Labour government no longer seemed remote and while industrial militancy remained a powerful weapon into the interwar years, its power proved less decisive than expected. The stirrings of 'Red Clydeside' were met by determined government action and a speeding up of plans for reconstruction, while the sectional and purely economic interests of many of the workers concerned sapped any support for revolutionary upheaval.[4] The failure of the Triple Alliance in April 1921, when its other two members withheld support from the miners, brought the postwar phase of militancy almost to an end. The collapse of the short-lived postwar boom also had its effect. Less favourable economic conditions, growing unemployment and falling wages took the edge off union militancy. Unemployment reached over 2 million in the summer of 1921, ushering in what was to be the familiar backcloth to the interwar years: mass unemployment. If trade union militancy in the last years of the war and its immediate aftermath touched the fabric of British political life less deeply than in some other countries, it was against the background of a trade union and labour movement which had developed strong and enduring institutional representation in both the workplace and the political arena. The readiness of the higher echelons of the labour movement to conform to the 'rules' of British society were shown clearly in the increasing absorption of the Labour Party into Westminster politics, confirmed by the formation of the first Labour government in 1924. Similarly, the General Strike of 1926 represented an important example of the unwillingness of the leaders of the Trade Union Congress to pursue with any enthusiasm a course which seemed to lead them into revolutionary confrontation with the government.

Crucially, for this potentially dangerous confrontation as for others, Britain had emerged from the war victorious while all over Europe, often assisted by the dislocation of war, defeat and the discrediting of the established order, monarchies were toppling and revolutionary movements were abroad. Economically speaking, it is true, Britain had been weakened by the war, through loss of markets and overseas investments and the run-down of plant and equipment. From a creditor, Britain had been turned into a debtor nation and its trading position, hitherto buttressed by the returns from overseas investments, was now exposed to the rigours of international competition in a more difficult market. But while economic difficulties loomed, the British political structure had withstood the strain. The existence of coalition governments from the middle years of the war had permitted the war to be fought with a high degree of national unity. Dissenting voices there were, with a brave and persecuted pacifist movement maintaining its opposition, but right up to the end there was little evidence that the war did not enjoy the at least tacit consent of the bulk of the home population and its political representatives. Unlike in Russia or Germany, and even in the darkest days, the issue of whether the war should be pursued to its end failed to become a major item on the political agenda. There is little evidence, either, from the serving soldiers on the Western Front of a parallel to the profound disillusionment which brought mutiny to large sections of the French, German and Russian armed forces in 1917.

Victory, bought even at heavy cost, freed British politics from the bitterness of recrimination and festering resentment which defeat, and still more dismemberment and humiliation, might have brought. In spite of the strong anti-war and pacifist feeling resulting from the war, it is striking that the most influential wave of anti-war literature, produced by the likes of Robert Graves and Siegfried Sassoon and containing not just anti-war sentiment but also a vehement indictment of the society which had given rise to the war and its continuance, appeared a decade or more after the actual conflict had ended. During the 1920s, at least, horror and a sense of 'never again' were the more characteristic features of the British response to the Great War than a corrosive and divisive assault upon the old order.

The survival of that order and the relative stability of British politics were reflected in the development of party politics after 1918. A still powerful Conservative Party dominated the postwar coalition government led by Lloyd George; in 1922 it was able to ditch the prestigious wartime leader and embark upon one of its most successful electoral periods. The Conservative Party showed a continuing ability both to act as a representative of established interests and to appeal to a wide mass electorate at local and national levels. For Britain the presence of a solid, reliable party of the established order was an important prerequisite in preventing the fragmentation and polarization of middle-class voters. On the other side of the political spectrum the Labour Party increasingly gathered to itself the votes of the organized working class but with an important admixture of middle-class and intellectual supporters. In the electoral sphere, the story of the interwar years was of the pressure upon the Liberal vote and the success of the Conservative Party in becoming increasingly *the* dominant party of the middle and propertied classes or those who aspired to them. The Conservative Party's sustained strength and electoral success – it held power either alone or in coalition throughout the period, save only for the two brief interruptions of 1924 and 1929–31 – represented an important ingredient in the political stability of interwar Britain.[5]

During the 1920s, then, there was little opportunity for extremist parties to gain any purchase on the political system. The Communist Party of Great Britain, founded in 1921, remained self-consciously a minority organization, dwarfed by the greater influence of the trade union movement, the Labour Party and, in some areas, working-class Toryism. The government's firm handling of labour unrest in 1918–21 and the more cautious approach of the trade unions in the 1920s left the Communist Party to make what headway it could through local trade union activity or through front organizations. As such it posed little threat of revolutionary upheaval to the country as a whole and was effectively marginalized. Denied formal expression through the Labour Party and the organized labour movement, and harassed because of its connections with Bolshevik Russia, the Communist Party by the late 1920s had dug itself deeper into a bunker through its adoption of the then Moscow line of 'class against class', involving vehement attacks on the 'social fascists' of the trade union movement and the Labour Party. As a consequence it entered the worst phase of the depression, after 1929, with only a few thousand members and only patchy support amongst sections of organized labour. Moreover, in so far as a 'Red Scare' existed in the 1920s it served, as in the case of the 'Zinoviev letter', to assist the Conservative Party as the bulwark of order. Similarly, the Conservative Party had little difficulty in outfacing the threat posed by the General Strike of 1926, rallying public support to itself as the party of the constitution and of national unity.

In spite of the onset of depression, which had already before 1929 become a permanent feature in some of the older industrial areas, and the bleak prospects for many agriculturalists with the removal of price support, there was no parallel in Britain to the devastating inflation which in Germany during the early 1920s ruined large sections of the middle class and prompted so high a level of political insecurity. In this context, the early fascist movements had little scope to operate. The British Fascisti, founded in May 1925 by Miss R. L. Linton-Orman, pursued a programme of patriotism and anti-communism, aiming to defend the constitution against attacks from communists and to preserve a disciplined organization in case of emergency. Later changing its name to the British Fascists, in the late 1920s and early 1930s the movement adopted a more clearly defined programme, borrowing from Italy an emphasis on a corporate state and advocating large-scale reforms of the economic and financial structure and the exclusion of Jews and aliens from public office. In industry strikes were to be declared illegal, compulsory arbitration introduced and trade unions reformed. Externally, a pro-Imperial policy was to be pursued. A largely middle-class movement, deriving its basic appeal from its militant patriotic stance, the British Fascists had a membership of only a few hundred. The National Fascists, who seceded from the British Fascists in the 1920s, had a similarly small membership concentrated mainly in the London area, while Arnold Leese's Imperial Fascist League never had more than a thousand members. All these groups remained on the fringes of politics, upstaged in their vehement patriotism by the solid, broad base of the Conservative Party and deprived of the national crises or threats which might have given them a recruiting ground.[6]

The persistence and deepening of the depression after 1929 seemed to some to threaten a more difficult time for democratic politics. With Russia and Italy already under totalitarian government, the Nazis growing in strength in Germany, and barely concealed instability in countries such as France and Spain, there was a distinct sense of democracy in danger. For Marxists there seemed first-hand evidence that the 'final crisis of capitalism' was looming, and men like John Strachey contemplated the need to wield totalitarian power in the event of a breakdown of the established order.

Events proved these dramatic scenarios false, however. The most significant political effect of the deepening world depression on Britain was the break-up of the Labour government elected in 1929 and its replacement by a 'National government', headed by the former Labour Prime Minister and some of the former Labour ministers, supported by a rump of Labour MPs but depending chiefly for House of Commons support on Conservatives and Liberals. The landslide election victory of the National government in October 1931, providing it with a majority of over 500 seats, gave a massive guarantee of stable, conservative government during the worst years of the depression. The sense of national crisis, undoubtedly present in the summer of 1931, was met in effect by a device not dissimilar to the coalition which had taken power in the midst of the First World War. It meant that the way was open for the National government to pursue policies which simultaneously reassured establishment opinion and secured a broad measure of consent to the view that there was no alternative to them.

The National government was able to use its 'honeymoon' period to take some of the steps which had proved unacceptable to the Labour Cabinet. A cut in unemployment benefit, including the introduction of the means test, was simply the most notable of several spending cuts imposed in order to balance the budget, comply with the recommendations of the May Committee and, ultimately, satisfy business and financial opinion. Notwithstanding a mutiny in the fleet and protests from the unemployed and from professional groups severely affected by the cuts, such as teachers, the National government stubbornly pursued its policies of economic orthodoxy: to balance the budget, economize on government spending and restore business confidence. Direct economic intervention was eschewed; capital expenditure on public works was regarded as wasteful, diverting investment from natural channels where it was believed it would prove more effective. The government's attitude was summed up by the Chancellor of the Exchequer, Neville Chamberlain: 'The quickest and most effective contribution which any Government can make towards an increase of employment is to create conditions which will encourage and facilitate improvements in ordinary trade.'[7]

Even as opposition grew in the later 1930s to the economic *immobilisme* of the National government, its policies remained in tune with the majority of orthodox economists, rather than with the untried and, some felt, potentially disastrous policies of heavy capital investment to solve structural unemployment in the depressed areas, or the kind of economic management advocated by Keynesians. The government expected unemployment to remain high; Chamberlain predicted, rightly as it turned out, that in the medium term the combination of 'structural' and 'frictional' unemployment was likely to remain as high as a million.[8] What was looked for was an upturn in the trade cycle from the 'Great Crash' of 1929–31, a view which received some support with the beginnings of a revival in world trade after 1933 and, by the mid-1930s, what has been called 'the largest and most sustained period of growth in the whole of the inter-war period'.[9] The government sought to hold fast to policies which it was hoped would facilitate 'natural recovery' while avoiding anything which might damage confidence in the business or financial world. In this it was assisted by the swift abandonment of the Gold Standard, unthinkable for a Labour government but possible for a 'National' one. With the introduction of a degree of protection in 1932, stabilization of agriculture through guaranteed prices in some areas of production, the reduction of interest rates, and encouragement of reorganization and rationalization in some of the older staples, the National government was able to claim, without obvious hypocrisy, that it was doing the best it could to see the economy and the country through an extremely difficult period.

The first fascist movements thus found themselves irrelevant in the face of a government which took its stand solidly upon the status quo and offered no significant challenge to the interests of property and privilege. Nor could the tiny Communist Party be regarded as a serious challenge to the stability of the country; effectively cut off by its acrimonious relations with the trade unions and the Labour Party from greater support within them, it had insufficient strength and influence to provide an important catalyst for right-wing groups. Sir Oswald Mosley's evolution towards the formation of the British Union of Fascists in 1932 was in part a response to the frustration of marginalization in this period. Having had what were considered his unorthodox solutions to the problem of unemployment rejected by the Labour Party, Mosley then found that his New Party was also swept aside by the electorate in the 1931 general election. Although earlier in 1931 the New Party's candidate, Allen Young, had polled respectably in the Ashton-under-Lyne by-election, at the general election its twenty-four candidates polled only 36,777 votes between them, with twenty-two losing their deposits; at Ashton-under-Lyne the New Party vote fell from 4,472 to only 424.[10]

Electoral disaster, which left the New Party shattered, was an important step in Mosley's adoption of a more avowedly fascist stance. Mosley's visit to Italy in January 1932 confirmed his drift to the right, impressed as he was by the 'modernity' of Mussolini's regime. As Robert Skidelsky has noted, the sense that the old order was in inextricable 'crisis' and that its collapse was inevitable, leaving communism to take over in the ensuing vacuum, was a major stimulus:

> since the 'old gangs' could not avert the situation from which commun-
> ism would benefit, the challenge to communism would have to come
> from a new movement with an alternative faith and an alternative system
> capable of winning mass support. Such movements had already arisen
> on the Continent. It was necessary to organise a similar movement in
> England.[11]

The launch of the BUF on 1 October 1932, then, represented Mosley's attempt to replicate in Britain the success of Italian and German fascist movements in mobilizing a coalition of patriotic and populist forces against the inadequacy of the old order and the threat to it from communism. Fascism was, according to Mosley, to offer the constructive alternative of the corporate state to the muddle of the existing situation. The BUF stood ready to prevent a communist takeover in the event of a descent into economic and political crisis. As Mosley wrote in *The Greater Britain*:

> In the final economic crisis to which neglect may lead, argument,
> reason, persuasion vanish and organised force alone prevails. In such
> a situation, the eternal protagonists in the history of all modern crises
> must struggle for the mastery of the State. Either fascism or Communism
> emerges victorious; if it be the latter, the story of Britain is told …
> In the highly technical struggle for the modern State in crisis, only
> the technical organisations of fascism and of Communism have ever
> prevailed or, in the nature of the case, can prevail. Governments and
> parties which have relied on the normal instruments of government
> … have fallen easy and ignoble victims to the forces of anarchy.[12]

Mosley went out of his way to repudiate the charge that his movement was organized to promote violence. Organization was required to defend the BUF's right to free speech and its meetings from systematic disruption. Mosley stressed that the BUF sought to achieve its aims by methods which are 'both legal and constitutional'. National reconstruction would be attained through Parliament, though parliamentary power was not an end in itself. Initially, the movement was to concentrate upon building up its strength and 'invading every phase of national life and carrying everywhere the Corporate conception'. It was recognized, however, that whether the fascists would come to power through the parliamentary system or in the aftermath of a crisis which had passed beyond parliamentary control depended upon the speed with which the crisis developed and how rapidly the 'British people accept the necessity for new forms and for new organisations'.[13]

For a time the BUF prospered. Meetings and rallies helped to recruit members, the backing of Rothermere's *Daily Mail* provided an influential outlet for views, and the movement's own newspaper, the *Blackshirt*, was launched in February 1933 to act as its main propaganda vehicle. Mosley was called to speak at debates and to write articles in the press, and was ever ready to enunciate his views to all who would listen. However, although its membership figures remain one of the BUF's most obscure features, 1933–4 probably represented its peak in terms of membership.[14] Critically, the BUF's early phase coincided not with a breakdown of the established parliamentary system or of the National government itself, but with the latter's consolidation of power. An 'old gang' which commanded a huge popular mandate, showed no desire to surrender the reins of power, and, apart from the demonstrations of the National Unemployed Workers' Movement, encountered no serious left-wing challenge, presented Mosley with a massive and growing obstacle to his hopes of building a mass movement of consequence.

Indeed, events conspired to make 1934 a watershed year for the BUF. By now the Nazis had been in power in Germany for over a year and indications as to what kind of regime the Third Reich promised to be were beginning to have an effect upon British opinion. As the BUF became more active during 1933 and 1934, it was the violence at its meetings which most frequently attracted publicity. The Home Secretary had already delivered himself of the opinion that it was the Fascists, through their provocative 'semi-military evolutions ... their marching in formation and their general behaviour' who had been responsible for provoking disturbances in Bristol.[15] Mosley did little to assuage opinion by his openly stated position that he would meet violence with violence. Although the majority of meetings were peaceful and well ordered, there was in their style and potential for organized violence something which caused serious disquiet across a broad range of opinion. The combined use of mass meetings, uniformed parades and the trappings of continental fascism, all at the command of a charismatic leader, had no antecedents in British politics. Mosley's self-conscious adoption of the style of continental fascism generated more suspicion than support. Even Rothermere was more of an anti-communist than a supporter of continental-style fascism. He flirted with Mosley's movement, playing down Mosley's fascist label and giving prominence to his pro-Imperial and defence policies, because he saw it as providing the leadership which conservative forces required in the face of a left-wing threat to established interests.

The Olympia meeting of June 1934 served to bring the disquiet of even conservative opinion into sharper focus. Whatever the rights and wrongs of the events surrounding the ejection and manhandling of hecklers and anti-fascists at the meeting, the most important aspect of the event was the furore it aroused amongst not just the obvious opponents of Mosley on the left but also Conservative MPs, *The Times* and the *Daily Telegraph*.[16] When Olympia was quickly followed by Hitler's 'night of the long knives', with its clear illustration of the brutal character of German fascism, the BUF found itself increasingly alienated from respectable opinion. Rothermere dissociated himself from the movement, depriving it of one influential supporter; Mosley now began to turn his eyes towards a new policy which might help to gather support.

Anti-Semitism became an increasingly prominent feature of BUF activity from 1934 onwards, although from the beginning there had been evidence of the attractiveness of anti-Semitism to some of the regional membership, and incidents had occurred of Jew-baiting and assaults on Jews by blackshirts. There was little doubt that the anti-Semitic campaign mounted in the East End of London did reap some rewards for the BUF. Fascist branches were set up in Bow in 1934, in Bethnal Green and Shoreditch in 1935, and in Limehouse in 1936. During 1935 reports of Fascists terrorizing Jews and attacking Jewish property became more numerous, and there was increased surveillance by the police of BUF meetings as well as a more rigorous policing of their marches and demonstrations. For the police, the BUF was becoming a serious nuisance, a drain on time and manpower which had already led them to discourage the movement from using venues such as White City for its rallies.[17] Whatever the feelings of individual policemen and their immediate superiors concerning the Fascists, it was increasingly evident that at least some form of prohibition on marches and uniforms might be necessary. The issue was clinched for the police by the 'Battle of Cable Street' on 4 October 1936, involving the mobilization of between 6,000 and 7,000 police in the East End in an attempt to protect the BUF's route of march from anti-fascist demonstrators.[18]

The passing of the Public Order Act did not in itself inflict a serious defeat on the BUF. The police reported that Mosley was still able to attract large audiences and that the Fascists were still steadily gaining ground in the East End. It was reported that there were no fewer than 131 Fascist meetings in London in November 1936, with an average attendance of 240. In January and February 1937, 325 Fascist meetings were recorded in London alone, though the number was closely matched by the number of anti-fascist meetings.[19] The London County Council elections of March 1937 provided the BUF with an opportunity to test its popularity in its strongest area of support. In January it was announced that six candidates would contest three two-member divisions, all of which were Labour-held: Bethnal Green North-East, Shoreditch and Limehouse. Mosley poured the resources of the organization into the campaign, the main focus of which was anti-Semitism. The result was a disappointment, for although in Bethnal Green the Fascist candidates came in third and fourth places, ahead of the Liberals, overall the BUF had taken only a fifth of the vote. Further attempts to make an electoral impact also failed. Sixty-six candidates contested the metropolitan boroughs and provincial towns in November 1937. In the East End the results were not very different from those recorded before, but in the forty-eight seats contested in London as a whole the results were very poor. The position was no better in the provinces, with BUF candidates coming bottom of the poll in several major cities. In further municipal contests in November 1938, the BUF put forward twenty-three candidates; they polled significantly in a number of wards, but not nearly well enough to gain seats or to set an electoral bandwagon rolling.[20]

If the electoral picture was disappointing, other evidence of the BUF's strength provided scarcely more encouragement. Regular meetings were held in the East End, but there was little evidence of renewed enthusiasm for fascism. Indeed, by the end of 1938 anti-fascist meetings in London were reported to outnumber significantly those of the BUF. By January 1939 the Metropolitan Police reported fewer Fascist meetings with smaller attendances.[21] The restriction on uniformed marches and the hiring of halls made both publicity and recruitment difficult. The BUF was also suffering from internal dissension and financial difficulties. The removal of all but thirty of the 143 salaried staff in 1935 included a purge of William Joyce and John Beckett, both of whom were critical of Mosley's tactics and turned to founding a rival fascist organization.

The 'Stop the War' campaign mounted by Mosley from March 1938 did achieve some support, at least to judge from the large and successful rally held at Earls Court in July 1938, but there is little evidence that Mosley was any nearer a practical route to power in 1939 than in the early 1930s. His position might, of course, have been transformed in the event of a humiliating climbdown or peace with Hitler in 1939–40, while the possibility of a successful German invasion raises hypotheses about which it is futile to speculate. One thing is striking, however: that the sense of unpreparedness, and of the inadequacy of the foreign policy associated with Chamberlain and the appeasers, was met in 1940 not by the abandonment of parliamentary government but by the installation of a coalition government drawing upon the leading politicians of the major political parties. Certainly Mosley and his followers were considered dangerous enough to be rounded up in May 1940 and effectively denied participation in the national struggle against the forces of continental fascism.[22]

Ultimately, the failure of the BUF and of the earlier fascist movements to gain greater support must be attributed to the established parties' success during the interwar years in maintaining and even increasing their support. In so far as fears of Bolshevism and of economic ruin for the propertied classes played a part in British interwar politics, they served to maintain and increase support for the Conservative Party. Even after the peculiar circumstances of the 1931 general election had passed, the Conservative Party was able to secure a comfortable victory in that of 1935. Electorally it was able increasingly to 'squeeze' the Liberal vote, evident both in by-elections and in municipal contests after 1935.[23] There was no obvious reason for large numbers of middle-class voters to seek refuge in a new party of the right, when the Conservative Party offered a safe bulwark to property and order. Unlike in interwar Germany, where there was no single, strong party of the right until the Nazi rise to power, Britain's strong Conservative Party virtually monopolized the ground on which any fascist movement might hope to base itself.

Nor did Labour, in spite of its humiliation in 1931, disintegrate. Its voting strength was much less reduced than its parliamentary representation. By the mid-1930s the Labour Party and the trade unions were undergoing something of a revival. Electoral recovery was evident in the 1935 general election, and the traditional strongholds of organized labour remained safe for Labour's municipal and parliamentary candidates. The legacy of bitterness from the Communist Party's 'class against class' line of the late 1920s and early 1930s effectively limited its ability to challenge Labour's electoral dominance in industrial areas or the grip of labourist or reformist trade unionists in the industrial sphere. Hampered by the 'first past the post' system of parliamentary and municipal elections, both Communists and Fascists found themselves unable to break the stranglehold of the major parties at the polls. While Communist influence was substantial in some places, particularly as the 'popular front' line from the mid-1930s made for better relations, or at least common cause, between Communists and Labour, this brought little direct benefit to the BUF. If anything the opposite occurred. Fascism at home and abroad offered an issue on which some form of unity of the left could be obtained. Support for Republican Spain, anti-fascist activity directed against the blackshirts and a greater politicization of youth and influential sections of middle-class opinion created a left-wing culture that the BUF was unable to counter.

Mosley envisaged that he would come to power in the event of a deepening crisis: either the BUF would be swept to parliamentary triumph or it would take control in the aftermath of a communist bid for power. The BUF was founded, however, at the trough of the depression and was only struggling into life when the depression began to ease. Although there were still 2 million unemployed in 1935, the BUF, like the Communist Party, found the unemployed not the volatile, ready-made material of a sweep to power, but an amorphous, scattered and often apathetic audience. In fact, the major period of active campaigning by the BUF was undertaken in the mid-1930s when prosperity was returning to many parts of the country. With the percentage of unemployed in single figures in many parts of the Midlands and the South-East, with a consumer-led boom taking place particularly in housing, electricity supply and consumer goods, and with a measure of revival even in some of the old staples, the BUF was a fascist party seeking support when conditions were improving. As living standards for those in work improved and the unemployment totals fell in the country overall, Mosley was in an increasingly unfavourable position to capitalize upon frustration and discontent; the BUF found itself waiting to take power in a crisis which was indefinitely postponed. Mosley's attempts to recapture the initiative as the worst of the slump passed, through anti-Semitism, the 'Back the King' stance in the Abdication crisis and the 'Stop the War' campaign, proved insufficient to mobilize the kind of support that could seriously disturb the status quo.

The adoption of a style of politics which seemed to include a readiness to resort to violence and occasionally deployed it against its opponents served to alienate Mosley and his followers quite early from much of the mainstream of liberal, educated opinion. The discipline and organization in which Mosley exulted did not strike as responsive a chord in British opinion as it did elsewhere, where traditions were different. The violence with which the BUF came to be associated, whether Mosley or his opponents were to blame, meant that the Fascists were regarded with concern even by Conservatives. While it is doubtful that the treatment meted out by the BUF to its opponents was more severe than that which the police on occasion gave to, for example, the National Unemployed Workers' Movement or anti-fascist groups, the BUF appeared to offend against the British 'myth of themselves' as an orderly, civilized people. Tough action by the police against demonstrators raised protests, certainly, but there were many who turned a blind eye to it or even condoned 'just deserts' for mischief-makers and subversives.[24] But this licence was not to be extended to the BUF; the same political culture which accepted police baton-charges as necessary if regrettable, looked askance at a fascist movement which appeared to organize political thuggery on its own behalf. However contradictory the public attitude to the 'civility' of British politics, it had an important effect in condemning the BUF to the political wilderness. There were few in Britain, certainly amongst influential opinion, who were ready to welcome the use of paramilitary organization and the cult of force as developed by Mosley. Whether accurately or not, the majority of British people chose to regard themselves as living in a relatively well-ordered and tolerant society, one with which the public style and behaviour of the BUF did not accord.

Mosley's most controversial policy, the playing-up of anti-Semitism, should be regarded in a similar light. Although it could trade upon a residual upper-class anti-Semitism and upon anti-Jewish feeling in some working-class areas, notably the East End, it offended far more people, and far more influential people at that, than it won over. Many Jews themselves took an active part in the anti-fascist organizations which increasingly dogged the BUF's steps during the 1930s. Growing support for 'popular front' causes, of which anti-fascism was the fundamental component, brought Jewish and other anti-fascist groupings into increasingly direct confrontation with the BUF. The ability of these groups to mobilize mass opposition on the streets to Fascist marches, and to bring out the worst in the behaviour of the BUF towards its opponents, played an important part in persuading government and police to focus upon the BUF as a 'problem' in the field of public order. Opposition to fascism at home and abroad provided common ground upon which left-of-centre parties could agree, and brought both the Communist Party and the Labour Party a growing following in the late 1930s. But even amongst those who were not natural members of a 'popular front' alliance, anti-Semitism provided a line of demarcation between conservatism and fascism. Continental examples exerted an important influence. A. J. P. Taylor has written that 'the Nazi treatment of the Jews did more than anything else to turn English moral feeling against Germany' and it was a 'moral feeling' which extended well beyond the lines of socialists and Communists.[25] Jewish and non-Jewish bodies such as the Academic Assistance Council and, later, the Movement for the Care of Children from Germany were actively engaged in assisting the 80,000 or more immigrants and transmigrants who came to Britain between Hitler's accession to power and the outbreak of war. Prominent Conservatives gave assistance. Ex-Premier Baldwin launched an appeal fund to aid refugees, while Harold Macmillan was active on parliamentary committees and other bodies on behalf of refugees as well as sheltering, with the assistance of friends, some forty Czechs in his house in Sussex.[26] Open anti-Semitism, like the BUF's taste for 'street politics', distanced the movement from those whose opinions mattered if the Fascists were ever to achieve a breakthrough in support.

No less striking was Mosley's failure to capture the large-scale support of the unemployed. Many reasons can be adduced for this, primarily that the unemployed in Britain generally failed to become a radicalizing force in politics. The longevity of the depression in the older industrial areas bred a certain fatalism and apathy, and even the descent into a deeper slump after 1929 failed to dislodge the unemployed from their existing political allegiance. In the worst affected areas, like South Wales and Scotland, Labour support remained strong and unbroken by the depression. Although the Communist Party and the National Unemployed Workers' Movement made significant inroads in some areas, even this was limited in terms of voting strength and membership. The survival of the Labour Party as a viable focus of political allegiance and the deep roots of trade unionism left poor pickings for the BUF. Indeed, in some areas, notably South Wales, the mid-1930s were a very active period on many fronts for Labour, trade union, Communist and other 'left' organizations. Campaigns against unemployment relief regulations, culminating in mass protests against the Unemployed Assistance Board regulations of 1934–5, against company unionism, in support of Republican Spain and against fascism in general gave South Wales a militancy which offered little scope for the Fascists.[27] Hence Mosley's strongest and earliest appeal – that he had a solution to unemployment – fell on deaf ears in one of the most depressed and stricken parts of Britain. Although the BUF opened a campaign in South Wales in 1935, with Mosley addressing meetings in several mining towns and opening branches at Cardiff, Newport and Swansea, little support was attracted. The picture was little different in other depressed areas such as Scotland and north-eastern England. There was virtually no evidence that unemployment generated mass support for fascism.

Ultimately, too, it is proper to place Mosley's views on the economy within a broader context of political opinion concerning economic policy in the 1930s. Mosley's contempt for the 'old gang' was based in large part upon their inability to provide a solution to mass unemployment. It was a view shared by others; alternative economic policies were being canvassed by Lloyd George from the late 1920s, and the early 1930s saw the first flush of enthusiasm for 'planning' in economic matters. The 'planning movement', launched in a supplement to the *Week-End Review* in February 1931, and the formation of the pressure group Political and Economic Planning (PEP) later in the year marked an important line of thought which shared with Mosley a conviction that the current state of affairs required action. *A National Plan for Great Britain* condemned the 'hopeless confusion of the post-war years and the extended active life of elderly men with elderly ideas' which had created the risk 'that in incompetent hands this country may go drifting on either towards a sharp crisis which might have revolutionary consequences or to dictatorship, or perhaps worse still to gradual decline'. PEP's aim was to promote a planned, rational approach to the country's economic and other problems, but 'on lines consistent with British traditions of personal and political freedom'.[28] PEP was explicitly opposed to totalitarianism, even to the extent of wariness in using the word 'planning' which was beginning to acquire some unpleasant overtones from Russian Bolshevism and Italian Fascism. PEP, along with the Next Five Years Group, formed in 1934, represented a fusion of still vital liberalism and social idealism with the scientific and technocratic tone of the twentieth century. Between them these groups were to embrace a broad range of what Arthur Marwick has called 'middle opinion', pursuing progressive causes in a number of important areas, including finance, industry, social welfare, housing and education. The list of those involved in PEP and similar groups in the 1930s represents almost a gazetteer of progressive opinion – 'a young man's consensus' which included a much more prestigious and wide-ranging group than could be found in the BUF. Liberal and Conservative in inclination as many of them were, they represented a vigorous alternative to both fascism and the caution of the National government.[29] Labour too, in the works of people like Barbara Wootton, G. D. H. Cole, Douglas Jay and others, supported planning as against the chaos, irrationality and waste of the capitalist system.[30] Capitalism was indicted as a gigantic muddle, whereas socialism stood for rationality and a co-ordinated approach to economic and social questions.

It was these views, held by a growing section of opinion, which provided the real intellectual challenge to the policies being pursued by the National government. They attracted far more support and greater intellectual weight than was ever mustered by the BUF and were to find their apotheosis in the war years in what Paul Addison has called 'Attlee's Consensus' – a convergence upon a reformed and, it was hoped, more efficient style of capitalism combined with greater state intervention and rationalization of provision in the social sphere. Planning in the sense of the utilization of resources for the social good, broadly conceived, on scientific and rational principles, provided the really effective alternative ideology to the conservatism of the National government. Often more radical-sounding than genuinely radical, it none the less provided the dominant new strain of thought to emerge from the slump. As Paul Addison has written:

> In general, the reform programme originated in the thought of the upper-middle class of socially concerned professional people, of whom Beveridge and Keynes were the patron saints. To render capitalism more humane and efficient was the principal aim of the professional expert. In World War II the humane technocrat provided a patriotic compromise between Socialism and Conservatism which virtually satisfied the desire of the Labour Party for social amelioration, without in any way attacking the roots of exploitation and injustice.[31]

Even in the intellectual sphere, then, British fascism found itself squeezed out by the voices of 'middle opinion', many of them Conservative reformers who could share Mosley's dissatisfaction with the status quo but not his means of changing it. In other conditions, at another time, it is not impossible to conceive of a British variant of fascism attaining significant support. A defeated and demoralized country either in 1918 or 1940, a ruined and threatened middle class, a more alienated intelligentsia than appeared in interwar Britain, and the reduction of the Conservative Party to a powerless minority representative of propertied or established interests: these conditions might have provided Mosley or someone else with their chance. It was not to be. Both the continuities and the contingent circumstances of British politics between the wars conspired to frustrate a significant fascist movement.

NOTES

1 Sidney Low, *The Governance of England* (London, 1904), p. 132, quoted in M. Bentley, *Politics Without Democracy, 1815–1914: Perception and Preoccupation in British Government* (London, 1984), p. 334.
2 See M. Farrell, *Northern Ireland: The Orange State* (London, 1976), pp. 66–97; F. S. L. Lyons, *Ireland Since the Famine* (London, 1973), pp. 439–68.
3 Bentley, *Politics Without Democracy*, pp. 340–1; see also B. Harrison, 'Women's Suffrage at Westminster, 1868–1929', in M. Bentley and J. Stevenson (eds), *High and Low Politics in Modern Britain: Ten Studies* (Oxford, 1983), pp. 80–122.
4 On Red Clydeside, see I. McLean, 'Popular protest and public order: Red Clydeside, 1915–1919', in R. Quinault and J. Stevenson (eds), *Popular Protest and Public Order: Six Studies in British History, 1790–1920* (London, 1974), pp. 215–42.
5 On the Conservatives in general, see J. Ramsden, *The Age of Balfour and Baldwin, 1902–1940* (London, 1978).
6 R. Benewick, *The Fascist Movement in Britain*, 2nd edn (London, 1972), pp. 27–38 and J. Morell, 'Arnold Leese and the Imperial Fascist League: the impact of British fascism', in K. Lunn and R. C. Thurlow (eds), *British fascism: Essays on the Radical Right in Inter-War Britain* (London, 1980), pp. 57–75.
7 Cited in D. Winch, *Economics and Policy: a Historical Survey* (London, 1969), p. 221.
8 See F. M. Miller, 'The unemployment policy of the National Government, 1931–1936', *Historical Journal*, vol. 19, no. 2 (1976), p. 455.
9 D. H. Aldcroft, *The Inter-War Economy: Britain, 1919–1939* (London, 1970), p. 44.
10 C. P. Cook and J. Stevenson, *The Slump: Society and Politics during the Depression* (London, 1977), pp. 198–9.
11 R. Skidelsky, *Oswald Mosley* (London, 1975), pp. 288–9.
12 O. Mosley, *The Greater Britain* (London, 1932), pp. 15–16.
13 ibid., pp. 149–60.
14 See Cook and Stevenson, *The Slump*, pp. 211–12. A peak of 40,000 active members is likely by 1934, though higher figures of looser contacts were cited; see J. Strachey, 'Fascism in Britain', *New Republic*, LXXVIII (2 May 1934), p. 331. For a more recent review, see D. S. Lewis, 'The British Union of Fascists', PhD thesis, University of Manchester, 1983, pp. 169–71.
15 *Hansard*, vol. 288, HC Deb., 5s (1934), pp. 14–15.
16 Cook and Stevenson, *The Slump*, pp. 203–4, 235–6.
17 ibid., p. 237.
18 For the evolution of the police's attitude to processions, see J. Stevenson, 'The BUF, the Metropolitan Police and public order', in Lunn and Thurlow (eds), *British Fascism*, pp. 135–49.
19 Public Record Office (PRO), Mepol 2/3043: Report on fascist and anti-fascist activities, February 1937, item 37B.
20 Cook and Stevenson, *The Slump*, pp. 208–10.
21 PRO, Mepol 2/3043: Report on fascist and anti-fascist activities, January 1939, item 133A.
22 Skidelsky, *Oswald Mosley*, pp. 447–53.
23 Cook and Stevenson, *The Slump*, pp. 260–64, esp. Table 13.6.
24 ibid., pp. 218–33.
25 A. J. P. Taylor, *English History, 1914–1945* (Oxford, 1965), p. 420.

26 B. Wasserstein, *Britain and the Jews of Europe, 1939–1945* (Oxford, 1979), pp. 9–10.
27 See H. Francis and D. Smith, *The Fed: a History of the South Wales Miners in the Twentieth Century* (London, 1980).
28 J. Pinder (ed.), *Fifty Years of Political and Economic Planning* (London, 1981), p. 6.
29 ibid., 'Select Biographical Data', pp. 201–21.
30 J. Stevenson, *British Society, 1914–45* (Harmondsworth, 1984), pp. 324, 326–7.
31 P. Addison, *The Road to 1945* (London, 1975), p. 277.

List of contributors

Martin Blinkhorn is Senior Lecturer in History at Lancaster University. His publications include *Carlism and Crisis in Spain 1931–1939*, the edited collection *Spain in Conflict 1931–1939. Democracy and its Enemies* and numerous essays and articles on nineteenth- and twentieth-century Spanish history. He is also editor of *European History Quarterly*.

Roger Austin is Director of the European Studies Project, Ireland and Great Britain. He is the co-editor, with Roderick Kedward, of *Vichy France and the Resistance: Ideology and Culture*.

David Close is Senior Lecturer in History at the Flinders University of South Australia. He is the author of several articles on British Conservatism and co-editor (with C. R. Bridge) of *Revolution: A History of the Idea*. He is now working in the field of modern Greek history.

Geoff Eley is Professor of History at the University of Michigan. He is the author of *Reshaping the German Right. Radical Nationalism After Bismarck*, *The Peculiarities of German History* (with David Blackbourn), and *From Unification to Nazism. Reshaping the German Past*.

Tom Gallagher is Lecturer in Peace Studies at the University of Bradford. He is the author of *Portugal: a Twentieth-Century Interpretation* and of several articles on the history of modern Portugal.

Stein U. Larsen is Professor of Political Science at the University of Bergen. He is the co-editor of the important collective volume *Who Were the Fascists?* and has contributed articles on Norwegian national socialism to several volumes.

Jill Lewis is Lecturer in Social History at University College, Swansea. Her book, *Fascism and the Austrian Working Class*, is now in press awaiting publication.

Irina Livezeanu is Assistant Professor in History at Colby College, Maine. A development of her University of Michigan PhD dissertation, 'The Politics of Culture in Greater Romania: Nation Building and Student Nationalism, 1918–1927', will be published by Cornell University Press in 1991.

Jeremy Noakes is Reader in History at the University of Exeter. His publications include *The Nazi Party in Lower Saxony*, *Intelligence and International Relations* (with C. Andrew), and, with G. Pridham, the three volumes of *Nazism 1919–1945*.

John Pollard is Senior Lecturer in History at Anglia Higher Education College. He is the author of *The Vatican and Italian Fascism, 1929–32: A Study in Conflict* and co-editor (with L. Quartermaine) of *Italy Today: Patterns of Life and Politics*.

Paul Preston is Professor of History at Queen Mary and Westfield College, University of London. He is the author of many books, notably *The Coming of the Spanish Civil War* and *The Triumph of Democracy in Spain*, and editor of *Revolution and War in Spain 1931–1939*.

Roland Sarti is Professor of History at the University of Massachusetts, Amherst. His publications include *Fascism and the Industrial Leadership in Italy 1919–1940*, *Long Live the Strong. A History of Rural Society in the Apennine Mountains* and, as editor, *The Ax Within. Italian Fascism in Action*.

John Stevenson is Reader in History at the University of Sheffield. Among his many publications are *The Slump* (with Chris Cook) and the Pelican social history of interwar Britain.

Index

Academic Centre for Christian Democracy (Portugal) 158
Academic Karelia Society 250, 251
Accão Escolar Vanguarda 163
Acción Española 5, 131, 140
Acción Nacional 128
Acción Popular 128
Acerbo Law 35, 47n.
ACNP *See* Asociación Católica Nacional de Propagandistas
Action Française 122, 127, 178, 179; influence in Portugal 157, 166
Adorno, Theodore 16–17
Agrarian League (Austria) 99, 107, 110, 111
Agrarian League (Germany) 58–9, 61, 64, 72
Agrarian Party (Finland) 257–8, 259; and Lapua 258
Agrarian Party (Greece) 204
Agrarian Party (Spain) 130
Albiñana, José María 129
Alcalá Zamora, Niceto 125, 127
Alfonsism authoritarianism under Spanish Second Republic (1931–6) 127, 131; influence of Italian fascism upon 127; influence within Nationalist Spain (1936–7) 133, 138; in Franco's Spain 139, 142. *See also* Renovación Española
Alfonso XIII, King of Spain 142
Almänna Valmansförbundet (Sweden) 247
Alpine Montangesellschaft; sponsorship of Heimwehr 112–13; sympathy for Nazism 113
Alvarez, Melquíades 125
Amzalak, Moses Bensabat 167
Annala, Dr Vilho 240
anti-Semitism in Austria 104; in Britain 274, 277–8; in France 183, 192; in Germany 51, 59, 60, 63, 72; in Greece 203, 213; in Portugal 166–7; in Romania 222–37 *passim*
Antivenizelists 200, 201, 204, 212, 213, 214; and ethnic minorities 203; anti-parliamentary wing of 203
aperturismo, -istas (in Franco regime) 152
Areilza, José María 154
Aretin, Erwein von, and Nazism 77–8
Arias Salgado, Gabriel 147, 149
army, French 191
army, German and Nazism 85–7, 88, 89–90
army, Greek 201, 204–5
army , Portuguese 163–4, 173

army, Spanish 123
Arrese, José Luis 149
Asociación Católica Nacional de Propagandistas (ACNP) 120, 125, 141, 143, 145
Association of Christian Students (Romania) 228
Austrofascism 11, 98; nature of 102–3, 114
Averescu, Alexandru 219, 220, 227, 230

Bakos, George 212
Balbo, Italo 23
Baldwin, Stanley 278
Banco di Roma 37, 38–9
Beck, General Ludwig and Nazism 89–90
Beckett, John 275
Bentheim, Prince 79
Blomberg, General Werner von 86, 87, 90
Bloque Nacional 131
Blueshirts (Portugal) *See* National Syndicalists
Boncompagni-Ludovisi, Prince Francesco 34, 38, 39, 47n.
Bonde Førbundet (Sweden) 257
Bondepartiet *See* Farmers' Party (Norway)
Bose, Herbert von, murdered by Nazis (1934) 83
Bottai, Giuseppe 14, 21; and Fascist syndicates 25; and corporatism 26
Bratlie, Jens 254
Bredow, General Kurt von, murdered by Nazis (1934) 87
British Fascisti, -Fascists 269
British Union of Fascists (BUF) 6, 8; founded (1932) 264, 271–2; and violence 273–4; and anti-Semitism 274, 277–8; and elections 274–5; limitations of 275; and 'stop the war' campaign 275; and unemployment 278–9. *See also* Mosley, Sir Oswald
Brochman, B. Dybwad 253
Bruck, Moeller van den 73
Brüning, Heinrich 83, 84
BUF *See* British Union of Fascists
'bunker' 153
Bygdefolkets Krisehjelp (Norway) 258, 259

Cabral, José 166
CADC *See* Academic Centre for Christian Democracy
Caetano, Marcelo 165

285

Polícia Internacional e de Defesa do Estado, *See* PIDE
Polícia de Vigilancia de defesa do Estado, *See* PVDE
Political and Economic Planning (PEP) 279–80
Popitz, Johannes, and Nazism 84–5, 88, 91, 92
Popular Front (France), Conservative opposition to 183–4; Parti Social Français and 185; opposition of Church to 192
Populist Party, Populists (Greece) 7, 200, 204. *See also* Antivenizelists
Portuguese Catholic Centre (CCP), foundation and conduct of 158; and Salazar 158
Portuguese Legion 163, 173
Poulos, Colonel George 214
PPF, *See* Parti Populaire Français
Pradera, Víctor 126
Preto, Rolão 9, 162–3
Primo de Rivera, José Antonio 129, 148; relations with monarchists 130
Primo de Rivera, General Miguel, pronunciamiento of (1923) 122, 123; dictatorship of (1923–30) 8, 123–4, 131; and fascism 123–4, 159
Primo de Rivera, Miguel 142
Progressive Party (Spain) 125
PSF, *See* Parti Social Français
Purschel, Victor 249, 251, 252
Puşcariu, Sextil 230
PVDE 163, 166

Quisling, Vidkun 8, 240, 242, 247, 258

Radical/Radical Socialist Party (France) 177, 181, 182, 185, 186; and Parti Social Français 190
Radical [Republican] Party (Spain) 125; – governments (1933–4) 128, 130
Rallis, John, head of Greek collaborationist government 213
Redondo, Onésimo 129
Reichdeutscher Mitellstandsverband, *See* Imperial-German Mittelstand League (RMDV)
Renovación Española, foundation of (1933) 127, 128 (*see also* Alfonsism); patronizing of Falange 130–1; 'fascistization' of 131; compared with Italian Nationalists 131, 134; dissolved (1937) 139
Riksførbundet Landsbygdens Folk (Sweden) 258–9
Rocca, Massimo 21
Rocco, Alfredo, and theory of state 21; and Italian Fascist state 24–5, 27, 28; and Catholics 38, 43

Rocque, François de la, *See* La Rocque, François de
Röhm, Ernst 87
Rosón, Juan José 149
Rossiter, Clinton, and conservatism 15, 16
Rossoni, Edmondo, and Italian Fascist syndicalism 22–5; compared with Spanish JONS 129
Rothermere, Lord 7, 273
Ruiz Giménez, Joaquín 145, 147, 149, 154

SA *See* Sturmabteilung
Sabetay, Sabetay 233–4
Sáinz Rodríguez, Pedro 130, 142
Salandra, Antonio 19–20, 34
Salazar, António de Oliveira 11; and Portuguese Catholic Centre 158; Minister of Finance 158–9; and *Estado Novo* 159–62; and economy 160–1, 168–9; and National Syndicalism 9, 163; and army 163–4, 173; -'s regime compared with that of Dollfuss 163; personal power of 164; hostility to liberalism, democracy and communism 165–6; rejection of fascist totalitarianism 167–8; and Axis powers 169–70; and Spain 170; and Second World War 170–2; relations with extreme right 173–4
Sallengro, Roger 183
Samfunnspartiet (Norway) 253
Santos Costa, Fernando dos 163, 165, 171, 172
Santucci, Carlo 32, 38, 39, 43
Sassoon, Siegfried 268
Satrústegui, Joaquín 148, 154
Schacht, Hjalmar 90
Schleicher, General Kurt von 84; murdered by Nazis (1934) 87
Schulenberg, Fritz-Dietlof von der, and Nazism 85, 88
Schutzbund (Austria) 110
Schutzstaffel (SS) 11, 71, 89, 90
Schwarz, Samuel 166
Security Battalions (Greece) 213–14
Seipel, Ignaz, and theory of 'True democracy' 106; and Heimwehr 107, 110
Service du Contrôle Technique 195
Service d'Ordre Légionnaire 194
Sima, Horia 232
Sindicato Español Universitario 149
Sintra, Alfredo 170
Skilakakis, Theodore 203, 211
Sleswig Party 252
Social Democratic Party (Austria) 98, 99, 100, 107–8, 111, 112, 113
Social Democratic Party (Finland) 251
Social Democratic Party (Germany) 52, 53; compared with Italian Socialist Party 56, 60